I0846861

THE LYNCHES
OF SOUTH CAROLINA

THE LYNCHES OF SOUTH CAROLINA

From Reconstruction to Redemption

Edited by Robert Emmett Curran

Voices of the Civil War | Michael P. Gray, Series Editor

The University of Tennessee Press / Knoxville

The Voices of the Civil War series makes available a variety of primary source materials that illuminate issues on the battlefield, the home front, and the western front, as well as other aspects of this historic era. The series contextualizes the personal accounts within the framework of the latest scholarship and expands established knowledge by offering new perspectives, new materials, and new voices.

Copyright © 2026 by The University of Tennessee Press / Knoxville.
All Rights Reserved.
First Edition.

Library of Congress Cataloging-in-Publication Data

Names: Lynch (Family : 1818- : Lynch, Patrick Neison, 1817–1882), author | Curran, Robert Emmett editor
Title: The Lynches of South Carolina : from Reconstruction to Redemption / edited by Robert Emmett Curran.
Other titles: From Reconstruction to Redemption | Voices of the Civil War series
Description: First edition. | Knoxville : The University of Tennessee Press, [2026] | Series: Voices of the Civil War | Includes index. | Summary: "This collection of letters comes from the Lynch family, an Irish Catholic immigrant family who first settled in Cheraw but over the generations would become active, both in commerce and religious leadership, in larger South Carolina cities such as Charleston and Columbia. The University of South Carolina Press published *For Church and Confederacy* in 2019, a collection of letters from the Civil War years and just prior. In The Lynch Family of South Carolina, Curran follows the Lynch family from the outset of Reconstruction to the Redemption efforts by Southern Democrats to undo civil rights gains made in the postwar period, approx. 1866–1882. These letters show a once prosperous, Confederate-sympathizing family navigating the Southern loss alongside a divided clergy and an uncertain way forward for Catholicism in the South"—Provided by publisher.
Identifiers: LCCN 2025027941 (print) | LCCN 2025027942 (ebook) | ISBN 9798895270394 paperback | ISBN 9798895270417 adobe pdf | ISBN 9798895270400 epub
Subjects: LCSH: Lynch (Family : 1818- : Lynch, Patrick Neison, 1817–1882)—Correspondence | Lynch family—Correspondence | Catholics—South Carolina—History—19th century | Reconstruction (U.S. history, 1865–1877)—South Carolina | LCGFT: Personal correspondence
Classification: LCC F273.L96 A4 2026 (print) | LCC F273.L96 (ebook) | DDC 975.7/041—dcundefined
LC record available at https://lccn.loc.gov/2025027941
LC ebook record available at https://lccn.loc.gov/2025027942

To John Hirsh (1943–2024),
A Scholar whose Love of Learning Led Him
to Open its Pathways to Those on the Margins
in DC and the UK.

Contents

Acknowledgments   xi

Abbreviations   xiii

Lynch Family Genealogy   xv

Introduction   1

1. "Everything Starts Anew Now": January–May 1866   17

2. "Practice Free, Times Hard, Money Very Scarce and Getting Scarcer": June–December 1866   37

3. "In All Probability This Will Never Be a State Again but Be Part of a Kingdom": January–June 1867   51

4. "You Have No Idea of the Scarcity of Money Here": July–December 1867   63

5. "These Attacks I Think Indicate Consumption": January–June 1868   75

6. "The Rub with Us Now Is Wether We Can Get the Necessaries of Life": July–December 1868   89

7. "I Feel as if I Were in the Embrace of a Boa Constrictor": January–June 1869   101

8. "Sr Borgia Believes the World Is Near Its End": July–December 1869   109

9. "Rev Dr Meriwether Hopes It Is Not True You Have Not Gone for the Immediate Definition": January–June 1870   115

10. "No Man Seems to Know Whether He Is Standing on His Heels or His Head": July–December 1870   123

11. "How Long, O Lord, How Long?" January–June 1871   135

12. "It Looks Like Antebellum Times": July–December 1871   143

13. "To Me It Appears More Difficult to Regain Than to Have First Gained": January–June 1872   151

14. "The Idea of a Religious Invoking a Malediction on the Head of Anyone!" July–December 1872   163

15. "The Taxes Seem to Carry Everything Before Them!" January–June 1873   175

16. "Our Privations Are So Great That I Think Our Enemies Would Take Pity on Us" : July–December 1873   183

17. "I Am at the Mercy of Creditors": January–June 1874   195

18. "The Wind Seems to Be Veering Now": July–December 1874   203

19. "Our Blessed Little Angel Breathed Her Last on Monday Morning": January–June 1875   215

20. "Our Poor Hearts Are Broken": July–December 1875   221

21. "No One Thinks Her Converted": January–June 1876   227

22. "Very Much Enthusiasm Prevails for the Success of the Democracy": July–December 1876   233

23. "God Is Good!" January–June 1877   245

24. "Everybody Seems Pleased with the Return of Home Rule": July–December 1877   253

25. "There Is No Mistake That Farming Is Ever a Failure": January–June 1878   265

26. "When You Shall Live at Home, Your Diocess Will Become a Perfect Hotbed of Catholicity": July–December 1878   271

27. "This Deprives Me of the Last Frail Plant I Had to Lean On for the Support of My Family": January–June 1879   279

28. "Just Now Everything Looks Gloomy": July–December 1879   287

29. "I Fear I Am Lost in the Labyrinth": January–June 1880   291

30. "The Pope Did Not Do Right Towards Bishop Lynch": July–December 1880   297

31. "The House Would Fall Down If You Had Not Been Its Prop and Support": 1881–1882   303

Epilogue   313

Notes   319

Index   347

Illustrations

Lynch Home, Cheraw   15

Postcard of St. John and St. Finbar   20

Ruins of St. John and St. Finbar   21

Ellen Baptista Lynch   54

Patrick Lynch, Catholic Bishop of Charleston   65

John Hugh Lynch   103

Lieber College, University of South Carolina   185

Acknowledgments

As with *For Church and Confederacy*, my greatest indebtedness is to the Catholic Diocese of Charleston, and specifically to Brian Fahey, archivist, and his associate, Melissa Maybry. Indeed, their assistance was even more central to my work of locating, selecting, and transcribing documents for this volume than it had been for the previous one. Unlike the correspondence during the war, the postwar letters of the Lynches had not been scanned and made available online. Brian not only steered me to all the postwar Lynch materials held in the various sections of the archives but was most generous and expedient in scanning documents for me to transcribe and annotate. Of particular value were the Lynch genealogies to which he introduced me.

Once again, I am deeply grateful to the following: Tricia Pyne, director, and Alison Foley, associate archivist of the Associated Archives of St. Mary's Seminary and University; Connie Fitzgerald, OCD, archivist of the Baltimore Carmel; Martha Jacob, OSU, of the Ursuline Sisters of Louisville Archives; and Stephanie Brooks, Library Express Leader, Eastern Kentucky University.

At the University of Tennessee Press, the critiques of the anonymous reviewers contributed significantly toward making the story of the Lynches more accessible. A dozen years ago, I had the immense good fortune to have Thomas Wells oversee the publication of my *John Dooley's Civil War*. I have especially appreciated this second opportunity to benefit from his editorial wisdom. For this volume of the Lynch family correspondence in the postwar period Jonathan Boggs has been an invaluable asset as the editorial coordinator, assisted by Jeffrey Saba as copyeditor. Maliea Ruby's sure hand guided the work through its critical final stages.

On the home front, I can only repeat what I have too many times said: that I can never adequately thank my wife, Eileen, for her above and beyond support of my scholarly projects that have lasted far longer than either of us envisioned when we retired to Kentucky two decades ago. She deserved better.

Abbreviations

agt.	Agent
AMDG	*Ad Majorem Dei Gloriam* (To the Greater Glory of God)
Archbp	Archbishop
B.C.	Brown County
Bk	bank
Bp. Q	Bishop Quinlan
BVM	Blessed Virgin Mary
chk	check
Col	Colonel
Col	Columbia
Compt.	Comptroller
cr	credit
DV	Deo Volente (God Willing)
Dolls	dollars
dft	draft
Exch.	Exchange
fav	favor
Gentm.	Gentlemen
inst.	instant (this month)
Jgments	judgements
Mme	Madame
MF	Methodist Female
NA	National Archives
Paymt	payment
p^{ct}	percent

Penty	Penitentiary
r^{cd}	received
rect	receipt
Revd.	Reverend
Rt Rev	Right Reverend
Rev. Dr. M	Reverend Doctor Meriwether
Shffs.	Sheriffs
So Ca	South Carolina
Sr	Sister
SS	Saints
Statmt	statement
TG	Thank God
Treasr	treasurer
yrs	yours

Lynch Family Genealogy

§
Conlaw Peter Lynch | Eleanor Neison
(1790–1870)   (1796–1877)

Patrick Lynch | John Lynch | Francis Lynch | Mary Lynch
(1817–1882)   (1819–1881)   (1820–1901)   (1822–1878)

Ellen* Lynch | James Lynch | Catherine⁺ Lynch | Conlaw Lynch
(1823–1887)   (1825–1860)   (1827–1873)   (1830–1856)

Hugh Lynch | Bernard Lynch | Anna Lynch | Julia Lynch
(1833–1863)   (1835–1859)   (1835–1870)   (1838–1861)

*name in religion: Baptista
+name in religion: Antonia of the Purification

§
**Children of John Lynch
and Elizabeth Steele Macnamara (1823–1903)**

Robert Lynch | Conlaw Lynch | Elizabeth Lynch | John Lynch
(1843–1928)   (1845–1880)   (1847–1929)   (1848–1915)

Mary Lynch | Eleanor Lynch | Anastasia Lynch | Louisa Lynch
(1850–1947)   (1852–1943)   (1855–1924)   (1857–1938)

James Lynch | Julia Lynch
(1860–1945)   (1862–1944)

§
Children of Francis Lynch
and Henrietta Mulligan Blain (1830–1888)

Marie Lynch | Conlaw Lynch | Eleanor Lynch | Francis Lynch Jr.
(1856–1930)　　(1857–1930)　　(1859–1897)　　(1862–1930)

James Lynch | Henrietta Lynch
(1864–1865)　　(1866–1875)

§
Children of Mary Lynch
and Charles Spann (1812–1886?)

Bernard Spann | Ellen Spann# | Martha Spann | John Spann
(1842–?)　　(1843–1865)　　(1846–?)　　(1846–?)

James Spann | Caroline Spann% | Marian Spann | William Spann
(1850–?)　　(1852–1931)　　(1855–?)　　(1857–?)

Maschal Spann
(1858–?)

name in religion: Gertrude
% name in religion: Michael

§
Children of James Thomas Lynch (1825–1860)
and Mary Augusta Pinckney (1838–?)

Mary Elizabeth Lynch | James Thomas Lynch
(1858–?)　　　　(1860–?)

§
Children of Julia Anna Lynch
and Eustice Bellinger Pinckney (1835–1925)

Conlaw Pinckney | Sarah Bellinger Pinckney
(1858–1932)　　　（1860–1940)

Introduction

The Lynches of South Carolina

When, in the late fall of 1818, Eleanor McMahon Neison and Conlaw Peter Lynch set sail with their one-year-old son, Patrick, from their Irish homeland for the New World, they were seeking the opportunity to regain the status and fortune which British occupiers had stripped from their distinguished Irish families, historic leaders of the Gaelic and Old English communities respectively. That voyage, on which Eleanor gave birth to a second son, John, eventually brought them to Cheraw in upcountry South Carolina, which, so they had been told, had the most promising future in the state. Utilizing his skills as carpenter and millwright, Conlaw became a major contributor to the town's development. As the patriarch of an eventual dozen children, Lynch struggled to provide for his family, much more to regain the wealth and prestige their families had once known in Ireland. But if the Lynches lacked the means to provide financially privileged lives for their many children, they very effectively implanted in their cultural genes the fundamental drive to acquire it. As the third oldest son once explained, all of them had developed "a taste for business."[1] The four youngest sons all apprenticed as clerks. Tragically, consumption (tuberculosis) claimed this quartet before any reached the age of thirty-five. The three oldest—Patrick, John, and Francis—trained for the professions of ministry, medicine, and law respectively.

Patrick studied for the priesthood in Charleston and Rome. Ordained in the Eternal City in 1840, he returned to Charleston where he quickly gained a reputation both as a preacher and polymath. The latter renown gained him entrance into the network of local and national associations that defined America's antebellum intellectual community. When Rome appointed him Bishop of Charleston in 1858, the city's Chamber of Commerce hailed him as "the scholar, the gentleman, the American bishop."[2] John Lynch graduated from the Medical College of Charleston and took up practice in Cheraw. In the sectarian climate of upcountry Carolina where persons tended to choose physicians of their own faith, there were simply too few Catholics in the area to support a doctor with an ever-growing family. Finally, in 1856 John relocated his family and practice to Columbia, the state capital, where, with its greater Catholic population and two medical institutions, he hoped to find patients and official appointments which would at last provide financial security. Francis Lynch read law in Charleston but never began its practice. Instead, he opened a tan yard and dry goods operation in Cheraw. Heavy investment in innovative technology enabled him to enjoy some early success, albeit at the cost of heavy debts which threatened to bankrupt him. Schemes to gain financial solvency through speculating in California gold mines and local coal beds proved unproductive. A late marriage (in 1854) and five children in short order compounded his financial difficulties. Banks grew wary of extending his credit. Rescue came in the person of his bishop brother whose vouchers and loans enabled Francis to stabilize his finances by 1860.

The oldest daughter, Mary, in 1841 had married Charles Spann, a struggling farmer. Six years later, Spann sought to better his prospects by starting a law practice in Galveston, in recently annexed Texas. Failing at that, Spann purchased land in east Texas to grow corn and cotton. By 1860, the Spann family included ten children. In 1847, Ellen, the second-oldest daughter, took a steamboat down the Great Peedee River to Charleston, where she entered the novitiate of the Sisters of Mercy. A year later she decided to pursue her religious vocation with the Ursulines, from whose Charleston academy she had graduated. After a peripatetic decade in Ursuline houses from Louisiana to Ohio, in 1858 Ellen Lynch, now Mother Baptista, led a group of six Ursulines from Brown County in Ohio to Columbia, South Carolina to found a convent and academy which her newly consecrated bishop brother had made possible. Two years earlier, her younger sister, Catherine, had entered the Baltimore Carmel Monastery at the relatively advanced age of twenty-eight.

In 1857, two of the youngest Lynches, James and Julia, had, within a week, married siblings of one of the first families of South Carolina, the Pinckneys of Walterboro. It represented a short-lived coup for the Lynches' social/financial aspirations, which the family's killer angel, consumption, all too soon upended. Consumption stalked the Lynches. Conlaw Lynch, at twenty-six, had succumbed to it a year before the twin weddings. Three years later, in 1859, Bernard Lynch died of it at the same age. The very next year, James, thirty-five, was its victim. The year after that, it claimed his youngest sister, Julia. Meanwhile Bernard's twin, Anna, displayed her own troubling consumptive symptoms, but continued the Irish tradition of the stay-at-home daughter caring for aging parents.

The War and the Lynches

For Church and Confederacy: The Lynches of South Carolina (2019) covered the correspondence and other writings of the Lynches during the war years and those immediately preceding it. The Lynches' political involvement was minimal before Confederate guns opened on Fort Sumter. Once war was declared, the family became, in Baptista Lynch's words, "strong secessionists." They demonstrated their patriotism according to their station. Hugh Lynch was the only one of his generation to enlist. He had barely begun to serve as an aide to General P.G.T. Beauregard when he became the latest family member to die of consumption. Francis Lynch suddenly had an enormous market for his shoes and secured government contracts to supply as many as he could produce. For the first time, steady profits replaced long-standing debt. In eastern Texas Charles and Mary Lynch Spann, with fourteen enslaved Blacks, became fervent Confederates, but none of their five sons was old enough to enlist. In Columbia, South Carolina, the Ursuline Baptista Lynch welcomed the war, not least because of the opportunity it offered for the region's elite families to place their daughters in the Ursuline academy, far removed from the fighting. By 1863, enrollment at the academy had soared from barely a score of students in 1861 to well more than a hundred, many of them, if not most, children of the first families of the Confederacy. That influx of students complemented the unprecedented number of women seeking to become Ursulines.

Patrick Lynch, as Bishop of Charleston, ordered a solemn *Te Deum* at the cathedral to celebrate the fall of Fort Sumter. Although priest-poor, Lynch assigned priests to be chaplains, enabled the Sisters of Mercy to establish a military hospital in western Virginia, and quickly became the chief Catholic apologist for the cause of the Confederacy. That led to his commissioning by the Davis Administration in April 1864 as a special agent to the Papal States, with a mission to secure recognition of the Confederacy by the pope as well as the principal Catholic powers in Europe.

As the superior force of Union armies eventually began shrinking the Confederacy, so too did hitherto safe havens, like upcountry Carolina, become targets for the invaders. Columbia had its reckoning in February 1865, when Sherman's army made sure that a Confederate-started fire would do its worst to the state capital. Among its victims were the Ursuline convent and academy. Then it was Cheraw's turn. Francis Lynch's tan yard and shoe factory both went up in flames; his enslaved workers took their freedom. The charred ruins in Columbia and Cheraw were stark visual testaments to the enormity of the loss which the Lynch family had suffered in supporting the Confederacy.

"If He Would Only Be a Bishop"

When Leo Fillion, vicar general of the Charleston Diocese, died in February of 1865 from typhoid fever contracted while attending Federal prisoners, the leadership of the diocese fell upon the thirty-year-old John Moore. Moore was deeply disturbed that their bishop had abandoned them to be an ambassador extraordinaire for the Confederacy. Two days after Fillion's death, Moore pleaded with Archbishop Martin Spalding of Baltimore, under whose jurisdiction the Charleston Diocese fell, "to hunt [Lynch] up . . . and send him home to us." Their bishop had been absent for nearly a year. They had no idea where he might be. In the new position of authority he had been forced to assume, Moore came to see ever growing evidence that Lynch's failings as bishop preceded his mission for the Confederacy. He had allowed priests too much independence, even to the point of insubordination. He refused to discipline those who needed it, a consequence of his failure to be a pastor of his clergy. And the same was true of his relationship with the lay Catholics of the Carolinas. "If he would cease to be 'a digger of artesian wells, a Railroad engineer, an architect . . . a diplomatist, a politician, a banker, &c and be—a Bishop,' Moore lamented. No wonder that Lynch was more popular with the Protestants in the region than he was with his own Catholic people, who "have some knowledge of what a Bp should be."[3]

Stranded in Europe, Patrick Lynch feared that he would be treated as a traitor by Federal authorities. The Catholic involvement in the plot to kidnap Abraham Lincoln that culminated in his assassination only worsened the bishop's plight. Through the intercession of other Catholic prelates, Bishop Lynch obtained a pardon from now-President Andrew Johnson, freeing him to return to South Carolina in December 1865. His brother Francis, who was deemed to have played a significant role in sustaining the rebellion by providing shoes to the major Confederate army, also successfully appealed for a presidential pardon the following April.[4]

A Diocese in Need

From Reconstruction to Redemption picks up the Lynch correspondence and other writings at the beginning of 1866 as Bishop Lynch and his siblings faced the gargantuan challenge of rebuilding their lives from the physical, financial, and emotional wreckage that the war had left. Not to mention the accommodations that the war's losers had to make to the new biracial order. For Patrick Lynch, the most pressing business was raising the funds needed to retire the debts incurred during the war and to rebuild what had been destroyed. Charleston, as a missionary diocese with relatively few Catholics, had always depended on Europe, not only to provide clergy and sisters but also funds to provide for spiritual and social outreach. During the antebellum period, the Austrian Leopoldine Foundation had been a significant benefactor, giving the diocese more than $30,000 (over $1,000,000 today) between 1846 and 1860. That all stopped with the war. It resumed in the fall of 1865 but with the warning that the allotment of £275 was likely the last the diocese could expect to receive for the foreseeable future.[5] That made it all the more imperative to secure greater aid from the other European benefactor the diocese had historically depended upon: the Paris-based Society for the Propagation of the Faith. The society became the mainstay of foreign assistance during Reconstruction. In 1866 it appropriated 40,000 francs ($10,760; $212,187 today) for the diocese, the high-water mark for the SPF's assistance. By 1871, due to the devastation and upheavals of war and revolution, it fell to 6,000 francs. Thereafter, its annual appropriations were barely nominal, despite Lynch's pleas that Catholics were becoming poorer by the year, their needs ever greater.[6]

Fortuitously, the bulk of the revenue that Patrick Lynch raised came not from the gifts of foreign missionary societies, but from the bishop's own domestic fund-raising. Beginning almost immediately upon his return from Europe in the early winter of 1865-1866, Bishop Lynch began a systematic nationwide effort to give lectures on religious or scientific topics or addresses for any occasion for which people were willing to pay him to speak. His main market proved to be the Catholic-rich Northeast, now also the wealthiest region which had surpassed the South in that distinction with slavery's demise. In addition, Patrick Lynch produced articles on religious, historical, or scientific issues for various journals and magazines, for which he was paid as much as $200.

Reconstruction

By mid-February of 1867, Mother Baptista Lynch thought she knew well enough the direction in which the winds were blowing through the halls of Congress to conclude that South Carolina, along with the rest of the former states of the Confederacy, would be under quasi-permanent military occupation. Northern and Southern opportunists would be controlling the vote of the soon-to-be enfranchised Black Americans to establish biracial governments which would spell economic and political disaster for not only the white South, but even their churches, as the taxing of ecclesiastical properties quickly showed. This radical disordering of the social and political landscape, in the Lynches' view, was wreaking havoc with the economy. All the more reason to court the favor of their conquerors. To what extent could they collaborate with the enemy in pursuing God's greater good? Baptista was open to probing the limits. Her siblings proved to be of the same mind.

Baptista Lynch and her Ursuline Community had already benefitted from one of the first instruments of Reconstruction which Congress had established in the final month of the war: the Bureau of Refugees, Freedmen and Abandoned Lands. The bureau became the main government channel for the distribution of food, clothing, and fuel to the destitute, whether Black or white. In South Carolina the Ursulines were among the grateful beneficiaries of the bureau's biracial relief program. As for the reintegration of the South into the Union, President Lincoln's successor, Andrew Johnson, determined that white Southerners themselves should have the responsibility to form new governments in their respective states. The Lynches, along with white southerners in general, had welcomed this development, especially when President Johnson appointed Benjamin Franklin Perry, a good friend of Patrick Lynch, as provisional governor. Catholics such as Ellison Keitt, Thomas K. Ryan, P. J. Coogan, and Franz Melchers were all elected members of the South Carolina constitutional convention.

But self-reconstruction all too quickly proved to be a defiant attempt to reestablish the old order in a new form, outlined by Black Codes which Southern legislatures passed to set severe limits on the newly acquired freedom by the former enslaved Blacks. Massacres of scores of Blacks carried out by local police in Memphis and New Orleans in the spring and summer of 1866 spelled the end of Johnson's reconstruction program. In March 1867 the Republican Congress effectively took unto itself the responsibility for remaking the South by organizing the states of the former Confederacy into five military districts. Andrew Johnson (as had Abraham Lincoln, for the purpose of avoiding the need to treat the Confederacy as a belligerent nation), had never recognized that the seceding states had left the Union. Congressional Republicans had no reason to share that view. To their mind, the repressive legislation and flagrant violence that had marked self-reconstruction showed all too well the continuing refusal of white Southerners to accept the war's results. Clearly, they needed to be under military commanders whom the Congress directed to oversee the calling of conventions to establish governments which could satisfy the stipulations that the Congress set down for their states' readmission into the Union.

The Lynches had already established friendly relations with the military heads of the Freedman's Bureau, as Patrick Lynch did with General Dan Sickles, in attempting to establish his colony for freed people on one of the sea islands. They now cultivated the new district commanders as well as the Republican officials elected and appointed under Congressional Reconstruction. John Lynch was especially active in using his government connections to secure a faculty position at the Medical School of the University of South Carolina as well as to be named medical director of the penitentiary.

Rebuilding

Amid the wreckage and anomie that dominated the South in the summer and fall of 1865, Baptista Lynch had sensed an extraordinary moment for the diocese, not only to rebuild and repair what the war had devastated but to carry out an unprecedented institutional expansion which would include not only establishing satellite Ursuline academies in other Southern cities, but a Jesuit college, an industrial school, a hospital, an experimental isolated community for the freed people, and the erection of churches in the upcountry, where Baptista was sure harvests of converts were simply waiting to be gathered.

In constructing new churches and repairing those damaged in the war, Patrick Lynch knew considerable success, as diocesan statistics attest. When Patrick Lynch became the third Bishop of Charleston in 1858, there were nineteen churches, forty mission stations, fifteen clergy, one college, two academies for girls, and one orphan asylum. At his death in 1882, despite the diocese's loss of North Carolina, it counted virtually the same number of churches and substantially more clergy, schools, and orphanages.[8] But the main components of Baptista's dream for Charleston's Catholic future failed to materialize: the Jesuit college, the industrial school, the hospital, the model African American community.

Pater Familias

By the spring of 1866 Patrick Lynch was providing vital financial support for family members. Over the next fifteen years, Patrick Lynch proved, at most times, to be a reliable beneficiary to his siblings. His brother Francis fared the best, receiving at least $10,500 ($207,060 today) in the form of gifts or loans. As both a planter and owner of a business destroyed during the war, Francis's need for financial assistance was immediate at war's end. The bulk of that outlay, $6,300, consisted not of loans or gifts but the bishop's assuming responsibility for the loans being paid back within an appointed time. That arrangement between the siblings became all too common over the next decade. Francis's wife, Henrietta, secured at least $400 for tuition, household needs, and other special needs. Baptista Lynch, having responsibility for an academic institution as well as a religious community, understandably had large finances to manage. From her correspondence, we know that Baptista sought at least

$11,135 ($219,582 today) from her brother in loans or direct outlays. John Lynch first had cause to appeal to his bishop brother in the spring of 1868, nearly three years after his siblings had first sought Patrick's aid. That spring, John had received at least $1,000 from his brother. Over the next dozen years Patrick gave his brother a minimum of $6,376 ($152,609 today).

Nor was the family's dependence on Patrick Lynch confined to his siblings and their wives. It extended to sisters-in-law and to nephews and nieces. A particularly persistent supplicant for Patrick's financial assistance was Henrietta Lynch's sister, Louisa Blain (1835-1907), who, from the early 1870s to the bishop's last days, regularly pleaded the desperate, if unexplained need for cash, with the recurring promise to cease such dependency in a future that never arrived. By the late 1870s many of the students at the Ursuline Institute at Valle Crucis were nieces of Patrick Lynch who was paying their tuition and fees. Conlaw S. Lynch, Francis's oldest son, received nearly $900 in gifts or loans. Patrick also paid for the medical expenses and institutionalization of Lillie Lynch, the orphan daughter of James. All in all, it seems likely that Patrick Lynch was able to provide his extended family well over $30,000 ($718,049 today) during the postwar period. When one considers that the bishop was on the road fundraising for most of any year, it is remarkable that his family was able to reach him enough to secure aid of that magnitude. How he managed to do so he may have revealed in a letter he wrote to the Archbishop of Baltimore, James Roosevelt Bayley, to whom he confessed something he would never disclose to his own family: "I have got through this year so far only by borrowing . . . and now I must *pay* or go to jail or be disgraced or bankrupted."[7] One gets a sense of the financial straits which Bishop Lynch found himself in by the late 1870s from the relatively meager amount of one hundred dollars he was able to contribute to the bishops' effort to rescue Archbishop John Purcell of Cincinnati from the collapse of the archdiocesan bank.[8]

Nonetheless, all the travel and lecturing and article-writing that Patrick Lynch engaged in during the last seventeen years of his episcopacy bore the results which he had set out to realize: a virtual elimination of the overwhelming debt which had greeted him upon his return to the country at the end of the war: from $400,000 ($9,573,984 today) to about $10,000 ($307,000) What we don't know is how much debt, if any, remained from the bishop's philanthropy in behalf of his extended family.

The Lynches Adjust to the New Order

Patrick Lynch fully expected that emancipation would inevitably, sooner than later, lead to racial conflict that would force the former slaves to seek refuge along the coast. That involuntary migration would provide the opportunity for Catholic leaders to establish, on some remote island, a colony for former enslaved Blacks, administered by the members of a male religious order who could prepare the Blacks to live virtuous and productive lives through education and working their own plots of land. At one point in 1867, Bishop Lynch secured a promise from General Dan Sickles, the local head of the Freedman's Bureau, to secure funding for the project.[9] But, before Sickles could deliver, President Andrew Johnson removed him for being too accommodating to those formerly enslaved. With no funding and no religious order willing to commit personnel to pursue such a utopian undertaking, Bishop Lynch dropped the project. Even had he obtained the wherewithal to begin such an enterprise, it is questionable how many freed people he might have persuaded to inhabit his ideal colony. In general, upcountry Blacks in South Carolina displayed a certain inertia when it came to geographic movement. As Julie Saville notes in *The Work of Reconstruction*, "most stayed behind." "Freedpeople wanted land," the land they had traditionally worked. Although South Carolina led the way in Black land ownership, for most Blacks in the state, land was not a commodity they could own. That being the reality, share cropping became the favorite means for Blacks to have control over their own labor, as white landowners, if reluctantly, abandoned the gang labor of slavery for family-based plots on which staples were raised, of which the family received a share of the production.[10]

For the senior Lynches, Conlaw and Eleanor, the war proved to be a Year of Jubilee for their bonded workers, all of whom took their freedom with the arrival of Sherman in February of 1865. The loss of their household servants put more pressure on Anna, the youngest surviving sibling, to assume her expected role as caretaker for her aging parents. That effectively brought an end to her long-held desire to join her two older sisters, Ellen and Catherine, in the convent. She stayed in Cheraw, despite her fragile health, to manage the homestead.

The pervasive poverty throughout the South in the war's wake affected all the Lynches, none more so than John Lynch, who found himself no longer lacking for patients, only those who had the means to pay for his medical care. Pressed for money, John sought to dispose of the real estate in which he had chosen to protect his assets amid the economic uncertainties that war produced, only to discover that his property in low country Beaufort was now under water and the mine in the upcountry might be worthless. That made all the more critical his cultivation of the Republican government which Congressional Reconstruction established. Such efforts finally brought him, in the summer of 1869, the medical school appointment he had long sought, as professor of physiology and materia medica, with an annual salary of $2,000 ($51,401 today). The hitch was that the legislature needed to appropriate the money. Years passed without any appropriation, as John's debts continued to mount. His barely surviving medical practice was further impeded when John lacked the money to replace his deceased horse. He found himself a doctor without means of transportation to attend to a dwindling number of patients, virtually none of whom could afford his care. On top of all that, he was served with a lawsuit that threatened to ruin him. No wonder he began to deteriorate physically and psychologically.

In the 1870 census, Francis Lynch, fifty, listed himself as a "manufacturer." In reality, Francis was still functioning as both planter and tanner, a dual career commitment which had, in the antebellum era, set him apart as a member of the antebellum Southern economic elite. With his plantation as well as tannery, Francis Lynch reflected the diversified economy in the upcountry which tended to raise wages or their equivalent for workers with options beyond field labor.[11]

None of this gave Francis any immunity from the loss of the status and wealth he had briefly achieved during the war. For a decade he attempted to recover them by raising cotton as well as by reestablishing his tannery. Like his Ursuline sister, Francis sought compensation from the US government for the losses he had incurred when Sherman's troops burned his plant in Cheraw and caused his Black workforce to abandon him. All he got for his troubles were unreliable harvests, mounting debts, and psychosomatic ailments that drove him to contemplate suicide. It is perhaps revealing of Francis's frustration that in the 1880 census, he listed no occupation.

Valle Crucis

When the burning of their convent and academy had forced the Ursuline community to relocate at Valle Crucis, there was no thought of making the rural site their permanent home. Day students had always constituted a significant portion of the academy's enrollment. Initially there was the frustration of failing to raise the funds to build anew, either in the form of compensation from the federal government, or in a subsidy from the diocese, as had enabled them to acquire the American Hotel for their quarters in Columbia just before the war's onset. Congress proved to be unwilling to make restitution for Sherman's failure to protect their property, and Patrick Lynch no longer had the financial means to be their all-providing benefactor. In 1872, they opened a free day school in Columbia, which lessened the likelihood that locals would have their daughters' commute to Valle Crucis. Then in the late seventies, a new nativistic movement revived the boycotting of Catholic institutions, especially girls' academies. For the first time in their history, the Ursulines had no Protestant students. And of the diminishing ranks of Catholics in the school, aside from the Lynches whose uncle financed their education, too few of the parents were able to pay. As Baptista informed her bishop brother, every year they lost anywhere from $1,000 to $14,000 ($25,000-$359,809 today) in unpaid tuition and fees.[12]

Baptista came to appreciate Valle Crucis' bucolic environment as a much more congenial setting for establishing a pervasive convent culture that bred conversions and vocations. Baptista seemed also to realize that they could never replicate the halcyon years when their academy had become a precious refuge for the Confederate elite. Better to set their sights more modestly, no longer in terms of hundreds of students, but merely a few score. On the eve of the war, indeed, there had been but twenty-three students and a faculty/staff of seventeen Ursulines. A decade later the Ursulines had added a member, with an even split between "teachers" and "domestic servants." Student enrollment had dropped to sixteen boarders, all but three South Carolinians. By 1880, student enrollment was static, at seventeen, outnumbered by the Ursulines at Valle Crucis.

Valle Crucis's cramped quarters were a catalyst for Baptista's decision to establish satellite communities in other Southern cities, at least until the Ursulines secured the means to enlarge their quarters outside of Columbia or returned to a new site in the city. Having a critical mass of students was a prerequisite for cultivating the vocations upon which the Ursulines' future expansion depended. If Valle Crucis could not accommodate enough students, then they would have to look to multiple foundations. In September 1866 Baptista accompanied three of her community to start a new foundation in Tuscaloosa, Alabama in quarters provided by Bishop John Quinlan of Mobile. Tuscaloosa, over the next fourteen years, proved largely to be but another source of frustration for the Columbian Ursulines' hopes to attract students and candidates for their religious order in the postwar South.

In the postwar period, psychological disfunction in the Ursuline community seems to have become more endemic. No nun gave Baptista Lynch more trouble for a longer period than did Augustine England, the niece of John England, the first Catholic bishop of Charleston. Augustine evidently had been a community thorn as far back as the 1850s. Baptista Lynch, apparently at her brother's urging, had reluctantly included Augustine in the band of Ursulines that laid the foundation in Columbia in 1858. For the first four years in

South Carolina, Augustine had become Baptista's mainstay in the new community, until the entry of Baptista's niece, Ellen Spann, as a novice, triggered a latent jealousy in Augustine that drove her, in a persistent passive-aggressive manner, to spread discontent, if not opposition to Baptista, within the community. Not until 1868 was Baptista able to remove the perennial underminer from the community. Sadly, Augustine's departure did not bring peace. In the postwar period, the community experienced a rise in contentious members, which gradually took a toll on Baptista. One wonders how much the outcome of the war—defeat and occupation—spurred the psychologically impaired to seek shelter in the ultra-ordered life of the cloistered convent.

Whatever the cause, dealing with disturbed nuns and sisters became a major occupation for Baptista. One interesting note about Baptista's governance, particularly in dealing with unstable members, is its democratic character. She was accustomed to consult her community about the dismissal, transfers, or returns of members. The community, if informally, served as the final determinator of a nun's fate in the community. It should also be noted that Baptista's confidence in the community's support stemmed from her knowledge that "they rarely differ or dissent from any thing I propose."[13]

Despite the relative isolation that a country setting imposed, Baptista never abandoned her audacious commitment to convert high Carolina society to Catholicism. The war had rendered improbable, if not impossible, the institutional expansion which was key to her vision. The loss of their Columbia quarters had forced the relocation to Valle Crucis which could accommodate few students. Nor did they any longer enjoy the peculiar circumstances of wartime which had made their academy such a desirable sanctuary for the children of the Confederate elite, the vast majority Protestant. Still, even as non-Catholic enrollment steadily declined at Valle Crucis, Baptista kept alive her evangelization of Catholic prospects among neighbors and parents of current and former students, as well as alumnae of the school and even the former enslaved people who remained in the area.

Baptista's evangelistic vision extended far beyond Valle Crucis's orbit. From her network of parents and alumnae, the Ursuline kept hearing of the openness to Catholicism, particularly in the upcountry. Given her brother's prowess as a preacher, Baptista was sure that a rich harvest of conversions and revitalizations of faith would follow Patrick's visitations to the upcountry of his diocese. Becoming a true shepherd of his lay flock was a theme Baptista would increasingly sound as the cycle of her brother's fundraising tours occupied more and more of his annual schedule in the postwar years. But Patrick Lynch was much more at home researching and lecturing on a broad variety of religious and scientific topics. He was much less so visiting the parishes and missions of his far-flung diocese and bringing the full complement of blessings which a sacramental church offered. When the Charleston Chamber of Commerce had hailed Patrick Lynch at the outset of his episcopacy as "a scholar, a gentleman, and a Bishop," they had unwittingly caught Patrick Lynch's instinctive priorities. John Moore noted in 1865 that, seven years into his episcopacy, the bishop had yet to make a visitation of his diocese, something prelates were required to do periodically. Fifteen years later, despite his sister's persistent urging, that charge against Bishop Lynch still held.

Baptista was, in her evangelistic aspirations, out of sync with an American Catholic Church turning inward, creating a parallel set of exclusive institutions which would make American Catholics a people apart. Tribalism, not evangelism, came ever more to set the course of the American Catholic community in the Carolinas, as elsewhere.

Vatican Council

After the death of Eleanor Lynch in September of 1877, the collective financial straits of the extended Lynch family made it imperative that they sell the family homestead. Two months later, when Patrick, still recovering from multiple operations in Boston, returned to Charleston with nothing to show for his latest fundraising trip, Baptista consoled her brother, "What matter is it about your empty pockets," so long as he was healthy enough to return home, knowing how greatly he had reduced the crushing debt that kept him in the North so much of every year since the war? That was the long view which Patrick, all too aware of his pressing debts, could not indulge. Travel perforce became a near constant in Patrick Lynch's postwar life. Most of it was domestic, but there were occasional returns to Europe, as in 1867 when he addressed the annual meeting of the Society for the Propagation of the Faith in Rome. His major foreign trip came in 1870 when he participated in the Vatican Council. Upon his return to Charleston Bishop Lynch claimed, "I felt more than ever the unity, the Catholicity of the Church, . . . from every quarter, there was heard one faith, one baptism, one Church of Christ there assembled in her majesty, and there about to declare the faith of Christ to this world." What the bishop failed to mention was the discord which had surfaced in the council over the attempt to define infallibility, not as a fundamental character of the Church itself, but as a charism centered in the pontiff. It was emblematic of the ultramontane movement to center all authority in the Bishop of Rome. Patrick Lynch himself chose to interpret the council's definition as merely a clarification of the Church's tradition, not an inversion. Most of the American hierarchy were convinced that declaring such a doctrine as papal infallibility would gravely threaten to undo the progress that Catholicism had made in the United States. In the end, all but one, Edward Fitzgerald of Little Rock, either signed the decree or got permission to leave Rome before the signing. Lynch was among the latter.

Redemption

Most of the Lynches welcomed Wade Hampton's Red Revolution in 1876 which promised to end the decade of Republican rule. As Francis Lynch reported to his absentee brother bishop, "Very much enthusiasm prevails for the success of the Democracy." His doctor brother, for one, did not share that hope, if only because he realized all too well that the Redeemers would treat him as a scalawag, no matter how extenuating were the reasons for his co-operation with the enemy. For his sister, Baptista, not facing the prospect of any retribution for collaboration, her friend Wade Hampton's triumph represented the re-establishment of the proper order marked by white supremacy and honest government. "Is it not a comfort," she wrote Patrick at the close of 1877, "to see the work [the legislature] is doing and realize our grand old state is again in the hands of those interested in its welfare."[14]

Text and Illustrations

As I related in the introduction to *For Church and Confederacy*, in the spring of 2013 my research for the book that eventually became *American Catholics and the Quest for Equality in the Civil War Era* took me to the Archives of the Catholic Diocese of Charleston, South Carolina, where I intended to work with the papers of Patrick Lynch, who had been the Bishop of Charleston during the war. As I was orienting myself to the collections of the diocese, Brian Fahey, the archivist, asked whether I had ever seen the correspondence of the Lynch family. "No," I replied. This was my first visit to Charleston. He thought I might find it useful in illuminating the Catholic involvement in the war. A few minutes later he returned with a calendar of Lynch family correspondence that ran on for pages and pages. There were more than 1,600 itemized letters, spanning a forty-year period, the vast majority of them written to Patrick Lynch by his siblings and other relatives. Since I had but one day to spend in Charleston, Brian recommended that I access the Civil War letters online, where the South Carolina Historical Society had scanned the correspondence

Modern-day photograph of the historic Lynch home in Cheraw,
South Carolina. Photo by the author.

between 1858 and 1866. Back in Kentucky, when I had the opportunity to
view the scanned letters at the Lowcountry Digital Library site, I quickly got
caught up in the Lynches' war experience. Caught up so much, in fact, that I
decided to put on the back burner my volume on the Catholic community's
war involvement in favor of a volume editing the Lynch family's wartime correspondence and other writings. That meant reaching beyond the Charleston
diocesan archive for family letters, to other dioceses, religious communities,
and institutions of higher education. In the end I transcribed and annotated
approximately a third of the letters (561) of which 336 made it into print.

Since none of the approximately 880 letters written after 1866 had been
part of the Lowcountry Digital Library Lynch Family Letters project, I needed
to access them directly at the Charleston diocesan archives. As noted in my
acknowledgements, Brian Fahey and his staff made possible the task of transcribing such a massive volume of correspondence. In my earlier introduction
I discussed the challenge of deciphering Baptista Lynch's scrawl, which fatigue
and neuralgia only worsened. In the 1870s Baptista's script suddenly became
larger and more legible. It was her attempt to compensate for her brother's
failing eyesight.

The letters in this volume total 532. Readers of *For Church and Confederacy*
will quickly notice an abundance of ellipses in *The Lynches of South Carolina*.
The much greater volume of the postwar letters necessitated a comparable

abridgment of the text. The first volume covered a span of eight years; the second's span of years more than doubled that. The upshot was a great deal of rigorous pruning, not only of mundane details but also of much material that was interesting, but, to my judgment, of less importance than that which survived.

As in *For Church and Confederacy*, the six surviving siblings of Patrick Lynch account for the vast majority of the letters. But two other relatives, Henrietta Lynch, Francis's wife, and her sister, Louisa Blaine, figure much more prominently in this volume than they did in the former one. The glaring absence is that of the eldest Lynch sibling. Patrick Lynch kept few copies of his correspondence, especially that to members of his own family. That was compounded by his notoriety as a chronic procrastinator in responding to his brothers' and sisters' mail. We can only be grateful that they persisted in writing, despite the one-sided nature of their correspondence.

Among the illustrations in the first volume there was none of Mother Baptista Lynch, even though her letters dominated the text. At the time, it was believed that there was no credible portrait or photo extant of Mother Baptista. Since then, I have come to conclude that the photo of the portrait of an Ursuline nun in the diocesan archives is that of Ellen Baptista Lynch. The photo, it turns out, became part of the archive's collections by way of Monsignor Richard C. Madden, most likely around 1985, the year that Madden's history of the diocese was published. Brian Fahey, who became the diocesan archivist some years later, recalls David Heiss, the biographer of Patrick Lynch, telling him in the mid Nineties that, while interviewing a Lynch descendant in Cheraw, he had seen the original portrait in that person's home.[15]

How did a cloistered nun come to have her portrait done? Mother Baptista Lynch had an artist friend in Charleston, Rosina della Torre, who kept a studio close by the Cathedral. In 1877, when Patrick wanted to have a portrait made of his parents, Baptista recommended della Torre. She might very well have had Della Torre do her portrait, perhaps at the bishop's initiative.[16] In the event, the portrait seems to date from the period and, to my eye, the habit is the one late-nineteenth-century Ursulines were wearing. In the event, for this volume I have included this reproduction of that portrait, wherever it may be.

1

"EVERYTHING STARTS ANEW NOW"

January–May 1866

After more than a year-and-a-half in Europe, Patrick Lynch returned to a Charleston left in ruins by war and natural disaster. Within weeks, the bishop was on the road again, to begin the fundraising which would occupy much of his calendar over the next fifteen years. His first trip to New York proved far less productive than he expected, a net of some $3,000, less than a tenth of what Archbishop John McCloskey had predicted.

Initially Bishop Lynch faced a serious threat to his fundraising from newspaper articles accusing him of being a rabid Confederate who had, among other treasonous actions, tried to induce Pope Pius IX to recognize the Confederacy as a nation. In March, in a letter responding to one critical article in the *New York Tribune*, Lynch tried to put the best possible face on his controversial actions during the war. If his response fell short of silencing his critics, it was more a matter of what he did not say, rather than what he did. We know, from his own words, that he wrote the pamphlet on slavery precisely to remove the stigma regarding the South's peculiar institution which was impugning efforts to gain recognition from European governments, especially the Papal States. In that pamphlet Patrick Lynch had predicted that racial warfare would be the inevitable consequence of emancipation. To avoid that bloodbath, at least to some extent, the bishop had proposed that colonies, ideally in Central America or some tropical locale, be established for Blacks where they could be prepared for freedom under the supervision of re-ligious orders. It was intended to be, on a vastly larger scale, the Paraguay Reductions which Jesuits in the eighteenth century had conducted in South America for indigenous people.

Bishop Lynch brought out the final edition of his pamphlet a month after the US Congress had passed the Thirteenth Amend-ment abolishing slavery. Nonetheless, Lynch continued to pursue his dream of a sanctuary for enslaved people, or formerly enslaved people, where they could make a guided transition into a free so-ciety. Aware of the strong expectations within the Black commu-nity that January 1 would bring, at last, the broad distribution of the land promised them toward the end of the war, Lynch calcu-lated that the US Government would not honor its word which would trigger violent clashes, particularly in upcountry South Carolina, where Whites would eventually drive out the formerly enslaved Blacks, forcing them to the coast. By the beginning of 1866, Lynch had secured, through a friend, a spacious site on one of the Sea Islands to house several thousand freed persons. He solicited various religious orders or congregations for the person-nel to conduct the experiment.

As Bishop Lynch tried to construct a utopian refuge for the newly emancipated, his family was reeling from the consequences of defeat. Francis Lynch's shoemaking plant, as well as the Ur-sulines' convent school in Columbia, had been reduced to skeletal walls. Many of the family's assets which survived the war were of dubious value, such as John Lynch's mine and seacoast property, the latter now under water. As for John's medical practice, he had more than his share of patients, but few had the cash to pay for his care. Securing labor in the wake of emancipation became the first challenge. The Lynches' labor force in the Carolinas had largely fled when Sherman's army swept through. When January 1 did not ring in a Year of Jubilee in which all the former enslaved would be awarded land for all their years of faithful service, the freed people in the Carolinas reluctantly settled for working on plantations for wages or a share of the crop. Francis managed to hire some fifty freedmen to work his plantation, while contem-plating mechanization and other elements of agricultural reform as the key to prosperity in a slaveless economy.

In the fall of 1865, the Ursuline Academy had reopened, three miles south of Columbia at the former Keitt plantation which Bishop Lynch had acquired during the war. Baptista Lynch named the estate Valle Crucis (valley of the cross). The estate's former bonded workers had secured land nearby on which to share crop but remained on good terms with the nuns. Mother Baptista, who very much preferred Irish labor over Black, delighted in their chaplain's hiring a quartet of Irishmen to work the fields of their new rural location. In East Texas, Charles Spann was trying to cope with the new order which emancipation had wrought by implementing a sharecropping system for the Black labor he still needed to work his fields. Sharecropping, Spann had reason to believe, would benefit both planter and field worker: for the latter, greater family control over the labor of its members; for the former, liberation from the unwritten rules of paternalism to provide for one's workers from cradle to grave. Now his sole obligation was the provision of a fourth of the crops.

With very limited quarters, Valle Crucis could accommodate far fewer students than the American Hotel, for all its defects, had allowed them. The reality was that the war had left most of the academy's former patrons unable to afford the luxury of a convent education. With revenue greatly diminished, Baptista found it all the more imperative to maintain good relations with their military occupiers, who could supply rations and other necessities for the school and community. She quickly cultivated the regional commanders and Freeman's Bureau personnel to assure that the Ursuline Academy would fare well under their Yankee overlords.

Meanwhile Baptista undertook to solicit funds from likely contributors both throughout the now reunited states and abroad. To facilitate the project, through her bishop-brother, Baptista engaged a full-time fundraiser to seek donations throughout the North. Within a few months, the supposed fundraiser's paltry results gave Baptista cause to suspect that he was exploiting their needs for his own personal gain. More promising was the widespread effort to secure full compensation from the federal government for the loss of their convent and academy during the burning of Columbia. Baptista prepared an account of the fatal event which she hoped to publish. Through various secular and religious channels Baptista made her appeal for justice to all three branches of the government.

PATRICK LYNCH, TO MARTIN SPALDING,
CHARLESTON, 12 JAN.[1]

... I find my hands full here, and my heart over full. What misery! What suffering! How much to do! How little to do it with!

I have not yet got a house to live in. . . . I have arranged to commence at once the erection of a temporary pro-cathedral, in such shape as to serve for a part of a future Boys Orphan Asylum, when we will have the Cathedral restored. Labour and materials are so high that I almost shrink from this undertaking.—Then the Sisters' convent, and the female Orphan Asylum are still unrepaired. We have finished the repairs of the injured Churches or nearly so but we want more church room. I would like also to have a negro church.—I have the ground for it. The Ursuline Convent is so big a job, that as yet I do not see my way to set about rebuilding it, with any means now before me. And yet it is so necessary.

About the negroes . . . I have a plan, . . . I think the negroes will be driven as fast as possible from Virginia N. Carolina and the upper parts of S. Carolina and Georgia, and will be pressed down to the coast and the Sea Islands, which they now hold almost exclusively.—There is an Island, some eight miles long, and from half a mile to 3 ½ miles in width entirely owned by a Catholic friend of mine. I think I could get it on good terms. I would put a religious commu-

Postcard, Ruins of St. Johns and St. Finbar Cathedral, Charleston, South Carolina. No date. Library of Congress.

Cathedral of St. John and St. Finbar after the Great Fire of 1861. Library of Congress.

nity on it, and would start a Paraguay village of Catholic negroes which might grow into a community of four or five thousand souls under the fathers. I have written to F. Sorin[2] on the subject. Also to the Benedictines of Latrobe. If both fail me, I will try the Maristes[3] who go from France to the African Missions. What does your Grace think of the plan? . . .

FRANCIS LYNCH, CHERAW, 7 JAN.[4]
. . . Now for the all-absorbing topic the employment of the freedmen—I have employed near forty of them, I think select hands, hoping to be able to make a crop with them—Of course it will require a heavy expenditure to make a crop. . . . If you have a few thousand dolls. that you would put on interest until Fall, do be mindful of me; . . . I have filed my application on the Govt which if

collected will give me over 20,000$ [$395,647.80 today] but of this, tis perhaps well not to be too sanguine. . . . The first of Jany, long looked for by the negroes has come and past, and many of them are homeless. Here generally the disposition is to seek employment. . . . I think the erroneous impression made on the negroes that they were to be invested with lands, is in a great measure dispelled. And there is much reason to hope that things will work tolerably well in this neighborhood. . . .

BAPTISTA LYNCH, URSULINE CONVENT AND ACADEMY
"VALLE CRUCIS" . . . JAN. 8th[5]
. . . Daniel and the negroes—(who are very agreeable to us)—will leave this week . . . The negroes have gotten land about three miles from here owned by a Mr Arthur.

   . . . Anna writes all are well at home. . . . Just to think that on the 2d inst every servant left the yard—and mother and father had not one to do a thing for them . . . I wish you could get a good Irish Catholic girl to live with them and do their cooking and washing.

   . . . Of course every thing starts anew now—there is no binding engagement of any kind—I received a very pleasing letter from the Ursulines of Quebec a few days since expressing the pleasure they felt in giving into the safe hands of our friend Mr Jones[6] the small donation they had wished to send us—Mother St. Andrew said that we had the sympathy of all the Bishops and clergy. From such gratifying intelligence, we will hope ere long to be enabled to begin the building of our convent so that we may resume our labors as heretofore . . .

BAPTISTA LYNCH, URSULINE CONVENT AND ACADEMY AT
VALLE CRUCIS . . . FEAST OF ST. AGNES [JANUARY 21][7]
I will only write a few lines to say how much we are pleased with our new chaplain. . . . I suppose he will tell you all about Charles Matthews and the four good, honest Irish Catholic workmen, who can be accommodated on the premises and about the good condition of the farm for raising vegetables for ourselves and market too. . . .

   . . . Genl Ames[8] has been very polite, and the rations generous.

FRANCIS LYNCH, CHERAW, 26 JANY[9]
. . . The Lyceum has revived, several schools are open here, and things generally are improving. I have about fifty field laborers and if I can manage successfully until Fall am sanguine of being in a more prosperous condition. . . .

MARY LYNCH SPANN, WASHINGTON COUNTY, JANY 29[10]

... Your letters my dear Brother came most opportunely at a time when we were bowed down with grief at the sad news which reached us a few days before, it consoles us not a Little that all bear testimony to the extreme piety and purity of life of this dear Child and we try to be reconciled that she is happy in gaining an early crown and that though her illness was short she was not unprepared for the summons. We ... believe Almighty God disposes all things well, she has gained all that we could wish for her and we must be resigned.[11]—

... Poor Charleston and Columbia they must be mere wrecks of their former beauty and prosperity. I trust my dear Brother you have returned strong in spirit for surmounting the difficulties which may present themselves in your efforts to reprieve the ravages caused by this cruel war—I am confident that you are able for the emergency and though it must take years before things can be restored to their flourishing condition the work will be gradually progressing. ... What heavy cares rested on Sister Ellen. ... The loss of our dear Ellen[28] ... adds greatly to her affliction, but your coming will give her great consolation and assistance by your counsel. ... We are much blessed in having a Pastor with us nearly all the while, it is a blessing which has repaid us for all our privations in this distant land. The mission is pretty extensive but our house is headquarters we have Mass frequently during the week and almost every Sunday. ... Mr Spann enjoys good health with the exception of the shock he received last spring in the failure of our cause. ... As to the labor system he does not mind it, as he hopes to do better with some able hands giving them one fourth of what is made than heretofore and we are relieved of having responsibility So far he is well satisfied with their dispositions for work which I hope will continue—few have stood the changes of twenty years better than Mr Spann. ... Our son Conlaw will be 18 years of age in the Spring. ... All who see him say that he is destined to be a Priest but that's in the future. ... I commit the matter to Almighty God only wishing that he may serve him in the state most conducive to <u>his</u> salvation—We sent Caro to the Convent at Galveston last week. ...

BAPTISTA LYNCH, URSULINE CONVENT AND ACADEMY AT "VALLE CRUCIS," SUNDAY EVENING 27th JAN.[12]

... You will be pleased to hear that we received another payment for our pupils in gold $161°° and I hope gradually we will get on as much as before. ...

... [In New York] You will see Messrs Wm and Jas. O'Brien, who have done so much in their sales for us—I sent them by today's mail a check draft for $200—in U.S. coin from the good Sr. Mercy's collection in San Francisco—

She writes most kindly and hopes to be able to send us more—We will begin to think of building soon—

. . . I received a letter from Messrs Will and Chisholm telling me of the furniture, it began "Holy Mother &c" Genl Preston called me the "dear blessed Lady" before, I'll soon have a Litany—won't I? . . .

BAPTISTA LYNCH, URSULINE CONVENT AND ACADEMY, AT "VALLE CRUCIS" . . . FEB 3rd[13]

. . . D[r] Meriwether told me last Sunday . . . that you expected to leave for New York on Wednesday . . . I trust you may have success. It was very kind of the Abp[14] to hasten your going on a questing expedition in his own archdiocese.

. . . Yesterday we . . . received among our pupils Judge Aldrich's two daughters—He brought them himself, and seemed to commit them to our care with great pleasure. . . .

BAPTISTA LYNCH, URSULINE CONVENT AND ACADEMY,
AT "VALLE CRUCIS," FEB 12th[15]

The same mail brought me your welcome letter and one from Bp Verot[16]—since I do not enjoy the pleasure of consulting you verbally, I enclose the copy of a letter I forwarded to him by today's mail—It would consume too much time, I feard, to await your judgment and reply—and moreover I thought you might have left for N.Y. and so I consulted my council and with the best I know how I'm hoping it would please you. . . .

When the Hutchets come who are in town, we will have eighteen pupils and we are daily expecting more. . . . Genl Ames too is very civil, so I do hope this week will be a propitious one—Our prospects are growing daily brighter—Parents are paying the little they owe us, and so nicely in gold accompanied with such gratifying letters—I do think if we had room for them, we would next year be as large a school as ever. But to make room either for them or Postulants, to whom we now wish to open the doors of our noviciate, we must form a Branch House—and we are therefore the more satisfied to sacrifice our feelings and make the Macon establishment until we rebuild. . . . We have also contemplated a day school in Columbia, but of that too we will speak. . . .

BAPTISTA LYNCH, URSULINE CONVENT AND ACADEMY,
AT "VALLE CRUCIS" . . . TO FELIX VEROT, FEB 12th[17]

. . . I am very anxious that we should establish a Branch House in Macon and although the same necessity for the move does not now exist, as when I proposed it, my judgment and desires remain the same. But my health of body is such at present, that I am *totally unable* to travel, and I am truly sorry to say, I fear I could not find three Sisters in our Community able to undertake the journey to Macon at present—

Eh bien! L'homme propose et Dieu dispose.

We are five less in number, than we were—two of our Sisters our Lord has taken to Himself and three left who were in their probationary period and found our privations too much for them—

I would like that we waited until the close of this session—and until we made our usual annual retreat, by which time we will (D.V.) be rested and strong—Then I could accompany our Sisters to Macon, and they be ready for the session of Sept.

BAPTISTA LYNCH, URSULINE CONVENT AND ACADEMY AT "VALLE CRUCIS" . . . FEB 13th[18]

. . . I see that in your regulations for Lent, that you are more requiring than ever before, since you do not allow the use of *milk* and *eggs*—this will be hard in this diocese and through the country, where light diets are so much needed and often where little else can be procured—I see you have followed the "Baltimore Mirror" but you know they have not suffered there, as we have in your Diocese. However, I am not at liberty to plead the cause of any but our community. . . . We still draw rations and received about thirty pounds of coffee and sugar last week. . . .

Genl Ames sent out an orderly with a polite note this morning, to let me know the cause of the detention of our chairs &c—the steamer or boat "George" had some accident and her freight had to be transferred to another boat—He said his Q[uar]t[er]master had the chairs and would give it his immediate attention. That was very polite and attentive, was it not? But it needs all this to help to heal the wound they gave us nearly one year ago and I am sorry to say although for individuals I have no resentment—for the people or nation—such is my feeling, that I am forced to stand *close* to our Blessed Mother at the foot of the Cross and often repeat the sublime lesson "Love your enemies &c in order to cultivate the right and Christian sentiments. But it is *all* God's holy will and for the best—Faith and reason assure me of this, and the heart will feel it after a while also. . . .

BAPTISTA LYNCH, URSULINE CONVENT . . . , FEB 21st[19]

. . . you have had such a rough time of it at sea, I suspect, that I have been very anxious about you and will look daily for a letter telling me of your . . . safe arrival in New York.

. . . I hope you will . . . see often—Miss Kate Harris, niece of Mr Dr Robert Emmet—and our former pupil, devoted to our dear Sister Gertrude and with us during the fire, &c . . .

We have had two *very pleasant* visits from Genl Preston[20]—truly he is a *nobleman*, his sense of profound gratitude seems not at all abated. . . . I hope he may meet you in New York on his return to Paris, where his wife and daughters are residing very pleasantly—I will tell you in my next what he is able to do for us—I fear not much, as he expresses so much regret at his inability to follow the promptings of his heart and wishes—We had quite a long talk about Religion, and he really edified me by his humility and deep sense of unworthiness in the sight of God. I believe he is a Catholic at heart—I gave him an Ursuline Manual. . . . He had met some sick Catholic lady on board of a steamer when coming over the last time, I believe in Jany, in whose "prayer book" he became very much interested . . . We concluded by my telling him, that I would ask our Sisters to pray that he might make a *good confession*—I had sent for Dr. M—and introduced him and the Genl said—now when the Rev. Father hears your confession, no doubt he has to rack his brain to find out a sin, but if *I* went to him, I should take his head off. . . . I would not be surprised any day, to hear that he had approached the Sacraments . . . We received very generous rations this week D.G. . . .

We are receiving regularly contributions which keep us with funds in hand (D.G)—yesterday we received $200 from various sources, and accompanied with very kind and sympathising letters. . . .

. . . I am glad that Father and Mother have things so comfortable at present. I feared it would not be so—In Texas too, things are better off than I thought—ultimately all these changes will no doubt be for the best. . . .

BAPTISTA LYNCH, URSULINE CONVENT AND ACADEMY, AT "VALLE CRUCIS" . . . , MARCH 1st[21]

. . . I told you in my last letter of Genl John S. Preston's visit to us—Since then he left for N. Orleans but before doing so, wrote me a note, enclosing $100 and saying it was all he could now spare, but on his return he hoped to quadruple it . . . and send us some provisions which he has ordered for us from N. York viz—a bag of coffee—a B[arre]l of sugar &c—

. . . John proposes that we would buy that lot of ground near the M. F. College which he has always had in view for us—and as you are not here to advise, I follow his advice with the agreement of my council, and will buy it on Monday (March 5th) at public sale. Mr Desaussure,[22] who was our friend in the "American Hotel" case, will be again, and if we will now purchase the second half of this square, will undertake to buy back from two parties who have it, the first half sold in Jany. I hope you will approve of this—John says it will be a good investment if we never use it to build upon, and if we do it will be a very desirable locality, and cannot be bought for perhaps five times the amount, when we want to build, or feel able to do so—The terms are $4,000 for the whole—with Bond and Mortgages on the lots—payable annually in 4 years—$1000 cash—We can give $1,000 draft on Mr O'Brien Bros. . . .

We received yesterday two more pupils . . . I expect we will be closely packed by warm weather. . . .

PATRICK N LYNCH TO HORACE GREELEY, MARCH 3[23]

Sir: . . . I have ever endeavoured to stand aloof from angry, political discussions, deeming that course most in accordance with my ecclesiastical character. . . . You will allow me, however, to correct some mistakes as to facts, relating to myself, into which the writer of the paragraph has fallen.

He states that I "was an original acrimonious, efficient and persistent pro-slavery Rebel." This charge will, I think, surprise my personal friends, as it certainly surprises me. So far as *acrimony* is charged, it does not tally with sundry notices of me and my acts published in the Tribune itself in 1861, 1862, and 1863. However let the charge pass. To discuss it, would be to discuss politics from which I abstain.

The Paragraph states that I had a *Te Deum* celebrated on the reduction of Fort Sumter in April 1861. In reply I state that the *Te Deum* was specially, to give thanks to God for the wonderful fact, still incomprehensible to me, that not a single life had been lost in the artillery duel of those two days; and the accompanying prayers implored a continuance of the Divine mercy—that the land might not have to mourn the loss of many lives. This, it seems to me, was a Christian appeal, not inappropriate in a congregation, where many near and dear to us, had passed through the dangers unscathed, and might again be exposed. I am not responsible for newspaper versions or newspaper comments. The paragraph states in the third place that I went to Europe next summer (1861 and "*did* induce the Pope to recognize Jeff. Davis as a potentate." Now, I did not go to Europe for nearly three years after the date assigned, and, in fact, the Pope was not induced by me or any one else to recognize the Confederate Government. It is incorrect to say that such recognition was ever given by the Holy See. . . .

BAPTISTA LYNCH, URSULINE CONVENT AND ACADEMY "VALLE CRUCIS" . . . MARCH 5th[24]

. . . I have just received such a kind letter from Mrs. Garesché . . . Mrs G . . . tells me she has about fifty-volumes promised to her, which she will forward to the

same. How much we have to be grateful for—I think if we were to publicize
our pamphlets, with list of losses &c &c—We would have so many donations,
as not to have a house large enough to keep them in . . .

. . . John has bought the "six lots" which he proposed and of which I wrote
to you—They cost on an average $633, instead of, as he expected $460. I yesterday evening, gave him for D.B. DeSaussure, Esq a draft . . . for $948:75
[$1,876,854 today]—the first payment . . . If you think it a good investment, &c
&c, we will endeavor to meet the other payments—if not, John thinks it can be
sold to advantage agn almost any time. . . .

BAPTISTA LYNCH, URSULINE CONVENT AND ACADEMY "VALLE CRUCIS" . . . , MARCH 15th[25]

. . . We have all given three general communions besides *ever so many* prayers
since you went on your questing expedition, but it does not seem they have
had much effect. Only $3000! And that for the great commercial emporium
of the North—that promised $50,000—if you would go on! I'm almost sorry
you took the trouble, and exposed yourself to the cold by going on—However
it must be all for the best in some way though it may not appear now—At all
events, it . . . is something to make a harvest of for Heaven. . . .

. . . God is very good to us, and we are daily growing stronger. . . . We are
working all the time—and our school is increasing a little. . . . John too is looking well and has considerable practice. . . .

Today we recd a barrel of crushed sugar—a present from Genl Preston—
We have received by our letters as much as you have by going north I do believe
. . . but I ought not to say that . . .

FRANCIS LYNCH, CHERAW, S.C., 1st APR[26]

On yesterday morning your telegram was received. . . . However I hope the
rect. of my second letter relieved your anxiety about Sister Anna's sickness.
She has improved so as to sit up some and is highly elated with the idea of
accompanying Bro. John to Columbia, on Wednesday next.

If able to go doubtless the change and travel will benefit her health.

. . . The sixth of May will be the anniversary 50th of the wedding of our
dear Parents. It will be well if we can have a happy reunion.

Your kindness in advancing the 500 dolls, to pay for Mules has obliged me
much—as I intimated to you, my Budget calls for 5000$ to set me right for the
Fall, with it, I will be able to fix up my several interests and return the same
during Sept and Octo next and will have quite an effect on the productiveness
of my pursuits. I hope with the use of it for 5 or 6% not only to repay the same

with ease, but to add 1000$ thru contribution to your funds. So if your calculations will admit of such disposal, without inconvenience, of your funds I am sure you will consider the matter.

. . . I wish much to aid your funds, and will D.G. do so, yet it is so important in my present circumstances to provide for the necessities of the interim till harvest, its fruitfulness will be increased thereby and means more at command.

BAPTISTA LYNCH, URSULINE CONVENT AND ACADEMY "VALLE CRUCIS' . . . APRIL 2nd[27]

. . . And so you return to New York! Well . . . it is for the best. I am glad for we need it all to rebuild and your chapel will I hope soon be so completed as to admit of service in it . . .

When may we expect you—and when will you go up to Cheraw? John is over there and I am anxiously waiting to hear how Anna is getting on—What a dreadful affliction to Father and Mother would her loss be—I do hope and pray she may soon recover—if it be the will of God

HENRIETTA LYNCH, CHERAW, APRIL 5th[28]

Your sister Anna has requested me to write and tell you that she has been dreadfully disappointed at your not coming up to see her just after Easter. She has been very low indeed and your Brother John has waited for her more than a week to see if she would gain strength enough to go with him but he will not risk it in the end. . . . on this evening she is in agony with the pain of her back. . . . The least disappointment throws her back. . . . Do come to see Anna as she desires it so much and as she is so dangerously sick. . . .

P.S. Anna expects you by return of car.

BAPTISTA LYNCH, URSULINE CONVENT AND ACADEMY AT "VALLE CRUCIS" . . . APRIL 6th[29]

. . . I was particularly anxious to consult you about the publication of our manuscript concerning "the burning of our convent"—I told you before, about Genl Hill writing to me for an account of it—and perhaps the Rector told you of Dr Treymonts visit requesting us to give a statement as to how we got possession of the "Preston Place" and saved it—which statement will be published—Today I received a message from Professor Le Conte[30] of S.C. College, asking for the same—I did the amiable to them all and unless you will correct and revise our manuscript and have it printed, others will have us in print anyway—Genl

Preston offers to print it for us in April, but I cannot accept his offer without your consent and I would be sorry to do anything that would militate against religion or the future interests of our Convent—You know that when Abp Purcell gave me such "a slap in the face" about Sherman and Hampton, I just enclosed him the pamphlet "sack and burning of Columbia" by Sims—[31] He seems to have been staggered a little by it and sent it on to Capt Cornysen—(the Commissary who gave us rations and $50. in greenbacks)—for corroboration. He however answers it I think evasively and his letter has been published in the "Cincinnati Telegraph" the Abp's organ—and is now going the rounds of the papers south I am told.

I believe Mr Cornysen to be a man of *undoubted probity*, and yet his statements are not true—I suppose thro- ignorance—The subject has become so agitated, that a certain set of respectable citizens will attest to the fact of Columbia having been burned by the Army under Sherman, and our account is to be a sort of corroborative evidence, together with that of a hundred others—I feel some timidity about this. . . . They are all very warm on the subject just now—and it is really wonderful to me, that an attestation is required of a thing as plain as that the sun shines! . . .

BAPTISTA LYNCH, URSULINE CONVENT AND ACADEMY
"VALLE CRUCIS" . . . TO SENATOR MANNING, APRIL 9th[32]
I take the liberty of addressing myself to you in the hope of interesting you in behalf of the rebuilding or our "Convent and Academy" which were consumed in the general conflagration of Columbia by the Army under Genl Sherman Feb 17th 1865—

Although our Institution was established in Columbia only about seven—now nearly eight—years, I do not hesitate to say that it had become one of the most flourishing and popular educational institutions in the whole country. Our sisterhood have devoted their lives to the advancement of education and religion and are well qualified for the duties which they assume—

I will not detain you by a rehearsal of the dreadful consequences of the burning of our "Convent and Academy"—our pupils dispersed—our selves reduced to abject poverty—&c &c—but only ask your attention to our earnest wish to engage ourselves anew in our work of education—and for that purpose, to rebuild our convent and academy—We wish to petition Congress for $150,000 to be appropriated to the erection of a house calculated to accommodate two hundred students (young ladies)—with their corps of teachers (our Sisters–) It is our earnest desire to offer at the earliest possible date such advantages of education to rich and poor, as, we believe, only such institutions as ours can give.

It is our firm belief that government, which so generously fosters education, could not more nobly or advantageously disseminate its funds for that
purpose, than by such an endowment—I beg your interest in this petition
Honored Sir, and will gratefully receive your advice upon the subject. . . .

BAPTISTA LYNCH, URSULINE CONVENT AND ACADEMY "VALLE CRUCIS" . . . APRIL 14th[33]

We have been *very much disappointed* in not seeing you during your short return to your Diocese. . . . But then of course it was better that you should go to
see Anna and our dear Parents . . .

You did not, as you said, enclose me Mr Jones letter and I hope you will
not give him any more credentials—I have lost all faith in him—He sends us
nothing, and I think goes travelling over the country on what he collects for
us . . .

If the Macon House is dropped, I will regard it as the will of God, and turn
our attention all the more rigorously to the establishment of a day school in
Columbia—next fall, if you approve. . . .

I am very glad you think of starting the Miscellany[52] again, no doubt with
the combined support of the Carolinas Georgia and Alabama it will be a success—and Charleston who was the pioneer should not resign entirely to others
the glory of disseminating Catholicity by that means. . . .

"Prudence is the better part of valor" But I cannot imitate Genl S[herman].
and tell an untruth about the burning of the convent—I simply gave the letter
of M—to Mrs Dr Darby—the daughter of Genl Jno S. Preston and his letter
in reply concerning the saving of his house—the object of that is, to show that
private property so far [from] being respected as promised, was ordered to be
burned—

Prof. Le Conte sent to us for an account of the burning of our convent &c,
but I will of course as you say let them manage their own affairs—I would be
truly sorry for anything which might militate in the slightest degree against
our *religious interest*, which is paramount to every thing else. I will enclose you
a circular letter I wish to send to "the powers that be"—

I wish I could show you a letter from Sr. de Chantel at Washington—who
says—send your Petition soon, you have warm friends here—who will support it, &c—

As mother says—"Nothing ventured, nothing harmed" and I suppose no
harm will be done by sending the enclosed to various members—especially all
the prominent ones—we do not know one party from another and will just
select the names from the Almanac—shall we? From President Johnson? . . .

As soon as we get our furniture and things a little straightened, we will begin to look around for Postulants but just now, we are not quite ready to give one a shelter. We have twenty one Boarders and the four little Lynch pupils—all busy preparing for the Distribution[53]—and want to know when it will be your convenience to preside? . . .

BAPTISTA LYNCH. URSULINE CONVENT AND ACADEMY, "VALLE CRUCIS" . . . APRIL 21st[34]
. . . Anna continues to improve and will come over to see us, as soon as able to travel. . . .

I love this "Association of Prayer"[35] and have affiliated our Community to that, of which Rev. F. Sestini[36] is the Director—I hope you have no objection—You see, I forgot to ask you—I have so long been accustomed to act for myself, and yet I love to be directed—perhaps I should say *advised*.

We are receiving congratulatory remarks on *your* promotion to the cardinalate! The Tribune[37]

BAPTISTA LYNCH, URSULINE CONVENT AND ACADEMY, "VALLE CRUCIS" . . . APRIL 29th[38]
. . . I hear through the paper and other peoples letters of your success, but I fear reports are exaggerated. I hope you are not *overworking* yourself—remember "Rome was not built in a day"—Do you expect to go to Boston and Philadelphia before you return? I hope you have heard from Cheraw as we have done, that Anna is improving. . . . At one time she was so low as to receive Extreme Unction, but immediately after, she fell into a comfortable slumber and has continued to grow better . . .

Brother John is talking of going on to New York and trying to sell his share in the gold mine to some company—He is so much in want of money, that he seems to think this his only resource—Francis seems to be doing well . . . I sent him a Draft for $100—last week. He wrote me that he would be glad to get $200 for immediate use—I know he will repay the Convent generously when he sells his crops—

Poor "Daniel" is coming to us, in a half-starved condition to get provisions, to be paid for at harvest season. Dr Merriweather was shocked by his appearance and hollow voice—Daniel says he is "mighty sorry" now, that he left here and did not accept your offer. . . .

Monday Evening 30th April—
. . . I do not understand why you say you will not be able to go to Cheraw for the 6th May? . . . I have no fears of the Cholera myself, having been in Cin. in 49—When it raged to such a fearful extant, but at the same time, I hope

you will not remain in its neighborhood. It will no doubt decimate the whole
country this summer. The smallpox which I dread more, is raging in Charleston—considered an epidemic. . . .

By todays post we received $100 in one letter and two Drafts from our Sisters in Galveston—one $210 in currency, the other $51—in gold—You see how
much more fortunate we have been than Mr Jones. I think he would do well
to *resign* the business (he has travelled enough) . . . You could then send some
Priest to travel for his health or otherwise who would do much between . . .

BAPTISTA LYNCH, URSULINE CONVENT AND ACADEMY
"VALLE CRUCIS" . . . ASCENSION DAY [10 MAY][39]
. . . Anna continues to improve T.G. and is full of the notion of visiting Columbia—I hope she was able to approach Holy Communion in 6th inst on the occasion of the Golden Wedding[40]—I'm so sorry you could not be at Cheraw at that
time and say Mass for, and give Holy Communion to our dear venerated Parents—I know it would have given them great happiness—John sent them over
a large handsome wedding cake made to order and we put up a box of trifles and
sent them per express, I hope in time to reach them on Saturday evening—I cut
some "Altar breads" and enclosed them in an envelope and tied it up with white
ribbon after the fashion, in which worldly people send wedding cake, and sent
it for their "Celestial Banquet." . . . Just to think—fifty years of mutually shared
anxieties and responsibility—and what a retrospect As Sister Antonia . . . says
"May we serve God, were it but with a small share of their fidelity"! . . .

BAPTISTA LYNCH, URSULINE CONVENT AND ACADEMY,
"VALLE CRUCIS" . . . MAY 16th[41]
. . . There is a good deal of sickness about, and John has his share of practice
. . . We know very little of what is transpiring in the world outside of "Valle
Crucis"—our school and ordinary duties occupy our time and attentions, so
that we are as perfect recluses. . . . It will be our own fault, if we do not become
contemplatives.
. . . When you have finished your "questing expedition" and have leisure
to turn you attention this way, I want to consult you about selling the lots in
our burned district—all around is now rebuilt—and hauling the bricks to the
square which we have bought, to begin at once the erection of a part of our
convent? I do wonder if Jones will ever do anything for us. He has sent us $150
in six months! We have sent our letters to Washington, but unless the Blessed
Virgin and St. Joseph bring about a miracle, we have no hope of success in that
quarter—we pray and hope anyway. . . .

It is just about four months since you were here—that is the longest time you have ever staid away from the convent, when you were on this continent—but I feel so unlike my former self, that I do not blame you for finding us dull—Visitors in general however compliment us on looking well and on our cheerfulness in contrast with the world outside. . . .

FRANCIS LYNCH, CHERAW, S.C., 20 MAY[42]

On yesterday I was favored with your kind letter of 14th inst. with chk for $1250. So timely too, that I will not attempt to express my thanks. I am also pleased with your attention to the matter of cotton pickers, they may be really good, and perhaps will become better, as the inventor suggests. My planting is about through with, and promises a good stand of cotton on a little over 300 acres. I wanted to plant 400 acres but consented to increase the quantity of land first allotted for corn, thus cultivating the area estimated, say about 650 acres in corn and cotton. . . .

. . . Father and Mother are as well as usual. Your letter to them, with others from Bro John, Sister Ellen and Catherine were received just prior to the *6th of May*, and while we all dined with them, the receiving of the letters so timely, added greatly to the enjoyment of the occasion; enlivened by remembrances from sister Ellen and Bro John . . . [and] from Sister Mary about same time—The happy accts of all being well, and many uniting in Holy Communion seemed truly a reunion. . . .

BAPTISTA LYNCH, URSULINE CONVENT AND ACADEMY VALLE CRUCIS . . . MAY 20th[43]

I have just received a letter from Mr. L. Jones (with $200 enclosed) . . . I am in correspondence with Sister de Chantel Cummings and she through Miss Meade is trying to aid us—Miss M wrote to both Genl Sickles about the rations, and to Genl Sherman to get him to recommend our case at Washington and they have sent me the reply of each, which I much appreciate—All is pleasing with Genl Sickles as you know, and with Gnl S[.] who again denies his acts—I will try and be prudent—of course I write only to Sr. de Chantel.

I also recd today a letter from the secretary of Chief Justice Chase, who altho he can give me no advice thinks our petition would receive a kind and careful consideration! I am agreeably surprised. . . .

BAPTISTA LYNCH, URSULINE CONVENT AND ACADEMY, "VALLE CRUCIS" . . . [FEAST OF] CORPUS CHRISTI, 9 P.M.[44]

. . . This is the first day since we came south that we have had "Exposition of the Blessed Sacrament"—and we enjoyed it so much! Our pupils (twenty-one) have just concluded their "Annual Retreat" with a general communion and renovation of their baptismal vows. They seem perfectly happy and were as good and satisfactory as we could wish them to be—I am very much pleased too, with the manner in which Rev Dr. Meriwether gave the meditations to them &c. . . . Several of the children are . . . ardent now about entering our noviciate . . .

I suppose you will spend the great part of the summer in making the visitation of your diocese all through South and North Carolina where I am told there are many scattered Catholics who have not been confirmed—and some of whom feel neglected—the war having prevented you from making your visitation before.

Brother Francis and Miss Louisa Blain[66] accompanied Anna over to Columbia last week—I have not seen Anna yet, but hope that under the kind and judicious care of brother John, in whom she has such unbounded confidence, she may soon be strong enough to come out to see us—I was sorry that Louisa Blain could not stay with Anna—she appears such a nice sensible girl; I was very much pleased with her—Francis looks *very well* indeed although much grayer than when I saw him last. . . .

The heavy rains so destroyed the greater part of the crops that [Revd Dr Meriwether] had to begin over again, which he is doing with a very good grace—we have three or four plows running but Francis does not seem to think the farm will pay for itself. . . . We have received a very kind letter from Mother Baptista Ursula—Sup Srs Mary California, with Draft for $55 in gold—and another from Rev. Fr. Blake the Catholic pastor in Hessian, Ohio—He writes warmly, and feels assured that "if Bishop Lynch would send a Priest in to beg in our behalf: we should soon be enabled to rebuild a splendid convent—"videmus"—we also recd by the same mail the final payment for Miss Mary Cuthbert of Petersburg Va. . . . Miss Cuthbert was with us at the time our convent was burned, and is the niece of Genl Bragg[45] . . . Col Green gave us good rations today and moreover hauled our corn from the Depot—How much we have to be grateful for . . .

2

"PRACTICE FREE, TIMES HARD, MONEY VERY SCARCE AND GETTING SCARCER"

June–December 1866

"The Negros are creating some apprehension around us." Baptista Lynch's opaque comment in the summer of 1866 likely reflected the growing unease among white Southerners about the efforts to organize the Blacks as a political force, in anticipation of Congress recognizing their right to full citizenship. That troubling development made all the more necessary the Ursuline's cultivation of the local federal commanders who represented the only safeguard against the race war which her brother had predicted that emancipation would eventually produce.

Despite these unsettled conditions, Baptista's long-range-planning for her community remained extremely ambitions: a multiethnic group of seventy-five religious women, which would have made the Ursulines of Columbia the largest Catholic religious community, male or female, in the country! Pursuing such an expanded community made for aggressive recruitment of candidates and the decided reluctance to dismiss candidates who gave little or no evidence of having a religious vocation. To realize such a goal required a major capital investment in a new facility. Given her extreme disappointment in their northern agent's fundraising. Baptista explored all possible sources, both domestic and foreign, for donations to their rebuilding campaign. Not even Empress Eugenie of France was off-limits.

Meanwhile, the Ursulines were not even able to fill the relatively few student accommodations available at Valle Crucis. The widespread inability of parents, including those of Baptista's immediate family, to afford such an elite education, caused Baptista to reduce the tuition and boarding rates for the school. Nonetheless, she remained optimistic. The productivity of their Valle Crucis farm under the able care of their chaplain was one positive indicator that better times lay ahead. Even though donations toward a new building continued to fall far below expectations, Baptista kept the faith that construction was just around the corner.

The inability of their now-isolated academy at Valle Crucis to serve the local Catholic girls of Columbia led Baptista to the conclusion that they needed to start an in-town day school, to preempt the Presbyterians from poaching for their own academy. Baptista was ever keen to broaden the scope of their educational outreach. One of her more avantgarde proposals involved the giving of retreats to secular women. She also ruminated about a preparatory school for girls interested in a career in teaching, as well as a trade school for Blacks. In mid-September, Mother Baptista led three other Ursulines by train, steamboat and carriage on a grueling, four-day five-hundred-mile trek from Columbia to Tuscaloosa. The outreach to Alabama was the consequence of Baptista's intention to open a satellite community beyond South Carolina.

In Texas, the Spanns gamely persisted in attempting to adjust to the new order. Mary Lynch Spann's brothers-in-law had abandoned planting after one season, to seek their fortunes in Galveston. In contrast, her husband was willing to try a bit longer to cultivate cotton with free Black labor. Still, as Mary ominously observed, echoing her Ursuline sister, people—both Blacks and whites—were very unsettled. Particularly disturbing to her was the failure of the thirty or so now freed persons to attend Mass and other Catholic services which they had previously done while in bondage.

In Columbia, Mary's doctor brother, John found his "practice free, times hard, money very scarce, and getting scarcer." Unsettled times were poor soil for economic recovery. Meanwhile, Anna Lynch, under the personal care of her physician brother in

Columbia, had improved sufficiently by October to accompany Patrick Lynch to Baltimore where the American bishops were holding a plenary council. Bishop Lynch, as the "first promoter" of the gathering, had been responsible for the planning of the council. No surprise, then, that the evangelization of the freed people became a major item in the prelates' agenda. Despite the support of the host, Archbishop Martin Spalding of Baltimore, and a few other prelates, the council participants refused to do anything to promote an outreach to Blacks beyond encouraging dioceses to do so. Internal evidence suggests that Patrick Lynch was assigned the task of writing the pastoral letter that the prelates issued following the council. In that letter he attempted to move the Catholic laity to take the actions regarding the exenslaved in the country which his fellow bishops failed to decree.

BAPTISTA LYNCH, URSULINE CONVENT AND ACADMY
"VALLE CRUCIS" . . . FEAST ST. BASIL [JUNE 14][1]
. . . Anna is at Johns and feels very well, goes to Mass and only needs strength to come out here in the hot weather—the heat is very great and debilitating . . . Friday 15th June,

   . . . Just to say that we will wait to speak with you before giving any answers about the candidates—you know my wish is to see a *full* house—a community of seventy five—one third lay sisters and the remainder choir sisters, of every nation . . .

   What do you think of our giving a "retreat" to secular ladies during vacation? You always seemed to desire it, and we were never so well situated for it as now—

BAPTISTA LYNCH, URSULINE CONVENT AND ACADMY,
"VALLE CRUCIS' . . . JULY 8th[2]
This will be handed to you by Mrs Brisbane with whose visit to us we are so much pleased.

   She has made a retreat of three days, and I see no obstacle to her joining us, so far—She certainly is an exception for one of her age—Just to think—fifty eight years of age, and not a grey hair or artificial tooth! While I, fifteen years younger, am as grey "as a Badger," and am condemned to an entire set of artificial teeth. She makes me change my opinion respecting widows and old ladies becoming nuns—We each day admired her more and more, and she seemed equally pleased with us and our mode of life—So I suppose we belong to the

"Mutual Admiration Society"—(!) Of which Dr. Meriwether does not seem to be a member, judging by the way he went off with John this evening, and left the old lady to find her way down to the Depot and to Charleston as best she could. . . .

BAPTISTA LYNCH, URSULINE CONVENT AND ACADEMY,
"VALLE CRUCIS," JULY 16[3]

. . . As Anna was here until yesterday evening and John came occasionally to see her, I have seen more of him than usual—Anna improved during her stay . . .

. . . I am willing to add to the number of our lay-Sisters, whose labor is needed very much. You proposed some from Philadelphia, who had been dispersed or disbanded at the close of the war—I think perhaps those from that city of *quiet cleanliness and industry* are preferable to those from money hustling *fast* New York—We prefer for Lay Sisters "*neat orderly* thrifty servant girls— or as the northerners say "*help*"—accustomed to do general work for a small family. . . . Small in person—healthy, and between 18 and 21 years of age. (I feel like adding—light brown hair and blue eyes—but that sounds ridiculous, to those who do not believe as I do, that these are indications of temperament.)

For Choir-Sisters we are not so particular as to age—they may range from 18 to 30—and in exceptional cases, more, and I wish very much we could get a real German lady to teach that, to me, mellifluous language, in our Institute— and we want also another French lady—It would be all the better if they know music well, and could sing.

You see my dearest Brother we are just doing as we did seven years ago— settling accts—arranging matters—planning for the next session, plunging into business and saying "Now I begin." We bury the last seven years with its many, many joys—in the Bosom of God—and forgetting its few but heavy sorrows, we will press forward in our *supernal vocation.* God is very good to us in supplying our daily wants, and we may expect a good school I think. We will circulate our prospects during the month of August as heretofore, and leave nothing undone to ensure our usual success—D.V.

. . . Do you wish, or approve of our having a day school in Columbia or do you think it at all feasible? We have thought that under the exigencies of the times, we could send in two sisters every Monday, who could return every Friday evening to "Valle Crucis.". . . This would afford instruction to the Catholic children of Columbia—and perhaps others would come who would pay the expenses. . . . We lay this before you and will be glad to know your decision by the time we enter into retreat if convenient. We fear that Protestants will supersede us in the city and we ask ourselves, if the Ursulines of New Orleans of Vincennes and of London did this in the beginning, shall we be less generous in the same cause? . . . Sr. Ursula and Sr Joseph[70] who are both good and steady are willing to undertake it also. But I . . . do not wish to agitate the point in public, until it is settled by your decision.

Regard us as ready, willing and anxious to do whatever will *contribute most* to the greater glory of God and good of souls, by the Instruction of young girls. . . . We are willing to have a normal school—a school for negroes—any kind that you may think advisable, to carry out the above mentioned end—And we are willing, if you so decide, to have none. . . .

I wrote to Abp Purcell acknowledging the $1000. . . .

BAPTISTA LYNCH, URSULINE CONVENT AND ACADEMY,
SUNDAY MORNING, 29th JULY[4]

I received your welcome letter with the photograph and am not surprised at your taking a favorable view of the proposition, coming from the source it does, and it seems to me, with such advantageous offers of property—We may well say "no one knows what a day may bring forth" How little we expected this—and what will the Maconites say—and good Bp V[erot]? Though there is a vast difference between the opening prospects of the two places. It seems to me that it will not be necessary for us to go and see the places—It would be so expensive and fatiguing, besides it would consume time.

. . . I will send our circular to Bp. Quinlan immediately. I will also mention to him the requirement of our rule on the point of foundations—and . . . see how far he can conveniently meet them—notwithstanding the good will of Bp. Q.[72] and your high esteem of him, I think it would be prudent to have everything "fair and square" before we make a move, and you could do that much better than I could—will you or can you conveniently? . . . Sr. A[ugustine] is at her games. All the rest are as usual, but will be *very angry* with you if you go north again, without coming to "Valle Crucis"—I hear that you are respected in Boston, so I hope you will do better there than you have done in N.Y. . . . If you see Genl Hartwick there, I hope you will make a Catholic of him—
I hope there is no danger in your going north—I see the cholera is in N.Y., Brooklyn, Philadelphia—and even Baltimore. . . .

Will you not drop in during the convention here next week, or do you steer clear of all such?[73] . . .

BAPTISTA LYNCH, CONVENT, AUG 4th[5]

I wish we knew your whereabouts . . . and I might have telegraphed you, had

I been certain that you were in Charleston—Rev Dr Meriwether . . . is very anxious to see you. . . .

The negroes are creating some apprehension around us. . . .

I want to consult you about the choice of subjects for Ala—What do you think of making Sr J[osephine] local Superior? and sending Sr. Augustine with her. . . . Of course I do nothing without consulting the counsel of sisters, but they rarely differ or dissent from any thing I propose—

. . . What is Mr. *Luke Jones* doing? Whatever he may collect never reaches us—so that the poor people have the merits of doing a charitable concern, but it is something like the Fenian bubble[75]—goes into the wrong purse. Please look after him. . . .

HENRIETTA LYNCH, CHERAW, [AUG 16th][6]
I write you this to thank you many thousand times for your kindness in attending to our wants in the purchase of the articles we asked for. They are all beautifully fine and much to be admired. It must have given you great trouble to get them and therefore we appreciate your kindness the more. . . .

My health is very wretched I have never known before such exhaustion joined to inexpressible feelings it makes me very sad for what my destiny may be by end Sept. I stand much in need of prayers. You know the one subject it still troubles me. Anna and Mr Lynch arrived last week the latter speaks of going North by end of Aug. Anna is far from being well she gives up to her nerves almost as much. There is a fair share of fever in Cheraw fatal to some. Mr Henry McIris has lost a child of 12 yrs being the second since my return. . . . There is a very great Methodist revival in the town and no other news. . . .

[P.S.] Oblige me by destroying this after reading.

BAPTISTA LYNCH, URSULINE CONVENT AND ACADEMY . . .
AUGUST 23rd[7]
The enclosed letter (or rather Bp Q's letter of which this is a copy) speaks for itself—Is it not beautiful? . . . The only writing I would like drawn up is the legal papers respecting the property—you know how timid I am on the subject of being "turned out of house and home" or whatever you may call the action of eviction—I suppose I am decidedly *weak* on that point—

. . . I have spoken to nearly all of the Srs about it, and find the right spirit— all goes well in general—but all so far, are afraid to have Sr. A[ugustine] go out there and think she would do a serious injury, therefore I will not take her out to mar the good work . . .

I expect great things for you in Boston—the *Athens* of America. Should you see any of our friends—you know—please say every-thing kind for us. . . . "God speed" Jones and to our advantage—as well as his—

BAPTISTA LYNCH, URSULINE CONVENT AND ACADEMY
"VALLE CRUCIS" . . . SEPT 2nd[8]

. . . Hope you received mine enclosing that of Bp Q . . . The papers I want him to write are those, such as you gave me for the "American Hotel"—He, to hold a mortgage on the house, and we, to hold the deed.

. . . We have received our delightfully toned, and prettily made "American Organ with tremolo attachment"—the partial gift of "Messrs S.D. and H.W. Smith, Fremont Street opposite Waltham—Boston. . . . We are expecting the Bell every day and are having the tower for it building—the carpenters will raise it on tomorrow.

. . . Rev. F . Crogan[9] sent up a first rate watchman from "Libby Mills"—as respectable looking as Genl Scammon[?]—His name is Scanlon—is (I suppose) fifty years of age—good Catholic and has a rich Hibernian voice! He hears Mass every morning after his night watch, and then takes his rest. . . .

BAPTISTA LYNCH, URSULINE CONVENT AND ACADEMY
"VALLE CRUCIS" FEAST OF THE NATIVITY [OF THE BLESSED
VIRGIN MARY, SEPT 8][10]

. . . I am very glad that you are getting in some means—every little is a help and besides you know that at this time, it is so scarce everywhere, that our dollars count for five almost. . . . We will soon look for our school to bring us in something, and we will settle all when you return. . . .

Now is the time I would thrill for South Carolina to be rec'd well in Boston since at the Peace Convention "So Ca and Mass were arm in arm"—[11]

Mr. Jones sent me a draft for $400—and I hope he will be useful to you in collecting. . . .

The even tenor of the school continues—and pupils are dropping in slowly—we now have twelve interesting girls, among whom are Judge Aldrich's daughters . . .

And today we received "Meneely's Bell.". . . It will be hung in the tower just erected in the yard, on Monday D.V.—But you can bless it afterwards, can you not? . . . I wrote to Genl Green (Comm. of this post) and asked him to have it hauled out for us. He did so with great promptitude and politeness—

Gen Sickles is in Columbia during the session, and came out to Valle Crucis on the *second day* after his arrival, to pay his respect as he so genteelly said—I was quite charmed with his conversational powers, which are equal to Genl Preston's. His visit was made in the style of a perfect gentleman's—he enquired particularly for you. He, Gov Orr and almost all who speak seem interested in the cultivation of the negroes. . . .

. . . Dr. M thinks your visit to Edgefield did so much good and hopes you will finish the good work begun—I heard him narrate to John, how several highly intellectual men were perfectly convinced by your sermon of the truth of the doctrine of Purgatory and now only wanted to hear you on Transubstantiation. . . .

I will leave for you, and packed in a Box—a biretta (made by Sr. Charles)—a small cap (made by Sr de Sales) and a mitre [(made by myself)—all of which I hope will fit you. I have fastened on slightly as an ornament to your mitre the *relic* sent me by the Princess deSay in Whittenberger—I hope it is not contrary to the rules—I would like to fix on the reverse side that beautiful medallion given you by the Holy Father—You can have that done yourself—I would fix it in the centre of the crown of thorns. . . .

BAPTISTA LYNCH, WEST POINT ALA, SEPT 18th[12]
You see I am on my way with Srs Josephine and Stanislaus to Tuscaloosa—and under the kind and attentive escort of Rev Father Pellicier who reminds me of yourself as a travelling companion foreseeing every want and never intrusive. . . .

Yesterday we all felt sick—the effect of broken rest the night before, which we spent at John's, leaving at 4:30 a.m. but we slept well in the delightful cars—the "night train" which we took at Branchville and remained in until this morning we reached West Point—Dickens' Valley of Eden with its many dirty, green mouldy puddles and miserable rickety old wooden houses and farms—The country was beautifully luxuriant in its wild verdure, but the corn and cotton crops are poor or indifferent—We will start D.V. in two or three hours—

FRANCIS LYNCH, CHERAW, 19 SEPT[13]
. . . My anticipations were too sanguine in regard to my crop yet will gather a fair one perhaps 100 bales. So far as I have tried the cotton pickers, my hands have not found them to do well and claim the efficiency of the fingers the more. . . . I would prefer . . . to return the picking machines if permissible. . . .

BAPTISTA LYNCH, TUSCALOOSA, AL, 22 SEPT[14]
We left West Point on Friday 18th about 1 ½ P.M. and arrived at Montgomery about 7 P.M.—took the steamer "Prairie State" and arrived at Selma about 4 ½ a.m. Wednesday 19th. We rested at Selma (with Mrs Cath Cochran for-

merly Julia (Sullivan) until about 3 ½ P.M. when we took the cars under the escort of Rev. Fr. McDonough . . . We took the stage coach at Newbern about 8 P.M. and traveled in a very unpleasant condition until about midnight—then rested for two hours and started again—worse off than ever—the nine passenger coach having been changed for a six passenger one, without any diminution in our party, . . . Such a time as we had of it! We stalled ever so often—had to get out and walk through the mud up hill and down dale—the stage turned over &c &c—a chapter of accidents—but T. G. no one seriously injured. . . .

About an hour before we reached Tuscaloosa the rain began to pour in torrents and the stage to leak—We concluded that our convent here is to effect much good—seeing so much had to be encountered in establishing it . . . It is a wonder to me, how we escaped as well as we did—and here I am instead of being over at the Convent which we went to see, not able even to receive visitors down stairs—so knocked up neuralgic and bruised in feeling from cold contracted—Srs Josephine and Stanislaus being young and lighter are doing very well, though both suffered considerably. . . . I could not venture the stage again unless obliged to do so, and would prefer the boat and cars all the way to Columbia.

We are much pleased with Tuscaloosa and with the convent. . . . It has a fine respectable appearance, but it not only has neither gas and water—which no house has in Tuscaloosa—but is in a much more unfinished state than Rev. F. Pellicer had any idea of—we found the plasteurs and painters busy, and the Revd Father McDonough indefatigable—We are most fortunate in having him here to attend to the business and he leaves nothing undone. . . . I am very sanguine of our effecting much good here A.M.D.G.

JOHN LYNCH , COL., S.C., SEPT 24th[15]

. . . Dr. M . . . feeling more secure *one* night than usual . . . slept soundly, knowing the moon was shining bright and Mr Scanlan on the watch, . . . behold the next morning the first thing presented to his view on entering the field was a shuck of suspicious appearance, on feeling which, he became convinced he had been robbed, on examination he found some person or persons had brought a waggon to the side of the field and had taken about *eight* bushels of corn, he determined to pull it the first day afterwards, that the weather would permit, and in the meantime . . . guns and pistols, were put in order and every man at his post . . .

JOHN LYNCH, COLUMBIA, S.C., OCT 2nd[16]

. . . Practice fair, but no money coming in, it appears to be getting scarcer and scarcer here.

Oct 5th

I have been delayed in sending off my letter. . . . If you find time to write to Mr. Wright, it might not be amiss to let him know that the Mary Copper Mine Co—is a chartered institution, with all the privileges granted by the Legislature, . . . I am much obliged for the interest you have taken, and am sorry my partner did not respond. I will see more of him in a few days, and let him know I . . . can sell his part with mine. . . .[17]

BAPTISTA LYNCH, URSULINE CONVENT AND ACADEMY TUSCALOOSA, ALA., FEAST ST. FRANCIS ASSISI [OCTOBER 6][18]

The convent is still in too unfinished a state to receive boarding pupils, but . . . we have fifteen day-scholars . . .

Since Education is one of the grand topics of the Council, why did you not invite a representation by letter from the various convents devoted to education. A few leading questions might have been proposed and answered perhaps with profit. Do not think me presumptuous, or a believer in women's rights. I am very far from it.[19]

BAPTISTA LYNCH, URSULINE CONVENT AND ACADEMY, TUSCALOOSA, ALA, OCT 16th[20]

. . . We have as yet only three boarding pupils one of whom is a beneficiary—a respectable poor girl who makes herself very useful about the house in return for her tuition &c, but as soon as the house is finished and ready to receive others, I have no doubt they will come—as then we will send out "circulars" and canvases for them as we have done in Columbia.

Our day scholars number twenty but they too will increase after awhile I have no doubt—We must here as elsewhere creep before we walk. I expect however that the Rt Revd Bishop will have to do for our Institute, what you thought you would have to do for ours in Columbia during its first few years— viz—support us—But you know how unwilling we will be for that, and what exertions we will make to obviate such circumstances.

"THE EMANCIPATED SLAVES," PASTORAL LETTER OF THE AMERICAN HIERARCHY, OCTOBER 21[21]

We must all feel . . . that in some manner a new and most extensive field of charity and devotedness has been opened to us, by the emancipation of the immense slave population of the South. We could have wished, in accordance with the action of the Catholic Church in past ages, in regard to the serfs of Europe, a more gradual system of emancipation could have been adopted, so they might have been in some measure prepared to make a better use of their freedom, than they are likely to do now. Still the evils which must necessarily attend upon the sudden liberation of so large a multitude, with their peculiar dispositions and habits, only make the appeal to our Christian charity and zeal, presented by their forlorn condition, the more forcible and imperative.

We urge upon the Clergy and people of our charge the most generous co-operation with the plans which may be adopted by the Bishops of the Dioceses in which they are, to extend to them that Christian education and moral restraint which they so much stand in need of. Our only regret in this matter is, that our means and opportunity of spreading over them the protecting and salutary influences of our Holy Religion, are so restricted.

ANNA LYNCH, CHERAW, NOV 1st[22]

I arrived safely last evening and found Robert at the Depot waiting for us. I need not say that all at home, were greatly disappointed that you could not come up with me—Mother had been sending for us every night for a week. . . .

BAPTISTA LYNCH, URSULINE CONVENT AND ACADEMY, [TUSCALOOSA], NOV 22nd[23]

. . . I suppose this House is to flourish some day or other since it is founded on the Cross. Were it not for the exertions and support giving us by the young priest here . . . I do not know what we would do. Besides coming to an unfinished and unfurnished house—a part of which was occupied for more than a month after our arrival by its former owner, we found everything at sixes and sevens—and as I said would have been very much embarrassed had we a clergyman here, less energetic and willing to aid us . . .

. . . Two sisters can very easily do all the teaching necessary for our present school and even twice as many pupils—but lay sisters are much needed for the domestic duties—and I hope Bishop Quinlan will follow your good example and exert himself to get us postulants both choir and lay sisters. . . .

It will be my first care upon my return to ask you about the erection of a chapel and *glebe* or parsonage, as we spoke of before—a cheap but useful building which will give us a proper choir—and sanctuary—the Revd Dr more room—and at the same time give us the use of that which he now occupies and the chapel . . . The bell rings for school—I'm obliged to go—I have not worked so hard and been so tired out in body, in a long time. But it is good for me spiritually and corporally. . . .

BAPTISTA LYNCH, URSULINE CONVENT AND ACADEMY,
TUSCALOOSA, ALA, NOV 27th[24]
... We have secured the aid of a sister from Opalousa—or rather the promise
of one, who will come on soon—I knew her in BC as a white-veiled novice—
Therefore, I am ready to start for "Valle Crucis" ...

My idea is, to propose to Bp Q to cancel all debts for us, that may be necessary for the purchase of "the ways and means" for conducting our Institute—and give us the wherewithal to get "well under way"—and we promise
to return payment through the income of our Institute as soon as possible.
We must have the proper means and surroundings—statues pictures—chapel
furniture &c &c to produce "convent education effect" before we can have such
success as we have in S. Ca—And I am for pushing ahead, as you know. ...

MARY LYNCH SPANN, WASHINGTON CO [TEXAS], DEC 14th[25]
... I hope my dear brother your untiring exertions on behalf of the diocese has
met with a warm response and that it will not be a great while before the Cathedral will be seen in greater beauty than ever and other improvements also.
... But there is little in our country to work with just now—people seem to be
very unsettled in all quarters, the merchants it is said have overreached themselves, planters are generally discouraged from the past years experience and
fearing worse for the next—very many are renting out their lands perfectly
disgusted with trying to work the negroes, among the number are Mr. Spann's
two brothers. I believe they will both live in Galveston.

As for ourselves Mr Spann will try again this year and hope for the best.
Conlaw will superintend the field-closely and if the seasons are favorable I
think we will have better success. I would be sorry to leave this place principally on account of our little Church which has been a great consolation and
happiness for us during many years, in good times and during the Confederacy we had a good congregation for the country; besides the whites there
were about 30 communicants among the negroes but since their freedom I am
sorry to say that scarcely one remembers the church—were we to leave I am
satisfied the Church would be removed as there is no other Catholic family in
the neighborhood and this I would be grieved to think of so I live on the hope
that the negroes will come to their senses and that some Catholic families may
settle near by. Our Pastor probably will be removed to a village 9 or 10 miles
from here where some Catholic families have settled and where they speak of
building a Church but he has promised us that anyhow he will try to let us
have the Holy Sacrifice offered up once a week which will be a great blessing
and privilege.

And now my dear brother I will speak of a subject of importance—we received from the Bishop through Dr. Spann your truly kind and generous offer relative to Conlaw. Mr Spann and I would be very glad to see him accept at once but something seems to hold him back, I do not know what[;] all the clergymen who see him, think he ought to have a vocation for that life—considering his age and that he knows our desires. I suppose it is better to leave the decision to himself as he has reflection and sense enough but is not very quick to act ; he told me this morning that Father Bellaclas our pastor whom Conlaw likes very much and to whom I believe he speaks freely had advised him to write to you and thank you for your kindness and also to ask you for a year to make a decision So my dear brother you can form your own judgment of what is best. I do not despair yet having always had the thought for him but I commit the matter wholly to

Almighty God whose honor and glory and the eternal happiness of Conlaw is all I have in view . . .

In my last letter to Sister Ellen, I spoke of our wish to send Caro to her convent but seeing no opportunity of effecting this we sent her to Galveston now that this favorable occasion has offered, we regret much that she is not there, but perhaps it is all for the best and she may go later. . . . I will now conclude as I believe Mr Spann wishes to add a few lines . . .

Right Revd Sir
Dear Brother,
. . . Owing to bad seasons and the new character of our labor system, I have been only partially successful in planting this year. But with better experience for the coming year, I am not discouraged from trying again, and hope with the blessing of God for more successful results.

My motto is "Nil desperandum dum spiro, spero." . . .[26]

BAPTISTA LYNCH, URSULINE CONVENT AND ACADEMY
VALLE CRUCIS, FEAST HOLY INNOCENTS [DEC 28][27]
Sr Etienne and myself have been "posting up our accounts" and yesterday we saw the Dr and talked over the expenses of the farm—and according to my calculations—the yield of corn, peas, vegetables &c make, or very nearly makes, all expenses of stock—agricultural implements—fencing and hire of hands—of course every thing is in a much better condition—and next year will probably do a great deal more. I had no idea that planting was so remunerative! when it affords us, a plenty of milk—poultry &c lessening very much our expenses . . .

What about the Building plan? I hope you will soon set it in operation so that we can hold our exhibition in it. I think that by that time, we could get 40 pupils—so, I leave my plan entirely, and take yours if you think best.

. . . I wish to subject to your inspection our terms for next session, reduced as you wish—and which I hope will bring us in more pupils.

BAPTISTA LYNCH, URSULINE CONVENT AND ACADEMY
VALLE CRUCIS NEAR COLUMBIA, S.C. SUNDAY 30th DEC[28]
. . . Please give me if you can—the address of the person in Paris to whom I should address myself about the loan—Perhaps Mr. B. Lafitte could be of some assistance in that matter—It was the Visitation Convent of Paris that loaned the Ursulines of B. C. the money they used in building, and Sr. Etienne will be very much obliged for the address of Empress Eugenia to whom the Visitation Nuns of Mobile applied and who sent them a donation—(we hear a handsome one). We can do nothing more in this country, so must try elsewhere—What about Jones? He might as well *return* his papers to you and find some other employment than living off us. I'm tired of him, the mean fellow! . . .

3

"IN ALL PROBABILITY THIS WILL NEVER BE A STATE AGAIN BUT BE PART OF A KINGDOM"

January–June 1867

By 1867 Patrick Lynch had committed himself to retiring the diocesan debt by accepting invitations to speak for a potpourri of occasions, ranging from the dedication of churches to the meetings of aid organizations to lectures at lyceums. The bishop developed a collection of talks on scientific or religious topics, which he gave, like an evangelical itinerant preacher, across the Midwest, South, and Northeast, especially the New York metropolitan area. At the same time, aid societies, both domestic and foreign, were sending money to Charleston, to aid the diocese's recovery effort, and to provide relief for those still suffering from the war's devastation, particularly women and children The most constant benefactor of the diocese was the largely Catholic New York Ladies Southern Relief Association, which sent money and clothing monthly to Patrick Lynch to be distributed to "the suffering women and children of your See without distinction of religious beliefs." Of course, with the bishop on the road for months at a time, money and clothing tended to pile up in Charleston, awaiting the bishop's return. With the informal, intersectional Catholic network once more fully operative, the association's leaders quickly heard from friends in South Carolina that aid was not reaching the needy, Catholic or otherwise. By April, having found they could not depend on his taking the initiative, they were designating to Patrick Lynch particular recipients for relief

By mid-February of 1867, Mother Baptista Lynch thought she knew well enough the direction in which the winds were blowing through the halls of Congress to conclude that South Carolina, along with the rest of the former states of the Confederacy, would be under quasi-permanent military occupation. Northern and Southern opportunists would be controlling the vote of the soon-to-be enfranchised Blacks to establish biracial governments which would spell economic and political disaster for not only the white South, but the churches in particular, as the taxing of ecclesiastical properties quickly showed. The radical disordering of the social and political landscape, in the Lynches' view, was wreaking havoc with the economy. All the more reason to court the favor of their conquerors. To what extent could they get in bed with the enemy in pursuing God's greater good? Baptista was open to probing the limits.

Rebuilding was an obvious necessity, which Baptista, at the year's start, took to be an imminent undertaking. For whatever reason, she assumed that her brother, as he invariably had done in the past, would provide the funds. Baptista had a builder at the ready, awaiting only her brother's go-ahead. Then, by February, she gradually realized that the wherewithal to build was beyond their present reach. Baptista was reduced to the improbable expectation that an improving economy would enable parents to meet their financial obligations for keeping their daughters in the academy and thus provide the funds to build within the next few years. Or that a benefactor/benefactress would miraculously appear. But money had largely fled the South. Their reduced circumstances at Valle Crucis compelled Baptista to make the most of the farmland which now comprised their campus three miles south of Columbia. She maximized their self-sufficiency by making their "domestic economy" as productive as possible, under the management of their chaplain, William Meriwether. Her sights remained fixed on a near future in which they would have a grand academy, now in a rural setting which would draw, as they had during the war, the children of the Southern elite. On their new site, they would also provide free education for the area's poor, both Black and white. Baptista's optimism was fueled in part by her continuing belief that Irish freeholders would inevitably replace Black tenants in the agrarian economy of the uplands and quickly Catholicize the region, just as the Famine Irish had transformed so much of the Northeast. She saw Valle Crucis serving as the center of a vibrant Catholic community. On Sundays, more in anticipation than in recognition of any current reality, the Ursulines' great bell signaled to the surrounding countryside the beginnings of Mass and Benediction.

The Reconstruction Act of 1867 enabled about a million Blacks in ten former Confederate states to secure the franchise.[1] Those intent on undermining the integration of the freedmen into the Southern polity searched for ways to control this group of voters to whom they could no longer deny the ballot. In March, 1867, at the very time Congress was enacting its own Reconstruction plan which recognized the right of suffrage for the freedman and punished states who took action to suppress that vote, Wade Hampton and former US senator William F. Desaussure, along with a freedman, William Beverly Nash, formed the Union Brotherhood Society, a bi-racial political bloc, in which certain whites attempted, in making the most of a new order stacked against them, to control these new voters. It would take nearly a decade for such cooptation to create a viable force to overthrow Reconstruction in South Carolina.

Francis Lynch, all too aware that his economic recovery lay not in planting but in the revival of his shoemaking business turned to the latest technological development in the tanning process as the means to re-establish himself as a successful industrialist. In Texas, Charles Spann had experienced enough frustration as a postwar planter to move his family from Washington County to Galveston to take up the practice of law for which he had been trained.

BAPTISTA LYNCH, URSULINE CONVENT AND ACADEMY, VALLE CRUCIS NEAR COLUMBIA, JANUARY 2nd[2]

... The hands are [tasking?] their Christmas.[3] I believe there has been a backing out on their part, and Daniel, his son-in-law, and Lee are engaged for this year on the terms which they refused, Green is here by the month His wife obliges him to go to the low country, and so he cannot engage for the whole year as he wishes.

I have not seen John lately—he fell in the streets one night last week, and bruised his face very much.

Ellen Baptista Lynch.

I suppose you will Pontificate on Epiphany but we will expect you *for certain* during the Octave—we haven't killed the pigs yet! So you must be sure and come. Let us know when to expect you—please? We are planning to have the new building ready for a Distribution Hall (temporary and going ahead as usual!) . . .

BAPTISTA LYNCH, VALLE CRUCIS, JANY 14th[4]

. . . What about our building? By commencing in time we could perhaps use it for a "Commencement Hall"—We are receiving applications from new pupils from Georgia. I think I told you one had arrived—We must get more furniture. . . .

BAPTISTA LYNCH, URSULINE CONVENT AND ACADEMY,
VALLE CRUCIS, JAN. 25th[5]

John brought me out your letter—no envelop, with numbers estimate, which he and Rev. Dr. M. [discussed] over at the Dinner table and afterwards. Both consider it a freely made out estimate, and beyond what is actually necessary— Dr. M. wants to know if he shall turn the order over to Mr Dent at once? and seems to think no time is to be lost about the Building. . . .

I told you in my last about John giving the drawing to a responsible white man and a good builder, to calculate as Mr Devereux did for you the amt of lumber necessary. . . . If Johnson is satisfactory both to Dr. M—and John shall we go ahead?

Where is the money to come from to pay [for] this building? . . .

BAPTISTA LYNCH, URSULINE CONVENT, VALLE CRUCIS
NEAR COLUMBIA, JANY 27th[6]
. . . Who is this distinguished visitor Hon. J.F. Maguire[7]—and where did you pick him up? Is he the gentleman whose speeches I have so often seen in the London and Dublin Tablet? Why is he travelling in this country? I hope he will advise his countrymen to come and settle in the South, and Catholicize it—You ought to have heard Bishop McGill . . . and ourselves on that subject.

. . . I hope Anna will be able to take charge of James' children for awhile, but it would never do to have her, like so many maiden aunts . . . I pity Augusta, . . . her husband may incite her to work on our feelings, so as to relieve himself of the expenses of supporting them in after life, as well as now.[8] I am far from wishing to be unfeeling towards our poor dear James' little ones, but at the same time, I have learned to distrust representations—however affectionate they may be. . . .

BAPTISTA LYNCH, URSULINE CONVENT AND ACADEMY, VALLE
CRUCIS . . . JANUARY 29th [9]
. . . I have nothing of interest to communicate—except the death of that young negro girl in whom we were so much interested—who washed for us, &c, who was baptized by Rev. Dr. M—on her death bed: A few days ago she was at work here—was taken with a hemorrhage next night—sent for physician and priest—was baptized—and last night expired very suddenly and happily in her Baptismal innocence. This is the third negro we have instructed and I trust been the means of serving since our convent was burned—Hester's death is a source of great consolation to us. . . .

. . . Dr. M. . . . is such an utilitarian, that he tries my patience—While I wish to beautify our grounds, he is only interested in making them *fructify*. I hope we will both succeed to your pleasure. Sr. Theresa tells me he suffers with neuralgia very much. I have not seen him since Bp McGill left—nor heard him either for he does not *exhort* every Sunday as he should. . . .

Col. Bauskett told Bp McGill that he had never been Baptised and was awaiting your visit, that you promised to come up and give him these and receive him into the Church.

BAPTISTA LYNCH, URSULINE CONVENT AND ACADEMY,
VALLE CRUCIS NEAR COLUMBIA, S.C., FEBRUARY 5th[10]
I received your short but truly welcome letter, with enclosed Draft of Mr
Roman returned—I wrote at once to Belle's Father, acquainting him of it, as
we have no time to lose—and we have sent out Bills for pupils, hoping to collect $1200°° by the 6th of March when we will owe that sum or nearly it, for the
second payment on those lots near the M[ethodis]t College

I do not apprehend any difficulty in raising it for our Sisters are praying
earnestly, and it seems to me, that our Lord always answers their prayers. . . .

. . . John dined here on last Friday when he and Dr. M talkd over the building, lumber &c and—and I believe men are cutting the "stocks in the woods
and Mr. Dent is sawing the lumber. . . . I am so glad that you succeeded in
paying that Bill of $3000" Is not Divine Providence good to us, who devote our
lives to His worship and greater glory? Some how or other, He manages our affairs just as we want, without our having much trouble. What a work and fret-
ting worldly men should have, to raise that sum, and it came to you so easily.

What was the success of your scientific lecture? I should think that would
take well in this country, and at this time—When RRs are the mania—and
the great source of wealth to our country. That would take well in Cincinnati
and St. Louis—and Louisville too—or something like it. Also in Boston. Often lecturing on Religious subjects or such scientific Lectures now and then,
would do good I have no doubt. . . . I received a kind and friendly note from
our righteous Miss Hampton the other day—in reply to my note of sympathy
after the death of her sister.

. . . And as for John, I wish he could sell that *mine* and get money enough by
it, to put his mind at ease, not that I think he would allow it to remain so long,
but I cannot bear to hear him talk so constantly about money and debts—He
must have "picked up Eliza's *tune*." I'd try and choose a merrier one, if I were
he—for I tell him he has so many blessings to be grateful for, he ought to
recount those to himself, then he would feel and speak differently—After all
prayer is the grandest thing. But I must stop. . . .

BAPTISTA LYNCH, VALLE CRUCIS, SUNDAY FEBRUARY 10th[11]
. . . We are all as well as usual (T.G) notwithstanding the *Blow* of last night—I
am very [breathless ?] with the *nipplers* around, the whole set of whom are
not as valuable as "Carlo" were it not for their immortal souls—if they have
any(?) . . .

I have written to Hon W. Aiken[12] for some G. Peabody[13] money of which
he is the trustee—for education in the South. . . . As mother says "Nothing
ventured nothing had." . . .

BAPTISTA LYNCH, VALLE CRUCIS, WEDNESDAY 13th FEBRUARY[14]
I telegraphed you yesterday evening, hoping if there were a night train you would take it—and if not, that you would come up today. John and Dr. M as well as myself think if we are to have the house built, your presence is imperative here *now*—We must engage the Builders *now*, or relinquish them to an indefinite period—that is to say, the firms of Keitt and H whose estimate I enclose. They have taken more trouble and seem more interested than any one else—are strictly honest responsible men—and it seems, every way desirable for the work. They have just finished Agnews new and larger store on Main Street, and will engage at once for ours upon enclosed terms, or undertake at lowest bid, their work—It is for you to say "yes" or "no" after calculating the difficulties—but a more advantageous offer and arrangement cannot be expected any time—so John and Dr. M think and it seems so to me. . . .

All the letters from Augusta[15] to the children speak in the most complimentary style of your lecture. . . . I hope you have your pockets filled in Atlanta and Augusta—I was particularly gratified to hear of your sermon in the church—Religion and science are the grand "motive powers" and keep pace with steam—cables and telegrams—Well "put on another Engine" and get into "fullblast"—A.M.D.G. . . .

BAPTISTA LYNCH, URSULINE CONVENT AND ACADEMY,
VALLE CRUCIS . . . FEBRUARY 16th[16]
. . . Today I received . . . a very kind [letter] from Sr. de Chantal Carmel[17] of Washington, who says—"No doubt the general sympathy and the intense interest manifested by various Religious Communities for you, is a source of great annoyance to some of the Generals. Indeed, the feeling for you is like that entertained for Holy Father Pius—Secretary Staunton[18] is so kind. I think (Miss Meade[19] says she knows) we can quietly get him to do something. If there are any gov. buildings that would serve you until you can better accommodate ourselves, we could ask him for them. In case you did not wish to occupy them, they might be sold for your benefit—Bishop Domenec[20] of Pittsburg—a stranger to the Secretary, asked for a House wherein to hold the Freedwomen for instruction (by Srs. Mercy) and immediately an order was given, for all unoccupied Government Buildings to be surrendered to the Bp—also $900 to commence a promise of a regular annual sum to Srs. Mercy here which they sold for a considerable amount, &c. If any place in Columbia can be found belonging to the U.S. which would answer for a chapel temporarily—let us ask for it, and by giving the use of it to the Bishop, he might be thereby enabled to build you a house—"

I quote all this and lay it before you for consideration—what about the

"Arsenal" building—You may remember, that although the Arsenal was blown up, the Residence of President was left standing and is a very nice building— would do for our day school—shall we ask for it—We could sell it afterwards. In all probability this will never be a state again but be part of a kingdom—so we may as well come in for some of the spoils, if we can do so with out injury to religion—What do you think? So many good day schools are starting in C[olumbia] that I fear our competitors.

BAPTISTA LYNCH, URSULINE CONVENT AND ACADEMY,
VALLE CRUCIS . . . FEB. 20th[21]
I enclose you two letters—replies to mine enquiring respecting the Loan in France—you will see for yourself how little prospect there is for success, and why—

It occurs to me that under existing circumstances, it would be better to wait six months or a year, and see what turn matters will take, before going far- ther into a debt which we may find it very difficult to liquidate—We are well off compared with thousands—and contrasted with what we were this time two years ago—the number of pupils we have would I think (with the farm) support us, if they could pay—And neither your condition or ours, seems to warrant the embarrassment consequent on building at present.—it seems to me—however you are the best judge—and the weight must (I am sorry to say) fall on you.

I find not enough coming in to meet our March payment but we do not in any degree lose our courage or faith, and expect before the date of payment to be enabled to meet it. John says Mr Boman [?] was mistaken about the sale of MF College. And that the Arsenal was a State affair and not U.S. therefore the proposition of Sr. de Chantel is useless. . . .

ALGERNON, NEW YORK, MAR. 9[22]
Enclosed please find a cheque for $200 to your order which the association requests you will use as previously informed with other remittances, either in your vicinity or elsewhere as your judgement may direct.

An early acknowledgement is requested.

BAPTISTA LYNCH, VALLE CRUCIS, MARCH 12[23]
. . . I wrote you a long Birthday letter and sent it on North to care Bishop McFarland[24] . . . and I wrote another . . . telling you all about the [illegible] about drawing up papers and beginning Building, on acct of your forgetting or not sending the Draft of $1200 as you said. I hope my letters has [sic] reached you . . . ere this so that if you wish the building to go on, you may know how

things stand, and take measures to effect your wishes. It seems to me that the readiest and quickest way will be for you to borrow for immediate use from some other Bishop $10,000—or so to build it and repay it gradually and by collections. But of course you know best. . . .

BAPTISTA LYNCH, URSULA CONVENT AND ACADEMY, VALLE CRUCIS . . . MARCH 14th[25]

. . . I told you in my other letters how the building affairs had fallen to the ground.—was an unmentionable subject—and John and Dr. M deemed to feel cheap. An agreement could not be drawn up, until funds in hand for first payment warranted such a proceeding—You had forgotten the $1200 deposit, spoken of, to be placed in E.J. Scott's hands, for that purpose and so—I thought it would be better to pay Messrs Kirk and Howell something for their troubles and let the matter drop, since you must have met with some unexpected difficulty.—But today, John writes me, that Mr. Kirk called him again, and seems anxious to carry out plans suggested hoping to hear favorable accts from you by the time first payment will be due.

As yet things are just as you left them and if the Building is to be done this year, there has been a great deal of wasted time and talk about it and the hall can hardly be done for the close of scholastic year. . . .

BAPTISTA LYNCH, URSULINE CONVENT AND ACADEMY, VALLE CRUCIS . . . MARCH 31[26]

What a relief your letter of today—or rather just received—has been. . . . It is a great relief to me also to know, that your wishes are not deviated from—for I feared you would be disappointed and displeased at not finding the building going on—But I suppose that you also prefer that it should not be begun, if you can not raise funds to complete it—Indeed I would much *prefer,* that it should not be begun, than that you should be harassed or embarrassed by it—it sometimes strikes me that my plan of the chapel would be more suitable to our present circumstances—and even to the circumstances since we have so few pupils.

But of course your judgment is so much superior to mine and you have so much more comprehensive views—and see so much, that I do not see or understand. I will be glad if you can effect a loan of $1400 in St. Louis—and I do hope you will raise a fine collection—somehow or other I think you will—and then you will return, ready to start for Rome. . . . Rev. Dr. M. says you might happen to come across some rich body, just waiting for a chance to build up your dioceses, and you would come back ready to go ahead! John is afraid not—We'll see. . . .

Our Sisters will pray most cheerfully for success to your mission but some of them will not grieve, if you postpone building until we can build in town. . . .

BAPTISTA LYNCH, URSULINE CONVENT AND ACADEMY. VALLE CRUCIS . . . APRIL 5th[27]
Your telegram reached us today, and I am happy to say not one sister expressed disappointment. On the contrary we felt relieved, that under existing circumstances and prospects, you have not embarrassed yourself with the building—especially too, as after the expenditure of so much money we could promise ourselves so little comfort or gratification from it. I am sure it is all for the best. We all feel that it is—and perhaps after awhile, you will be able and willing to let us carry out our suggestion of a chapel which we all prefer. . . .

BAPTISTA LYNCH, URSULINE CONVENT AND ACADEMY, VALLE CRUCIS . . . APRIL 26.[28]
I write you a few hasty lines . . . to let you know that notwithstanding my resolution to the Contrary, I have been obliged to cash some draft in my favor. From "E.M Donan and Co Mobile in Howe's and Macy Bankers, 20 Wall Street. NY.

I tell you this at once, that you may not draw on them a second time and be disappointed. . . . We were for several days without a dollar bill in the house, and began to feel like we were . . . very neuralgic. So I thought it best to draw it before every body got sick.

Judge Aldrich was here a few days ago, and told me that planters would have to suspend their work, unless Factors would forward money to meet the expenses of the labor. . . . The great destitution of the state and country is almost inconceivable—and no one seems able to meet payments—they are mortified and pained, but that does not pay us—we feel for them—but our dependence is on the rations and we feel more for ourselves than for them—

You will be glad to hear that Revd "brother Ambler"[29] is sending us a sort of a postulant, whose money may be useful to us . . .

NEW YORK LADIES RELIEF ASSOCIATION, [MARY MILDRED] SULLIVAN, NEW YORK, APR. 27[30]
I enclose you a cheque from the Society for one hundred dollars, to be given to Mrs. Phillip J. Porcher , and Mrs. William McKensie Parker (fifty dollars each), in case you have not already given them that amount, if you have given them this amount already, the society will be happy to have you appropriated the enclosed to such cases as your judgment may approve.

Hoping to hear from you at your earliest convenience.

NYLSRA, [Mary Mildred] SULLIVAN, NEW YORK, MAY 10[31]
I forwarded to you from this Association on March 9th a cheque for two hundred dollars, March 30th one for three hundred, April 8th two cheques, one
for five and one for three hundred dollars, May 1st one for one hundred dollars.
I have recently learned that you are absent from your diocese, and therefore
that these amounts are unappropriated. The Society feels that as the need of
the people is so great (this money being intended to relieve present suffering),
and this the hour of their extremest need this amount of fourteen hundred
dollars, should not be lying idle, they therefore ask that if you are to be detained any longer from Charleston, that you will send for these cheques, and
transfer them either to the very Rev. Dr. T. Bermingham, or to whom ever you
may select to disburse them. . . .

BAPTISTA LYNCH, URSULINE CONVENT AND ACADEMY,
VALLE CRUCIS, May 16[32]
After all our work and management to prevent it, we are obliged to be a burden to you—in pecuniary matters—the answers to our Bills presented, are all
unsatisfactory (with one exception)—asking time and declaring their inability
to pay, &c &c—so that for our present needs and until our school reopens in
Sept. we must call on you for support. I calculate that $2000 will meet our
wants, but do not know exactly—You will be the best judge of how we should
manage this—It may be, that some parents may be able to pay us something,
but since the "Rations" have stopped (which they did May 1st) we have to spend
much more money and have used the Draft you sent me from Mobile, . . . I
cannot tell you how much I feel our having to call on you—especially as I do
not know the result of your collections either in New Orleans or St. Louis, nor
have we heard from Jones. . . .

  Moody (who is a splendid Boy) and Smith went fishing this afternoon to
provide for tomorrow's table but brought back only a bunch of "Bay magnolia
flowers" for our Blessed Lady's Altar. . . .

FRANCIS LYNCH, CHERAW, 21 MAY[33]
. . . I would be glad that something could be done for Mr. James Fer, an industrious man, but very unfortunate this year. $100 to him and family would not
be misapplied. There are many in this section that would be benefited with a
little aid a dozen at least, of moderate farmers.

  Besides these, among my laborers there are about thirty to forty families of
Negroes, with no subsistence other than I may advance to them. If through me
an appropriation, say of ten dolls per family would be made to them, I would
be better prepared to continue to buy supplies of corn and bacon for them,

the appropriations so made to inure to the special benefit of the respective families. This would aid in furtherance of a crop of some importance. My own means in money, is partly well nigh straightened and a relief to these laborers would be the more graciously received, as their necessitous wants for the next three months ought to be supplied. . . .

BAPTISTA LYNCH, URSULINE CONVENT AND ACADEMY, VALLE CRUCIS . . . MAY 26th[34]

. . . I hope this cold and damp weather is not affecting you as it has done so many of our household. The screams of one of our Lay Sisters could have been heard a square night before last—we feared she would die—her exhaustion was very great after the pain had subsided—Several others have had less violent attacks of cholera morbus and Rev. dr. M. is quite sick, and under John's care. . . .

BAPTISTA LYNCH, URSULINE CONVENT ANDACADEMY, VALLE CRUCIS . . . JUNE 18[35]

Today we presume you are nearing the eternal City and will spend there the beautiful feast of Corpus Christi.

We received your letter with cheque of $1,500 and placed the sum in Mr. E.J. Scott's hands as you desired. . . . We have received our small rations of meat and corn meal, suitable for the farm hands.—but now that Genl. Green has been removed to the Indian Frontier and Genl Burton of Fortress Monroe stationed in Columbia (Is he not the same who was so courteous to President Davis and polite to you when on your visit to him?) we may get more—we will see what our *Father* as Sister Antonia calls Gen S[ickles?] will do for us. . . .

June 22. . . . Next Thursday we hold our "Commencement"—at which his Excellency Gov. Orr[36] says he will with great pleasure confer the Honors on our pupils &c &c &c How I would like to shut myself up in our room for that occasion—But that is not "generosity in God's Holy Service": . . . You will be gratified to learn that the daughter of late Mayor Barry thinks of entering our Novitiate. I received a beautiful letter from her mother expecting it. . . .

To our surprise Belle Roman returned the Eve of "Corpus Christi" . . . I do not think she is very long for this world, and although unfit to enter the Noviciate, I think it a charity to let her remain where she can enjoy the sacraments. I must not forget to tell you about the old "Ex-officer" whom you sent us as "Guardsman". . . a restless imaginative devout man—but I like him all the same. . . . We will be happy to get as many relics as you may collect . . .

4

"YOU HAVE NO IDEA OF THE SCARCITY OF MONEY HERE"

July–December 1867

Speaking to the assembled delegates of the Congress of the Association of the Propagation of the Faith in Rome, Bishop Patrick Lynch laid out his plan for the utopian community of Black Catholics. The bishop placed his undertaking within the church's long history of religious communities serving as the center of populations drawn there by the hope of gaining the education and spiritual nurture that would enable them to build productive, prosperous lives. As the Jesuits did with the endangered indigenous peoples of Paraguay, so Lynch envisioned their nineteenth-century successors doing with an equally vulnerable group, the recently emancipated. On a coastal island where climate had erected a natural barrier against white intrusion, Lynch planned to carry out a domestic colonization enterprise in which Catholic freedpersons could acquire the education and land enabling them to live virtuous and independent lives. It would be a self-sustaining community, providing for one's changing needs from birth to death, including schools, orphanages, facilities for the care of the aged. As he told his audience in Rome, those who joined such a community "would soon come to look on the Island as a second Paradise." One might reasonably ask why Patrick Lynch would have expected Black Catholics to be more favorable than American Blacks historically had been to colonization of any kind? When one wants to believe something badly enough, one can be quite selective in mining history for confirmation.

From the beginning of Congressional Reconstruction, there was a backlash against the expansion of government bureaucracy, of the services it administered, and the taxation it imposed to fund them. Cries for retrenchment quickly ensued. Anti-taxation movements to undermine the ability of government to provide for education and other social services sprang up. Patrick Lynch, in a letter to the Charleston City Council, put on his scientist's hat to demonstrate, by hard statistics, the penny-wise, pound-foolish thinking which such reactionary politics could generate. The bishop might have shared much of this sentiment about activist government. Still, he was too civic minded to jump on the "least government is the best government" train. If government had any role whatever in promoting the public welfare, minimalist governance was incapable of doing that. In a letter to the Charleston city council, Bishop Lynch made his case that increasing the government's bureaucracy could paradoxically cut costs from the municipal budget.

A year after she had led a trio of Ursulines to begin an academy in Tuscaloosa, Alabama, Baptista Lynch had second thoughts about the wisdom of a satellite community so far removed from Columbia. Despite expectations, the urban location in Alabama proved no better able than their rural setting in South Carolina in generating sufficient revenue to support a convent academy. With no reliable income from tuition which virtually all parents lacked the means or will to pay, the Ursulines were forced to look to benefactors, wherever they could be found. As self-subsistence became a greater necessity, the farm more and more served as their major food supplier. The lack of revenue precluding their hiring any laywomen to offer classes the nuns were not prepared to teach, Baptista was under greater pressure to accept candidates who aspired to be choir nuns and thus potential faculty.

PATRICK N. LYNCH, LECTURE ON THE CHURCH IN THE UNITED STATES

... I have come to devote myself to a special subject—the work of the Catholic Church in regard to the Negroes in the Southern States formerly slaves, now emancipated. . . . A Protestant Minister of America lately summed it up by saying that those multitudes were ... ready to belong to the Church that would first take possession of it and called on the Protestant Churches to act promptly and vigorously, else the Catholic Church would precede them. . . . Would to

Patrick Lynch, Catholic Bishop of
Charleston. Reproduced by permission
© Catholic Diocese of Charleston.

God their idea of our zeal were true.... I think that the entire number of Catholic Negroes in the United States is not above 150,000 ... The population of 3 ½ million of Negroes then is the [mission] field in which the Catholic Church has to labour. I may well speak of it for in my dioceses of Charleston there are over 700,000 of whom only about 2,000 are Catholics. In our late Council of Baltimore ... the most serious exhortations were made to the several bishops to do for these poor people everything that Christian charity and apostolic zeal could accomplish.

We shall continue to do all that we did before. They [the Blacks] have a portion of each church set apart for them. They have special catechetical instructions and sermons suited for their capacity. We foster among them pious confraternities and associations. But if owing to the fewness of our priests in the Southern States, and the ever increasing work of the ministry, little has been accomplished hitherto, ... we hope for greater results now.

We have gone farther. In various cities we have established separate [sic] churches for the Negroes exclusively.... In addition to this, I am now striving to obtain a religious community or clergymen to undertake a special mission among the Negroes, on a portion of the Diocess where I have two small churches or chapels. There are fifty thousand Negroes in that region and not 500 whites. This too I hope to inaugurate soon....

As I look back on the History of the Church seeking a parallel, I come on the disorganized society of the seventh, eighth, and ninth centuries. I see there monasteries and convents, on the plains, in the valleys, on the mountain side . . . and the people gathering around them, for religious instruction and aid and protection, learning to be moral and industrious, in the cultivation of the earth and in every necessary trade. By this means was the heritage of literature and civilization preserved and handed down through those ages to us. . . .

If I turn to America, I find the Jesuits of Paraguay, gathering the Savage Indians into saintly communities, teaching them religion, and industry, and prospering beyond all expectation, until modern infidelity more barbarous than any feudal chieftain of olden times in the name of philosophy and Progress, loaded the Jesuits with chains or put them to death, and sent the Indians back to their forests, where still amid their barbarism and in the fifth generation, they baptize their children and teach them to recite the Pater and Ave and Credo [torn]

. . . Cannot this be done for the Negroes in my Dioces? . . . It is now not only feasible but comparatively easy. . . . The coast of South Carolina is as you know flat and filled with swamps. Except in a few places, white men cannot pass the summer months there without great danger. The Negroes on the contrary enjoy perfect health . . . Along the coast are a large number of islands of various sizes from one hundred to ten thousand hectares. The soil is fertile, and the climate almost tropical. . . . I have determined to purchase one of such islands, [and] . . . place on it some suitable religious order, divide the lands into small suitable farms or gardens, to be inhabited and cultivated by the Negroes under the guidance and control of the good and fatherly religious. In such a home, sufficiently secluded to prevent the idle interference of the outside world, we would soon see how the holy influences of our religion can elevate this poor race. The community would prosper in a temporal point of view, for such is the mildness of the winter and such the fertility of the soil and such the conveniences for the ready sale of profitable productions, that . . . the whole outlay would be paid for in three years. Even the Negroes with ordinary prudence, could do it in eight or ten years, purchase a home, we might soon see orphan asylums, [hermitages?] for the aged, schools perhaps even for a higher education. It might in time be religious houses for their own race. One such colony established and prospering, others will follow. The Protestants will imitate it, as they often try to imitate the noble deeds of Catholic charity. . . . The Catholic missions for the Negroes will stand, and I see a race saved from ignorance and superstition, from immorality, perhaps from Extermination by the only influence which under Divine Providence has ever wrought, or can work this miracle—the power of His Holy Church.

. . . The General[1] in command in my dioceses . . . warmly entered into it, and just as I was leaving for Rome, wrote me a letter, urging me to take action if I could. On the part of the Negroes there would be little or no hesitation. They would soon come to look on the Island as a second Paradise.

. . . I have spent hours on the calculation and I shew that 300,000 francs ($70,000) would be ample sufficient to purchase the Island, to put up temporary buildings, sufficient to commence the establishment.

. . . I . . . am poor. . . . Yes, I am poor enough to commence this work—I am forced to rely on God, and on him alone. The holy Father knows my plan, and approves of it, and will bless the undertaking. . . . Will my words be in vain? My words? It is not my words you hear. It is the cry of those poor Africans. It is they who stretch forth their hands to you as in a vision the Irish stretched forth their hands and cried to St. Patrick, my patron, to return from Gaul to the land where he had been a slave, and to bring to them the light of the Gospel. Who will hear the cry of the Negro[?] Who will come to his aid? . . .

BAPTISTA LYNCH, URSULINE CONVENT AND ACADEMY
VALLE CRUCIS, AUGUST 4th[2]

. . . On the 1st of July, we—that is Sister deSales, Belle Roman and myself—set off for Tuscaloosa—and reached there on the 6th. . . . I was very much gratified with the efforts they had made. . . . Having settled up the business of the House spiritually and temporally . . . we started back on Tuesday 30th July— and reached Columbia Saturday, 3rd August. . . .

While I was in Tuscaloosa the R.R. contract was concluded . . . for the completion of the great Meridien and Chattanooga R.R., via Tuscaloosa. . . . It is estimated that property will advance very much by this—therefore I wrote a letter to Bp. Quinlan, at the suggestion of Rev. F. M D and left it for him to present—asking a settlement &c . . . I promised to send some teacher to aid our two sisters . . . I also wish to send a Lay Sister to help them . . . Sr. Camilla[3] who if thrown on her own resources will be much more useful there, than here—and the *Teacher* I propose sending is Sr. *Augustine*—for one year, at the expiration of which period, she could return, and I hope we could spare some one less dangerous—But I am exercised very much on that point, by the unwillingness of Sister Josephine and Stanislaus to have [her] . . . Rev. Chaplain Rev. Mr. M. . . . also thinks it would be better to employ a secular teacher than send such a person—I do not agree with them—but . . . What do you advise? . . . The Tuscaloosa Institute *must* have a *French* teacher and should have a teacher of drawing and painting—Parents expect and wish it, and it must be given their children or the Institute will fall through and other schools rob us justly of our pupils—We have to compete with good schools, and *must* work our way . . .

Our school does not promise to be self-supporting, this year, therefore we have suggested the idea of a "Fair" given this winter for our benefit, in this Diocess as has been done elsewhere—You know that concerts and fairs, together with charitable contributions have made our principal support since our convent was burned. . . . You will be sorry to learn of the effects of the continued heavy rains—Sr. Theresa tells me this morning that the Rev. Dr. said we would have only two thirds of a crop—I suppose we will have to get Rev. Father Bermingham who is—what you my dearest Brother are not—a splendid "Questor" to go on a questing expedition for us, and we must be content to live on such charities for the next two or three years, until the condition of the country will enable persons to pay for the education of their children. . . . Rev. F McDonough . . . says you are splendid for the *pulpit* but the last man in the world, to go begging—why a poor man would be ashamed to offer *you* a small sum—you are . . . too great a personage—whereas if you had some humble little Priest with you, to go among the people—while you were seen and heard in the pulpit, you could have gotten thousands where you got hundreds.

. . . I cannot begin to tell you how the prospect of being a burthen on you for a few years *frets me* and makes me regret so much that I did not carry out my plan of sending a few sisters to Macon and a few to Raleigh to start schools, that would mutually support one another.—that was a great mistake in my opinion—preferring Tuscaloosa which is so distant and by no means as desirable a locality in my opinion. . . . We are praying for the receiving of your Carpet Bag.

BAPTISTA LYNCH, VALLE CRUCIS, VIGIL OF ST. THERESA
[14 OCTOBER][4]
. . . John and family are quite well—Robert and Kate Bauskett are to be married 21st Nov—I suppose if convenient to you—Old Col Bauskett[5] has been baptized—John standing God-father for him—The old gentleman is very low—expresses himself anxious to see you before he dies—he may linger as he did last year—and even get up again—We will certainly expect you as soon as you visit Cheraw and look around.

PATRICK N. LYNCH TO CITY COUNCIL OF CHARLESTON, N.D.[6]
Inasmuch as the attention of the Committee on retrenchment, has been or may be directed to the office of Civil Engineer and as, outside your honourable body, it has been said that the office itself is unnecessary, and might be altogether dispensed with, I take the liberty of presenting to you a few facts which in my judgment will full show the propriety of the office, and its economy to the city finances, especially at the very moderate salary.

. . . I wish to call your attention to the mode in which the work now assigned to this office was done for the city before its creation in March 1867. . . . The City of Charleston in the past has had much of such work to be done, for which it paid generally according to professional rates, and will always have more or less to be executed, for which so far as it may be properly entrusted to and directed by a salaried civil engineer, it will have to pay far less. In those years the city was disbursing on average over $12,000 a year for ordinary professional work, three fourths of which, [crossed out: if not all] would now fall to the charge of the salaried civil engineer. . . .

BAPTISTA LYNCH, V.C., ALL SAINTS DAY[7]

. . . The provision of the Farm is being laid by—I suppose you know every thing was prolific sweet potatoes in abundance and I wish we had a good man to take care of the stock—and to milk the cows for us. We ought to have much more milk but I think the Negroes don't take so much care of it for us as for themselves—John and Dr. M have tried in vain to get one in Columbia—$10 per month wages. . . .

JOHN LYNCH, COLUMBIA, SC, NOV. 2[8]

. . . You ask me why it is better for all parties to have the wedding late, for the best of reasons. Robert has *very little* money. I know, and Mrs. Bauskett has not a dollar in her house, neither do I see where she will be able to get any for some time, I tried to get some for her but signally failed, her friends and those who owe the Col. have no money. You have no idea of the scarcity of money here, I went out today to persons owing me, over six hundred dollars, all I collected was ten dollars, and that was from a man owing over one hundred dollars. I do not know how I am to get on. I am not able to raise my insurance . . . Mrs Caldwell sends me word she will be down in a few days, and every one I owe a dollar to is continually dunning me. It unfits me for my business, as I remarked to you before If I could find any one who had money to lend, who has a conscience, I would borrow enough to pay all my little debts and consolidate them, it would give me a chance of attending to business and making something, have a chance of collecting some that is already due, I intend to try, until I find such an opportunity. If you know or come across such a person i.e. one who has money to lend, at a reasonable interest, I would like to borrow One thousand dollars payable in twelve months, and will give as security a mortgage on either my house or on the Copper Mine, if the money matters of the country do not improve I might wish to extend the time to two years. I have plenty owing to me, but the money is not in the country. I have not a judgement against me, except the Eighty five dollars to Robinson, and there is no lien on any of my property, this I mention to you, that you may speak knowingly if you find any one you think there would be any probability of my getting a lone [*sic*] from, you do not know the kindness you would be doing me, ... I know what I am offering is as good as any one could desire, who has money to lend.

... Dr. M says I must hold on and persevere to the end, with the help of God. I will try and do so, but I fear my distractions are too numerous. ...

BAPTISTA LYNCH, URSULINE CONVENT AND ACADEMY
VALLE CRUCIS, NOVEMBER 4th[9]
Enclosed I send you a "document" or "billet-doux"[10] such as many are receiving down here, but none relish—I am sorry to send it to you, but think you would prefer it—and you can shew it to your friends, and let them see how the "Church property" is situated in your Diocess—and I expect, very generally in the South.

I was so anxious to see you and consult you about "Tuscaloosa Foundation," and as I cannot write what I would say, I suppose I must make use of the "obedience" I have for Sr A and send her with Sr. Camilla—as soon as I can get free "passports" or free "tickets" in the several RRs. I wanted to tell you that we had not been able to meet the payment due some months ago, for those lots in town near the M.F. College, consequently we are paying compound interest. I was speaking of this to John, and he said we need not distress ourselves about that, for he and many others would willingly pay that and more than that of interest for money nowadays—that they are paying 20 per cent interest for loans and even more in Columbia—Happily, that is our only debt and we have much more owing to us, if ever we get it—The cotton planters are very dispirited, owing to the season and ravages of the "worm"—therefore our school remains in "statu quo.". ...

BAPTISTA LYNCH, URSULINE CONVENT AND ACADEMY
VALLE CRUCIS, NOVEMBER 8th[11]
... Mrs Huchet[12] brought back her three daughters ... But the failures in Liverpool have affected Mr. Huchet. I have no doubt in a month hence, business will brighten and people look more cheerful. We are expecting two more pupils and as the season advances I hope their number will increase—as yet however no one has entered, who has not asked time wherein to meet payment but of course as prices advance cotton will press into market and we will come in for a share of the proceeds.

Mrs. Huchet is full of our Fair, ... We think to have it open Feb. 2nd under the protection of our Blessed Lady.[13] What do you think of that arrangement?

It will give a sufficient time to ladies to work, and I hope the people will have arisen somewhat from their depression, now caused by stagnation in business &c . . .

If Miss Eliza S. Mason,[14] to whom I proposed sending us some of her protégés would do so, and let me select the recipients of her zealous efforts for the education of Southern young ladies—the two families of Bland would be with us—But I could select many others. . . .

Nov. 9th

John has just come and tells me that he wrote to you respecting your "Taxes" and thinks that $75—or 100 will cover them—He asks me to lend him the $100 . . .

Capt. Keitt has placed in John's hands this week the deeds of land adjoining but the proper deed has not been drawn up yet. . . . Capt. Keitt is one of those who believes the "war of races" is approaching and that all property will greatly depreciate—Then he ought not to ask $25 per acre for his land . . . I suppose you have seen a notice of the Convention held in Columbia?[15] . . .

MARY LYNCH SPANN, GALVESTON, NOV. 15[16]

. . . Mr. Spann, was greatly relieved to find a position, in which he could make a support without trying to plant, which proves a very losing business, these times . . . Mr. Spann is doing his best, to adapt himself to his new life and succeeds pretty well, and what contributes most, to our happiness is having our first Texas pastor, who is now Vicar General, living in the house with us; he is as a very considerate Brother; so that we have much to feel grateful for. . . .[17]

BAPTISTA LYNCH, VALLE CRUCIS, NOVEMBER 19th[18]

. . . I heard from Anna yesterday . . . Mother worried by *independent servants.* Elections began today in Columbia—hope all will be quiet . . . Francis, like all the rest of the planters is disappointed in his crop.

Human feeling seems to be at its *ebb* just now. I suppose after the elections are over we may expect its *flow.* . . .

. . . This morning's post brings me a letter from Capt. Ellison S. Keitt (who by the by) has never paid that $200—to us that he told you he would . . . He writes wishing to send a niece of his on the same terms as his daughter—both to be paid for by interest on bond for lands and wishes to meet you in Columbia and perfect the business of drawing papers, deeds &c &c I think it a real swindle to ask $25 per acre for waste lands, it deprived of wood, except pines and unsalable unless to us.

Mr. K advised John as trustee of Col. Bausketts estate, to sell off as speedily as possible all property, for times in the South, he said, will be getting worse and worse, so that in a year or less, no sale may be found for them ... No wonder at $25. per acre when such are his views!

I must say I do not agree with him though, for I believe although there may be a few years in which the finances of the South will be in a very trying state, it will be *only a few years*, after which the South will be in a much better condition for the people generally, than ever it was. Your philanthropic view of colonizing the Islands with Negroes withdrawing there from the uplands and introducing white foreign labor instead, will contribute largely to the future prosperity. I hope to the culture of silk and wool with the grass and other articles suitable to our climate, will supersede cotton in a great measure.

As for us, we can *pray* as well, with the country in its present condition as in any other—therefore we can save our own souls and be instrumental to the salvation of others in the same way. And *that* is now our work. If left to our own choice, we might prefer to see our Convent sheltering a great number of holy recluses—our Institution giving instruction to a large number of these noble minded southern girls who love truth and virtue as if by instinct. A large free school on our premises for all who need instruction whether white or black—a chapel wherein all might hear the word of God and attend the Holy Sacrifice. But we must know that our choice is not the best, and that circumstances manifest the Holy Will of God and true piety, in conformity to it. How many blessings do we enjoy? The daily Holy Sacrifice, frequent sacraments and so much that other convents are deprived of in various parts of the country. Every Sunday we now ring the great Bell for Mass and Benediction. ...

I have told you before, I think of the piles of sweet potatoes that Rev. Dr. M has stored away for winter use—and the quantity of peas and vines for the cows—now, he is stall-feeding three of the cows, and has one of these "Farmers Boilers" from "McNeely's founding" N.Y. in which he had the feed properly boiled for them. So we have plenty of home-made butter as well as milk. ... The Dr. has fixed the "pigeon house" so that it will accommodate two hundred pigeons—and frequently furnish a breakfast table. Sister Agnes' poultry yard gives us eggs for the table, ... this sounds very material, but you will also see by it how we exercise domestic economy. ...

BAPTIST LYNCH, CONVENT, FEAST PRESENTATION BVM [NOV. 21][19]

... This morning before Mass, "Daniel came over for some medicine for his wife "Aunt Darkey" saying that the Dr. [Meriwether] sent him ... that the Doctor had been to see her before day and Baptized her! They thought she was dying but she was better then. I had Sister Theresa to enquire from the

Dr. at the Breakfast table if it would be well for some of us to go and see here. If her sickness were contagious, we would not go; He said it would be well he thought. So . . . I took Sister Theresa with me, and carrying a bottle of holy water, a crucifix and prayer book, we started . . . When we got over to the big gate . . . I felt quite in a strange place, so changed is every thing since I was in that yard about two years ago—quite an improvement.

. . . You just ought to have seen how polite those Negroes were—I suppose Moody or Dr. M. had told Daniel that we were going over to see Aunt Darkey, so they had raked all the pathway and swept it to the house and had everything around and in the house so orderly and for them clean. Milly came out to meet us and show us in—We found the poor woman quite sick and frightened—thought she should die—but said she was much better since she was Christened by the Dr.—(I do not think they sent for him otherwise than as a master and physician, but he did not let the opportunity pass) We gave her some little medicine, talked kindly with her, knelt down and said aloud some prayers—sprinkled the room with "Holy Water" hung our crucifix near her—Then gave some general instructions *to* her daughters and grandchildren and *at* her, for she was too feeble to hear much—and left. They respectfully accompanying us out of their yard, and expressing ever so much thanks—*"more dan dey could 'spress"*

Rev. Dr. M. had sent for John and now Darkey is much better. . . .

The planters of cotton tell me they are worse off this year than they were last—Mr. Mikell called today to say unless we could keep his little sister for $200 per annum he would be obliged to take her home—which he would regret exceedingly to do. Not one dollar has been paid in this session—and much that is due for the past is unpaid—so it seems we must either wait and live on other resources, or have no pupils at all—Those who have offers made them from institutions will accept, if obliged or if we cannot have the same terms. . . .

FRANCIS LYNCH, CHERAW, 28 NOV.[20]

. . . If convenient, while in Boston, learn what you can as to this need made of obtaining ext[tract] of Bark for tanning; In the Shoe and Leather Reports of 14th and 21st insts. an article from H. W. Johnson Boston on this topic; also one in reference to the requisite machinery, for the production of it, being prepared at the South Boston Iron Work. I look with much interest to this matter being of opinion, that. . . [by] the advantages to be derived in tanning [by this method] I may in a good measure retrieve my losses—and in ways honest and honorable to myself and highly beneficial to every interest therein concerned. . . .

BAPTISTA LYNCH, URSULINE CONVENT AND ACADEMY,
VALLE CRUCIS, DECEMBER 18[21]

. . . We have examined the vocations of our two postulants—Your president D[avis]'s housekeeper and Cecilia Barry, and accepted them in Chapter for investing with the Veil. When will it suit you to give it to them? . . .

JOHN LYNCH, COLUMBIA, SC, DEC 22nd[22]

It seems that I can never write except it is to bother you, but I am in a quandary, and have no one else to advise with. You know I am one of the Executors of Col. Bauskett's Est[ate], the estate is large, but very much in debt. Since the war the Col. had to borrow money—which he did . . . at an exorbitant price, in some instances as I am informed, at *twenty percent a month* . . . the creditors, some of them, have ordered the sheriff to sell his dwelling and office in this place. I have filed a bill in Equity for the settling of the whole estate, and have asked the Commissioner to grant an injunction on the sale which is advertised for 6th January, this he has refused. . . . Mrs Bauskett wishes to pay every dollar that is *justly* due, but wants to save her house. I am satisfied there is plenty to pay out without touching the house, if a little time is allowed to arrange the affairs. . . . I am now in treaty with a party in N.Y. (P M Wright) for the sale of North Island (12000) acres) which sale I expect to complete, in less than a month, . . . With the proceeds of this sale, I can pay all the pressing creditors. . . . Can I . . . apply to Genrl Canby[23] to restrain the Sherriff [*sic*] for a reasonable time. . . . The sale must be stopped some way. I must defeat the swindling for the widdow [*sic*] and orphan of my old friend, . . . Please advise me soon. . . .

5

"THESE ATTACKS I THINK INDICATE CONSUMPTION"

January–June 1868

Having lost his business to Sherman's avengers, Francis Lynch, despite his initial intentions, was forced to turn to planting to recover economically. He soon discovered that conditions could not have been worse for producing the South's traditional agricultural staples. Compounding that challenge were his wartime debts which no peace settlement could forgive. Hence Francis's convoluted attempts to stave off the debt collectors, to the point of selling part of his plantation to New York investors. What the Yankees failed to take by war, they now alone had the financial wherewithal to buy up, such as the indebted property of Southerners like Francis Lynch. Still, he put the greater part of his estate in his bishop brother's name, just in case he was forced into bankruptcy. Francis even found himself saddled with the debts of his dead brother, Hugh, who may have long since been buried, but his financial obligations lived on, now as additional weight to Francis's crushing fiscal burden. As do Francis's outstanding debts for his purchase of enslaved people, despite emancipation. And yet, for all his financial woes, Francis retained his entrepreneurial ambition.

Nearly three years after the guns had gone silent, the Ursulines not only continued to fall short of filling their limited facilities at Valle Crucis, but saw their student numbers plummet, as parents were increasingly unable to afford the tuition. With debts continuing to mount, the Ursulines were forced to resort to any and all mechanisms to raise money: from fairs to circulars sent to all the women's religious communities in the United States, to a lecture by Abram Ryan, to the recruiting of candidates for the order who could bring with them a substantial dowry.

The proclivity of the Lynches to follow the money in order to survive led a few of them to seek employment from the Republican government of South Carolina, since the Republicans now controlled patronage, as well as the rations and other supplies which the Freedman's Bureau administered. Two members of the third generation, Robert and Conlaw, both turned to their bishop uncle to obtain government positions for them. John and Francis, of the second generation, were also willing to use connections to secure government posts or to obtain relief from debt.

Increasing episodes of weakness convinced Baptista that her time on this earth was drawing near its end. One definite force undermining Baptista's health was Augustine England who, for over five years, had waged psychological warfare against her religious superior. After Baptista's attempts to get Augustine into another religious community failed, the satellite community in Tuscaloosa provided an opportunity for Baptista to at least remove her physically. But changing states did nothing to change Augustine, whom Baptista was forced to recall. Upon her return, the troublesome niece of Bishop John England was subjected to extraordinary punishments in the hope they would produce reform: enjoining that she wear lay clothing; excluding her from the community's daily recreation; barring her from receiving the Eucharist at Mass. All this physical and spiritual ostracizing failed to accomplish its purpose. "The engine," as Baptista informed her brother, "is off the tracks." Finally, by the consensus of her own consultors and directors, Baptista was forced to impose the ultimate punishment upon her once close friend.

HENRIETTA LYNCH, CHERAW, 2 JANUARY[1]

... I heard Mr. Lynch say he was expecting you here and had to see you about his property. He is in a great deal of trouble and if you have business calling you off for a month I wish you would come before you go away. I cannot write explicitly as I do not know if you will get this but I know that your visit should not be delayed too long for Mr Lynch's sake. He would not write to ask you because he says he is sure you are coming but delays are dangerous, I know. His health has somewhat improved since cold weather but he has had trial after trial, Job's trials, since Sherman's entry into Cheraw. . . .

FRANCIS LYNCH, CHERAW, 12 JANY[2]
Your valued letter was received by Friday's mail with ck for five hundred dolls with many thanks. . . . Your trip here will be anxiously looked for, as for my own part I will state to you what I have in need.

The ineffectual efforts on my part in planting, resulting in much loss and leaving indebtedness unsatisfied, may result in my being sued for much that I owe. On account of my indebtedness to yourself, I would suggest my making titles of my home place, tannery and so much of other real estate as will mark its sum to trust to me when I can repay you, thus securing to me the possession of it if matters go to the worst.

I will offer the lower portion of the plantation for sale in N. York and if sale can be effected I will straighten matters. The proceeds of my past years crops, about reach the cost of fertilizers expended on it. Having laborers working on shares, they are all paid. With this experience I have rented a portion of my land and will work a small portion and I hope realize more from it. And will endeavor to rebuild my tannery . . .

Father was sued by Messrs. Caldwell and Robinson for the indebtedness of Bro. Hugh to them because of his having given them his guarantee—and rced 900$. Messrs I and Hudson their attys. have told me they thought that about 200$ would compromise the claim—it was my purpose to have tendered it, but circumstances have overruled me—truly, you may say this is the winter of our disappointment! I would not desire to trouble you with these matters, only I suppose you would prefer to be apprized even though the matter is distasteful.

. . . Robert is [testing some experimental tanning machinery] . . . about 50 miles up the river I can procure large quantities of Oak Bark at 3¢ per cord and a marketable production of the Extract might prove a highly lucrative business, besides enabling me to make my tannery house of first importance both as to quantity and quality of production. . . .

BAPTISTA LYNCH, URSULINE CONVENT AND ACADEMY,
VALLE CRUCIS . . . JANUARY 12th[3]
. . . I was quite indisposed on Saturday night, and worse on Sunday morning, When I had as violent an attack as when you were here, or even worse so—I ventured to get up for the Holy Sacrifice but had to be helped back to bed, from which I was unable to raise until about two hours ago. I am still in my room but will D.V. leave it after the day warms—These attacks are becoming much more

frequent of late—say twice in every three weeks, and I think indicate consumption—so, that I will be very happy to receive several promising candidates and have the holy privilege of training them for Religion, before my strength fails—especially as all say I possess the capacity of inspiring others with a love for our holy state—a love which I possess to an enthusiastic degree. . . .

BAPTISTA LYNCH, URSULINE CONVENT AND ACADEMY,
VALLE CRUCIS NEAR COLUMBIA, S.C., JANUARY 24th[4]
. . . I have spoken again with Sr. A—about going to Tuscaloosa and am happy to find her more reasonable—I do hope she will go agreeably and think she will if only assured that she may hold on to this community and return to it—Of that there will be no difficulty of course—The same charity that brought her here will continue to protect and shelter her—and for that she is indebted to you—I also thank you for the same, as I feel it has been a means of purifying me. . . .

BAPTISTA LYNCH, URSULINE CONVENT AND ACADEMY
VALLE CRUCIS, FEBRUARY 6th[5]
. . . The chain which you so kindly sent Rev. Dr. Meriwether and of which you should not have deprived yourself if you use it, was in town several days before John or any of us knew of it.[6] . . . Our prayers have been heard somewhat, and the affairs of the Bausketts estate proved more satisfactory than John expected . . .

BAPTISTA LYNCH, URSULINE CONVENT AND ACADEMY
VALLE CRUCIS NEAR COLUMBIA, FEBRUARY 15th[7]
. . . I hope you will see Kate Harris—Dr. Robert Emmet's niece by marriage . . . She has just returned from China, whither she accompanied as one of the suite—Mr. McLane—Mrs. Garesché's brother. We expect her to join our Novitiate some day perhaps—I wish too you could see Mrs. Garesché who is my particular friend and now lives in Astoria—they are all busy for our Fair.
     . . . Miss Denison . . . has . . . written asking formally to be admitted as a candidate into our novitiate. Miss Denison like Mrs. Brisbane will I calculate pay her board ($25) per month which will also support Cecilia Barry and Natalie Brownfield. And in this way we feel no difficulty, even under present circumstances, in receiving them—especially as they are so respectable and accomplished young ladies and so highly recommended. I feel truly thankful to our Lord in permitting me to be His instrument in helping to rebuild the spiritual edifice and I trust that by the time you can give us a proper monastery

and institute we will have a corps of efficient nuns and mistresses. Valle Crucis will be a great place yet.

I enclose you the copy of my correspondence with Mr. DeSaussure (the same who has ever been our friend and spoke so forcibly with Gen. Marcy Gregg at the time the American Hotel was stoned).[8] It will explain itself. I have not heard from him since but upon reflection and consultation we doubt if it would not be best to relinquish our hold on those lots even at the sacrifice of the one installment paid, than continue to make payments year after year or have the same anxiety year after year and with such a poor prospect for the country and us ahead.

I do not like to pay such a high price for land, in times like these and I feel the same about the Keitt place, over the road. . . . I wish you were near enough to give me your decision about offering to give up town lots to Mr. De Saussure sacrificing our past payment and get release of our bond and mortgage—John with the best will in the world has not proved a successful money manager so I rather think we will make the offer to Mr. D—S Trusting that you will approve. If the parties will not accept we must only do the best we can. . . .

[DeSaussure] and John both advise our holding on to those lots and Mr. DeSaussure says most amiably "The Ladies shall not be troubled." . . .

I am so sorry that you will not return to your own Diocess for the Holy Week and Easter services and it looks strange too. Will you not write and send a newspaper from time to time that I may know how you are and where . . .

PATRICK N. LYNCH, THE CHURCH'S RESPONSIBILITY TO EMANCIPATED NEGROES[9]

I will speak on [a] subject, the most interesting perhaps the most difficult task now before the American Church—the work of evangelizing the recently emancipated Negroes—this people, the descendants of those Africans who in the last two centuries, and in the first eight years of this century were brought from Africa to America, amounted in 1860, to nearly 4,000,000 of whom little more than one in 20 was free. The vicissitudes of the war, and the condition in which they now live has reduced that number to about 3 ½ millions. All now emancipated. This emancipation though previously decreed during the war, was only carried into effect at its conclusion in the spring of 1865. The time has not yet come to discuss its practical results for as yet the Negroes have not been placed in the position which it is intended they shall occupy. By the emancipation they were made free. By subsequent legislation, they are declared citizens, and are clothed with the privilege of universal suffrage. During these two last months the electoral registration of voters has been actively continued, and it appears that in many of the southern States the Negroes formerly slaves, form now the majority of the voters and may therefore hold in their hands the power of legislation. Until this has been effected, and until we shall have shown in what manner they will use this power, it would be premature to speak decisively on the subject.

Still in America, the friends and the opponents of this change each declare their opinions and appeal to the facts that have so far occurred.

The friends of the Negro appeal to the fact that the Negroes are working for wages, that on the whole they conduct themselves quietly and have not shown themselves vindictive against their former owners, but on the contrary continue in many cases to work for them as before. That tumults and homicides and other weighty crimes are rare among them, that they are rapidly being educated in the many schools established for them and that there is abundant reason to hope that from slaves they will become orderly, quiet and industrious citizens.

The enemies of the Negroes while obliged to acknowledge most of these facts, yet say that the industry of the Negroes is greatest and they are more orderly in those portions of the country where the emissaries of the northern states have scarcely entered to disturb their minds and thus in those portions on the contrary, they have been much at work, the Negroes are idle and turbulent and they call attention to the fact that even under the stimulus of prices for cotton and rice, nearly twice as high as in 1860, the cost of those articles produced this year will scarcely exceed one half of the crop of that year. In fact about 2/3 of the Negroes are working, and their work is often very negligently performed. Nor, is this the fault of the southern planters. For the most signal failures are seen in the cases of northern men, who have come south and have had to [torn] undertaken to cultivate large plantations with the aid of Negroes.

They point to the fact that the Negroes are living in a state of indigence and misery unknown when they were provided for by their former owners—that thieving is universal among them, that millions are spent each year in providing food by the Government and by charitable associations in providing food and clothing for the poor among them. . . .

They further point with alarm to the fact that political emissaries have been for months actively at work enrolling the Negroes in a distinct, political organization, often in secret, oath-bound societies—all in preparation for the time, now near at hand, when the military power will be withdrawn, by the United States government, and the several states left nominally to their own civil government—that is, in many instances, where the Negroes are in a large majority to such government as they may establish.

For myself, while I do not think the extravagant hopes of the friends will be soon realized, neither do I entirely coincide with the exaggerated fears of the second class. It is unfortunate that there is a mutual distrust of each other—perhaps not without foundation. It is to be hoped that this distrust, so dangerous in itself will not increase and pass into action, but will be . . . repressed and die away, not only in view of temporal interests and worldly policy, but chiefly through the benign influences of our Holy Religion.[10]

BAPTISTA LYNCH, URSULINE CONVENT AND ACADEMY, VALLE CRUCIS, FEBRUARY 23rd[11]

. . . I see the Dr. going about as if the fate of a nation depended on his crops—himself and his men indefatigable. Our invalid Sisters are out again—our pupils merry as the birds and all, T.G. giving me satisfaction.

. . . Mrs. Brownfield spent a couple of days and left Natalie who is still, as you advised, a visitor, but I think will be a very happy and useful member of our Noviciate.

You just ought to have heard Mrs. Brisbane! . . . She begged me to say to you that she is the only one living now, who can give you some practical information—of your "Georgia Lands" which you perhaps would wish to colonize with Catholic emigrants. She has placed hers in the hands of an Auction Agent for sale and I suppose wishes you would do the same as it would enhance the value of all to have an industrious and enterprising colony together. . . .

. . . I think I told you that Mrs. Brisbane offered to invest her $1,000 (greenbacks) in it. But where would the installment next due come from? However I am incompetent to judge and refer to your better judgement and experience the whole statement. I have just received a letter from that interesting Mrs. Emma Denison from Richmond that splendid musician of whom I wrote and she purposes entering our Noviciate in about three weeks. . . .

BAPTISTA LYNCH, URSULINE CONVENT AND ACADEMY, VALLE CRUCIS, MARCH 8th.[12]

. . . This (Sunday) morning I of course heard Mass at which [I] received Holy Communion. Gave meditation to Natalie Brownfield from 9 to 10. At 10 ½ gave half an hour's instruction to novices as usual, and now come to give you my regular "Bulletin" . . . I only fear that we will harass you about our various wants. I . . . now must say, as yet I failed to collect monies and it will be disastrous to our farm, I fear, if we do not succeed in time to purchase the fertilizer necessary, and keep the hands on it to work. Last month is first that Rev. Dr. M was unable to pay the men and I greatly fear he will lose his popularity which he had purchased by his prompt payments, if he can not continue them. If you could conveniently, and without detriment to your other Diocesan wants, send me a check of two or three hundred dollars as a loan I would feel greatly indebted and perhaps the Fair would repay you. I am told it will be a success if held before the Northerners who now crowd the Mills House and other Hotels leave Charleston. The Ladies seem to have gotten into the spirit of it and express themselves quite interested for us. . . .

. . . I think I told you about Mr. Fleming's son calling on John for the interest due on "American Hotel." But John told him you were not in the state. As I did not hear to the contrary from you, I have requested John to say to Mr. DeSassure [*sic*] that we would return the lots in town and lose the $900 sunk in paying the first installment rather than be harassed by a law suit and our inability to pay the other installments due, one of which comes due this month, making another this month due = $2,229.57

. . . If you think it well, and that it does not look too independent of you, we could write as before to the different convents and Bishops asking charitable aid, alleging the cause—a threatened law-suit &c—shall we? I have been advised to do so by outsiders but that was one word for us, and two for themselves since they could not pay for their children—But every body is [so] poor, and willing now to beg that the shame has worn away from even the most respectable. . . .

Although we have only fourteen pupils we are teaching them music for our "Annual commencement" with the same steadiness as if we had a houseful. I received a note and formal application for admission to our Noviciate from Natalie Brownfield at the end of her fortnight visit, to which I replied, in equally as formal a manner and put her into a Retreat of three days, and will give her the Postulant's Cape and receive her into our Noviciate on your Birthday—Friday 10th inst.

. . . Has no old sinner left you a legacy for us and died yet?!!! . . .

BAPTISTA LYNCH, URSULINE CONVENT AND ACADEMY,
VALLE CRUCIS, MARCH 15th[13]
. . . The young lady in R[ichmond] whom we expect is a devotee of the Poet, Rev. F. Ryan[14]—expects him in Richmond about the 20th when he is invited to lecture and visit for a fortnight and then, she purposes returning under his escort.

. . . The Fair may give us enough to pay for [the lots].

. . . Why do you not advise immigration to our delightful climate and healthy section of the state? That is what we most want—an industrious, intelligent, lively class of foreign Catholics. . . .

BAPTISTA LYNCH, URSULINE CONVENT AND ACADEMY,
VALLE CRUCIS, APRIL 2nd[15]

... We have been expecting you daily for so long, that we are anxious about you. I always feared that cold snowy North for you but did hope that by care and avoiding exposure after preaching, you would escape sickness. I still hope the Doctor is mistaken about your lungs being effected [sic] I have happily seen so many cases in which physicians were mistaken. I do hope the sea voyage will rest and benefit you. Let me beg of you, my dearest brother, not to undertake the services of Holy Week which are so fatiguing but depute Rev. Dr. Persico to officiate for you, and you rest. ... Come up and enjoy our delightful and refreshing country air at Valle Crucis, which is looking lovely now in its fresh spring verdure and flowers. ...

BAPTISTA LYNCH, URSULINE CONVENT, APRIL 17[16]

We are very happy to hear from various sources ... that you are so much better in health and preached on Good Friday and Easter day. ... I am so glad that you will start for Columbia on Monday (day after tomorrow). ... With our expected postulant from Richmond—Miss Emma Denison and her escort Rev. Fr. Ryan (the Poet)—it will be such a relief to me to have you here to entertain him and I would like to secure his influence and friendship for our Institute. I have been *very anxious* to see you here for the last few weeks—things are not running smoothly. The engine is off the track and I'm afraid you will find it more than 3 hours good work to get all right again.

ELIZA LYNCH, [COLUMBIA] TO CONLAW LYNCH,
SUNDAY EVENING, APRIL 19[17]

... The election days passed very quietly. Many Negroes voted the Democrat ticket. The Negroes had the majority (Bevely [sic] Nash)[18] is a senator, what would *Solon* think if he were living.

    With much love, I remain your affectionate Sister. Eliza.

HENRIETTA LYNCH, CHERAW, TO PATRICK LYNCH, 29th APRIL[19]

... Mr. Lynch's health is good. He is very much bothered about 700$ that he is trying to raise to finish off the Medlin note. ... Daughter is in Charleston on a visit hope she will enjoy it. She has been at home ever since she arrived here, helping me. We keep so few servants and 5 children need help. I was pretty sick in February, have lost 15 pounds of flesh. Ma is ever uncomplaining and always busy. What an example have I not had! But it is all lost on me

    And there is Mr. L a perfect saint. ...

BAPTISTA LYNCH, URSULINE CONVENT AND ACADMY,
VALLE CRUCIS, MAY 10th[20]

... The old lady—Mrs. B. is determined to take the Veil—I represented to
her politely the inconveniences of assuming it during the warm weather &c,
and that she could wait until Sept.—or Oct. But she is not to be dissuaded so
easily. ... She certainly knows how to take care of *No 1* but I suppose all old
people do—What does the "Gazette" mean by calling you the *Old* Bishop?
Hurumph! If it had said *"venerable* Bishop that would do very well and respect-
ably"—but "old" to a man in the prime of life and just fifty—I like the tone of
the "News" better.[21] Rev. Fr. Ryan sends his paper regularly.[22] ...

ROBERT LYNCH, CHERAW, MAY 12th[23]

... It has been my desire for some time to have a home of my own. The place
spoken of in the letter I am desirous of purchasing at present, but have not the
means to do so. If you can let me have the amount I will give you a mortgage
on the place, until the amount is refunded to you. As long as I hold the office
of Ast. Assessor, I can pay you monthly installment of one hundred dollars.
After which I would be willing to pay interest on the sum still due. Please let
me know, Sir, as early as possible if you will comply with my request. ...

BAPTISTA LYNCH, URSULINE CONVENT AND ACADEMY,
VALLE CRUCIS MAY 15th[24]

... Poor Mrs. de Bertheville writes me today of her condition. It is a blessing that convents are freed from such good, demented persons. Poor Sister
Martha is in the moon at present and as to Mrs. England,[25] I have come to the
conclusion that it would be true charity to give her a certain amt and send her
under proper protection to her mother and brothers. She is more dangerous
than either of the other(s) ... , because more subtle and ...

BAPTISTA LYNCH, URSULINE CONVENT AND ACADEMY,
VALLE CRUCIS. MAY 22nd [26]

... We are all so glad to hear of the success of your "Fair" and hope it may
relieve you of some of your embarrassment and let you rest and strengthen,
before setting out on your questing expedition again. That is a recreative way
of collecting, whereas appealing to the sympathies of people, is exhausting and
depressing. ... What do you think of a Fair in Columbia during some assembly?

... Every body and thing seems to be getting on very well, excepting Mme
A who I fear will bring upon you as upon me, and all the Superiors she has ever
had, the odium of being tyrannical and unfeeling. ...

CONLAW A. LYNCH, COLUMBIA, JUNE 10th[27]

Having heard that you are daily expected in Washington city, D.C. I will beg you, while there and at your earliest convenience, to see Mr. St. John B. L Skinner asst Postmaster Genl to whom I sent necessary papers for obtaining the position as business Mail agent on the Columbia and Augusta R.R. now running to Graniteville and lend me your influence in securing that business. . . . The contract for carrying the mail over the road has been made and the agent to carry the mail will have to be appointed before 15th inst.

BAPTISTA LYNCH, URSULINE CONVENT AND ACADEMY, VALLE CRUCIS, JUNE 12th[28]

. . . Rev. Dr. Meriwether gave our pupils their "Retreat meditation" as usual although very feeble ____ and at our request received into the Church and baptized Miss Octavia Chaires—who for two years, has asked of us and her father this privilege. Her father left it to herself and she being nineteen years of age, we thought it advisable to delay no longer.

On yesterday she together with Anna Lynch and Bessie Ahern made their First Communion so that all the children (except four) as well as the nuns (except one) approached Holy Communion on this beautiful Festival of "Corpus Christi." and we had Exposition of the Blessed Sacrament all morning followed by Benediction at 3 ½ P.M. . . .

. . . Mary Enright received a letter yesterday from her father who says " . . . I am certain there is not in any part of the state, another town, where the people are better disposed toward Catholicity at present than here. If Bishop Persico or some other good Catholic preacher would come here (to Abbeville) and preach say three sermons on the principal doctrines of our Church, I am surely of the opinion he would gain many converts. I have been begging the old Doctor to come up but it seems he cannot leave home. I suppose it would be out of our power to get our own good "Bishop" to come. There is no doubt if the effort were made to build a "Church:" we could get good assistance to do so in this district. . . ."

Of course, you received my letters by Dr. P—Sr. Etienne will send you by today's mail the first letter given up by Madame A. . . . We could not endorse the letter which contains so many imprudent and uncharitable personalities— artful subterfuges and distortions and several positive untruths. . . . She ought to be called "the Agitator" or "The Weakener" Such a contradiction of life and words! . . .

. . . You know that we did not pay for those "Lots" since it would not be of any advantage to John. But when Miss Denison gives me her money $1100 I will use it for the payment if you approve (although I do not count on her perseverance notwithstanding her assurances) as it seems to me better to lessen the debt . . . We got excellent "Rations" D.V. yesterday . . . We are very thankful for those Rations and the *manner* in which they are given. . . .

BAPTISTA LYNCH, URSULINE CONVENT AND ACADEMY VALLE CRUCIS, PENTECOST SUNDAY[29]

. . . John wrote to you respecting the use of your draft for $772.73 and being in such straits, I told him to use it unless he heard the contrary from you—he promising to pay it back to the Convent by August. The Sisters Notre Dame, East Boston are the first to answer our "Circular Letter" to convents and send us $10. If each will do as much, we will be aided in our difficulty. Emma Denison, who is a very excellent "Business woman" and very ardent in whatever she undertakes, writes to Rev. F. Ryan, urging him to give a lecture for our benefit in GA or rather the proceeds of a lecture. . . .

. . . Mme A . . . was at our general recreation yesterday. I will enclose you the opinions as expressed *informally* to Mother Assistant, who at my request communicated informally and prudently as much to each, as it was necessary for them to know. She does not receive H. Communion until Trinity Sunday. I will also enclose you the effusion of her crazy sarcastic mind, at the time she was deprived of her religious Habit—indeed on the very morning. The more I hear of this affair and of her conduct of which I did not take cognizance the more desirous am I, that she should be out of the House, and I pray our Lord and His Blessed Mother to remove *peacefully* so dangerous a person.

Monday: I had a conversation with her on Saturday, but tried to be watchful in my words, so as to give her no opportunity of making mischief, and promised to finish it today, but have been both sick and busy. Indeed the thought of it makes me sick. Another Band of the Soldiery visited us on Sunday, and told Mother Assistante who saw them, that it was very thoughtless in them, not to have remembered us on their pay-day before, but they would do so in future. (Monday evening) we have sent for the "Rations" and hope to get them- . . .

(Friday) Sr. A. said to Sr. Agnes "No Sr. Agnes I *have not* to go—possibly I *may go* but probably I *may stay*. . . .

BAPTISTA LYNCH, SUNDAY AFTERNOON (TRINITY)[30]

Before sending off your letter, or rather *my diary* to you, circumstances induced my sister counselors to advise my showing to Dr. M[.] this rhodomontade [*sic*] of Sr. A[.] and he advised or rather suggested the prudential act of sending it to you by hand not by mail—I see Rt. Rev. Dr. Persico . . . just now driving to Dr.

M[.] so I will hand it to him together with your cameos and Buttons to take to you in the morning. Please excuse haste. . . .

BAPTISMA LYNCH, URSULINE CONVENT AND ACADEMY.
VALLE CRUCIS, SUNDAY IN THE OCTAVE OF CORPUS CHRISTI[31]
. . . Mme A certainly has any amount of assurance and seems not to feel in the slightest degree her position. . . . Her manner towards me is defiant and disrespectful, but no one seems to mind her, nor do I. . . . The sooner she is out of the house the better. . . .

6

"THE RUB WITH US NOW IS WETHER WE CAN GET THE NECESSARIES OF LIFE"

July–December 1868

Pervasive poverty reduced most business transactions in upcountry Carolina to payments in cash, something the Lynches were sorely lacking. Francis Lynch was imperiling his health in his futile efforts to sell land in order to obtain the wherewithal for agricultural production that would support his family and workers. Worsening the condition of the Cheraw Lynches was the reckless speculation in the cotton market by Francis' son, Conlaw. In these dire straits Henrietta Lynch once again implored her bishop brother-in-law to provide the most basic necessities for her family: food, clothing, medicine. In the capital, John Lynch was in no better financial shape than his brother. His best option for obtaining cash was to sell a patent for the manufacturing of plasters. And so, John took himself to New York City where he calculated he was most likely to find an entrepreneur with the capital to invest in his invention. But even New York failed to provide a buyer, which left John concluding that all the talk about the riches awaiting newcomers to the city was "humbug." Meanwhile Patrick Lynch sought to extend his fundraising odyssey beyond the Northeast into the Northwest and Canada but found there much less support than he had previously realized in New York and other eastern cities.

At the Ursuline Academy, a lawsuit against the Valle Crucis property aggravated the financial pressures created by a chronic lack of revenue. The fall of 1868 brought some relief with the renewal of rations from the Freedman's Bureau. Meanwhile, the better-than-expected enrollment for the new academic year at their satellite academy in Tuscaloosa underscored the need for additional faculty. Which prompted Baptista, with the utmost reluctance, to send her most valuable member of the community to the satellite community to make the most of their opportunity.

After years of failing to find some appropriate way to remove Augustine England's divisive presence, Baptista finally managed, through others, to persuade the niece of Bishop England to start life anew in another Ursuline Community. To Baptista's great relief, an Irish Ursuline community consented to receive her back into her homeland. Patrick Lynch, through his Irish vicar-general, Thomas Bermingham, seems to have been responsible for the successful arrangement in which Sister Augustine herself made the appeal to the Irish prelate to take her under his jurisdiction. As part of the deal, Augustine got to have the final word about her case through letters addressed to Patrick Lynch and other officials which, to Baptista, merely provided an afterlife for her years-long campaign to undermine those in authority. Despite the concessions, Augustine's departure left Baptista exhilarated.

In the summer Mary Lynch Spann made her first return from Texas to the upcountry since before the war. So much in appearance had the Lynch sisters changed over the years that Mary failed to recognize Baptista upon arriving at Valle Crucis. But, if age had greatly affected their appearance, time had not severed the mental bond which the two women had forged in their youth. With Mary came her daughter Caro, who became the latest Lynch offspring at the Ursuline Academy.

As the country prepared for its first presidential election since the end of the war, terrorist groups, like the Ku Klux Klan, wreaked havoc throughout the South, particularly in the Piedmont region, as part of the effort to overturn Republican rule. After the November election, Baptista from isolated Valle Crucis reported to her bishop brother that "just as I expected, no disturbance of any kind worth mentioning," and welcomed Grant's victory as a boon for the country. In the man whose most famous campaign utterance was "let us have peace," perhaps the Ursuline

saw an instrument to realize the reconciliation which had so far
eluded the country. To Baptista, if Grant could bring about true
re-union, not just the absence of war, such an irenic environment
could not only cultivate economic revival but greatly facilitate the
spread of the Catholic faith in the South.

BAPTISTA LYNCH, URSULINE CONVENT AND ACADEMY, VALLE CRUCIS, NEAR COLUMBIA, S.C., JULY 12th[1]

. . . Miss Denison is writing today to Mr. Jas Dooley[2], a young lawyer in Richmond respecting the $1000—she will lend us at state interest 7 percent. . . .

Mme England has received but one response and that a negative (very
kindly worded) to her application.

BAPTISTA LYNCH, VALLE CRUCIS, ND[3]

Have you forgotten all about us? We have written several times and among
the letters to you was one from Mme Augustine, to which we had hoped for a
reply ere this. . . .

Please let me hear from you as soon as possible. The time is nearly up for
the departure of Mme A—and yet you do not aid her to go to the Convent of
Trois Rivièrs, which, as you see by the copy of letter enclosed to you by her
receives her most cordially. Am I to infer, from this that you prefer her remaining here? I asked Dr. Persico this. . . . But he said, no it was positively your
intention that Mme A should leave and he would say the sooner the better. If
so, my dearest brother, I must beg you to lose no time in sending her the proper
introductory letter. Which Dr. P—says you are too consistent to refuse her,
and also to send me $300 which will be necessary for her expenses and for Mrs
Brisbane who will be her escort to the convent of Three Rivers, Canada. . . .

. . . So what shall I do? This presses. I am without money and she without
the necessary letter for acting. . . .

HENRIETTA LYNCH, CHERAW, TO PATRICK LYNCH, AUG. 14th[4]

. . . It may well be said that misfortunes follow one by one for so it has been
with us since the war ended. The rub with us now is as to wether [sic] we can
get the necessaries of life. To show you how the tables turn even last night Mr.
L got a letter saying his cotton was sold at a loss of one half, he tells me this
is the money with which he expected to keep up household expenses. I refer
to Conlaw's speculation. If I tell you truly, we cannot get medicine needed in
sickness because everything needs cash and formerly an order would get us
any want. But for food, Mr. L is put to no straights [sic] by me, for I make the
children do with what they have had for years. Mr. L. has to provide for every

one he employs because they are all so poor, sometimes he feels like giving up. To give you an idea of the press of time upon him, he says he only weighs 120 lbs. . . . No one knows better than I do how much you have assisted him and to trouble you is indeed a trial sent me in another form. Mr L. has made a compromise with Judge Ingles and is to pay him $300 in 60 days and to return the land. He could do no better, he thought. This is to be paid with the new cotton. His friends seem very hard upon him. . . .

. . . We keep no house servant and I am always busy. I have become weak and thin since Jan last, . . . The children are studying under Josie[5] for the summer months. . . .

There is no one to whom I can open my heart but to you. . . .

JOHN LYNCH, COLUMBIA, TO PATRICK LYNCH, AUG. 20[6]
I write to let you know that sister Mary and daughter[7] arrived on Tuesday evening, are now at the Convent, will go over to Cheraw some day next week, perhaps Tuesday, do not know how long her stay will be there, but she will return by here, and spend a week or two. She will leave for Texas between the 12th and15 of Oct. She looks in excellent health, . . . Madame Charles met us at the carriage. I introduced them and drove around to fasten the horse. When I came back I found Mary and Ellen sitting together alone. Sister Mary had just asked Ellen for the health of the Community and her sister in particular. Then it was that Ellen found out Mary had not yet recognized her, they had quite a merry time over it.

. . . I may take a trip north myself, as soon as sister Mary leaves, to attend to the sale of my *Patent*; if I do I would like to get some letters from you, to some one who would give me an introduction to some of the most influential physicians in N. York, Boston, and Philadelphia from whom I would like to get recommendations for the use of the improvement. Armed with those, I could convince some of those large manufacturers of plaisters with confidence of success. . . .

BAPTISTA LYNCH, URSULINE CONVENT AND ACADEMY,
VALLE CRUCIS, AUGUST 27th[8]
At last your welcome and anxiously looked for letter has arrived! . . . Excepting your presence at the consecration,[9] we have not seen any mention of you whatever, and I begin to think you had attained your desire at last and found holy oblivion!!!

. . . You have of course received my letter announcing sister Mary's arrival in Columbia. She is a splendid woman! There is no doubt about it. She spent three days out here and all of our sisters are charmed with her and call her Sr.

Superior! Her daughter Caro is quite an interesting child. They are still in Columbia at John's but will leave for Cheraw tomorrow. . . .

BAPTISTA LYNCH, URSULINE CONVENT AND ACADEMY, VALLE CRUCIS . . . SEPT. 1[10]

Your welcome letter containing Draft was sent out by brother John and I am very thankful to you for both—The Draft of course I will not use unless as you advised and directed the proper letters arrive—and I wish you were near enough for me to consult you verbally—as Madam Augustine England is so anxious to remain even yet. Of course we wish to do the will of God as directed by you for the good of our Community. . . . Indeed I could not express to you how fully sensible not only myself but all of our Sisters are that this situation owes everything under God to you.

It is I who should speak of inefficiency and feel it when dealing with an underminer like Genl. Grant[11]—but on the other hand with so many good supporters I ought to be thankful. You too my dearest brother have devoted clergy who are happy in aiding your good work and if the general wreck of the country prevents your accomplishing all that you would wish and immediately—still look how much you have already done and I have no doubt with the blessing of God you will find means to continue your good work.

I am not at all surprised that in the West you did not succeed—It was not there but, in the East, I expected success and congeniality—as well as appreciation of you. I am very happy to learn that your cough has left you and that you are strengthened by your travels. . . .

[Mary] is . . . Considerably changed in appearance but the same beautiful character of mind and heart. . . .

. . . Natalie Brownfield's two sisters Mary and Frances are expected this afternoon. . . . We are also expecting three young ladies from Augusta as pupils by this same train. It sounds like old times to hear of new pupils coming in that way and I am truly glad to see it so. . . .

Sister Mary says Bishop Dubuis[12] asks why we do not like himself negotiate a loan in France? I told her it was our wish &c but we will soon *talk* about that &c

When will it be your convenience to give the white veil to Natalie and Emma (alias Denisen)—in October? One of those candidates, the protégé of the Semmes family, arrived last Friday. Made the retreat and was formally received into Noviciate on Sunday. . . . Our noviciate is certainly blessed and its members superior—So far from Mrs. Brisbane speaking of leaving she seems more satisfied than ever since the retreat. She edifies us very much notwithstanding her quotations of Carlyle, Rochefoucauld and such. . . .

ANNA LYNCH, CHERAW, SEPT. 9[13]

We received Sister Agatha's kind letter, a few hours ago, and are more than sorry to hear of your sickness. We expected you yesterday, and again today, when Bro. John arrived, and were quite disappointed that you did not come, but, far more so, to know that you have been detained by so serious a cause. . . . I wish very much I could assist in nursing you, and hope you will soon be well enough to come up *here*, where you can rest, and recruit without having anything to worry you, and be able to enjoy some of sister Mary's society. She is very anxious to see you, and much grieved to know of your sickness, as we all are. We will expect anxiously to hear from you, and also to see you . . . I am sorry you returned to Charleston, at this season, and while it is as hot, one great advantage you will have up here, will be to be free from the annoyance of mosquitoes. . . .

BAPTISTA LYNCH, URSULINE CONVENT AND ACADEMY,
VALLE CRUCIS . . . SEPT. 16th[14]

It seems that an "Extraordinary Confessor" (and Rt. Rev. Dr. Persico told us you had appointed him such) is necessary for Mme A[ugustine] E[ngland]. Each development which she makes causes the community to desire, all the more heartily, her departure from Convent. Since no letter comes to her from the Bishop of Trois Riviers and your sickness has prevented your meeting in the North the Bishop of Louisville, we think it well, if you approve, that the plan which she has mapped out, in her letter to Bishop Leahy[15] should be followed viz. to go to Ireland and place herself under his protection.

Mrs. Brisbane can leave with her on the 25th inst. Go to Baltimore and secure a passage in the "Bremen Line" steamer . . . Before that date she wishes to make a general Confession to Dr. Persico she says.

. . . Perhaps it would be well for Dr. Persico to be here at the date of her departure which would greatly relieve me and I suppose you also? This is a sad, sad case. By the "Bremen Line" it will cost $90 which is much less than the other steamers charge. . . .

Let me have as little to do with it as possible. Let Dr. Persico and Mme Etienne attend to all that is necessary. . . .

BAPTISTA LYNCH, URSULINE CONVENT, VALLE CRUCIS,
OCTOBER 1st[16]

. . . I had written to you in Charleston, not expecting you to go north so soon again, but I am glad you have gone now, instead of in mid-winter. . . . John is now in New York and feels dreadfully home-sick and alone in a crowd—I hope you may meet with him and assist him.

I am happy to say *at last* Mme England has gone! Deo Gratias. At her request Rt. Rev. Dr. P—came as "extraordinary" spent three days at her service and thanks to him after Divine Providence, she is gone. I have been filled with disgust, sadness and misanthropy, but I also trust have learned a salutary lesson of humility—from the developments to us made, by this revolutionist and schemer.

Mrs. Brisbane very kindly accompanies Mme E—as far as New York City and will see her on board, pay her passage and in which her nephews will attend to her wants. She will stay at the "Convent of Mercy Houston Street" until the vessel leaves. . . .

We gave Madame England, or rather Mrs. B. for her, $240°° in currency to pay expenses, $50°° in gold to use in Ireland (she will land at Queenstown) and some small silver coin to pay servants and She took with her as credentials your "Obedience" written for "Trois Rivièrs" and a letter which came to her about a week ago, and refusing her politely.

Before leaving, she Mme England wrote several notes of reparation for all the falsehoods she had told on you and myself and the fullest was to Rev. Dr. M. But as it is not possible for her to tell the truth, these notes read to me, rather as agitators and keeping herself as a subject of interest before others, than a reparation. . . .

I received a letter from Rt. Rev. Bishop Quinlan who declines inviting any or all of the Opelousas Nuns to Tuscaloosa, hoping still for aid from us. When we had been two years, at Columbia as they have been in Tuscaloosa, we had six white veiled novices. But as Sr Theresa says, that was under *Our* Bishop. . . . We are advised not to have our "Fair" until after the elections are over, as no lady will ever now venture out at night and we might as well be in Mexico it seems, as in the South. However, with us all is as quiet as ever, and I trust will continue so. I must say I am not apprehensive.

Rosie Ferre . . . has spent two days at the Convent going to the sacraments. She has "Ryan on the brain"[17] like so many other ladies and has given me a more exalted idea of the *ascetic knowledge* of this worthy Divine than I had before. . . .

BAPTISTA LYNCH, URSULINE CONVENT AND ACADEMY, VALLE CRUCIS, OCTOBER 12[18]

. . . I am so glad that you met John and cheered him up so much. . . .

I hope you fully approve of the entire settlement of the affair respecting Madame E—who did leave on the "Erin" for my only concern in the matter was to know your wishes, and yet I felt they must have concurred with ours, were you here, possessed of the knowledge we had on the subject. Since being relieved of her presence we all feel as if a heavy burden were removed. I look back on the ten years of suffering, with a sort of wonder at myself and how I stood it. But now I feel ten years younger and I trust will be able to do more A.M.D.G. . . .

How thankful I am to hear you say that if you make a good collection in Phila. you think it may be the last you shall have to make out of your Diocess. Then you can stay at home as you used to do when we first came to it and run up every now and then to Valle Crucis *to keep us all straight*. I really look forward to that time with a great desire and pleasure. I hope your trip to Canada will be to some purpose notwithstanding the great fire and floods from which they have suffered and that you may collect all that Mr Jones canvassed for and see our dear sisters the Ursulines of Quebec for whom we entertain an extraordinary degree of respect and affection and with whom we hold a close and confidential correspondence. We understand each other. . . .

Revd Father Cornette[19] of Mobile has taken quite an interest in our Sisters in Tuscaloosa and is canvassing for Candidates for their Convent. You know he gave a Retreat of eight days. I am very much gratified with the result of it. He has inspired them with a spirit of cheerfulness and holy joy in the service of our Lord. "Let every spirit praise the Lord" but *that* is the one I love, and if superiors I mean Bishops and Rev. Superiors, only knew how much the spiritual tone of a community is effected by the Annual Retreat they would never send these good, pious, *crusty* or *doleful* spirits to infuse themselves. Last year our Sisters there were told they were to bear the cross and a very heavy cross &c &c Their imaginations were filled with an indefinable fear, and the whole year was one of hardships. This year they begin in a different and cheerful, hopeful spirit, for which I am truly thankful. . . . The cold bracing atmosphere of this morning admonishes us that you might, as good Father Bermingham said, be driven here by the cold climate of Canada—a thing which he desired . . . We will all rejoice when you can stay at home and devote yourself exclusively to the duties of your office. . . .

BAPTISTA LYNCH, URSULINE CONVENT AND ACADEMY,
VALLE CRUCIS . . . OCTOBER 26th[20]
. . . Will you not be surprised to learn that our dear mother has been spending a week with us. . . . We are all delighted with her visit and she enjoyed it too. Our Sisters say she is such a personification of strength and sweetness combined, such calmness and intelligence! So reposeful in appearance, voice, and manner.

Brother John is expected home every day—says he has succeeded somewhat in his business but not as he expected or wished. However "a half loaf is better than none."

. . . Mr Spann has written to Mary to hasten home because Revd Father Assistant is appointed to go to San Antonio which may affect their prospects. She will be here in a few days. Caro came over with mother and Mary will leave on Monday 2nd. Nov. All Souls Day and Caro remain with us. That will be my birthday. I shall be forty-five years of age but mother says I look much younger especially when compared with Mary in appearance who is only eighteen months older than myself.

Madame Charles Weed and Sister Camilla Ahern will go on at the same time with sister Mary as far as Montgomery where I hope Revd Father McDonough will meet them. . . . I cannot express the regret I feel in parting from Madame Charles Weed. She has been my counselor and friend as well as sister in Christ for the past eventful eight years, and I have never known her to be anything but a most exemplary Christian lady possessing such a sweet and even disposition, never too much elated nor too much dejected. Always so kind and prudent and mortified. My heart and head both do her homage. She will be a splendid acquaintance to Tuscaloosa Convent and I will expect it to take a definite stand to have a noviciate for itself.

. . . We are again receiving "Rations." . . . I had no idea how dependent we were upon Rations until the issue of them ceased and now we are so thankful to get them again. . . .

I hope to hear from you and that you are doing well. Gleaming the harvest sown by Jones. . . . Mrs Brisbane will return next week. The N York physician pronounces her *dropsical* and her family tries to dissuade her from remaining with us.

. . . Cannot you get us one or two good *French* Lay Sisters in Canada. Young and strong for heavy work and a French teacher for Tuscaloosa? . . .

BAPTISTA LYNCH, VALLE CRUCIS, 6 NOVEMBER[21]
Sister Mary arrived here on Saturday last and spent All Saints with us, and Madam Charles and Sister Camilla left with her on the morning of All Souls day for Tuscaloosa. . . . We have receivd "Pencillings by the way" as far as Atlanta—"it goes well with them so far—As usual they have "Free tickets.". . .

. . . The grand subject of elections is seemingly over and just as I expected no disturbance of any kind worth mentioning not as much as we saw in Cincinnati—I said long ago that it would be the best thing for "the people" for the intelligent white working class and consequently for the spread of Catholicity in the South, if Grant were elected—although I know nothing of politics and have not read on either side—and now I am glad to see others think it will advance the "internal improvements" of the country generally which amounts to pretty much the same thing. . . . We are expecting the children of Mrs. Brisbane today—she has been detained in both New York and Charleston—partly by sickness or indisposition and partly by business—but with full permission, without which she will do nothing. . . .

I cannot tell you how thankful we are to Genls. Meade and Brainford for the rations—without which we could not manage at all. . . .

BAPTISTA LYNCH, NOVEMBER 21st[22]

. . . Sr. Charles picked up at Selma the two postulants about whom we have been corresponding lately and went on to the Convent in Tuscaloosa, to the great pleasure of Rev. F. McDonough and our Sisters. It is a very great relief to all to have Sr. Charles there and to know that they now number six, all told, besides a Lay Sister postulant . . . their pecuniary condition is not very flourishing but I think Mme Charles will be a better manager than Sr. L—and it would be well to place her in charge—May I do so?

. . . You will be glad to hear that we think our "Fair" or "Fete" will be a success. We invited Mrs. Dr Darby, oldest daughter of Genl. John S. Preston to manage the whole affair for us in the style of Patroness of the Institute (quite European like those noble ladies in Europe have done). She accepted with great grace and cordial politeness—came out to see us, and is doing everything in her power to make it a satisfactory elegant and profitable occasion. It would be held DV on December 1st—only one night and one day I believe. Mr. James Gibbons *with great pleasure gives* us the use of his hall. Mr. Jackson ditto—does the necessary printing &c &c. It is very amiable of them all and not one a Catholic. Of course John and Eliza are prominent. . . .

I am sorry you are not collecting as well as we had hoped, but as mother would say: "the worse luck may better again." So, don't stay in the cold and cause yourself to suffer as you did last winter. I am very surprised about the country now that the elections are over and "all's well that ends well." . . .

P.S. I forgot to tell you that Mrs Brisbane has returned . . . But is far from being well. . . . She edifies us very much. She is very anxious to sell her Georgia lands and thinks you can help her to do so, by seeing and cooperating with her brother in New York: Col. M. White. No 2, West 43rd Street, NY.

BAPTISTA LYNCH, VALLE CRUCIS, 15 DECEMBER[23]

What "under the sun" has become of you! Such a man I never saw! Spending winter at the north pole! Instead of at the sweet sunny south! I'll just not tell you another word!

JOHN LYNCH, VALLE CRUCIS, 21 DECEMBER[24]
Did you stop in New York on your way back, did you see Dr. Sims, or hear anything about the sale of my patent. I do not understand not hearing anything about it. New York is a humbug, as far as I am concerned. . . .

FRANCIS LYNCH, CHERAW, 27 Dec.[25]
. . . In business, matters are pretty must in statu quo. I have offered for sale my creek lands, through a New York house, which if effected, I trust will enable me to relieve much of my indebtedness and enable me to rebuild my tannery. Mr Blain continues his school and the children are learning well. . . .

7

"I FEEL AS IF I WERE IN THE EMBRACE OF A BOA CONSTRICTOR"

January–June 1869

No Lynch felt the impact of the new "hard times" as did John, who could no longer support his family through his medical practice. Before the war, it had simply been a matter of building up one's practice to the point that it could keep a family in comfort. Afterwards, no matter how many patients one had on the books, if they lacked the means to pay, numbers ceased to matter. To compound John's financial shortfall, the tax man cometh, a particularly odious feature of Reconstruction government. Whereas before the war, the planter class bore the brunt of the minimal taxation Southern governments imposed, now the tax burden fell broadly across society. Moreover, these postbellum governments were much more activist than their predecessors, engaging the state in a myriad of enterprises ranging from education to infrastructure to welfare that greatly drove up the budgets which were funded mainly through property taxes. John Lynch's inability to pay his taxes in full put his greatest financial asset—his home— at risk. As he told Patrick, his tax problems left him feeling "in the embrace of a boa constrictor . . ."

Baptista suffered from the same residual effect as John: parents unable to meet tuition payments and other educational costs incurred by their daughters. Nonetheless, the nuns began to operate segregated free schools for the neighborhood poor, both Black and white. As the community's Annals summed up: "Thus we try in our own little way to advance God's glory and the good of souls." In the rustic setting of Valle Crucis with its single manor house, the nuns did not attempt to maintain any semblance of cloister, bringing their sole French member, who knew the strict confines under which the Ursulines lived in her country, to remark: "What would our dear Mothers in France think of our Bohemian way of living?"[1]

Francis's hope of investing the profits of successful harvests into the rebuilding of his tannery was frustrated by his failure to accumulate any surplus. For the Lynches, the new financial straits forced them to appeal all the more to an old source of economic relief: their brother. Only now Patrick Lynch was in a far weaker position to come to their aid than he had been in pre-Confederate times. Patrick himself was spending at least half of the year on begging tours throughout the North and beyond, beset with his own immense challenge of restoring his diocese. Any plans of expanding facilities, including Valle Crucis, or adding new ones were on indefinite hold, much to Baptista's frustration.

Part of Parick Lynch's wartime strategy for protecting diocesan funds intended for future institutional expansion had been to invest them in real estate, particularly in Georgia. During the last phase of the war, the federal government had seized and put them under the Freedmen's Bureau. A novice of the Ursuline Community at Valle Crucis, a widow who held the title to lands in Georgia contiguous to those held by Bishop Lynch, became, in effect, the bishop's agent in attempting to reclaim them by paying the due taxes.

Baptista Lynch had a broad network of friends among the hierarchy. Even in their reduced quarters at Valle Crucis, the Ursuline superior continued to invite bishops and clergy to spend time at their new home, in the hope of having their guests become advertising agents for the academy, as well as recruiters for Ursuline candidates. So too, in the postwar period, Baptista remained on the alert for new targets for evangelization, not only those she encountered personally, but for regions in the Carolinas which, she learned from alumnae or friends, were ripe for the Church's harvest.

Having their academy and convent situated on a farm rather than in a former hotel meant much more manual labor, the kind

John Hugh Lynch.

that lay sisters traditionally had provided within the Ursuline order. So Baptista looked for any opportunity to secure new sisters
of this class. The hiring of a new overseer presented the occasion
to put his two adult daughters on probation as lay novices. Enrollment had increased to the point that Baptista expected that
they would reach capacity by next term. Still their revenue did
not match their expenses, forcing Baptista to seek the difference
from her bishop brother.

Three years after the war, they had begun to commemorate
the tragedy that had put them in their current straits. The night
of burning became a fundamental part of their history, the moment when God involved them in an extraordinary sharing in the
cross of His Son.

BAPTISTA LYNCH, [URSULINE CONVENT],
SATURDAY [JANUARY] 22nd[2]

I enclose you the circular which we forgot. I also forgot to tell you which I
promised Mrs Brisbane I would do—of your returns for taxes on Georgia
lands. Mrs Brisbane received a letter from some one in Georgia telling her of
the death of Mr Paulk, the former agent in the tax business and she wrote immediately and had your lands returned with hers. I wonder she did not think

to mention to you, as she is so very anxious that you would sell and colonize—or sell to some company—you understand me. . . .

Rev. Dr. M sent me word about the German family of which you spoke and Rev. F. Shadler wrote—I think we ought to exert ourselves to get them. It seems to be the very thing needed. But the convent is too poor . . . to promise to erect a house for them or incur any expenses. It does not even meet its own current expenses now. Never has, as you know since /65. Will do all we can though.

BAPTISTA LYNCH, URSULINE CONVENT AND ACADEMY,
VALLE CRUCIA NEAR COLUMBIA, S.C., FEB. 5th[3]
. . . You will be glad to hear that Dr. Meriwether was stopped in the street a few days ago and told that in consequence of your letter the "Convent and its farm would not be subject to taxation. I need not tell you what a subject of gratitude to you that piece of intelligence was.

You will be glad to hear we have two new pupils, daughter of Mr. Thos. McNally of Union C.H. who is a gentleman from the County Mayo in Ireland who married a Methodist lady some eighteen years ago—his children were baptized recently by Rev. Father McMahon, and he says if they only had a small church and some one to explain a few times, eloquently the doctrines of the Church, there are several ready to hear and accept its teachings—gentlemen who during the war were tended by "Srs. of Charity or Mary: and now prefer their religion to all others but don't know it. What would you think of Dr Persico who is so eloquent making a flying visit in the upper part of the state? . . .

BAPTISTA LYNCH, URSULINE CONVENT, VALLE CRUCIS,
FEB. 15th FEAST OF ST. SCHOLASTICA[4]
. . . I sincerely hope you are feeling as well and strong as I am. . . . We are expecting today the arrival of "Cecilia Kiernan," the sister of Sr. Anthony (President Davis' housekeeper) and I am very glad to have her come, for we need her very much. Rev Dr. M—has gone down to Charleston this morning, to see about getting "Fertilizer" for the farm and also to see about those Germans of whom Rev. F. Shadler wrote and you spoke. He told Sr Theresa that he would like to secure them for next year and wanted to know if I would take the girls for Lay Sisters. It seems . . . good parents do not want to leave them in the city. . . . Living in the country, we need more Lay Sisters, than when in Town, so if they come, I suppose it would be well to give them a trial?

A lady of Va is thinking of joining us as Choir Sister and I am told is a second Mme Charles—has a small fortune. We received those two McNallys and am much pleased with them. Expect two more which will be as many as we can crowd in.

Have had several visitors and apparently interested, inquiring about our Institute lately. Next session will hope for as full a school as we can accommodate. . . . The children are anticipating a day of recreation 17th into the anniversary of our being burned out. We make it a day of Thanksgiving for that blessing in disguise, that large portion of the Holy Cross. Our Communion is for the perpetrators of the act, and our pupils have recreation. This is in Faith and prevents either resentment or despondency. How deeply grateful we are and should be, to experience the contrast between our present circumstances and those of that time. D.G.

ANNA LYNCH, CHERAW, [FEB. 28][5]

I suppose you are very busy at this time with the work of the council in Baltimore[6] and hope you will enjoy the rest, or rather change from the constant preaching and labors of the winter to that of other duties. . . . Brother John paid us a week's visit, not long since, which we enjoyed very much. He was not very well, at the time. Cornelia[7] came over with him, for the change and benefit of her health, having been very sick. . . .

BAPTISTA LYNCH, URSULINE CONVENT, VALLE CRUCIS, MARCH 22nd[8]

. . . As you directed, Rev. Dr. P. came and Rev Dr. M went to Edgefield. . . .

A letter arrived from Mme England to Mrs. B—while Rt. Rev. Dr. P—was here and I gave it to him to read. She is not converted—the same bad spirits.
. . .

[Rev. Dr. Meriwether] is beginning to hint strongly for another mule to work the farm with as he often send[s] "Dick" to town—but we will turn a "deaf ear" to that as long as possible. I wonder if a "velocipede" would not be an economical horse to send into town. Are any made with a chair and pedals that a woman could use? I feel quite an attraction to and curiosity about the "velocipede."[9] . . .

BAPTISTA LYNCH, URSULINE CONVENT AND INSTITUTE, VALLE CRUCIS NEAR COLUMBIA, S.C., APRIL 14[10]

. . . They [Meriwether, Persico, Paquet, and Shadler] admire Valle Crucis so much . . . urge the building of an upper story—just as I proposed to you. . . . [we] are looking forward to the increasing of this house. I think you said the work should be begun in May, in order to be ready to receive pupils in next session.

I told you in my last of the $18,000 cash in greenbacks offered by Mr Hope or rather suggested for the town Lots (American Hotel) for the building of a post office and of Mr Ewd White saying that my offer to sell them for $28,000 (terms one fourth cash with bond and mortgage—balance in installments of $7000 per annum with interest from date) had a prospect of being accepted—he only wants the owners to empower him to sell it. He writes again for a reply but I think he wishes to charge 10 perct commission. Perhaps you could do better? . . . Please let me hear from you and if you prefer not selling now, or prefer to sell through other parties? . . .

. . . I hope to welcome to Valle Crucis those many friends of yours when they come south, especially my esteemed friend, Rt. Rev. Bishop Wood. If we could, as in Brown Co., receive such visitors, have them to make short but pleasant stays with our worthy chaplain, say Masses in our chapel, become interested in our Institute, I have no doubt they would increase the number of our pupils and perhaps noviciate, as well as bring a blessing on our Convent by the masses offered.

BAPTISTA LYNCH, URSULINE CONVENT AND INSTITUTE, [MAY 16, PENTECOST][11]

. . . You will see by my handwriting that I am not fully very well and am a little neuralgic—but am much better today than yesterday and the day before. I believe one cause is, that I have to ask you for money which I hate to do. It will take at least $600°° to meet our expenses up to the reopening of school in September and we have not $100 now to calculate and do not know if any one can pay us more than we have received this session.

Then John's troubles affect me. He tells me his house is advertised for "sale for taxes" and although his friends, many of whom are in the same condition hold an indignation meeting over it, that does not greatly meet the emergency. John says he wishes you would give yourself and him time to have a long, quiet sympathizing, brotherly and home-like talk about his prospects and give him the satisfaction of being listened to, by one who is interested in his condition, and possesses judgement to give him a suggestion. I proposed Francis, as being a better businessman than you, but John said, he had talked with him, and he could not suggest any plan for him—and he must do something to support his family.

Mrs Brisbane wants to have a long talk with you about those "Georgia Lands" which you—or the Church, seems about to lose. . . .

The old lady, who is daily sinking, is certainly indefatigable in the purpose of whatever she conceives to be her duty and that of preserving to the Church these lands—no doubt a very valuable property. . . . I wish you could sell them and rebuild our convent with the portion destined for Catholic education.

When I calculate that we received "Rations" until January '69 and that our present set of pupils do not support us, the balance of the year and on the other hand, see no workmen coming as you said in May to enlarge our House, I feel some anxiety for our support the next year. However, I ought to know well . . . that "God will provide" You see I am not well today and am looking on the dark side of the picture, but by the time this reaches you, I will be well and see only the bright side—so, as Mrs. Brisbane quotes: "We are all from critters after all."[12]

JOHN LYNCH, COLUMBIA, JUNE 4[13]

I recd yours of Monday on Wednesday. Called at once at the Sect Treasury Office but could not find what I wanted. Called the second and today the third time but without success. Cardoza[14] tried his best and even went or sent to Mr. Hunt, former occupant, who is quite sick, therefore can't assist him. I had called on Capt Fisher before receiving your letter, and told him, there would be no difficulty about his getting the place from you, that you only wanted a fair price, but preferred the arrangement you mentioned to him, and would write to him. . . . After concluding the purchase of the pine lands in Lexington at five dollars per acre which seems to me to be a fair price, I have no doubt if you offer the place to him at two thousand five hundred dollars he will be willing to give it. . . . Neither have I been able to collect anything to meet the balance of my taxes. What I am to do, I do not know. I feel as if I were in a vice, in the embrace of a boa constrictor, if you can imagine [sic] the feeling—how to release myself I do not know. . . .

8

"SR BORGIA BELIEVES THE WORLD IS NEAR ITS END"

July–December 1869

If there is such a thing as epistolary addiction, Baptista Lynch exhibited it, at least when it came to corresponding with her bishop brother. As she once candidly admitted to him, she simply did not know when to stop. It was as though she had this compulsion to be in contact with him. So long as she could continue to put pen to paper in addressing him, she somehow felt connected, whether he was in Charleston or Quebec. One recurring subject in Baptista's driven correspondence with her brother was the heroic commitment of the Ursulines' sickly chaplain, William Meriwether, to make Valle Crucis a productive estate. Successful harvests became imperative, not only for maximizing Valle Crucis's self-sufficiency, but also for supplementing the traditional income from tuition which source had nearly dried up since the end of the war. Given Meriwether's ambitious goals, he expected no less dedication from the freedmen whom he had hired to work the fields. When they did not measure up, the chaplain attributed it to the "indolence" associated in the white mind with Black character. Little wonder that Meriwether sought, like most of the Lynches, to replace the Black labor force with a white one. Meriwether was even open to bringing in Chinese immigrants, whose legal status fell well below the rapidly rising one for Black Americans.

Even in the unusually hot summer which dimmed prospects for an abundant harvest, the growth of the Ursuline community put more pressure on Meriwether to provide the basic components for an adequate diet. Since arriving in Columbia in 1858, the Ursulines had more than tripled in number, including eight members in formation. Indeed, the community outnumbered the students enrolled in their academy. Still Baptista remained upbeat about the institution's future, in part because her bishop brother continued to support it financially, including bearing the cost of the education of a growing number of Lynch siblings. There was also the encouraging environment of a South getting on its feet again. That this revival coincided with the implementation of Republican governance in the region went unconsidered.

In Tuscaloosa, the escalating difficulties between Bishop Quinlan and the Ursuline satellite community brought to a boiling point Baptista Lynch's exasperation with her brother's persistent failure to respond to her letters seeking advice and guidance regarding the matter. This, to Baptista, was the inevitable consequence of being a carpetbag bishop, more absent from his diocese than presiding over it. In a subsequent letter Baptista bluntly conveyed to him the widespread frustration that Patrick had generated among his people by spending so much time away from his diocese to retire the debts which war and natural disaster had wrought. Rather than abandoning his people and ruining his own health in order to relieve the diocese of its indebtedness, Baptista advised her brother that she should have contested the legality of war-generated debts in court. At the very least he might well have secured an arrangement by which the sums owed could be paid back gradually as the diocese, along with the country, recovered its financial footing.

John Lynch finally realized his decade-long quest for an appointment to the medical department of the University of South Carolina, with a $2,000 salary which promised relief from his financial woes. Lynch knew too well how precarious his appointment was. Radical changes were afoot for the university as the Republican government extended Reconstruction to the realm of higher education by integrating the institution at every level, from students to the board of trustees. John Lynch's keen awareness of the unsettled situation at the university made him all the more determined to establish his academic bona fides. The immediate challenge was to so excel in his classroom lectures as to diminish the likelihood that a newly installed radical administration would find cause to replace him. His late-hour appointment made it practically impossible to prepare lectures for his courses. In desperation he turned, once again, to his bishop brother to use his contacts with the intellectual elite of Charleston and beyond to "borrow" someone else's lectures for his initial classes. Although such plagiarism was all-too common in late mid-century American academia, John Lynch was providing to any impending radical administration convenient grounds for removing an ex-Confederate from the faculty.

In Cheraw, Francis and Henrietta, as though they had not enough challenges in their lives, found themselves caring for Lily Lynch, Augusta Lynch Ryan's troubled child. They turned to their bishop brother to find a suitable place for Lily, before he headed off to Rome for the first ecumenical council the church had held in well more than two centuries.

BAPTISTA LYNCH, URSULINE CONVENT, VALLE CRUCIS
NEAR COLUMBIA, S. CAROLINA, JULY 11th[1]
. . . I write now to thank you for your great kindness in remembering our needs and sending us the check $200 which is most acceptable. I hope you are feeling quite well ere this. . . . The thermometer stood 102 today and we want rain badly. The garden parched up. . .

Owing to the great drought and heat and to the indolence of the Negroes I believe Rev. Dr. M—is determined to have white or Chinese labor next January. If so, we will be all the better pleased to have a sufficiency of Lay Sisters but Sr. Ursula says you will have to give them a house to live in also. I think we can accommodate two though—unless they are like the last one who left proud and insolent—self-seeking,—and those we don't want. . . .

BAPTISTA LYNCH, URSULINE CONVENT AND ACADEMY,
VALLE CRUCIS—SEPT. 21st[2]
. . . We have had a visit from the clever Sister Xavier and Sister Agatha (now Sr Treasurer)[3] who came to secure to themselves that $6,000 which had been voted them by the City Council and mentioned in the newspapers. They had some work, but Sr. Xavier has, she thinks, pushed the matters thro with the clemency of Gov. Scott[4] who seems wonderfully Catholic of late.
. . . I was surprised to hear Sister X say like every body else, that you ought never to have subjected yourself to this mode of life of begging all the time—but just have paid a dividend on percentage, or placed the business in court and let the Law decide your indebtedness at the close of the revolution, and in after

years when the Diocess and its institutions had been set on a good footing, the country recuperated and gradually pay off the entire. . . .

This has always been my view of your case, but of course you know your own affairs best—now however that Bp. Persico is gone, where is the Head?

. . . Anna,[5] like myself, has been exerting herself to keep from calling on you for money to repair the church and so gave a concert at which Caro and Ellen sang, and Anna realized enough to pay for the repairing of the organ, making a platform for it and some $50 or $75 toward shingling the roof of church. . . .

You will be glad to learn that Columbia is being rebuilt rapidly, and the winter promises to be prosperous. But the planters seem to feel somewhat dejected on account of the long and severe hot spell of dry weather.

Sr Borgia[6] and myself have a talk every day about all the natural phenomena noted in papers and she believes . . . the world is near its end. . . .

LOUISA BLAIN, [CHERAW], OCT. 12th[7]

. . . I write this to speak of H[enrietta] and her health. You remember on your last visit to us, we acquainted you with the sad state she was in; for the last week or ten days she has not been so bad but for all that she does not allow Mr. L any more liberty and the sight of that child[8] always brings on fits of melancholy. Ma is anxious to send L to the city with me to see if the change should benefit her and I think it would but the trouble would still remain. My plan is this as the mother of the child has frequently written that she wished to have her child to visit her, I thought if I could take her down if only for a short time, it would make all things right, no one would suspect anything for not more than a few weeks ago, A[ugusta] wrote to know what would the expense be to send the child down. Now I beg of you dear friend to offer to pay her expences down as I know full well that her mother cannot do it. . . . I have great hope of her recovery. . . .

BAPTISTA LYNCH, [VALLE CRUCIS], EVE OF ST. URSULA'S FEAST [OCT. 20][9]

. . . I am so afraid that you are doing as Bishop England did and are allowing your mind to be harassed by money matters. What is the good of it? As mother would say, there will be money after we are all gone, and your health is of more value than "the mines of California."

. . . Mrs Brisbane is very ill. Wants you to administer to her Extreme Unction. Has made her will. I hear in our favor $6,000.

Oh! I wish I could tell you what I wish to say. Do come?

JOHN LYNCH, COLUMBIA, OCT. 22nd[10]

... I have been elected professor of Physiology and Materia Medica in the medical department of the S.C. University and will commence my duties on Monday 1st Nov. after that I cannot leave home until July next except at Christmas, when there will be holiday for one week, ... I wish to make my mark so as to retain the position, after the powers that have put me in the position have been removed, to do that will require ... hard study. I am doing that now, but fear I will break down under it. I find it a very difficult task to write my lectures and fear I will not be able at first to keep up, especially as I know there are jealous eyes on me, can you not amongst your many medical friends borrow for me for a while a course of lectures on each of the branches, that I could use, until I could write out a course to suit myself. It would be a great relief to me, and harm no one. ...

I was at the Convent this evening. All well, except Mrs. Brisbane, who proposed leaving us a few days ago, but has changed her mind. She was at Mass this morning. ...

HENRIETTA LYNCH, CHERAW, 25th OCT[11]

It was with great pleasure that Mr. L. received a letter from you about 10 days ago. It raised his spirits exceedingly to read your flattering promises. He has been trying so hard to obtain help first from one, and then from another, but without success.

I have been sick for about 12 days. I was in bed since Tuesday. I would have written to you long ago but was never certain of your whereabouts. I trust you will not put off your visit here till within a day or two of your departure because I wish to see you ever so badly, your visit here will be a great relief to me, I trust. ...

Please burn this letter.

BAPTISTA LYNCH, CONVENT, VALLE CRUCIS, NOVEMBER 12th[12]

I write *immediate* on my envelope because I want to overtake you in New York before you set sail.[13]

I thank you very much for your kindness in sending me the Bank Check of $800 to pay the balance due for shingling and help us over the winter.

All congratulations little [blotted out section] manner in which [illegible] lecture was given and the handsome sum raised to defray your expenses to the council. This shows that your people not only do not object and murmur at your absence but cheerfully acquiesce and can contribute to your departure. That is pleasant. ...

... Mme Borgia appears just the same, but is suffering all the time. ...

9

"REV DR MERIWETHER HOPES IT IS NOT TRUE YOU HAVE NOT GONE FOR THE IMMEDIATE DEFINITION"

January–June 1870

During the last year of the American Civil War, Pope Pius IX first raised the prospect of calling an ecumenical council, a gathering of the world's Catholic prelates that had last occurred more than two centuries before the establishment of the United States. When, four years later, a commission was formed to plan for the council, James Corcoran of Charleston represented the American bishops. Despite missing the first fifteen months of planning, Corcoran quickly discerned that ultramontanists, or proponents of a Rome-centric Church under an infallible pontiff, were dominating the preparations. Some of their proposals regarding civil government Corcoran found to contradict the fundamental principles upon which the American republic was based. Of equal if not greater import, Corcoran reported that defining papal infallibility as an article of faith was a foregone conclusion. Conservative forces wanted papal infallibility to become a litmus test for the loyalty of Catholics. The issue divided the American prelates, with the largest bloc arguing against the definition on the pragmatic grounds of the deleterious impact it would have on the Catholic community in the United States.

As Baptista Lynch inferred, her bishop brother was part of this broad middle group, between the ultramontanists and the conciliarists who denied that infallibility was a personal charism of the pontiff. Bishop Lynch did not participate in the extended discussion which preceded the vote on the definition. He did, serve, in effect, as the correspondent for *The Catholic World* in publishing eight reports on the council. In the end, the ultramontanists prevailed, and many of Lynch's bloc, including Lynch himself, received permission to return home without having to take part in the final vote.

Baptista wanted to take advantage of her brother's presence in Rome to have him secure a rescript from the pope which would give Bishop Lynch full jurisdiction over their community, eliminating the possibility of a Roman congregation or the Ursuline order itself from intervening in the apostolates and governance of the community. At William Meriwether's suggestion, Baptista also urged her brother to make time during his European sojourn to tap the unique sources available there—the missionary societies, royalty, the low-interest loans—to create an endowment for their institute which would enable students of all classes to enroll. There is no evidence that Patrick Lynch ever acted upon either notion. The only significant fundraising to take place was in the District of Columbia where former Bishop Michael O'Connor gave a lecture for the benefit of the Columbia Ursulines.

The community continued to receive almost too many applicants to become choir sisters. As eager as Baptista was to grow the Ursuline presence in Columbia to better staff their institute, she was wary of supporting candidates whose fragile health promised to make them burdens upon the community, particularly those bringing no dowry with them. The advent of the railroad to Columbia from Augusta, Baptista was quick to realize, offered the possibility of securing a station stop at Valle Crucis. Such a stop would not only enable them to get mail and supplies right on their doorstep, but also provide commuters easy access to their campus.

The situation of the satellite community in Tuscaloosa continued to deteriorate. The basic problems were a lack of personnel and chaplain services. Their five years in Tuscaloosa had yielded not one novice who proved worthy of taking the veil. That left two

options: merging with a nearby Ursuline community or bringing in Irish or French women to supplement staff, both teaching and support. Baptista much favored the first; the second had
proven to be a dependable source for candidates, but rarely dowry-
bearing ones.

John Lynch, unable to acquire any extant notes for his lectures to medical students at the university, perforce prepared his
own, which, at least in John's view, went over well. Buoyed by this
success, he made bold to secure an appointment for his Texas
brother-in-law Charles Spann, so as to have a supportive colleague. Francis, still trying to revive his tanning business, traveled
to Baltimore to secure backing. Meanwhile, the Cheraw Lynches,
like the Spanns in Texas, found themselves hosting their pastor.
The Catholic communities in both upcountry Carolina and eastern Texas were too poor to provide rectories for their priests.

By late April the Lynch patriarch, Conlaw Peter, his health
rapidly declining on the brink of his eighty-first year, became increasingly anxious to see his oldest son once more. Yet again, the
family found itself hoping against hope that Patrick would not
disappoint.

BAPTISTA LYNCH, URSULINE CONVENT VALLE CRUCIS
NEAR COLUMBIA, SOUTH CAROLINA, JANUARY 24th[1]
. . . Anna says . . . brother Francis has at last succeeded in obtaining a steam-
engine for his tanyard, and as usual, is very energetic. Lillie has been on a
visit to her mother in Charleston. Went down with Miss B and with Caroline.
. . . Brother John and family are as when you left and he looking better than a
short time ago. His lectures are good and his success gives him pleasure. I have
read two, which I liked greatly and am thankful he has this useful distraction.

Sister Mary will be pleased if Mr. Spann is elected to the Chair of Classics,[2] because it will bring her nearer to our dear parents. . . .

BAPTISTA LYNCH, URSULINE CONVENT, VALLE CRUCIS . . .
TO PATRICK LYNCH, FEB. 22nd[3]
. . . We have been reading as a Lecture in Community an article in the "Catholic World" on the Ecumenical Council and think we discover in it *your style* of
composition. Is it by you? Another piece from the same author appears in this
month's number . . .

Our Sisters in Tuscaloosa are not satisfactory. There must be something in the atmosphere of the place, to produce instability . . . To *give stability* it would be better to invite the Opelousas Convent to unite with them. . . . Or it will be necessary for the Bishop to bring over a *band* of *recruits* say 5—convent educated, intelligent, pious young ladies, capable of *forming a corps* of *teachers* and *carrying on religious observance*. I am told many such can be got in Ireland or France, if taken without dowers. Either one, I see, must be done. I prefer the first to give stability to that convent, if not, I see no other alternative than to recall our professed, which I will *regret exceedingly* to do after we have put the hand to the plough. . . .

BAPTISTA LYNCH, URSULINE CONVENT,
VALLE CRUCIS, MARCH 7[4]

. . . Yesterday I was doing the duty of "General Mistress" according to our Rule—and giving the pupils an opportunity of laying before me their wishes and views &c &c like the President of a College does with his students. You would really have been amused and pleased with Caro Spann . . .—so natural, so much simplicity mingled with true womanly delicacy and dignity! Caro will be 18 next month and after hiding behind my chair through bashfulness, ventured to ask a place in our noviciate! We can have no doubt of a vocation of four years standing, but she will have much to conquer in her witty wayward spirits—fun-loving as she is! She is so remarkable sensible, has such uncommon good judgement, just like mother, that I hope she may be a superior nun. Her talents are superior and her education advanced . . .

(Tuesday 8th March)

. . . I wish *very much* you would, while in Rome, get for me, or rather us—I mean of course *our convent* a Special rescript from the Holy Father, giving us the authority to establish our Convent in this diocese, where and as you, the Rt. Rev. Bishop judges best for the carrying out the end and object of our order of the Ursulines and Congregation of Paris—with full authority to use such means and adapt ourselves to such ways as you, the Rt. Rev Bishop may judge best for the advancement of Religious education. Now my dearest brother do not laugh at me, and throw this aside, but please humor my fancies and get the Rescript dated for the time of our Foundation—say August 15th 1858. . . .

BAPTISTA LYNCH, [VALLE CRUCIS], MARCH 17th[5]

I feel like saluting you with "a Patrick's day in the morning to you!" with a sprig of shillelagh [*sic*] and shamrock so green! . . .

I have on my desk a note or letter from Rev. Dr. Meriwether on various items of business, one of which is our *"prospects of rebuilding,* or of *"building ourselves up"* We are very much gratified to see him take up the interests of our Institute so warmly and identify with it . . . He is very anxious that you could get help from the "Society of the Propagation of the Faith[,]" from the Trappist Monks in France or make a loan, which our *newspapers say* can be done now at an interest [rate] of two or three per cent? Or if you could only meet "accidentally on *purpose"* the Marquis of Bute and get from him the wherewith! Or what shall I say next? Well, your own wise head and far seeing thoughts will suggest and we will echo your proposition.

Rev. D^r M—is ready and anxious to work, thinks no time is to be lost or we shall lose our chance of scholars now that planters have recuperated sufficiently to be looking around for a good school for their daughters and when once selected, will in all probability continue . . . "Salem" NC has 800 girls in its academy. . . .

Rev. Dr M—wants to see the Convent numbering as many if possible and like "Oxford" Eng. in its beginnings a Funded Institution—*gratis education* for all and cheap board—so that *Catholic education* may reach all classes. . . . This he proposes as the bulwark against the evils of modern society as existing and growing in this country. . . . We are happy if Divine Providence raises up in him an efficient co-operator with you, to whom he refers everything with so much confidence and respectful affection. I believe if you can raise the funds, you will find in him a right hand for your work. . . .

Do not think that we . . . on this side of the Atlantic are growing chimerical while the "Princes and Sages" of holy Mother Church are in Council. No, we are a unit in our work—however varied our conceptions respecting it. . . .

ANTONIA LYNCH, MOUNT CARMEL, MAR. 28th[6]
. . . You will be pleased to learn that I had the pleasure of seeing brother Francis about the first of February. He was looking very well. . . . I believe he is making much exertion to rebuild his factory. . . . Sister Mary also wrote me about Christmas.

. . . Brother John proposed to Mr. Spann to apply for a seat in the Columbia College. In case they do not succeed, Sister Mary said they would return to the country in the summer. At the present time Mr. Spann has charge of St. Mary College in Galveston. . . .

. . . I suppose you have heard that I have charge of the Community. I find all the duties much lighter, than I had anticipated. I am sure it is all owing to the many good prayers offered for me. . . . I am in very good health and growing more fleshy. . . .

BAPTISTA LYNCH, URSULINE CONVENT,
VALLE CRUCIS, GOOD FRIDAY[7]

Annie has wanted me to write and tell you how very weak our dear and venerable father has been. Her third letter makes me do so. Brother John and myself thought it useless to write because of the great distance between us and the slow European mails. John went over to Cheraw and remained from Thursday until Saturday, assisted father to receive Extreme unction, but was compelled to return to Columbia for his lectures in the University. Since then, father has rallied a little under the stimulants and tonics given him, but is unable to sit up or even take nourishment sufficient to strengthen him. He may last a month or he may be taken at any time. All seem anxious that he may see you, and are praying for that. . . .

BAPTISTA LYNCH, URSULINE CONVENT,
VALLE CRUCIS, APRIL 21st [8]

. . . Our dear and venerable father is very feeble—may not last even until this reaches you. They seem anxious that he should have the gratification of seeing you. . . . Father may rally as he has done before. Perhaps you may telegraph and inquire on your arrival in N.Y.

ANNA LYNCH, CHERAW, MAY 10th[9]

We are expecting, for a week past to hear of your arrival in this country and should be so much relieved to have you at home again, on father and mother's account especially. Father continues, *very sick*. We do not expect him to live, and he wishes most anxiously and continually, to see you before he dies. I hope you will come directly here, and that thro the prayers that are being said for father, he may be spared to see you as he so much desires. He has been ill, for more than six weeks and suffers very much lately; mother and the rest are pretty well and unite in much love to you, my Dear Brother, hoping you will come very soon . . .

BAPTISTA LYNCH, URSULINE CONVENT,
VALLE CRUCIS, MAY 16th[10]

. . . Rev. D[r] Meriwether hopes it is not true you have not gone for the immediate definition. John amused me, he says he will not read any newspaper accounts, for he is so sure all will be right, that he only awaits the decision to chime in with it.

Mr Charles Pelham called yesterday on Rev. Dr. Meriwether to know if we could *"give the right of way"* the surveyors are nearing Columbia from Augusta and the . . . RR will pass near us . . . of course the land will be enhanced in value, by the RR—but there are two sides to every thing. Mme Borgia Brisbane advises to *give* the right of way, with condition that they stop 5 min. to bring out to our institution pupils, express, mail and [marketing?] which will just suit us. . . .

You must be awfully tired of so much writing and debate—But of course, that is the way in all councils whether of state or Church . . . It seems to me I have outlived the age of being surprised at anything and I begin to fear I may live to be as old as our dear and venerable parents. . . .

BAPTISTA LYNCH, VALLE CRUCIS, MAY 27[11]

A telegram calls brother John to Cheraw. Anna says our dear venerable father was released from his sufferings this morning about 6 o'clock. May our dear Lord establish him in eternal peace and blessedness. So good a life must merit eternal happiness. The good Carmelites have been praying for your return but, as I told you before I am not sorry that you are spared this trial, when your presence was not necessary. Father had every spiritual and temporal consolation and while your strength would have been tried, he would have forgotten your person in a few moments. . . . Father, cheerful, peaceful, calm but very weak and his memory not retentive. I hope that mother may feel consoled that he is relieved from his sufferings. She and Anna have been very much exhausted nursing father, but neither they or he could be satisfied to have it otherwise.

BAPTISTA LYNCH, VALLE CRUCIS, JUNE 4th[12]

It was a true joy to us to receive your telegram . . . announcing your safe arrival in New York on 1st inst. . . . I am very glad that you are going up to Cheraw on Tuesday. . . .

ANNA LYNCH, CHERAW, JUNE 26[13]

. . . I write today, particularly on account of Mr Blain's accident . . .

On Thursday evening last, after giving his usual night lesson . . . , Mr Blain . . . met Theodore Neal, with whom he began wrestling in play, when he got his leg broken, in two places. This occurred about eleven P.M. and he was not brought home until about 3 A.M. after the bones were set and anodynes given by Dr. McLean. This gave, of course, his mother and sister a great fright, and occurred at an unfortunate time, too, when they were without servants about the house. Such high wages are offered for field laborers at this time, that the Negroes heads appear turned by it and many are left without house servants.

Aunt Roddy, whom we have, threatens every day to go, also, but, I hope, she will not. . . .

Mr Blain suffers a good deal . . .

ANNA LYNCH, CHERAW, JUNE 28th[14]

. . . Mr. Cullinan wishes me to make an effort to have music on Sunday, . . . But, I fear, I will not have much success, as I have so little heart for singing just now and will miss very much Mr. Blain's efficient help.

. . . I should have some courage to attempt, under better circumstances, church music, in your presence. But . . . I will not, if possible, ask Protestants to assist this time, fearing they may return the compliment.[15] . . .

10

"NO MAN SEEMS TO KNOW WHETHER HE IS STANDING ON HIS HEELS OR HIS HEAD"

July–December 1870

Five years after the war's end, Baptista Lynch became increasingly frustrated by her bishop brother's absence from his diocese for much of the year on fundraising tours. Particularly when there were so many opportunities for evangelizing at which Patrick Lynch, by his preaching and engaging manner, was so adept. And so Baptista continued to urge that he restrict his travels to reaching his own people throughout the Carolinas, so many of whom were longing for the blessings that he could bring them. Moreover, the diocese needed his presence to effectively oversee his clergy. Even a cloistered nun like Baptista heard the rumors about the scandalous alcoholic indulgence of some of his priests. "I do wish you could stay at home," she told him in July, when he was about to head north; "—hold your synods and Retreats, issue your Pastorals and fulfil the functions of a Bishop then your Diocess would not be, as I read, 'out in the weather' any longer."

Baptista herself was particularly active in her own sphere of ministry, not only in the classroom but as a spiritual counselor, particularly through the retreats she directed, both for students and lay adult females. Meanwhile the convent and institute continued its hand-to-mouth existence, barely meeting their current expenses, unable even to afford the travel costs of a retreat giver.

Nonetheless, Bishop Lynch, with his eye on future development, advised his sister to have her community engage in prayerful discernment about renovating Valle Crucis, building anew, or acquiring suitable facilities in Columbia. The community's other institution, the understaffed academy in Tuscaloosa, was financially in better shape than its motherhouse, with enough paying students to make ends meet. Still, for Baptista the ultimate success of an Ursuline academy was the number of vocations it fostered. It was clear to her that unless there were enough Ursulines to form a convent large enough to create a religious milieu in which students would become predisposed toward the vowed life, the vocations would not follow "as naturally as water flowing downhill." Reluctantly, Baptista concluded that Tuscaloosa was not sustainable as an apostolate.

Reconstruction had not favored Francis Lynch's business ambitions. Not only did he struggle to find the means to rebuild his tannery, but labor in the post-slavery South was simply a more expensive commodity. No longer could enslaved labor serve to keep wages depressed. Instead, freedmen and white workers both expected wages which would allow their families to lead decent lives. That affected the lifestyle of even a formerly prosperous businessman like Francis Lynch. Retaining his workers necessitated a certain belt-tightening for his family, something Francis obviously found embarrassing. Compounding Francis' financial woes was his failure to obtain badly needed credit from bankers, the consequence of Francis' inability to meet production goals and of cheaper prices than anticipated for his products. The upshot was to appeal to Bishop Lynch to underwrite another of his nieces' education at Ville Crucis.

Health crises for Eleanor and Anna Lynch occasioned their move from Cheraw to Valle Crucis where they could both be under John's care. The move seemed initially to benefit both mother and her youngest daughter. But when Eleanor Lynch regained her feet, Anna remained confined to bed. By late October, when John took his gravely ill sister into his own home in Columbia for constant care, Baptista feared that consumption, the family scourge, had returned to seek its first postwar victim.

BAPTISTA LYNCH, VALLE CRUCIS, JULY 10[1]

. . . Conlaw[2] and Josephine came out to see us and I am greatly pleased with Josephine. She appears to possess a quiet dignity of manner—sweetness of disposition and sufficient strength to meet and bear up under the vicissitudes of life.

. . . I wish very much you could make a visitation through the upper part of this state and preach in Union, Lancaster, Newberry, Abbeville &c I am sure you would do so much good and win so many to the Faith, who are just waiting to be called. Mrs McNally who was baptized some months ago, is waiting to make her First Communion and have her infant baptized. At Spartanburg poor Belle Roman writes us. She only waits for a priest to return to the church from which she apostatized . . . At Newberry Mrs Gist wants to learn the Catholic religion and . . . I know if they all heard your explanation and sermons, they and many others would come into the one true fold. . . .

Sister Charles writes from Tuscaloosa where Bishop Quinlan gladdens all by his presence, benevolence, and kindness. . . . Their commencement came off very well, and good humble sister Charles is so glad to have been able to have it and gratify the Bishop and Rev. Fr. McDonough who she says are so interested in the Convent.

Rev. Father Ryan[3] will be the substitute for Rev. F. McDonough for a while. No doubt it will be of solid advantage to him to come in contact with such a superior Religious as Mother Charles. . . .

I have not said anything about our "Retreat" because I have not the wherewith to pay traveling expences. . . . Must go in debt for provisions and until Sept. or next session. Could not wait for "Retreat money" in that way. . . . Well content with Rev. Dr. M—than whom I know no one suits us better—quiet, unpretending, solidly religious and nothing high-flown. But whatever arrangement you want my dearest brother will be most acceptable to us. . . .

BAPTISTA LYNCH, VALLE CRUCIS, JULY 18th[4]

. . . Rev. Dr. Meriwether I learn . . . is going away to rest or recreate awhile, and at the same time make a retreat at Frederick, MD. So of course, cannot give our Retreat, even if this bronchial affection allowed him to do so. I wish you had a half dozen men like him in your dioceses . . .

. . . Indeed I do not know any Bishop more calculated and few as much—to gather under his paternal roof all the clergy of the Diocess—console the weak, animate the faint hearted, patiently listen to the murmuring and tottering— as yourself. I do wish you could stay at home—hold your synods and Retreats, issue your Pastorals and fulfil the functions of *a Bishop* then your Diocess would not be, as I read, "out in the weather" any longer. . . .

Now, if you will just give the heads to Rev. F. Shadler and send him "Preaching and Teaching, thro all the towns and villages"—he will have "stumped the state" in the cause of Christ, and prepared the people for your advent next winter . . . [by] a delightful summer campaign for soul and body. . . .

BAPTISTA LYNCH, VALLE CRUCIS, JULY 22nd[5]

. . . Today I received from Mr Brennen $200 the balance due for educational expenses of his daughter and this will make us easy about the Retreat. We are so much obliged to you for procuring the service of Revd Father Boone, S.J.[6] You must be quite a favorite with the Jesuit Fathers, they always accede so readily to your wishes. . . .

We will make our improvements out at V.C. a subject of special prayers and thoughts, as you advise. After the war-devastation we were very reluctant to come into the country, foreseeing much more privation and suffering than we have been called on to endure temporally and spiritually. It was this made us work so hard, before your return from Europe, to rent or buy the MF College, now Nickerson House. Even now, that House is the only one in Columbia we could occupy with as much comfort as this at Valle Crucis. . . . Could that be bought, at what price if at all? If bought by you and for us, would it be like the American Hotel?

We enjoyed quite as good health in Columbia as at Valle Crucis—out door exposure was less and for house room, we were never so crowded as now. Yet we have never considered ourselves to have a voice in the matter, when speaking of the *pros* and *cons*—but I felt that Providence *forced* us out here, and took from us the ways and means of doing otherwise than remaining out here and making the best of it. So, we determined to make a virtue of necessity—daily grew more reconciled and finally to liking it. But at the same time we are not unmindful of what you suggest to our thoughts and hold ourselves in a state of indifference on the subject and ready to do, whatever you think best for the interest of religious education. The advancement of that, is our one object, next to our salvation. If you think better to suspend all action in the matter for a year or two, then, it will not be well to borrow money, because we ought not to borrow, unless to use in building.

But when once decided—[remain] here or buy M.F. College (Nickerson House) then the sooner we go ahead the better, I suppose. We will pray and depend on your judgement.

. . . No doubt a few years will accomplish a great deal for us, and if a war in Europe drives good French immigrants to our state, it will be to the advantage of Religion.[7] At all events, you my Dearest Brother, have given me two mottos, which I intend to keep before me: one—Serve God *well* today and He will take care of you tomorrow." So far I have realized the truth of this. The other is "Deus providebit," and so we find. He always gives us "our daily bread"—as to the future we thank Providence we have no children depending on us and we know each generation thinks itself the wisest—so, will let it plan and work for itself. You say, my dearest Brother "After I am gone." God grant I may *never* see that day. But weary as you may sometimes feel the burthen of life, I have no doubt that you possess a good constitution like that of dear mother and will long be the support and guide of us all.

At present we (I mean you and I) have our trials out of which to wear our crown, but a few years will change things greatly.

. . . Our noviciate . . . is busily engaged at study. Every morning I teach Latin from 8 ½ to 10 o'clock. Mme Etienne then teaches them drawing and Painting from 10 to 11 and at 11 they study the English studies of the various classes as needed. In the afternoon they study Mathematics and French and Music and feel the time short. in thus preparing themselves for the Institute.

JOHN LYNCH, COLUMBIA, JULY 24th[8]

. . . I am doing very little in practice but have had a few cases from the North, which are talked of a great deal amongst a certain class. One of them came on especially to see me from N.Y. where he has been under treatment for some months without benefit. He is now well. . . .

BAPTISTA LYNCH, URSULINE CONVENT, VALLE CRUCIS, AUGUST 2nd[9]

. . . What a time the people of Alma, North Carolina are having under Gov. Holden![10] John says he is very glad that you have a reasonable cause for being absent from home from now until the great excitement will be over. No man seems to know, he says, whether he is standing on his heels or his head, so hot is the political campaign for gov. to be decided in the Fall. It would be exceedingly difficult, he thinks, for one in your prominent position to steer clear of all parties, so, we never know what is for the best, and that reflection went a long way to reconciling him to your absence.

We trust it is to your own satisfaction and that you do not find every body's head turned on the subject of the European War. It seems to me there may be no war after all but only a show of one. But if one, will it not be Gog and Magog?![11] . . .

P.S. Caro Spann and Sallie Burt are spending a few days at John's. Caro's last visit to the world. She will enter noviciate August 15th, D.V. . . .

HENRIETTA LYNCH, CHERAW, AUGUST 9th [12]

... As Marie grows so tall that much more will be expected of her than she can accomplish I have had to make up my mind to let her go to the Convent by 1st Sept. and her father has such numerous calls on him for money, by his workmen that I find it difficult to get her wardrobe completed in time therefore, my dear never-failing Friend, I will dare make another call on your kindness asking as a very great favor the loan of $30, which, I trust some good fortune will enable me to return before I die. ... I hope that your goodness will make you overlook my taking this liberty again. I trust my children's prayers, on your behalf, from generation to generation will obtain for their remunerative Uncle all that he desires, and which the imperfections of their mother cannot let her hope to obtain for him. But, that by Heaven you will ever be blessed, ...

LOUISA BLAIN, CHERAW, AUGUST 12th[13]

... I am sorry to say Anna has been quite sick for the last five weeks. Is still in bed but not as sick as she has been. She sat up twice last week but today she complains of her side and sick stomach. ... It grieves me to see Anna sick, as I am not able to go over and see her as often as I would like. My brother keeps me very busy. I have not a moment to myself. ... As I am obliged to prepare every meal for him. ... I hear that Augusta has Lilly ready but for the want of money could not send her on. Could you dear friend manage in some way to send it to her. ...

BAPTISTA LYNCH, VALLE CRUCIS, ASSUMPTION DAY
[AUGUST 15] [14]

... Rev. F. Boone gave us an *excellent Retreat*—so calm, so earnest and Religious that all the Community enjoyed it very much. Are spiritually refreshed and strengthened. ... We all renewed our "Vows" this morning and feel ready for another season of work AMDG. I am very much edified by our sisters, who certainly do possess a beautiful spirit—of religious simplicity and humility ...

After the ceremony "Judicite vos" we received Caro Spann into our noviciate, and gave her the cape and she seems perfectly happy. Her mother wrote her a beautiful letter, which came just on the eve of her Retreat. ...

We are easier in money than when I wrote you and gave $60 to Rev F. Boone, ... and paid $200 to our grocer, so you see Providence provided. ...

FRANCIS LYNCH, CHERAW, 21 AUGUST[15]

Thinking that my letters have reached you, you must be anxious about mother, of whom I am rejoiced to be able to say, is quite better. Doctors Nelson and

MacLean have been in attendance this morning to us, to say that if the fever did not rise today, much of the danger will have passed, fortunately it did not rise. Constipation of the bowels, seemed to be the matter, with a bilious attack. And danger from inflammation was found. Mother and the family looked anxiously for you on Saturday. And hope still to see you here on tomorrow. It will be such a gratification. Although we consider the crisis is passed, it will be some days before our dear mother will be fully recovered.

Sister Anna is improving though confined to bed a large share of her time. . . .

BAPTISTA LYNCH, CONVENT, VALLE CRUCIS, AUGUST 23rd[16]

I forwarded a telegram to you, which brother Francis sent to us and I now send you his letter. John went over at once at noon today, after getting the telegram. I only hope he will find mother better. Though, why should we wish to prolong her exile. . . .

FRANCIS LYNCH, CHERAW, 23d AUGUST[17]

Thinking your anxiety must be very great in regard to our dear mother, I write to say that in the absence of fever, the chances of speedy recovery are improving. Of course, mother is very much prostrated from the severity of the sickness, yet being of so short duration, her strength would soon return. On yesterday I sent off telegrams[.] Today it would not seem so necessary to do so. . . .

BAPTISTA LYNCH, VALLE CRUCIS, SEPT. 4th[18]

I am writing near mother's bed where she is sleeping comfortably and Anna is not far from her in the same room. They both came out to the Convent yesterday after spending a few days at brother John's. Mother and Anna both appear feeble but say they are very much better and are cheerful.

Mother talks of father all the time which will do her good and I expect in a few days she will feel quite recreated. Anna too will no doubt improve by the change of air and scenery. . . .

As yet we have had few applications for pupils but the heat is so oppressive and there is so much sickness through the country, we cannot hope for many before October.

Sisters Angela Brownfield and Anthony Kearnan, the latter president Davis' housekeeper are both preparing for their holy *Profession* about All-Saints day—or at your convenience thereabouts. Sr. Angela will have worn the white veil of the novice the two years required by rule—on the 23rd of October . . . She is so good and satisfactory that we feel you will readily consent to profess her. Sr Anthony—the Lay Sister is a woman of good sense and piety—and will be four years in the Convent next January—her high temper has caused the delay in her profession But she is an invaluable servant and has never been otherwise than obedient and respectful to me personally but to her companions is sometimes a trial. . . .

Monday night—5th
Today John brought out Lily, who appears to be a very clever child. . . .

BAPTISTA LYNCH, VALLE CRUCIS, SEPT. 15th[19]
Many, many thanks for your welcome letter of date 8th inst just received and containing the cheque $100—payment in Lillie's acct.

. . . This is the first line I have received from you, since you went to Brooklyn, although I have bothered you with many of my letters—What is the matter with your eyes? . . . I hope you are not suffering like Bishop McGill of Richmond—if you would not overwork them, your eyes would not feel so weak. . . .

We are all so glad to have mother and Anna with us. Mother is very well and right cheerful, but Anna has been very ill. She is much better now however and John says has only to nourish herself judiciously and she will soon recruit. She is still confined to her bed however. . . .

I am quite surprised to hear you will return in October and truly hope you may be able to remain where your presence is *so very much* needed.

. . . I want to lay before you, the subject of recalling our sisters from Tuscaloosa, unless members to build up a convent are furnished to them. *Five years and not one novice!* A school, but not a convent. . . .

BAPTISTA LYNCH, URSULINE CONVENT, SEPT. 19th,
FEAST ST. JANUARIUS[20]
Mother says, that previous to her leaving Cheraw, Francis got a letter from Col. L.B. Northrop[21] asking him to look out for a place for him to buy &c &c. . . . She now thinks if Francis . . . offered him our Home-house it would just suit him and he would be a respectable and desirable purchaser and occupant of it. What do you think of that?

Mother intends remaining over . . . to see you here, and talk over her future arrangements. She says she could spend the balance of her days contentedly here, by paying her expenses and feeling independent. But if Anna prefers to return to Cheraw, they can with more economy live in the house next door where Mr Laughlin lived . . . than in the large house. Mother seems to dread going back to live in the same house.

Anna is improving very much, but not yet well enough to go about. . . .

P.S. Mother says you are the head now and she will do whatever you think best.

Anna thinks it would be better not to sell and sacrifice the Home house, but to sell the cottage. Yet will do whatever is judged best. I only write now that you may use this knowledge if you wish and prevent Mr. Northrop from purchasing elsewhere if you wish to so manage.[22] . . .

FRANCIS LYNCH, CHERAW, 4th OCTOBER[23]

. . . Dr. Brother when you asked me as to my meeting the acceptance of 400$ at the Peoples N. Bk. I answered too confidently. My purpose was to place with my leather factors—tanned leather to meet it, but sickness among my workmen retarded the preparation of the leather timely. So I sent to the Bank a dft at 30% on my factors, to cover. This however was not acted on further, than to return it to me. I am forwarding as fast as I can, to my factors to lift the obligation and next week will have forwarded them, I think, enough to pay it. Had my Dft been acceptable, things would have pleased me more. This paymt will run so closely on the next for 300$ at maturity 12/15 of this inst. I would like that you could aid me in a respite of 30% on it—if conveniently you can do so. The N. York House that sells for me, makes for me the fuller price sales; its rule of business however requires stock in store, on which cash advancements are readily made. This throws on me the onus of supplying the leather without their aid in its production. Some leather that I consigned to my friends in Balt. was sold at lower rates than is obtained in N. York. . . .

LOUISA BLAIN, CHARLESTON, OCTOBER 9th[24]

. . . It is now two weeks since I have been in the dismal City[;] every place is gloomy every visit I have paid has been one of condolence, or to listen to the sorrows of others so that my mind has not had the rest it so much needs. I feel the separation from my dearest mother. I do not know if I can endure it. I try oh so much not to think; particularly of the past, as for the future I have no hope. . . . Poor Augusta is in trouble again. Mr. R has been on a drinking spree for over a week. She does not know what to do, and says her life is in danger. James still comes to school and is improving very much. Now that I have given vent to my sad feeling I feel better do not be distressed about me. . . . If I can only hear from you all will be right. . . . Your devoted friend, 'D'[25]

BAPTISTA LYNCH, URSULINE CONVENT, OCTOBER 27th[26]

I am sitting in Mother's room, trying to write to you, while she is talking about you—for we want to welcome you home immediately on your arrival. . . . We are all so happy to hear that you intend staying in your own dioceses awhile for we know your presence will be such a consolation to your clergy and do so much good for Religion. . . .

Anna is at brother John's now—she was supported by pillows in the carriage and drove in on last Sunday with brother John and Eliza. She is improving but very slowly. I sometimes imagine she has consumption. But of course I am not a judge. She was seven weeks confined to her bed here and with a Sister's constant care night as well as day. Mother recovered wonderfully and is looking well. She will return home soon and I hope Anna may be able to do the same. Mother . . . talks of coming here to live, but I think she will be much happier in her own house. To visit is one thing, to live out of one's sphere is another and I am sure I have had ample experience. . . .

Lillie is doing very well in every way—is a very fine girl and pleases me so much in her manner towards mother and Anna, so respectful and affectionate. . . .

Hope the elections will not interfere with those Fairs which must contribute to the prosperity of the state and its general recuperation.

What intelligence from Europe!!! The Holy Father![27] We are so very thankful you are at home. . . .

BAPTISTA LYNCH, URSULINE CONVENT, V.C.,
FEAST OF ALL SAINTS [NOVEMBER 1][28]
. . . For the first time since the burning of our Convent, we suspended on this festival our "sanctuary lamp," although not perfect in its parts. It was stolen by the soldiery who sacked our Convent but rescued from there by a Catholic officer who returned it into my own hands. . . .

Anna is now at John's—still very feeble, but recovering slowly—sits up a little every day. Mother wishes to go over to Cheraw and see how things are going on, but is undecided as to her home for the future until she consults with you. Much can be said that should not be written—and expences must be calculated and Both John and Francis are like yourself struggling and the low price of cotton does not mend matters. Still they live on hoping for the best.

Sister Mary has moved into the country where Mr. Spann enjoys "otium cum dignitate. Reads every day the classics as a refreshment of mind and has a few scholars in English. They are gathering around their little comforts and are only desiring such religious blessings as they formerly enjoyed. That is one thing which comforts us so very much for which we are so much indebted to you under God. The daily Mass, the frequent sacraments and other religious privileges for which we cannot be sufficiently grateful and moreover for such a minister of them.—We cannot expect to have everything and surely we all would prefer the privation to extend to temporals rather than spirituals—and as for the temporals, as you say "all will come, right in God's own time." ...

... All this "hurry-cum-fuss, through the state will have been over too—by that time, and every body reconciled to take events as they come—or as our dear good mother says to "take the world as God sends it"—How wise, if we could only do it always. ...

BAPTISTA LYNCH, URSULINE CONVENT,
FEAST OF ST. GERTRUDE [NOV. 17][29]

... I hope you are well and doing well and have found more satisfaction among the good and simple country people of moderate means and feeling hearts, than among the city folks. It is only such as those, who know how to sympathize with us.

... Mother and Anna are now at John's—Mother is getting anxious to return and look after things in Cheraw, but is detained by Anna's illness. Poor Anna has never left her bed, we may say for the three months she has been over here now, for the three months before in Cheraw. Nothing seems to give her strength. She is truly to be pitied—such constant suffering.

... Will you please let Mrs. Brownfield as well as us know exactly when, in time, so that she can come up with you to her daughter's Profession? It is difficult to say who has most generosity—she in joining us, or we in adding to our number, under such embarrassing circumstances and pecuniary difficulties— But "God is at the helm" or as you say "Deus providebit." and she no doubt will be an instrument to give Him great glory in future. The good religious spirit continues to pervade our noviciate and Community, ...

JOHN LYNCH, COLUMBIA, DECEMBER 8th[30]

I promised to let you know how sister Anna's case progressed. There has been very little change since you left until last night. Her bowels were troublesome. ... Tonight she seems easier but has had a bad day. I think she had taken an idea that she was to die *today*, which made her worse. Mother also seemed more concerned for her today, than usual. If there should be any serious change before you come up, I will let you know at once. She certainly is getting gradually weaker. ...

BAPTISTA LYNCH, VALLE CRUCIS, [DEC. 15?][31]

... I am truly thankful you gave Extreme Unction to dear Anna and that she is so easy and comfortable ever since. Sister Agnes persists in thinking she will recover. But in that, as in all things else "Fiat voluntas Dei." . . .

[P.S.] Is there anything we can do?

BAPTISTA LYNCH, VALLE CRUCIS, DECEMBER 24th[32]
. . . We hope you are now comfortably enjoying home after a useful and pleasant visitation to the upper part of the state and your Diocess—we are sure wherever you went you did good.

All of our Community unite with me in wishing you a very happy Xmas and many, very many joyous returns—each replete with Heaven's choicest benedictions. . . .

BAPTISTA LYNCH, VALLE CRUCIS, DEC. 27[33]
Conlaw is giving way to so much feeling, that I have been trying to mother his feelings. He says that Anna called him to her bedside and told him the last time he saw her, that when she died, she wanted him to see that she was buried beside brother Bernard, and he promised her.

It distresses him to hear now, that you all are thinking of burying her in Columbia and he could not tell you what he now tells me. Of course I am not a judge, but I also feel that Anna should not be buried out of the family burial-ground where those to whom she was so devoted lie. If it is the expense, Conlaw says he will bear it all cheerfully, for his Aunt Anna who did so much for him and with your permission I will send $10 toward the same. But as I said, I am not a judge in the case. It is a relief to me to know that our dear Anna is out of pain, to know that she was in such a suffering state and be unable to relieve her was truly distressing. We will now do all we can—pray. . . .[34]

BAPTISTA LYNCH, VALLE CRUCIS, [DEC. 28–30?][35]
I need not say I am with you in all the services of today. Let us hope that this bright and beautiful morning is typical of the bright and beautiful heaven which our dear Anna is enjoying.

How is mother? . . . [36]

11

"HOW LONG, O LORD, HOW LONG?"

January–June 1871

At the Baltimore Carmel it frustrated Antonia Lynch no end that no one in her family had warned her of Anna's imminent passing. Given the Carmelite's strong belief that prayer, particularly from those who make it a cornerstone of their lives, is a powerful facilitator of a soul's final journey to heaven, she found it more than regrettable that she and her community were denied a vital occasion to "storm heaven," in this case for the sibling who was the perennial channel to their parents.

In assessing the tumultuous events of the Paris Commune in the wake of the disastrous French defeat by the Prussians, Baptista found some providential consolation in the prospect of this revolution producing a new wave of French religious emigres, seeking in the South a sanctuary, as their ancestors had done eight decades earlier. Such an influx would provide a new opportunity to advance the Ursuline's dream of Catholicizing her native region. That such emigres might not be attracted to a region that was undergoing its own sociopolitical revolution seems not to have occurred to Baptista.

As Baptista perforce put on hold any building plans until they could secure outside funding, it was necessary to tap as completely as they could interim sources of assistance. As Congressional Reconstruction entered its fifth year, Baptista continued to cultivate the chief military occupiers and their families, to maximize the opportunities for aid from the federal government, whether it be rations or compensation for the destruction of their convent and academy. Selling some of the vegetables and fruits that their chaplain raised became an immediate means of securing some income. William Meriwether made a further contribution by taking out a $10,000 life insurance policy with the community named as beneficiary, a transaction that Baptista found hard to believe that the health-compromised priest could have negotiated. It encouraged the Ursuline superior greatly that the Mercy Sisters had received $12,000 from the federal government for their losses during the war.

At St. Peter's Church in Columbia, years of growing lay resentment of an autocratic pastor culminated with John Lynch leading an effort to revive the tradition which Bishop John England had introduced into the diocese four decades earlier, by enacting a constitution establishing the rights and responsibilities of the various cohorts of the local church.

In league with the American episcopacy's support for papal temporal power, Patrick Lynch issued a pastoral letter. In recapping Pius' nearly quarter-century reign, the Bishop of Charleston focused on the first few years of his pontificate, when his reforms excited the western world. The letter skipped over the revolutions that shook Europe to its core in 1848, forcing Pius to flee Rome. As well as how the pope, after French troops restored him to the throne of Peter, quickly became the symbol of resistance to the forces of modernity and democracy that had occasioned the uprisings. Meanwhile, as his temporal power crumbled under the Risorgimento of Italian unification, Pius shored up his spiritual authority through his centralizing policies, culminating with the decrees of the Vatican Council proclaiming his primacy and infallibility. This consolidation of the church under the bishop of Rome Patrick Lynch chose to read as the unprecedented display of unity within the universal Church.

ANTONIA LYNCH, MT. CARMEL, 10th JANUARY[1]
I thank you so much for your kindness in writing so fully of dear Anna's last moments. May our Lord reward you. . . . I had been most anxious to hear all the week before. I suppose not being very well made me more so. On Wednesday, Thursday and Friday nights, I scarcely slept at all. So although I did not

know Anna was so low still I was mindful of her all that time. I was very much surprised to hear of Anna's death and almost impatient with the children of brother John's family for not writing me. But I suppose our Lord permits all this in order that the offering may be more acceptable. . . . I would beg so much the next time any of the family are dangerously sick, that I would hear it as soon as possible. It is a time they need all the help they can get, and it is a great consolation to help and hasten their entrance into heaven. In a letter I wrote mother, I told her, we would hope to see her in Baltimore next spring or summer. Altho' it would give me much pleasure, still I do not look for it. . . . I have now recovered from the severe cold I took some weeks ago and continue to grow more fleshy every day. I hope mother has not been sick. From Mother Baptista's silence I fear that she too is not well with all the consolations which a happy death should give one. It is astonishing how much nature will feel these partings. So I trust as time passes, the recollection of the great goodness of God may make us forget the feelings of nature under these trials. . . .

BAPTISTA LYNCH, URSULINE CONVENT NEAR COLUMBIA, S.C., JAN 18[2]

. . . I received such a kind and well expressed letter from Sallie Aldrich whose faith is so strong. I do hope you may be able before very long to visit Barnwell, and be the means of receiving into the Church the judge and Mrs Aldrich.[3] I feel very much interested in that family's conversion. . . .

I am sorry to say we have no more pupils and I fear we shall have to call on you for means, but I will tell you when and it may be we can do with out . . .

BAPTISTA LYNCH, URSULINE CONVENT, VALLE CRUCIS, FEBRUARY 8th[4]

. . . Our entire household has passed through a sort of influenza—the effect of the severe spell of intense cold—but we are now again enjoying our usual health and happiness D.G. I am sorry to say John is not at all well—looks very badly and seems greatly embarrassed by pecuniary matters. . . .

. . . Mother equals the Holy Father in her energy and fortitude! She delayed her return expecting you in Cheraw and was disappointed that you did not go. But now we will expect you to meet her here.

. . . We have made all but the last payment on those Lots, but cannot meet that and as we have decided it is useless to hold them with the view of building, we would have no object in building there, except to obtain a better price for them. . . .

BAPTISTA LYNCH, URSULINE CONVENT, VALLE CRUCIS.
ASH WEDNESDAY [FEB. 22][5]
... "Sister St. Michel"[6] looks so well and religious in her new habit and veil. ...

BAPTISTA LYNCH, URSULINE CONVENT,
VALLE CRUCIS, S.C., MARCH 1st[7]
Today Genl. Cash[8] brought us his daughter. I know you will feel gratified to hear his high opinion of our Institute and of all Catholic schools. ... The child is a bright, interesting little girl of ten years of age, and makes our eighteenth pupil and we expect two more this month—which crowds our house to excess.

If we send our circulars out for next term it is probable we shall have more pupils than we can accommodate ... Of course Genl Cash paid—Your letter made it work. I would not be at all surprised if Mrs Cash and the Genl both became Catholics eventually. ...

JOHN LYNCH, COLUMBIA, MARCH 2[9]
Enclosed I send you (as the chairman of the Catholic Church of this place) a Constitution and By laws, for your approval adopted last night. If they meet your approval we will organize under them. The first Sunday after Easter, Father Francis was present at the reading and adoption of them, therefore I suppose they are all right.

I hope to see you up before that time, as I have a grave subject for your consideration, viz. the Taxes on the Convent lot, and on more perhaps which I am not aware of. The city has assessed the Convent lot on Main St. at $20,000 which at 1 pct. will amt to $200. I would not return it; but the Clerk (Yankee) told me he would enter it and I could contest it. I told him I would leave it in the hands of one who I supposed knows more of the case than I did, meaning yourself. ...

BAPTISTA LYNCH, URSULINE CONVENT,
VALLE CRUCIS, ... MARCH 9th[10]
... Madam Etienne hopes you are praying for her people—the French and I am greatly pleased to hear that there is a prospect of French immigration south. ...

BAPTISTA LYNCH, U.C., V.C., APRIL 21st[11]
... Francis ... was able to pay only $35 at [Marie's] entrance. I hate to call on him too but must. For Lilly you sent us $100 at her entrance. Could you conveniently send us the other $100—for her? ...

JOHN LYNCH, COLUMBIA, APRIL 21st[12]

. . . I am doing my best to sell my mine. Agnew seems to have struck a vein, whether it will prove to be a profitable one or not, will have to be developed, but I have other prospectors out, certainly some of them will strike a profitable vein, after a while, that will be one of the points in the sale, to get cash enough to pay all my debts, including the $3000 guardian bond, I am anxious for the time to arrive . . .

JOHN LYNCH, COLUMBIA, APRIL 22nd[13]

. . . As I think I remarked to you before, I am on a warm trail for the sale of my mine. When I sell, we will all know it. . . .

BAPTISTA LYNCH, URSULINE CONVENT, VALLE CRUCIS, APRIL 29th[14]

. . . Did Col. Waring tell you of his visit to V.C. I did not insure my life but Col. W. told us that Rev. Dr. M—did endow our Convent, with his life insurance of $10,000. When we get surplus funds, we may do the same perhaps—We were much gratified at the evidence of kindness toward our institution on the part of Rev. D M . . . Are you not surprised that the Co. would insure the life of such a delicate man as Rev. Dr. M!

PATRICK N. LYNCH, PASTORAL LETTER ON SIEZURE OF ROME, MAY 3[15]

It is now nearly a year since the necessities of our poor and still suffering Diocess compelled us to withdraw as we then thought only for a season, from the Session of the Ecumenical Council, then assembled in Rome. What mighty events have marked the months that have since passed by. A gigantic war has slain tens of thousands, has filled hundreds of thousands of hearts with sorrow, has desolated one fair Christian land, and has left it a prey to horrors at the sight of which the world stands aghast, and has filled another with widows and orphans.

Taking advantage of this struggle and of the failing fortunes of France, the Italian Government, continuing in violation of justice and of international law, and in direct violation of the Treaty made with France, September 15, 1864, sent an overwhelming military force to seize the last remnant of the States of the Church and the city of Rome, and has annexed them to the Kingdom of Italy. . . .

The Council no longer able to hold its meetings in peace and safety, has been adjourned until the advent of happier times. The Holy Father has ever remained shut up in the Vatican, from which he cannot go forth save at the risk of insult, if not personal injury—or as yielding his assent to the wrong done to him and his people, and the Church.

... Each week brings us accounts of fresh insults to the Holy Father, fresh attacks on churches and the clergy, and faithful people, sometimes during the very hours of divine service, and by fresh outrages on morality, good order, and Religion. From Rome comes the cry, How long, O Lord, how long?

Each week too brings us evidence how deeply these events have stirred the Catholic heart throughout the world. Protests have been made by the Laity in every land. Addresses have been sent to the Holy Father. Governments are being appealed to by their citizens and subjects and numerous delegations are journeying to Rome, to express in person the veneration, the sorrow, and the hopes of Catholics of every portion of the Church. For the same Spirit which led the early Christians to pray with one voice for St. Peter, while he was in prison, still moves the children of the Church everywhere and increasingly to pray for his Successor, the venerable Pius IX in these days of his sorrow.

The Pontificate of the present Pope has indeed been remarkable, under many aspects. Elected June 16, 1846, at the very opening of the Conclave, and almost unanimously, his elevation was hailed with joy by the entire population of the Roman States. . . . Sparing no effort to secure a proper administration of law, to encourage and reward industry, to develop the resources of the country. . . . It was that truly democratic government in the best sense of the word. Talents and merit wherever found were sure of their reward. The son of the artisan stood on an equality with the son of the noble, and both might be surpassed by the son of the labourer. Even wealth, becoming elsewhere so powerful, and gradually the aristocracy of nobility in this century, could erect no barrier of exclusion at Rome.

As head of the Church, Pius IX has indeed done much to forward the interests of Religion, . . . drawing into ever closer and intimate union with the See of Peter, the Bishops and Clergy and Catholic laity throughout the world. Never, perhaps, in this past history has the Church rejoiced in such a manifest and cordial union of all its members with the Head. . . .

BAPTISTA LYNCH, VALLE CRUCIS, MAY 17th[16]
... The "Convention" of which Genl Cash and Capt Keitt were members have stayed the Tax from Nov- to March /72 and they think, effected other points for the state. . . .

... Rev. Dr. M. . . . made some $200 or more with his fine strawberries and has frequent visits from gentlemen attracted by the same. . . .

. . . We are praying for your success and indeed I think between the Fair in Charleston and the $12,000 from Gov. your Diocess is coming out right well. D.G.

As for us, what a contrast our peaceful Valle to the convents of France and Italy!!! . . .

BAPTISTA LYNCH, URSULINE CONVENT, JUNE 2nd[17]
. . . I thank you very much for the obituary of Revd Mr. Weed. I know it will console Sister Charles and I am happy to be able to render her any service especially at this time. . . .

I have been so occupied during the last fortnight that Mother was out here, I could not write many of those letters to Bishops—so my first response came yesterday from the Rt. Rev. Bishop of Boston $25 which I thought good. But John amused me with his Southern notions, asking if he strained his wrist! How would he feel if he saw the collection made in the Churches there. . . .

P.S. Conlaw and Josephine lost their infant—it lived only one month and died on Ascension Thursday. Happy little thing!

12

"IT LOOKS LIKE
ANTEBELLUM TIMES"

July–December 1871

More than five years after the war, Patrick Lynch was still spending months on the road fundraising where the money was: the North and Northwest. His sister shared the concern of others in the diocese, that by such prolonged absences, the bishop was neglecting his primary duties as the first pastor of his scattered flock. For Baptista, it was a matter not only of episcopal obligation but a familial one as well: a chronic failure to fulfill promised visits to Cheraw or Columbia. The harsh reality was that Patrick was finding benefactions harder to come by. His summer trip to the Northeast yielded but $20,000, an amount, Baptista reminds him, that he once raised in New York City alone. She suggested other potential sources of support, such as the Society for the Propagation of the Faith, which had provided funds in the past and that did not require his presence. But the disruptions of war had largely eliminated sources like the SPF as a viable provider.

If sororal pleading failed to persuade him to return home, yellow fever did not. Bishop Lynch cut short his fundraising to attend to the stricken in Charleston, a move that his sister could only applaud. Meanwhile the worsening health of Archbishop Martin Spalding sparked new rumors, at least within the Lynch family circle, that Patrick Lynch would at last be named by Rome to head the premier see of Baltimore, an anticipation they had first entertained eight years earlier with Francis Kenrick's sudden death.

The success of the Columbia Fair led Baptista to report to her brother Patrick that "it looks like antebellum times." Money was beginning to circulate again. People had the financial means to buy the goods upon whose sale the Fair very much depended for a profitable outcome. One threat to the economic recovery was the Ku Klux Klan terror campaign throughout the upcountry. When leading members of the Klan were brought to trial in Columbia, John Lynch worried about its impact on his real estate holdings. Baptista was all too aware of the hard times that plagued the region, if only by the collapse of student enrollment at the Ursuline academy. A wartime enrollment that peaked at 150 in Columbia had shrunk to a dozen or fewer in Valle Crucis, before staging a modest comeback. Of that greatly reduced number, Lynch children make up a sizeable portion.

The Lynch brothers in Columbia and Cheraw had not shared, to any degree, in the recovery. John Lynch continued to chase the invention that would at last solve his financial problems and provide the wealth which had eluded him all his life, even as his debts threatened to strip his home from him. John's many attempts to secure financial equity by investments ranging from mines to patents were not only failing but the prospect of economic failure was putting in jeopardy his university appointment as well. The financial noose he had gotten himself into was gradually tightening. Once more he reached out to his brother for rescue from his immediate financial shortfall. He was paying nearly $1,000 a year for insurance as well as interest on his many debts. Other household expenses exceeded $1,800 annually. His overall debts approached $9,000. His main source of income, the $2,000 per annum salary from the University of South Carolina Medical Department, the legislature was holding captive. The other potential revenue producer was the boarding house he and Eliza had opened during the war, Boarders potentially represented income up to $1,500 a year, but boarding was no longer the affordable option that it had been during the war. John Lynch's income from his own practice had shriveled to an amount so insignificant he did not even list it as an asset. . . .

Francis, having rented out most of his land, including his town property, was now concentrating on his tannery to enable him to realize enough revenue to cover his debts, but to date had been unable to reach that point. Desperate to cover his debts, Francis tried to get his bishop brother to vouch for his ability to meet them. Even his brother's episcopal status was not enough to secure credit for Francis. In the end, Patrick provided the required cash as temporary relief to his brother. On his own initiative, Francis laid out for Patrick, as John did, the details of his finances, in the hope that Patrick could invoke his experience as well as his scientific acumen to discern a path toward fiscal solvency.

BAPTISTA LYNCH, CONVENT OF THE URSULINES,
VALLE CRUCIS . . . , JULY 11[1]
. . . John was out yesterday with a letter from Mrs. C—[2] of whose daughter he is guardian and he is depressed greatly by money matters—I wish so much he could sell his mine or even some of those lots in town—would afford present relief. It seems the will of God that he should be tried just now—for little Eliza too is very feeble. . . .

I held the Chapter of which I spoke to you my dearest Brother and we have thought it best to receive for holy profession Sister Ignatia.[3] We put her in Retreat yesterday and she begins her *remote* preparation looking ahead. She appears very happy in the thought—God grant she may be always so, and not thankless for such a priceless boon, like Srs Theresa and deSales are at times, and greatly to our trial. . . .

BAPTISTA LYNCH, CONVENT URSULINES, [AUGUST][4]
We are *deep* in Retreat and delighted with Rev. Father Ward, S.J.[5]—think his character of mind something like yours. . . .

BAPTISTA LYNCH, CONVENT OF THE URSULINES,
VALLE CRUCIS, AUGUST 18[6]
. . . I do not think you have done so badly in collecting, considering it is the dull season of the year and I am quite compelled to think that $20,000 will enable you to stay at home for I remember you collected nearly that much in New York City once. We will pray for success to your efforts in the West. Will not the "Propagation of the Faith" society be able to give you some soon? . . .

BAPTISTA LYNCH, URSULINES, FEAST NATIVITY
BVM [SEPTEMBER 8][7]
The old lady is much the same—often suffering and rendered weak and

irritable—but at the same time edifying. We have as yet only ten pupils, three
of whom are new . . .

BAPTISTA LYNCH, CONVENT OF THE URSULINES,
VALLE CRUCIS, SEPT. 17th[8]

This afternoon brother John with his sons "John," and "Jimmie" came out
to the Convent and brought your telegram announcing your safe arrival in
Charleston! . . . I do not know whether I am sorry or glad you have come down
to work amid the Yellow fever. You have made our Sisters—especially Sisters
Theresa—good prophetesses by returning—for they all said you would be certain to do so, as soon as the Yellow fever made its appearance. Of course, I am
proud and happy to have you at the post of honor and duty but hope you are
not a subject for the Fever. Caro Spann says I must tell you to *take a little qui-
nine every morning*—that her Father and Mother were advised to do so when
in Galveston and as you know escaped the Yellow fever . . .

Columbia is crowded with refugees but if I hear you are sick you may certainly expect to see me—yellow-fever or not—I am not afraid of it—had it
before—and would not weight [*sic*] it in the balance—[9] . . .

How thankful we ought to be, to have this healthy, lovely country place
removed from City atmosphere and epidemics! . . .

JOHN LYNCH, COLUMBIA, SEPT. 27[10]

. . . Would suppose from the report, that you had been more successful in your
financial affairs than I have, for the want of success with me has produced a
state of mind I am afraid of, especially as I have to commence my duties in the
university on next Monday. I am satisfied I have taken a position which will
stand, if I can keep up my credit financially. I have placed my patent in the
hands of a party at the North, to *sell* irrespective of price, also offerd through
the same party: My mine for $10,000 cash, with royalty of 7% on profits, nei-
ther of which gains have as yet taken effect.

I have debts falling due, some secured by mortgage on my house. . . . Have
tried to borrow money from private individuals on mortgage of house &c but
have as yet failed. I have every prospect held out by the party—North that
Sales will be effected at the price named, but I specified the time, and they have
not come up to it. . . . Can you suggest anything better. I need advice and help.

If you will look into the last number of the *Scientific American* you will see
I have not been idle, but have taken advantage of the Westfield Excitement
to reproduce, curtailed, the article I submitted to you a few years ago, and
which you returned a few months ago on the Cause and prevention of Steam
Boiler explosions. I believe it is correct, and if properly pushed will not only

do a service to the world but perhaps to myself also, especially if after the cry is received, a means can be pointed out by which the capt or pilot may at any time detect the state of danger . . .

JOHN LYNCH, COLUMBIA, OCT. 5th[11]
I received your kind letter enclosing the check for $100 for present Emergencies and asking a full statement of my affairs. I have tried to give it to you on the other half sheet. . . . The note of $1,200 under protest was made at ninety-days not renewable, for the purpose of paying a part to Scarborough and my taxes, with the Expectation of a sale of my mine and patent, in Phila—before it became due. I have been disappointed. . . . I am also in treaty for a loan of $3500 here, on mortgage, 11 per cent pr annum but can count on nothing now. If I give a mortgage on the house for that amt, will not be able to make a second, to meet other debts; You must excuse my not entering more fully tonight on the matter, as I have *four* children sick in the house, am called on every minute about something, have been up three nights the past week, with Cornelia.

. . . About the Scientific article, I *can* explain it to you, the same difficulty you make is what has prevented the facts having been applied to the particular case, if you do not make it out before. I will take pleasure in illustrating (not by an Explosion).

If you see a better way for me than my borrowing the $3500 at 11 pr cent, telegraph me. . . .

Situation!

1	Balance on Scarborough Bond	$1800.00
2	Bank Note (Kinard and Dierks) Security (Protested)	$1200.00
3.	Bank Note (Bishop L and RK Scott)	$ 800.00
4.	Bank Note (R.K Scott)	$ 500.00
5.	Note to Kinard of Bank for Dry goods	$ 400.00
6.	Note to Dierks at Bank for groceries	$ 300.00
7.	Interest to Mrs Caldwell as guardian	$ 210.00
8.	Taxes due for Mrs Allen's property as trustee	about $ 320.00
9	Interest due on Mrs Allens bond, as trustee	$ 210.00
10.	Bond as Guardian for Sue Caldwell	$3000.00
	[Tot] $8740.00 [$225,334.39 today]	
11.	Bond for part of mine payable in 1st Nov.	
	three years out of Salary 1st paymt	3.33
		9.073

Assets: Mine	10,000
Patent	2,500
Beauford lot	1,000
House and Lot in Col.	8,000
Salary	2,000
Boarders	1,500 = 25,000
Practice	

BAPTISTA LYNCH, URSULINE CONVENT
VALLE CRUCIS, . . . OCT 6th[12]

. . . We are truly glad and thankful to see that you continue to enjoy your usual good health even when so fagged out as you must be in nursing the sick. Like yourself, my dear Brother, we are more than pleased, that you came back to Charleston in this Yellow fever season, not only because it is right and proper that the Shepherd should take care of his stricken fold but also for the moral effect it will have on your people. . . .

Does not Mrs. Brisbane hold out wonderfully and is getting gay again! Busy writing a sacred drama. . . .

BAPTISTA LYNCH, VALLE CRUCIS, SUNDAY MORNING, 22nd
AFTER PENTECOST [OCT. 30][13]

. . . What terrible conflagration in the N. West.[14] How will all this affect you? Can you expect a hearing at all for your Diocese, when such pressing claims are made for Chicago, &c &c.[15]

Perhaps you can get an [alternative?] for making collections north? I hope the "Propagation of Faith" may be able to help you this year. . . .

. . . This time *last year* we had 7 pupils. This year we had 14 but two left. . . .

People are beginning to talk of "state Fairs" which if KK does not interfere with, will I hope entice you to visit Columbia and at that time, be "all in all to gain all." As you usually are. . . . Madames Borgia and Ursula not at all well— the former *very poorly.* . . .

BAPTISTA LYNCH, CONVENT OF URSULINES,
VALLE CRUCIS, S.C., NOV. 10th[16]

. . . The "State Fair:" has brought *crowds* to the city, so that last night the night of the Ball, persons could not get beds, had to sleep on the floor—Robert and Kate, Conlaw and Josephine—with 4 children and nurse and Mr. Lord a cousin are all at Johns! . . . Mr. Josh Gray of Augusta was here today to see his daughter . . . He says he never saw such a brilliant crowd in Columbia and display of prosperity—It looks like ante bellum times. . . .

FRANCIS LYNCH, CHERAW, 29th NOV.[17]

. . . In the scarcity of money here, I hope the note of Mr Dargans to me for $180.24 as also my note in your favor for $175 may be discounted. The proceeds of both, covering the acceptances. Please endorse them.

If necessary, however, to use the ck, enclosed, for $152.25 do so. If not, I would like it to my credit in Bk. Besides Mr Kendall promised to deposit fifty dolls for me in same Bank on 30th tomorrow, perhaps 100$, so I enclose blank signature that you may fill out a ck, if needful and the deposit shall have been made as promised. I am anxious to make some other payments and hence ask the discount which I trust will be conceded. . . .

[Patrick Lynch's hand:] Fa. Exch: Bank refused any thing but money. People's National Bank discounted[18] Dargans note of 180 p. Jan1 '72 proceeds [$]178.20.

FRANCIS LYNCH, CHERAW, 8 DEC[19]

. . . The manner that you arranged the business in Bk shows me what I ought to be able to do, but until some of the clouds pass away I must consider myself under banns. I cannot sufficiently thank you, for your many favours, according to the measure of means, my business has done tolerably well. But after long efforts—with fruits less than anticipated, I feel that after all, my sanguine temperament makes me to hope for too much. And I feel the want of some good counsel from you. I will give you an outline of my actions, that knowing them you may favor me with your views of them.

Of plantation I run a small farm (4 plows) and rent out lands. My agt then looking after rents and works my crops—this arrangement will likely bring 6 pct on the cost of plant[ing.]

My town property rents for near 600$ pr yr. Near 30/wk. The Tannery is made the main feature, in this I feel the lack of capital, by nursing it, the stock now will almost resupply itself from its sales. I mean by this that the tanned stock may work out fast enough to pay for hides and labor—working in hides every week. This I am not so sure about as I wd wish to be. But even this attained, until I can return outstanding obligations, I am at the mercy of any creditor who may force me to the wall.

Now what appears to me the better course if practicable, would be to borrow enough money, on the Sanders tract of land 1180 acres as wd settle all the creditors, in two years time. Their claims could now be settled at 50. cts. or less. This with improved credit the way would be clear for better success. The long-continued strain on my limited finances makes me timid—and while my judgment directs, fears restrain me. If by some bold move, I could so gain the mastery, it would be a grand point, and when 3 to 5000$ would do everything, it appears to me so much real prosperity ought to suffice to its accomplishment.

    . . . I will be glad of your views. . . .

JOHN LYNCH, COLUMBIA, S.C., DEC 15[20]

. . . I waited a reasonable time expecting some word from you, not hearing, have been making efforts elsewhere both as to sale or lone [*sic*], have not succeeded as yet, further than hopes held out . . . I have been excusing your not writing from mortification of failure, and myself as the cause, therefore (after laying on my oars, perhaps too long) have taken to my own cause I may be swamped but there is nothing like self-reliance and independence. I wish I could feel the latter . . . I have another string to my bow about the sale of mine, but the Kuklux trial interferes for the present. . . .

BAPTISTA LYNCH, CONVENT, URSULINES, VALLE CRUCIS, DECEMBER 23rd[21]

We *all* come and Mother at our head to wish you a very Happy Christmas, and many, very many joyous returns. The examination of the children concluded yesterday evening and they are now busy and noisy over the Xmas crib and tree—and each feeling herself very important, which illusion, seems to make the secret of all children's (old and young) happiness.

    . . . Rev. F. Bermingham . . . ought to congratulate himself on not having "money" to take home with him, since all who have money are marks for the assassins nowadays. . . .

    Sister Antonia wonders in each of her letters, why you are such a stranger in the city of Baltimore and asks do you fear being made its Archbishop—which people say will be the case when the see is vacant? But add that notwithstanding the very poor state of health of the venerable Abp, he is likely to last some years yet, by all the good kind care taken of him by Srs. of Charity and others. So you can safely venture.

    . . . I would feel perfectly willing to give you up to the See of Baltimore, just to relieve you of those pressing, harassing debts and pecuniary embarrassments which seem to weigh heavily on you at times. In all things *Fiat voluntas Dei*. I have never said as much as that to any one, but after all, this is speculation. . . . Mrs. Brisbane has been quite ill this week—she was dying but has rallied again and is up today. . . .

13

"TO ME IT APPEARS MORE DIFFICULT TO REGAIN THAN TO HAVE FIRST GAINED"

January–June 1872

Francis Lynch's finances were, at their best, complicated. The war's outcome had rendered them virtually beyond redemption. Like so many of his fellow planters and industrialists, he had lost his most valuable financial asset, human property. As he told his bishop brother, "I am in the meshes. To me it appears more difficult to regain than to have first gained." Events had humbled Francis to the point that the self-confident entrepreneur now was overcome by feelings that destiny was no longer his servant but his persecutor. Once again, his bishop brother became his rescuer, from the imminent disaster of losing the family homestead, as well as from the psychological depression that had Francis expecting the worst. With decisive monetary assistance from his bishop brother, and with the prospect of selling good portions of his land to Northern purchasers, Francis' spirits managed to revive to a point he had not enjoyed since the war.

Or so he pretended to his bishop brother. Perhaps Francis felt he could not do otherwise with the sibling who had just saved their home. In the event, it took Henrietta to enlighten her brother-in-law about the reality that her husband's optimistic pose was obscuring. Unabashedly she spelled out how their impoverishment had reduced them even below the condition of hill folks. Their children now perforce went barefoot; they were dependent on their bishop uncle funding their schooling and putting food on the table. What neither Francis nor Henrietta thought to ask was how Patrick could be such a reliable benefactor. The reality was that Patrick Lynch had no special fund set aside for aiding relatives in need. He was raising money the same way as his brothers: by taking out loans. Whereas Francis's extensive history of troubled finances had cost him the trust of creditors and hence any new loans, Patrick's fear was that his own failure to pay off his growing debts would bring consequences worse than the loss of credit.

John Lynch's persistent efforts to sell his mine at last attracted the interest of a British investment firm, spurring in John the hope that his most valuable asset would finally enable him to achieve fiscal equilibrium. John was not above oiling the process with the offer of assisting one of the British partners in securing a faculty position in the medical school. His own standing at that institution, if measured by his continuing failure to receive the remuneration to which the position entitled him, was shaky at best. That four-year salary drought most likely bode poorly for the other government position to which he had been appointed: examiner of those seeking certification as pharmacists in the state. Those appointments had been the outcomes of working relationships which John Lynch has been able to establish with Republican officials, including governors.

The productive shortfall of the Valle Crucis farm convinced William Meriwether that the farm could no longer support the operation of the academy, even with a greatly reduced enrollment. Returning to Columbia, he urged the Ursulines, was their only option for survival. Baptista, resisting any such talk, proposed to her brother to sell some railroad stock the community had come by through a dowry in order to provide the cash which their chaplain needed to operate the farm. Meanwhile, she discovered the device of incorporating the academy as a means of avoiding the onerous property taxes under state Republican administrations.

The Ursuline Community's grand act of consecration to the Sacred Heart reflected the resurgence of the devotion as a prominent element in the Catholic spiritual culture in the postwar era, particularly following the fall of Rome and the transformation of Pope Pius IX from the ruler of the Papal States to the "prisoner of the Vatican." There was a very explicit linkage of the Sacred

Heart devotion and the papacy. The pontiff's post-Vatican Council experience, to Sacred Heart adherents, was the most conspicuous embodiment of the suffering which Jesus continued to endure through His mystical body. In the world of redemptive sacrifice, Rome also had primacy. Such unique surrogacy strengthened the pope's paternal power to safeguard the faithful from the acids of modernity. Paternalism writ large was the key to social justice and private tranquility. And yet, in the devotional realm, women held a peculiar superiority, precisely because of their humility in recognizing and accepting their lowly status in society's hierarchy as well as by making a virtue out of the suffering that their vocations as mothers or religious invariably entailed. For the Ursulines, there was the additional agency of controlling who would have authority over them by the power which their constitution gave the individual Ursuline communities to elect their directors.

At the Baltimore Carmel, Antonia found in these political and religious developments a paradoxical reassurance that God was yet with them. Still, she insinuated to Patrick, her faith in God's providence would be complete should her brother be named as the premier see's next archbishop.

JOHN LYNCH, COLUMBIA, JAN. 3rd[1]

If you are not coming up today, please endorse the enclosed note for five hundred. It is to take up my note with Gov. Scott as endorser which fell due yesterday. I did not wish to ask him again and Col. Childs says he will discount it for me with your endorsement.

Hoping to get some money very soon to take up the others. . . .

BAPTISTA LYNCH, CONVENT-URSULINES, VALLE CRUCIS, S.C., JAN 7[2]

. . . We are truly happy to hear that your health is buoyant for good health is a "Powerful lever."

Poor Mm Borgia is in a constant state of suffering so much so that she longs for the relief which death alone can give. Yet she sometimes leaves her room and gathers up her remaining strength. . . .

. . . Sister Charles Weed . . . seems to be anxious to have that settlement made about the House in Tuscaloosa . . . . Were I in their place I would *rent* the house only from the Bishop unless the rent surpassed the interest on principle charged for it and it should not and I would not be incorporated until a better prospect offered of building up a community. The only Choir novice they have was sent by Rev. Mr. Ambler Weed (R.I.P.) If Sister Charles should die, how could they carry on the House. . . .

Neither Bishop Q nor Rev. F. McD seem to know that we are not obliged by our Constitution to receive and obey as Rev. Father Superior anyone whom we ourselves do not elect. . . .

Mr Calman called on us for our "act of incorporation" to see if by it we could be relieved from Taxes imposed by Baldwin for not only this but past years and thinks all is right . . . we hope so truly. Our school is limited. When disturbances blow over, no doubt will be better . . .

HENRIETTA LYNCH, CHERAW, 9 JAN[3]

. . . The letter you last sent Mr. Lynch did cheer him indeed and he said "t'would be a comfort" if all his letters were like yours. . . . He has not been so low spirited since the second year of the War. His crop has proved a failure, he now owes to his hands and they do not want to begin work. He has of late been sued for sums of 20 and 30 dollars by men like Brock. It pained him very much. Mr. L repeats to me that if he does not win a prize[4] he does not know what he will do. The large debts he has been trying to pay all along, keep his family in great straits it is with hardship we keep the children from looking mean in dress. You would not believe that they are often without shoes. I have been schooled to poverty and this does not make me unhappy, if I am so. . . . I am nervous and somewhat irritable, when I see the children deprived in their youth, the only happy time of life. . . . Mr. Lynch . . . has always been so sanguine, as to make others believe him in a prosperous way while indeed, it was far from so, but he has lost this now. Taxes stare him in the face and swallow up everything. . . . Mr. Lynch never thinks of himself, he actually looks meanly in his business suit. But the War has brought these changes and keep us down. . . .

FRANCIS LYNCH, CHERAW, 21 JAN.[5]

Your very kind letter was received together with the ck accompanying it, much thanks for both.

Although, my dear brother, I cannot expect that you can do more, (already far more that [sic] I deserved, towards alleviating my difficulties. Still it seems to me I should apprise you. Prior to the judgment in your favor, there were others obtained against me, summing little less than 1000—besides these however there are two judgments for negro debts, one of them growing out of a purchase made in 1864; and the other a security debt, on which I was indemnified by mortgage of negro property. Perhaps the whole of the forgoing might be settled with near $1000, yet if I should be sold out, the proceeds . . . I infer would be applied in full satisfaction, before your judgmt would be reached.

This existing state of things brings vividly to my mind, the wise counsels of our Dear Father in urging me to file the judgment in your favor. So much time has elapsed, so many fond hopes disappointed, that I can hardly look for a continuance of the indulgence extended to me.

So little have I attained the past six years that the feeling comes over me that a punishment is on me. . . . My courage almost fails me. You are too good to be offended at my relating to you the state of things. If down to the wall and sold out, what then[?] If the older judgments were satisfied, the one in your favor would cover the rest; if not lifted until a sale, they might absorb near everything at sacrificing prices.

Then another matter, I have had a horror of the court of Bankruptcy, but if closed on it might be well to make avail of it, yet I almost shudder at the thought. So different do I find the state of my affairs, from what I would hope to have them, and I fear that . . . my confidence in myself is giving way. Pray for me and give me your counsel. . . .

BAPTISTA LYNCH, CONVENT—URSULINES, VALLE CRUCIS,
NEAR COLUMBIA, S.C, JANY 26th[6]
. . . Thank you for your few lines from Richmond and . . . I am particularly gratified that you paid Mrs. Weed a long visit and do hope that dear Sister Charles's family may all become Catholics. . . .

Mrs. Brisbane is very low has received the last Sacraments. I wrote to her family, and "Mr. Alonzo White" was here this morning. His visit did good to both. He will remain in Columbia tonight and come out tomorrow to see her. Mrs. B—may last Drs. White and Lynch say some time or she may die at any moment. I do not see how it is possible for her to survive—so weak and suffering all the time—not able to take any nourishment. She said before she got so very low, that she wanted your blessing before she died but now she could hardly discern you she is so weak.

What a happiness for her to die in Religion! She appreciates it and speaks beautifully to all our sisters. I will telegraph you when she passes away—though we expect you up very soon—perhaps Monday. . . .

FRANCIS LYNCH, CHERAW, 30 JANY.[7]
With this I send the statmt regarding settlement with Mr. Woodward—He held two notes as the statmt refers to each, one of them fully satisfied, on the other a balance of $353 88/100, appears [?] due on 1 Jany 1870, all of which I trust is correct.

On yesterday I learned that the judgmt to Prince Adml. could be settled at 25 prct and costs and the one in favor of Diggs in same manner. . . .

I thought that I had until the 15 Feby to finish up my taxes of which I lack 200$ of reaching, But today was advised, that the 20 pct penalty will attach after tomorrow if not paid by evening—I will try to have the Treasr wait a day longer, so that if you can assist me through this my "winter of discontent," I will have time to hear from you. This state of things feels unnatural, and if the storm is weathered, it must be if possible set right.

As an active man in the world my means ought to be at your call. Just now however I am in the meshes. To me it appears more difficult to regain than to have first gained. In the first case a good credit assisted me—while in the second it has to be acquired, after many disasters. . . .

FRANCIS LYNCH, CHERAW, 2d FEBY[8]

. . . Messrs GW Williams and Co through Messrs Buist and Buist of your city have sent to the sheriff here to press a claim of about 175$ due them. I have written Messrs G.W.W. and Co asking an extension of time . . .

My taxes if pd this afternoon will be free of penalty, if not $60 add[itio]n[al]ly will be added I lack 200$ of the required amt.

It does seem there is much danger of my being floored, and then what shall I do, crushed. My design was to pursue business as vigorously as practicable, buy up claims as I might find myself able and in time, perhaps not very long by the aid of sales of property, be all right again; but designs go for nothing when not carried out. And to be driven to the wall before having compromised the negro claims would frustrate them I fear entirely—for they are the oldest filed Judgmts. . . .

The past year I had to pay over 1,000$ in liquidation, which in my little business after meeting its expenses, was tight. . . .

Unless Messrs GW W & Co. instruct the sheriff to wait, he will proceed under present instructions to my ruin, and to the loss of their claim and many others.

Perhaps your requesting these Gentm. to withhold proceedings for the present might influence them so. Some one else might act, but perhaps not. I am very desirous to arrange the negro claims before being pressed, as they have precedence from their date. Sorely grieved to worry you. . . .

[PS] I got one day longer on taxes.

FRANCIS LYNCH, CHERAW, 7 FEB.[9]

How can I express my grateful feelings for your great kindness and most generous assistance [?] On yesterday I recd your telegram and forthwith called on the County Treasr and gave him a dft on you for $200 . . . One of your letters contained checks summing twelve hundred dolls for which I cannot thank you sufficiently [for the means] with which to lift the judgments prior to yours. As yet no reply is recd from the parties representing the McNair debt. Mr McIver who represents the parties recommends the acceptance of my offer and I earnestly hope it will suffice . . . This is the lion of the claims . . .

It will be my aim to get things in right shape as quickly as possible, and reanimate myself. What has borne hardest on me, has been a feeling of disappointment at the fruits of my endeavours for so many years—and my being a burden on my best of brothers. I do hope the tide will soon change and that with God's blessing my endeavours may prosper. At least as you so kindly say, I must have courage. . . .

BAPTISTA LYNCH, CONVENT OF THE URSULINES
VALLE CRUCIS, FEBY 13th[10]

. . . Sister Etienne and myself had quite a long conversation with Rev. Dr. M— on the Farm its necessities, its expenses &c &c and he seemed to regret that for the want of means to carry out what had been begun, the Convent should lose or sink what was already expended. Said he had explained to you, but did not think you took it in. If he employs men to work must pay them—cannot as a priest fall short of his word with them—he had expended on [the] Farm all that Convent placed in his hands for the last three years, during which he received therefore no salary. Now he is in need of clothes, and some other things and frets speaking of it.

I told him how we felt about that and also tried to make him take a more cheerful view of himself. But he takes rather a gloomy view and seems to think himself in an embarrassing position since our school is not building itself up and we have not the means of carrying on the Farm which might support the Community independent of the school.

For ourselves we are truly thankful if our school enables us to pay our grocer's bill and keep out of debt for our House expenses—more than that, we cannot aim at. . . .

JOHN LYNCH, COLUMBIA, FEBY 20th[11]

Enclosed I send you a blank to be endorsed by you for the renewal of the $700 note at Scotts. It is due 25th inst. Times I am sorry to say have not changed with me since I saw you. . . .

FRANCIS LYNCH, CHERAW, 26 FEBY[12]

It is my good fortune this evening to have received your cheering letter of yesterday's date, with enclosure of Bank check, summing three hundred and fifty dollars. I cannot Dr. Brother sufficiently express my gratitude and thanks—

Your kind and encouraging advice, as well as the material assistance so graciously bestowed on me, is enough to awaken life, and better energies.

I have been endeavouring to settle the negro claim with H. L. Moore and hope to do so some day this week. He is more exacting than I looked for, considering the purchase was made, in 1864. The settlement of this and a claim to W.F. Moore, will leave only the McNair debt for ending your judgmt. I would far prefer the buying off of this McNair judgmt yet fear to awaken an interest in it. . . . My depression was consequent on the ill success for several years, during which time . . . I had hoped to liquidate to a large extent my indebtedness. With results so contrary, a feeling of want of confidence in myself was gaining on me, until thanks to your encouragement it has been arrested. . . .

In regard to the future, . . . All must be left to the ruling of Providence. . . .

FRANCIS LYNCH, CHERAW, 28 FEBY [13]

. . . Accept my heartfelt thanks for your goodness. I hope that I may prove myself worthy of it, with yourself as a beacon to guide me.

So far as I have settled judgments, they have been transferred to you. . . . Of the cks received of you, $750 have been sent to the Bank, and one for 200$ was sent to you, as I had drawn this amt prior to the int of them. I have thought best to hold the checks, using them when necessary. . . .

BAPTISTA LYNCH, CONVENT OF THE URSULINES, VALLE CRUCES, FEB. 28[14]

. . . We have, as you know, about $2000 in RR &c stock remaining yet of Mrs. Brisbane's dowery and if you desire that we should sell $1000 and place it in Rev. Dr. M—hands, of course we will do it.

Our school is so very small or rather diminishing than increasing, so that he has taken the alarm, and wishes the Farm to support the Community independent of the school—and thinks town is the place for us We do not feel disturbed, poor as we are and small as our school is—We have been worse off and Divine Providence fed and clothed us. Our trust is in the same yet the thought of Rev. Dr. M leaving us is very depressing and we would make great exertion to prevent such a loss to our Institute—for where would we find one so well suited to his position.

He with considerable modesty and embarrassment told us (M. Assistante and myself, as we talked over business matters.) as he had not received any salary for the last three years he had gotten out of necessary clothing &c. and he thought if at the end of the year there were no better prospect of our Institute being built up, he would be forced to seek some other field of duty. Of course we could not blame him—for who would stand it buried alive and doing nothing for six years, as he has done? Especially now, when his improved health animates him to exertion. But for our Convent such a loss would be inestimable. . . .

JOHN LYNCH, COLUMBIA, MARCH 2nd [15]

Enclosed I send a blank for your signature for a renewal of the five hundred dollar note due 5th of March. . . .

Genl appropriation bill just passed the house. It now rests with the Senate. I hope it will not be fought there as it was in the house. There appear to be some apprehension that after it passes there will be no money in the treasury, but where it has gone no one seems to have an idea. . . .

BAPTISTA LYNCH, CONVENT OF THE URSULINES, VALLE CRUCIS, MARCH 7th [16]

. . . We received a very interesting letter from Sallie Aldrich, in which she tells us that her Mother has just been received into the Church and I am much consold by her taking in Baptism the name of "Baptista" saying, that I was the first to introduce Catholicity into her family. She was sure my patron assisted me—hence her devotion to him. . . .

People have not stopped congratulating us on your being chosen for Abp. of Baltimore! How little they understand about it! . . .

BAPTISTA LYNCH, CONVENT OF THE URSULINES, VALLE CRUCIS, MARCH 14th [17]

. . . I was sorry to have to trouble you about our business matters, but see you have the *honor* and the *onus* of being the Head, and it can't be helped. I have since talked to the "Council" [18] about the sale of stock to value of perhaps $800 in South Western R.R. to carry on our Farm, if that is to support our Community. But they seem to prefer waiting until you come and let us *talk* over our prospects and future. . . .

JOHN LYNCH, COLUMBIA, S.C., MARCH 25th [19]

I recd your letter of 22nd from Atlanta enclosing a check for Pope and Haskell for $1700 yesterday . . . I am very much obliged to you . . . If it was only possible for me to effect a sale soon. You have no idea the relief it would give me.

FRANCIS LYNCH, CHERAW, 2nd APRIL[20]

. . . Of your good health and return to the City, Daughter has apprized us. From the aid you have so generously extended me, and for which I cannot be sufficiently grateful and have settled Judgments &c summing about 3000$ among them an old judgment for about 1600$ on which Father was endorser, this I paid with $150 cash and my note for 75$ at 12 months . . .

So far as my lands are concerned I have concluded to divide the lower tract 767 acres into small sections, and sell in the Fall; the indications are that it will bring in this way from 15 to 20$ per acre 1/3 cash. The property being its security for the remainder—What think you of it?

I have sent plats of this land to NY and Boston without as yet finding a purchaser. So the plan of selling here in sections may be the better way. If it works well I may sell as much more off the upper plantation. . . .

HENRIETTA LYNCH, CHERAW, 23 APRIL[21]

. . . It is with so much difficulty that Mr Lynch can get the necessaries of life for his family. I think if a change is needed in any thing you can give advice. They would have dealt with him. . .—but for your timely aid—[by] selling the house over his head. Oh! My dear Bishop we owe everything to you. . . . Your last deed of benevolence seemed to have raised your brother as it were from the ground. . . .

JOHN LYNCH, COLUMBIA, S.C., APRIL 26[22]

. . . I am sorry to learn that the Executor of Lieber,[23] Richard L. Manning Jr. is living in Baltimore. . . . I feel pretty certain that Lieber never sold his interest but when his friends whom he induced to invest their money became dissatisfied, he silently withdrew his claim never having put in anything but his talent and labour. . . . I have a copy of L's will in which he gives a list of his effects; the mine is not mentioned, I can therefore safely claim having purchased the whole property. It might not be prudent [to] say anything to the father.[24] . . .

BAPTISTA LYNCH, CONVENT—URSULINES,
VALLE CRUCIS . . . APRIL 27th[25]

. . . Sister Antonia writes us that she is about to have her hands full as the Community have decided to sell their present Convent and build a new one in a more desirable and healthy locale. I do not envy her the responsibility and anxiety attendant on such a work. She herself shrinks from it, but it seems to be the will of God. I suppose the Community recognize in her the good business talents, for which our Brothers are remarkable. She says friends have

offered to lend them money at 6 per. ct interest. Every thing combines to facilitate the work. . . .

JOHN LYNCH, COLUMBIA, S.C., MAY 19th[26]
. . . Practice rather improving—Lectures, first rate as far as the class is concerned, but the State Treasurer has not paid one dollar of this year's appropriation, consequently &c &c.

BAPTISTA LYNCH, URSULINE CONVENT, VALLE CRUCIS,
FEAST SS HEART, JUNE 7th[27]
I know you would have been pleased if you had been here this morning and
witnessed how *grandly* we celebrated the Feast SS Heart this year. You may
remember that I spoke to you of the "Circular" from "Abbe Richandean" Blois
France. Who acting as the mouth-piece of various Ursuline Convents, invited
the whole Order of La Ursula to unite as one body on today, Feast SS Heart
7th June (1872) and make a solemn act of Consecration of themselves to the SS
Heart. The idea seems to be, to pledge the whole Order to offer themselves to
make reparation and to carry out in the fullest manner possible, through the
exercise of our *fourth vow*, our work A.M.D. G.
    . . . Rev. Dr. Meriwether . . . got quite into the spirit of it and you would have
been gratified to see his painstaking [devotion] in carrying out the ceremony.
. . . He sent for the Act of Consecration, which was too long and verbose and
wrote one for us, much better short and full. . . . We had the Holy Sacrifice as
usual, then Exposition of Blessed Sacrament with hymns, Pange Lingua. Then
followed Litany SS said by "Rev. Dr. Meriwether—Choir responding—then
he gave a soul-stirring exhortation on the subject!
    After the Exhortation I went up, with the two youngest of the Professed
Choir Nuns . . . bearing lighted wax tapers, and we knelt before the Communion table, . . . I read the "Act of Consecration" . . . to which we all . . . affixed
our names. Rev. Dr. M. then . . . announced the "Te Deum" which the choir
took up and finished. After the "Te Deum" . . . we sang the "Tantum Ergo" and
the Benediction of the Blessed Sacrament crowned the whole. . . .
    . . . I will write to "Sister Antonia" perhaps tomorrow and let her know
that you . . . [will lay the] cornerstone of their new Convent on 16th July. . . .
I hope you . . . do not over-exert yourself—You can *rest* yourself by writing
sometimes!

ANTONIA LYNCH, MT. CARMEL, [JUNE 16][28]
. . . My dear Brother, will [you] send me a few lines saying if you saw in N.Y.

Rev. Vaughan or if you have written or *would write* to him stating that he could have our present location for $25,000 with interest. If there is no prospect of his taking it we will have to make exertions in other directions. Those Asylum men are still anxious for it and we would be glad to get out of the affair without telling them what is our *objection* in *truth.* . . .

ANTONIA LYNCH, MT CARMEL, 25th JUNE[29]
At once I must tell you of the great consolation we have had during the past week—a visit from our own Carmelite Father—Father Patrick of the Cross (Kelly) from Dublin. . . . As it is the intention to found a convent of our order somewhere in this country during the coming year you may be assured, we all begged this Father very much that Baltimore would be the first location. Rev. Father Dougherty[30] is so much in favor of it and I may say the people for they flocked around him that we have the confident hope that our Lord will give us this consolation. Father Dougherty promised his [*sic*] to use all his influence with the new Archbishop for a Foundation. In the mean time so as not to miss a chance this Father has written to his provincial for leave to purchase our present location at the price we offered to the Missionary Fathers[31] $25000 with interest and if he gets that permission the property will be theirs. Should they fail in getting permission from the new Archbishop (which we will pray will not be the case) I am sure they can sell without any loss. This good Father is even *more opposed* to our selling to those Asylum men than you were. . . . If his answer from his Provincial will be in favor of his proposals he will return to Baltimore for the purchase. . . .

14

"THE IDEA OF A RELIGIOUS INVOKING A MALEDICTION ON THE HEAD OF ANYONE!"

July–December 1872

In their postwar location at rural Valle Crucis, the Ursulines may have struggled to attract students, but for many, if not most of those who did enroll, life in a convent academy still was a transformative experience, not only for the students but their parents as well, both Protestant and Catholic. The postwar curriculum combined an expanded core of liberal arts and sciences together with traditional elements of practical training for adolescent females, while maintaining the religious atmosphere which had characterized their academy in Columbia. Noting the heightened importance that German had come to have in the United States, not only from the continuing German immigration (now leading all other ethnic groups arriving on these shores), but from the prestige that German unification and the new country's double victory over Napoleon III and the Paris Commune had given the German community in the United States, Baptista, at her brother John's suggestion, wanted to include it in her institute's core curriculum.

Baptista had occasionally in the past presumed her bishop brother's permission about a minor matter when she had not had a response from him. Her patience with his dilatoriness finally ran out on the major matter of starting a free school in Columbia for both boys and girls. The academy's resident chaplain was evidently a major consultant, as was St. Peter's pastor in Columbia. In the event, Baptista seems to have determined that with the traditional starting month of schools—October—fast coming to an end, she could afford to wait no longer for her brother's approval. And so, she dispatched a trio of nuns to Columbia to begin the parochial school.

One decision she could not make regarding the new mission was the appointment of a Confessor for the nuns engaged in the operation of the day school. In an era in which Confession was seen as a necessary prerequisite for the worthy reception of Communion, being able to have regular access to the sacrament of Penance was a spiritual sine qua non, even for female religious. Hence Baptista's exasperation with her brother's failure to respond to her request.

Meanwhile, the Ursuline community continued to press their war claims in Washington. In the District of Columbia, the Barrys were among the staunchest advocates of the Ursulines' campaign to secure compensation from the federal government for the burning of their academy and convent. When Ellen Ewing Sherman, in a letter to Mrs. Barry, shared an account of Mother Baptista's reported face-to-face defiance of her husband, it became the occasion for Baptista to correct the record, with an eye toward gaining General Sherman's wife as yet another powerful advocate for the Ursuline claims for the community's war losses.

John Lynch, through a Byzantine transaction, cleared the title to his mine from the debts incumbent upon it thus putting himself in a far better position to attract a buyer which he desperately needed to do, if he was to rectify his financial woes. He was still without a salary from the university. His private practice had improved but still fell far short of meeting his expenses. Like his brother Francis, he had lost any standing for credit. So too his situation was threatening to wreck him psychologically. The upshot was John's disparate attempts to secure income, whether from his patents or as Examining Surgeon for insurance policies. In soliciting Patrick's influence toward shaping the medical department politics to protect John's status on the faculty, he let bare his conflicted feelings in being indebted to the Republican governor for his appointment. Indeed, John acknowledged that in adjusting to the new order he owed more to the governor than to anyone else.

Francis's hopes to better his cotton production through the acquisition of a gin were dashed when fire badly damaged his newly acquired machine. That disaster also scuttled any plans to realize quick revenue from the sale of lands whose value had been enhanced by the greater production which his gin was to make possible.

Antonia Lynch, as prioress of the Baltimore Carmel, encountered the painful reality that in a patriarchal church, women, even religious, were very limited in their ability to have their concerns factor into key decisions, in this case determining the purchasers of the monastery on Asquith Street. The Carmelite nuns had hoped that this property would be occupied by a male Carmelite foundation. When the Carmelite Superior declined to authorize the expansion, the local superior of the women Carmelites, a Jesuit, negotiated a sale of the property to the directors of the German Orphan Home. The nuns' scruple about the sale apparently grew out of their concern that their former home would become a place in which Protestant ministers would be responsible for the spiritual care of all the residents, including the Catholics. Antonia's protests brought no change of mind in either the Jesuit director or the new archbishop, James Roosevelt Bayley. Relief came to Antonia Lynch only when the German Orphan Home directors decided to raze the Carmelites' buildings and construct a new facility for housing youth.[1]

The Baltimore-based Antonia Lynch appeared to be the sole member of the family to want her brother to be named the next archbishop of the Premier See. Baptista, by contrast, was relieved to learn that Martin Spalding's successor would be James Roosevelt Bayley, the nephew of Elizabeth Ann Seton. When the new archbishop sided with their Jesuit superior in approving a sale to a buyer Antonia, as well as Patrick, considered unsuitable, the Carmelite had even more reason to regret that her brother was not heading the see.

As another year ended, Patrick could not but envy his Carmelite sister's good fortune in being relieved as prioress of her community. "I close one year of hard work and sorrow," he told Antonia, "and I scarcely see that the year we are about to enter will be of a different character, but we are all in the hands of God." For bishops, unlike Carmelite superiors, there were no periodic elections to free one from the persistent burdens they faced as prelates.

BAPTISTA LYNCH, CONVENT URSULINES,
VALLE CRUCIS, JULY 3rd[2]

... You will be astonished, as we all are, at the fine "Commencement" we had, considering we had only 13 *pupils* and none of them of the First Class in studies or *Music*. But we taught and drilled them so much, that we have not had so satisfactory a "Commencement" for four years at least and some of our sisters say since we came to Valle Crucis—I suppose 50 carriages were on the grounds! You see, the "College Commencement"[3] was over this year before ours, instead of clashing with it and so, we had a crowd. John read very nicely the names and prizes and Rev. Dr. M. gave them, or rather, gave the "crowns" and "cards" for we are *still* too poor to distribute prizes. ...

ANTONIA LYNCH, MT CARMEL, 9th JULY[4]

... Rev. Fr. Dougherty with our Agent Mr P Dugan and our Builder Mr Stack, have at our request taken the entire management of affairs on *that day*. We hope to collect a good deal towards our next payment on the occasion and will pray much for good weather, and a *happy success*. It may be that our Carmelite Father will be present. We have not heard from him since he left for St. Louis and the understanding *was* if his Provincial favoured the purchasing our property he would return to Baltimore and if not he would write us the result—so from the silence we hope the answer will be in our favour. ...

JOHN LYNCH, COLUMBIA, JULY 15[5]

I enclose this in a letter to your friend Mr. Courtnay, to awaken your interest in the matter of the sale of the mine. ... I am particularly anxious for a speedy sale, or arrangement—that I may get enough money to pay my debts; for my credit is gone, both in the stores and in Bank. I am not able to collect; either accounts or my salary, I know it is producing its effects on my body and if it were not for a great effort I would have been sick before this.

... My practice is improving but I do not *collect* enough to support the family. If you see any arrangement that can be made with the mine, so as to give me enough ready money to pay my debts; close with it, and I will agree. ...

FRANCIS LYNCH, CHERAW, 28 JULY[6]

... My business is improving and with the necessary capital for its masterly execution, would doubtless prove the best in this section. As I told you, my aim is to sell farms in the Fall. I am sanguine of doing so to the extent of 15000$ and to receive half cash for it. As the money for the purchase is to be derived from the growing crops, in the main, it will be late in the year before farmers will be entirely prepared to pay.

P.S., my pay[in]g off judgments will give greater confidence to purchasers of land, who might be dissuaded. You will note that the advancement in the price of land tends greatly to my advantage in selling . . .

BAPTISTA LYNCH, [URSULINES], TO MRS. M.C. BARRY, JULY[7]

. . . I admire Mrs. Genl Sherman's letter very much—it does honor to her head and heart. Nor am I surprised at the testimony she gives of Genl. Sherman's character -for even in the short interview I had with him, he impressed me very favorably and as one who regretted the military necessity and the stern measures he had been obliged by duty to adopt. It is not surprising to any one acquainted with History, that Columbia, the hot-bed of secession should have been a "doomed city" as one of the officers told me it was. But its destruction far exceeded Genl Sherman's wishes and intentions owing, I was told, to the fact that the soldiers became intoxicated on liquors secreted in cellars. Genl Sherman himself expressed to me his regret at the wholesale destruction of the city—as he looked upon its ruins.

However, such were the magnanimous terms by which peace proposed by Genl Sherman and such his frequent marks of friendship for the South since that event, that I should suppose all Southerners would regard Genl Sherman not only as a splendid General, but as a magnanimous enemy . . . whose generous heart knows no malice.

Mrs. Genl Sherman makes a mistake when she says that Genl Sherman sent her brother, Col. Charles Ewing to our convent. The Convent was burned on the night of 17th Feb 1865 and it was not until the morning of 18th about 10 o'clock that Genl. Sherman and staff and Col. Ewing came to us in the Catholic Church yard—into which we had fled during the night previous for refuge. Col. Charles Ewing certainly was most polite, kind and attentive from that time out. But what could he do—we were homeless and in every way destitute. He did all he could and with a manner which enhanced greatly the value of his attentions. He placed us under shelter in a pro-tem Hospital—saved from the flames—Genl Preston's House that we might be more comfortable in it and on Sunday just previous to the departure of the Army from Columbia he brought Major J.N. Corrigan to whom Mrs. Genl Sherman alludes—with him to arrange about giving us provisions—and they were both most courteous, kind and generous.

What shall I say, my dear Madame, of "the slander," as Mrs. Genl Sherman justly stigmatizes the assertion—The idea of a Religious invoking a malediction on the head of any one! Could such a hypocrite be found she would greatly deserve to be divested of her religious uniform and degraded from her Order for are not Nuns not . . . disciples of Him who when He was reviled did not revile—when persecuted "opened not his mouth"—but like a lamb was led to the slaughter? Whose doctrine is Love your enemies—do good to them that hate you—pray for them who persecute and calumniate you?

You will find in one of the South Carolina Papers of that period (1865) a different version. One of the Army Reporters had it, that I came out of the Convent surrounded by the Nuns and kneeling before Genl Sherman uplifted my crucifix imploring mercy of him.

But neither of these reports is true. I did carry my crucifix prominently as a protection for I feared to go out into the streets at midnight and meet the crowds of soldiery—even though the fires made it light as day. But we were silent and prayerful—God alone knows what have been our poverty and sufferings since.

... [There are] many details—too long for me to write yet which we have placed in the "Chronicles of our Order." ...[8]

BAPTISTA LYNCH, URSULINE CONVENT,
VALLE CRUCIS, AUGUST 18th[9]
... I hear that the Hamptons and Prestons were all at Church in Columbia today or Sunday to hear Mrs. Mahon sing and that Miss Preston is *nearly* a Catholic. Hope so, it is my daily prayer. ...

BAPTISTA LYNCH, URSULINE CONVENT,
VALLE CRUCIS, AUGUST 28th[10]
... Another idea we have is respecting taking the Parish school in Columbia. ... I am sure there is not a sister, whose zeal for the glory of Almighty God would not cheerfully go at the voice of obedience and spend herself and be spent in teaching the poor Catholic children of Columbia. Would you object to our making the proposition to Revd. F Fullerton, that if he and the Congregation would give us the use of the newly purchased house, rent free, we would go into town 2 or 3 and teach the parish school. This is the season of the year after Retreat, the "obediences" for the coming scholastic year are given out, and I am full of that thought, which we can accomplish, I think, without injury to Valle Crucis or to the interior spirit. ...

I saw in the Irish World that you were *visiting* in Mass. Thinks I to myself visiting! ...

JOHN LYNCH, COLUMBIA, S.C., AUGUST 31st[11]
... Mr. E.J. Scott ... agreed if I would pay three hundred on the present note leaving a note of three hundred, he would take your name singly as security,

thereby releasing me from the Gov. in full—an object to be desired at this particular time, although after accomplishing it I shall not only feel obliged to speak of and feel toward the Gov. as one who had done for me more than any one else since the war ended. I am only sorry I had to apply for assistance from such a source, but having applied successfully, am obliged to feel the obligation. . . .

I wish it were possible for you to push up your friend Mr. Courtney. I wrote him an urgent letter about four weeks ago, saying I was obliged to have money by the first of Sept. or I would suffer, begged him to try and use his influence to borrow me some on the security of the mine, but have heard nothing from him since. I fear he is looking too much to his own interest, or profit he is to make out of it for me to realize anything soon, but you know, the note to the Ins. Co. will fall due on the first of Decr and the only way I have to expect any money is from this sale. Try and find out has he any prospect of selling. If so, what is the cause of delay. . . .

I am afraid Dr. Michiac has declined the offer of the chair of Dr. Darby—if so Dr Gibbs of this place will be elected, if the College continues, this will be better for me personally, but I would rather the other, for the benefit of the School. . . .

BAPTISTA LYNCH, URSULINE CONVENT, VALLE CRUCIS, SEPT 26th[12]

. . . I am very glad you called by to see [Sister Catherine]—she has her hands full and is surely disappointed that you will not be her Superior directing the affairs of their convent and sustain her under her difficulties. Perhaps though, she may not be re-elected, and the burthen may fall on some one else, though I doubt it. . . .

I will write prudently to M. Charles at Tuscaloosa, and am very much gratified at the tone of the Rt. Rev. Bishop, but should he die tomorrow, would the Nuns be any better off than those of Charleston were, after Bishop England died (R.I.P.) *We* should look to that. I mean you and I. . . .

We are quite busy in thought about our Day School in Columbia. John and Mr. Colman have both spoken to us about it, but neither one is at all sanguine. On Monday morning M. Ursula and I will go in with brother John to see the House—which is being repaired and renovated. Rev. Dr. M—and Fullerton will be there to receive us and also our dear Mother with probably some ladies of the congregation and seeing the house we will judge whether or not, it would be advisable to go into it. . . . I think like yourself—if once started it will continue to improve. . . .

BAPTISTA LYNCH, URSULINE CONVENT, VALLE CRUCIS,
OCTOBER 5th[13]

. . . I have written more frequently than perhaps I would have done other-
wise to ask your permission and advice about a day-school in Columbia for the
Catholic children which this session we can undertake without detriment to
Valle Crucis Institute. No. 1; Will you give us permission to take in the day
school little boys of 10 ten years of age and under? No. 2: And will you appoint
Rev. Dr. M—Confessor to those of our Community who go into town? . . .

BAPTISTA LYNCH, URSULINE CONVENT,
VALLE CRUCIS, OCTOBER 7th[14]

. . . Revd. F. Fullerton and Rev. D. M. both seem to think a letter from you
authorizing [the day school] necessary. There is also a difficulty about our
taking Boys in the Parochial school with the girls. Rev. Dr. M—thinks we
cannot—while Revd F. Fullerton thinks the school ought to include *all* the
children of the congregation girls of all sizes and boys under 10 or 12 years of
age. . . .

LILLIE [ELIZABETH] LYNCH, URSULINE INSTITUTE,
VALLE CRUCIS TO [AUGUSTA LYNCH], OCT 13th[15]

Since I last wrote to you we commenced our annual studies, and as I know it
will give you pleasure to know mine, for this year, I write to tell you.

I am in the 2nd class, 2nd Div. . . . On Monday, we study Catechism, Bible
History, Dictionary, Grammar, Ancient History and Botany, we have Writing
also every day; In the afternoon French, Arithmetic and Drawing Tuesday
Catechism, Scripture Text, Spelling in Scholars companion, Familiar Science,
Modern History and Chemistry. In the afternoon Reading, Parsing, and
Latin. Wednesday, Catechism, Catholic Principles, Dictionary, Chronology,
Ancient History and Astronomy; in the afternoon the same as Monday.

Thursday, Dictation, Reading, Singing Class, plain sewing, crochet and
Embroidery, this day we have the afternoon recreation instead of Saturday.
Friday, Catechism, Saints of the month, Scholar's Companion, Modern Geog-
raphy, and modern Biography and Philosophy. In the afternoon French, arith-
metic, Musical catechism, and Tables. Saturday. Catechism, Prophecies and
Fulfillments, Common things, biography, American History, Mythology and
Rhetoric. In the afternoon Reading, composition and Latin. I take lessons on
the Piano, Harp and Guitar. . . .

BAPTISTA LYNCH, SCHOOL OF NAZARETH, COLUMBIA,
OCTOBER 24th[16]

As the children say, what under the sun is the matter [with] you! I have written and written to you and not one word of reply! We had to act on your *presumed permission* and act—at once—so you see we are at our Day school in Columbia and we are delighted with our work. There are about 40 fine intelligent Catholic boys and girls, who come daily and Mesdames Ursula and Thomasina are doing a beautiful work.

　　. . . Of course, the Parish Priest is the *Principal* of it. The *Trustees* of it are the gentlemen of the Catholic Association, and we the Ursulines are the *Teachers*. We teach gratis—if . . . it can be called gratis to receive a house rented and provisions—of course much more than the tuition of our scholars would bring in. The "Catholic School-Fund" is the payment of Parents and voluntary contributions. A very Catholic Spirit has been shown. . . .

BAPTISTA LYNCH, "SCHOOL OF NAZARETH,
COLUMBIA, OCTOBER 25[17]

. . . You are playing "hide and seek" with us all these days . . . How many times I have written to you lately!!

　　. . . Our "Catholic Day school" . . . is going on finely. . . . We . . . see in their future useful and ornamental members of Church and Society. . . . We feel only one draw-back. We want Rev. Dr. M__ to hear our Confessions and he "strict to the law," awaits your permission.　Please send it, or what is better, come and give it at once before they break s[ai]d Rule? . . .

BAPTISTA LYNCH, NOV 6th[18]

You will be happy to hear that our Parochial School is getting on finely . . . have between 50-60 scholars. Boys and girls—who would in a short time have lost their faith, whereas they [are] a bright intelligent set, just ready to drink in all we tell them of the Holy Faith.

　　We left Valle Crucis on the 14th of October . . . All that time . . . have Srs Ursula and Thomasina [had no confessor] . . . Which is growing to be quite a serious affair. As I fear they may disedify seculars by remaining away from communion and busy-bodies may think some difficulty exists between the Bishop and Priests. This is my fifth letter to you asking permission for Rev. Dr. Meriwether to hear their Confessions in town. Will you please telegraph him in Latin or Italian and relieve our Sisters. . . .

BAPTISTA LYNCH, URSULINE CONVENT,
VALLE CRUCIS, NOVEMBER 21st[19]

. . . I am happy to say our dear Sisters at the Day School are doing well—have 60 scholars and are doing a splendid work A.M.D.G.! . . . We *all* rejoiced when Rev. Dr. M got that letter which pleased him so much.

. . . Our school at Valle Crucis is as good as it was last year—we have 14 pupils . . .

The poor Bostonians! Have our sincere sympathy and prayers—The Pilot office the Cathedral! How sorry we are for all the sufferers—we offer our humble prayers for them and hope that in that prosperous country, they may soon find relief. Where were you, at the time of the conflagration? My first thought was that, . . . you were not in the city.[20] . . .

JOHN LYNCH, COLUMBIA, NOV. 24th[21]

This evening I recd yours of 22nd containing note for $2575⁰⁰. It will go in the morning. . . . I have not yet been able to get the county treasurer to take up my warrant as he promised, although I have been to Edgefield twice expecting the money. He will be here tomorrow or next day.

. . . Is it not possible by some means to raise some money on the mine property to relieve me, and yourself too if possible. I think, if I had the incubus off my shoulders, I would be quite a different man. I feel that I never will be able to do any thing satisfactorily, until I am relieved, and the only possible way of my getting relief, is through . . . this mine, in some way. . . .

BAPTISTA LYNCH, URSULINES, TO PATRICK LYNCH, DEC 9th[22]

. . . Miss Crenshaw from Richmond Va. is one of Mm Etienne's friends and quite a superior young girl. She is very anxious to continue her studies of German. We promised to try and get a German teacher . . . finally wrote to that German City Philadelphia to see if the Augustinian Father—your good friend and ours—Rev. Father Stanton could get us a nice German postulant. He has not replied, but is, I hope, working for us. I told him we are anxious to introduce the German element into our Community. . . .

. . . Brother John says a corps of teachers is not complete now, without a German teacher, and we ought to have a German Sister. . . .

ANTONIA LYNCH, MT. CARMEL, DEC. 21st[23]

Several times within the last month I attempted to write you but put off from day to day. It was painful to tell you our troubles when you could not help us . . . about the sale of our present location. When it was ascertained that the

General of our Order would not at the present time give his approval of a Foundation in Baltimore, our Superior (Rev. J. Dougherty) told the Agent to sell to the Asylum Company. The Community then required me to write to Newark to Bishop Bayley—this I did sending the letter up to Father Dougherty to send first. The answer to the letter was for us to follow the advice of Fr. Dougherty.

It is an exceeding great cross to us, but Rev. Fr. Dougherty has never seen any objection to its falling into that Party altho I told him your opinion . . . I have done all I could—even wrote the Archbishop your objections—but no one seems to care for what is called our scruples. . . . As yet no papers have been signed, but they are preparing—and it gives one a chilly feeling whenever I am called to the Speakroom[24] for fear I am called upon to sign the *Deed*. Wonderful are the ways of God! Had you been made our ArchBishop the Fathers would gladly have come and this place would have been in their possession.

. . . The Asylum Party offered twenty-five thousand with interest—The Agent thinks if we lose this chance of selling, the property will long lay on our hands. It is astonishing in a city where there are so many wealthy Catholics they have never [made?] an offer to buy. Blessed are those who expect nothing—they shall not be disappointed!!!

. . . Our consent was not asked—Father Dougherty told the agent to close the bargain. Of course he has all power when supported by the Archbishop. Our Lord seemed to desert us not heeding our prayers. I am very sorry to tell you all this, but you would know it sometime. . . .

ANTONIA LYNCH, MT. CARMEL, TO PATRICK LYNCH, [DEC 23?][25]
. . . You would be pleased my dear Brother to learn we have the consolation of learning that the Party who have brought our *Property* intend to level all the Buildings and build a new House. I trust they will not change their minds. Please pray that they may not. . . . Our Elections came around this latter part of last month, when Mother Ignatius was chosen Rev. Mother. . . .

FRANCIS LYNCH, CHERAW, 24 DEC[26]
. . . Thanks to you, I had succeeded in planning the foundation work leading to success. The earnings even of my ginning business were netting about 10$ per day while the other branches, the tanning and shoemaking were improving, and I had begun to feel brighter hopes every dawning—when the calamity befell me, unhinging in a measure my onward career. Fortunately the Engine was but slightly injured and the Boiler not at all . . . Still the loss, in my estimate, exceeds two thousand dollars in value; and besides, retards my attaining some ends I had in view. . . .

PATRICK LYNCH, CHARLESTON, TO ANTONIA LYNCH,
DEC. 27th[27]

I regret that I could not call on my return home. Still if I had known that the Archbishop was so unwell I would have made an effort to do so.

In regard to the sale I do not see that you need trouble yourselves on the subject. What your letter states you did seems to me amply sufficient for the peace of your consciences. Whenever we are called on to act on our responsibility we must endeavor to ascertain what is right and act accordingly to our best convictions. Whenever properly asked for our advice we give it sincerely, whenever others have authority and do act, even though their judgment run counter to ours, there is no reason why we should distress ourselves.

I suppose, my dear Sister, I may congratulate you on the conclusion of your term of office and your return to the quiet walks of obedience; it would be well for your brother if something similar could happen to him. I close one year of hard work and sorrow and I scarcely see that the year we are about to enter will be of a different character, but we are all in the hands of God. . . .

JOHN LYNCH, COLUMBIA, DEC. 27th[28]

. . . I will be glad that you come up before the first, Monday in next month, and *bring* with you the *mortgage*, which Dr. Boatwright returned to you, when the last payment on the American Hotel (during the war) was refused. If I remember rightly, Dr. B. felt indignant that the last payment was not recd by the parties (Mrs. Flemming &c) and on that acct returned to you your mortgage. We have spoken of this matter since, especially when young Flemming asked me to ask you, to renew the mortgage which was lost." I have accidentally learned that *they* Treadwell at the head, have gone into Court (at Chambers) *revived* the mortgage, obtained an order to foreclose &c &c sale to take place on first Monday in January. . . . The mortgage was delivered to you. . . . The parties undertaking to revive may place themselves in a very awkward position by the production of the original. . . .

JOHN LYNCH, COLUMBIA, DEC. 31st[29]

. . . I will be 54 on tomorrow a week, if I had not the cares of debt and duns on my shoulders, I would *feel* as able to battle with the world as I did twenty-five years ago. . . .

I wrote today to Dr. Rowe of N. York offering to give him an interest in a *Patent* . . . if he would bear the Expense of taking out the patent, and would manufacture and sell them. It is a scientific thing, which Dr. Sims would appreciate. If I cannot work with my hands must work with my brains, hoping to make something by the effort. . . .

15

"THE TAXES SEEM TO CARRY EVERYTHING BEFORE THEM!"

January–June 1873

From Henrietta Lynch's begging for a few dollars to put food on the table, Patrick Lynch discovered the extent of his brother Francis's financial woes. Indeed, Henrietta was concerned that Francis was so out of sorts that suicide was a distinct possibility. Meanwhile they were keeping up appearances, including Ellen's convent education, which Patrick was also underwriting. The Lynch's financial crisis mirrored the country's economic downturn, which condition had seriously worsened Patrick Lynch's prospects during the bishop's near-perpetual fund-raising tours of the North.

To secure the money needed for improvements at Valle Crucis, Baptista was prepared to sell their town lots; that failing, she would reluctantly mortgage Valle Crucis, but not at the usurious interest rates banks were charging. Instead, she, like her siblings, turned to Patrick to secure a loan under favorable conditions, from a Catholic source, ideally a "rich bishop or priest" somewhere in the North, preferably New York.

The makeshift arrangement for conducting the Ursulines' Columbia day school at the current parish building pointed up the need for more adequate facilities. That necessity revived the issue which had bedeviled the Charleston Diocese at its beginning. Who controlled church property, the members of the local congregation or the bishop? Baptista was willing to have lay persons front and center in any acquisition of property, which might have reflected her painful memories of the uproar over the Ursulines' acquisition of the American Hotel in the late 1850s. Better to court a renewal of trusteeism than to restir any residue of the virulent nativism which had plagued them two decades earlier.

That the free school in Columbia had the largest enrollment of the Ursuline schools in South Carolina or Alabama pointed up how far short they remained of Baptista's vision of a network of Ursuline academies in the South. In truth, their precarious position had left them more dependent on Bishop Lynch to keep them financially afloat than they ever had been since he had led them from Ohio to upcountry Carolina fifteen years earlier.

The resurgence of the Democrats nationally emboldened Baptista Lynch to renew, covertly, their attempt to secure compensation for the loss of their convent and academy to Sherman's avenging army. The revelation of new evidence pointing to the responsibility of Union soldiers for the conflagration that destroyed a third of Columbia provided a new occasion for soliciting reparations from the federal government, now at the figure of $100,000. Fortuitously, the Ursulines had a politically well-connected advocate in Washington, whose daughter had been a student at the academy when Sherman's army burned the city. Never had the Ursulines seemed closer to securing a settlement from the government which would enable them to rebuild and so become once more an elite educational institution for women in the deep South.

Scarcely four months after completing her second term as prioress of the Baltimore Carmel, Antonia of the Purification (Catherine Lynch) died suddenly on April 2, 1873, at the age of forty-six. As the Annals of the monastery noted, "She was remarkable for her great patience, charity and meekness. Although she was sick but a very few days she suffered intensely from hernia, but continued until her last moments to give the edification and good example she had always presented to us since her entrance in religion."[1] Family references to "the sainted Catherine" in the wake of her sudden death reveal her siblings' spontaneous recognition of how faithfully their sister had lived the vows she had professed in seeking to follow Jesus more fully.

HENRIETTA LYNCH, CHERAW, 12 JAN.[2]

I write to beg that you will advise Mr. Lynch, as you have before so frequently done, as to what can be done in his emergencies. . . . He says he will not be able to take up Mr. Waddell's note unless he has the good luck to sell some land. He has fair promises made him of purchasing but these have failed him on other occasions. . . . He also owes a large sum to Geo. W. Williams, and he will allow him no more time . . . Mr. Lynch offered to Wm's his crop next year, but he wrote that "he must look to his attorneys for any arrangement looking towards a settlement."

Dear good Bishop if you could get these gents to wait on your brother without committing yourself, Mr. Lynch would be relieved. I do not know what would become of us if you had not befriended us in the hour of Trial, not only on this occasion but whenever the cloud lowered. May the God of charity, who sees and takes down our smallest good deed, reward you a thousand fold for every action done our family in the benevolence of your heart. . . . I fear that Mr. Lynch 's health will fail him if he is beset by his creditors. . . .

BAPTISTA LYNCH, URSULINES, VALLE CRUCIS, JANY 13th[3]

. . . I sometime fret, thinking we are now a burthen on your hands—a "brake on the wheel" of your Diocess. . . . Those lots in town are again threatened, and Mr. Douglass Desaussure has certainly proved himself a friend, by fighting off, as long as he can—But he called on John a few days ago and says he can do no more, but that we must do all we can to keep out of court, this next month, the "Chapman estate" unless we pay at least $1000.

John says he will try and sell one lot to a negro for that and stop the suit . . . But may we not ask the lecture[4]—and also try elsewhere . . .

FRANCIS LYNCH, 20 JANY[5]

. . . The 300$ that you so kindly sent me, assists very much in making up state taxes—sumirg [sic] about 500$. I have placed with the agency of Messrs J. Chadwick and Co., Charleston, the disposal of 1200 acres of land, and the waterpower of Thompson's Creek and hope they will effect sales for me. . . . I am endeavoring to refit, as best I can, the tannery. My anxiety for the sales of the lands is very great, as enabling the placing my affairs in easier condition.

HENRIETTA LYNCH, CHERAW, TO PATRICK LYNCH, 22 JANY.[6]

. . . The Sunday after the fire and excitement, [Mr. Lynch] gave up, weeping. It was indeed sad to those who know how he has labored with his hands at that gin. He thinks of nothing but his business. . . . He tries in every quarter to sell his lands. . . . The Taxes seem to carry everything before them! I think he pays more than he ever makes. Your checks kept off many a sick turn this year. These sick turns come over him the moment he is troubled by debt, and I trust you would write to encourage him sometimes. I know how badly he feels at being so largely your debtor[;] he said he had paid some of his debt by January and was in a fair way of paying you at no distant day, so you may think if his heart was not full when that sad calamity befell him.

It grieves Mr. Lynch terribly to see Mr. Waddell's note unpaid, he had much hope on Mr. W. buying land to cover the debt but he backed out. . . . Most of the debt during the War and before that period were from security much in the kindness of Mr. Lynch's heart. He is too kind-hearted, and easy, and everybody is hard on him. . . .

JOHN LYNCH, COLUMBIA, S.C. TO PATRICK LYNCH, JANY 24[7]
. . . Have been striving to raise $1000 to pay De Saussure on the lots above Female College and prevent foreclosure of Mortgage—but so far have faild. . . .

BAPTISTA LYNCH, URSULINES, VALLE CRUCIS, JANUARY 31st[8]
. . . John is trying to do his best about those Chapman Lots, upon which we owe $3,020^{00} . . . I have also suggested that the "Catholic Association" come forward and relieve the convent, take the lots and assume the debt. Hold lots and sell to advantage at ad libitum.

Men can manage such things. Women cannot, especially nuns. I do not want to make a note in Bank nor mortgage "Valle Crucis," as John suggests, to save ourselves from the court. We prefer to lose what we have paid on them. John will cut them up into 1/3 acre lots and put them up at public sale on First Monday in March. If sale is not a success will want mortgage on V.C.

I will say it is your property, and not mortgage it to Protestant Bankers at such rates of interests and let the law take its course with those lots—shall I? We have sacrificed too much already. Although so entirely averse to mortgaging "Valle Crucis" to the Bank we would like very much to mortgage it to some rich Bishop or Priest for the loan of $10,000 so as to give ourselves a fair start. . . . With this view I asked Bishop Wood could he lend us . . . but he is now unable. . . .

JOHN LYNCH, COLBUMBIA, S.C., TO PATRICK LYNCH, FEBY 20[9]
. . . The Legislature adjourns on the 1st next month. They have not yet passed the appropriation bill, but have elected new trustees, 4 negroes, and 3 whites. The Negroes I do not know, one is from Charleston (a Senator) another from Edgefield (Speaker of the House), one from Georgetown, the other from Spar-

tanburg (both Members). The whites are Tillson (of the old board) Chamberlain, and Northrop, editor of an evening paper here (brother of Revd). We have quite a change. If it does not break up the University. I am not injured by the change, but rather strengthened in my position. . . .

Today I see a prospect of Robert's getting the appointment of county Treasurer for Edgefield. I have got all the influence to bear, I can, and expect as soon as the present incumbent resigns, or is relieved, to see Robt. appointed, it will be worth over $2000 a year. I believe he understands the duties. . . . Have only a note of $150 30 days in Scotts Bank and one for $450 90 days in Gulicks Bank with your endorsement alone. Both, I hope to take up on maturity by salary, if appropriation is made, which I expect will be this week. . . .

P.S. What has become of Courtney[?] I have not heard from him since 13th Decr. . . . He has not advised me whether Mr. B[aldwin] gave him my patent papers, nor whether his friend has been able to do any thing with the patent. I see the want of its application to the porous plaster every day, if it was once tried, it would prove itself, to anyone. The mine, I am afraid, will stick in the mud for some time. . . .

CONLAW LYNCH, LEXINGTON CITY, 9 MCH[10]

I wrote you a letter some time ago and begged of you if it were in your power to lend me a helping hand in my present trouble. I know not who else to call on. If you could lend me one hundred dollars for a little while it would put me on my legs again. My wife at present is in a very delicate state of helth [*sic*] and may be sick at any moment and God only knows my dear uncle if you do not help me in my embarrassed condition, who will. If you will lend me this amount I will return it the first money I get hold of which I am in hopes will be very soon. . . .

ROBERT A. LYNCH, EDGEFIELD C.H., MARCH 9th[11]

. . . I have applied in every direction to find employment, but to no avail. I am willing to do any kind of work, and am strong and hearty, all that I want is something to do, to support Kate. . . . My being first in an United S office and then in the State's employ, has given me the requisites of a business man: punctuality, neatness and dispatch, and my gymnastic exercises, which I have never given up, fit me for hard work. I have tried farming but have come to the same conclusion as Aunt Ellen, that the country is no place for me, where we have but seldom a clergyman and no associates, in a word, my dear Uncle, where we do not live but vegetate. . . . I . . . beg of you with your influence to try and get me something to do anything that will support Kate and myself. . . .

BAPTISTA LYNCH, COLUMBIA, 10 MARCH[12]

. . . Perhaps brother John wrote you he has an offer of $12,000 . . . for the Convent—alias American Hotel, lots in Columbia—he proposes to sell them and pay the balance due on "Chapman Lots" for Convent—so as to free the latter of Mortgage about $3,500 due on them. Then we would be somewhat relieved, and we hope, able to sell and give good titles. We are very harassed about those "Lots" and fear the threatened courts and suit—and would be truly thankful to get sale for them this month—or at least lift mortgage on them. . . .

FRANCIS LYNCH, CHERAW, 18 MAR[13]

. . . I have gone on refitting the engine and yard, though with much difficulty, in a few days I hope all will be in readiness for work. The hope I have indulged in, of selling lands through Messrs Chadwick and Co. has buoyed me. For succeeding in this matter I would be relieved of a burden, and lessen the weight I am on you my most generous Bro. but for your kind encouragement and help, I do not know what I should have done. . . .

PATRICK LYNCH, NEW YORK, TO BAPTISTA LYNCH, 25 MARCH[14]

. . . . My health is good.—My sight got a great deal better. But of late I have had to prepare so much for my lectures that I taxed myself severely, and I have to be careful again. . . .

HENRIETTA LYNCH, CHERAW, 4 MAY[15]

. . . My dear Friend, I am forced to call on your kind charity because we are in such straightened circumstances. . . . Mr. L. . . . is doing nothing to bring [in] money now. The fact is he told me he was so distracted he could commit suicide, every thing calls for money but none comes in. . . . I have made a fruitless attempt to teach music for two years. In the time I received only forty six dollars and most of it went on, right off, for Marie's board, as Mother Superior asked me to send, if it were but $5 at a time. . . . I will beg of you my very best Friend to give me thirty Dollars if you can . . . You are the only one that turns to us in need. People may make pretty speeches but they give you not a crust of Bread. If my poor prayers avail not, I trust, that my good Mother's will, for the blessing of Heaven in this life and an everlasting reward for it in the next. . . .

HENRIETTA LYNCH, CHERAW, 11 MAY[16]

I received your very kind letter and would have answered by the next mail but was sick enough to be in bed from weakness and sore throat. I cannot tell you how thankful we are to you, dear Friend, for the check, enclosed, and if you had seen how happy it made your Brother Francis to be praised by you, I know you would feel doubly repaid. . . .

I do not think you know, yourself, dear Bishop, the exalted Piety of your dear brother Francis, but I have been with him 18 years in the daily walk of life have never seen him to leave his room however pressing the call on one occasion without offering up a prayer. And in the evening he as regularly says the beautiful devotion of the Rosary. As I could never tire speaking of the virtues of your sainted Sr. Catherine so do I think that he is her living representative. . . . I have never, in fact, known a person come up so closely to perfection. . . .

JOHN LYNCH, COLUMBIA, S.C., MAY 17[17]

. . . Do you think there would be any chance for me to sell a portion of the property I own in Beaufort, as wharf lots. My title calls for seventy acres in the town of Beaufort on Bay Street. I learn that they are covered with water, which has no doubt prevented their having been sold for taxes. Not having recd, my Quarter Salary, and doubting if I do, before next Legislature, I will be compelled to sell something, in the meantime. For although I have as much to do, as I well can do, on foot, collections are very slow and demands pressing. . . .

JOHN LYNCH, COLUMBIA, SC, MAY 27th[18]

. . . If you can possibly see Mr. Courtenay, try, and push him up, to doing something for me, for until I can obtain money sufficient to pay my debts, and pay Mrs Caldwell's claims, I am miserable, as I wrote you. I will have to deliver my lecture tomorrow night. . . . But you know it must be quite an effort to me, in my embarrassment, and I would have refused, if I did not feel that this is an opportunity of being placed before the community in a position which may not happen again, and it is a necessity that I should be forced there. I hope I may acquit myself, so as to make my position permanent, if the School keeps up. There are some fears that it may go down. I hope not. . . .

BAPTISTA LYNCH, URSULINE CONVENT, VALLE CRUCIS, JUNE 17th[19]

. . . I told you in my last letter that we were expecting the two young daughters of Judge Aldrich and they have come—are remarkably fine looking, large girls, larger than Marie and sensible, pious girls—well advanced for their age having been taught by their sister at home. Mrs Richardson seemed delighted to bring them . . . She says you are just the sort of man to get hold of her husband, and make a Catholic of him. He and his family are good prospects—not finding in Protestantism what will satisfy them . . . Yet imbued with great reverence for all true religion. She hopes to send us a niece of his as pupil soon.

. . . The Misses Hampton and ourselves continue to have a "mutual admiration society" and they will be at our Commencement, which will be the best since we left town. . . .

I cannot imagine a more lovely spot than Valle Crucis is today. . . . No wonder Mrs. O'Neill exclaimed . . . A paradise on earth! How thankful we feel for the enjoyment of such a sweet country place and when in a few years as of course will be the case, we shall build a proper monastery and Institute, we cannot desire for religion a more suitable place for the education of young girls. . . .

BAPTISTA LYNCH, URSULINE CONVENT, [JUNE 29?][20]

. . . It occurs to me that now, it is incontestably proved, that the Federal Army under General Sherman burned Columbia. This incontestable proof was brought about by the "mixed Claims" and without our interference or concurrence. Now is our turn to push our claim for indemnification we ask no favor, simply demand justice and claim 100,000^{00} one [hundred] thousand dollars.

Sallie [Aldrich] fully agreed with me, and said she did not think that $100,000 [$2,161,226 today] would cover our loss judging from what she saw at the time. . . . She and her two younger sisters were under our care, during the burning of Columbia and the Convent. I then requested her to ascertain "sub rosa" thro her father and Senator Stephens of Georgia, the probability of success in such a move—after which, I would ask your permission if there is any chance for us to push the matter with success.

We offer to give one fourth—$25000" to the lawyers or parties who win the case for us. Sallie is sanguine—has laid the case before her Father; who has not however written to Mr. Stephens of Georgia as I suggested but to Mr. Boyce. . . . As I told Sallie the work must be done entirely by others without either the Convent or bishop seeming to know it as far as possible. Nor would we wish it moved, until others had proved incontestably the fact of the burning of Columbia. This has now been done without our testimony. We take advantage of the tide and hope to win our claim. . . .

16

"OUR PRIVATIONS ARE SO GREAT THAT I THINK OUR ENEMIES WOULD TAKE PITY ON US"

July–December 1873

John Lynch continued to suffer from the financial consequences of the war, now compounded by the panic that devastated the national economy and by the death of his horse. The latter event made him a doctor without means of transportation beyond his own feet, about the worst situation for a physician whose practice was already suffering from the inability of so many people to afford a doctor. A revival of the economy, he came to realize, was key, not only for his potential earning power as a physician, but to improve the real estate market, even for unproven mines or underwater lots.

Economic growth, John Lynch recognized, very much depended on the survival of local Republican governments committed to public investment. So did his salary as a university professor. The new constitution of the state declared that all universities should be "free and open to all the children and youths of the State, without regard to race and color." In 1869, a biracial board of trustees formally adopted that policy for the University of South Carolina. Still, for four years, no blacks applied. Finally, in October 1873, the mixed-race Secretary of State, Henry E. Hayne, enrolled in the medical department of an institution of higher education that had historically been an aristocratic preserve. That enrollment touched off a boycott by both students and faculty, of what came to be known as "The Radical University." John Lynch found himself in the awkward position of serving on a faculty of which he was the only non-radical member in a medical school whose only student was counted as Black. "Matters are getting from bad to worse," John told his brother Patrick. Only the slim hope of the legislature releasing funds to pay his salary kept him in a situation which he found "disgusting." Still, despite his racist instincts, he admitted to feeling shame about his silent complicity in the resistance to the integration of medical education. He appealed to his brother Patrick to find some competent physicians in the North to fill the chairs boycotted by the local medical elite. Such an infusion of talent might not only "save the university," but give it a prestige it hitherto lacked. And provide him with at least one white colleague.

Money was certainly a driving force in his decision to become part of this social experiment. Nonetheless, he was willing to become a pariah in the white community, not only by being on the university's faculty, but also by agreeing to organize a school that might as well be for Black students only. In violence-prone South Carolina, the willingness to be labeled a "scalawag" qualified as heroic, no matter the financial motivations involved in his decisions.

Taxation to enable the Republican government to expand its efforts to provide for the public welfare affected seemingly everyone in South Carolina. The Lynches not only resented being forced to pay without the means to do so, but could only conclude that a corrupt administration was insisting that they were in arrears for taxes the family was certain they had paid.

Taxes were but the tip of the financial ruin Francis Lynch faced. As his wife, Henrietta explained to her bishop brother-in-law: "Our privations are so great that I think our enemies would take pity on us." Equipment for his tannery sat at the railroad depot. Francis lacked the means to redeem it by paying the shipping costs. Again, it fell to Henrietta to appeal to her brother-in-law, not to rescue the uncollected equipment, but to provide food for their table and clothing that will enable their daughter Marie to continue to be a part of the tiny utopia that Baptista and Patrick had fashioned at Valle Crucis. Even though the enrollment was pathetically small and too thick with Lynches, it was still a place insulated from the ills of the postwar South.

Lieber College, originally constructed in 1837, is the office of undergraduate admissions at the University of South Carolina and is listed in the National Register of Historic Places. Courtesy of the University of South Carolina.

In a tight money market afflicted by the panic that had spread nationally from New York across the country, it is no surprise that Francis' attempts to sell property or secure loans were failing, particularly given his own poor credit history. When the sheriff informed Francis that creditors were pressing him to seize Francis's business and home to redeem his debts, Francis in desperation turned to Patrick to provide the $5,000 that was threatening to crush him. A week before Christmas, Francis received the best gift that his brother could give him.

Unlike her older brother, John, Baptista Lynch was buoyed in her campaign to secure federal recompense for war-incurred losses by the changing tide in favor of the forces of redemption, which, by the summer of 1873, through propaganda, terror, and Northern fatigue, were steadily undermining the revolutionary government that had plagued white Southerners over the past six years. As Southern states were "redeemed," Baptista increasingly had powerful Democratic advocates in Washington, including Georgia Senator Alexander Stephens. But with U.S. Grant still in the White House, Baptista calculated how she could get his close friends, such as the Shermans and the Ewings, to intercede on the Ursulines' behalf.

BAPTISTA LYNCH, VALLE CRUCIS, JULY 11th[1]
… We disappointed so much Miss Renshaw by not securing a German teacher for her during the past scholastic year that I fear she will not return and the Misses Hampton are equally anxious to study that language. Will you my dearest Brother try and send us an educated German Postulant by Sept 1st and also a good Lay Sister postulant. …

JOHN LYNCH, COLUMBIA, SC, July 28th[2]
… I see very little prospect of receiving salary. Have recd none since 1st Febry—on 1st Augst. will have due me $1000. … I went to Beaufort, saw the marsh land.[3] If it is a Phosphate bed, as is said, it will be worth 5 or 6 thousand. I have offered it for 7 thousand, without the phosphates—as Wharf lots, it may be very valuable, when Beaufort becomes a city …

I must turn my attention to the sale of this, as it seems there is no chance for selling the mine. I am afraid my spirit will be broken, before the spell that seems to surround me, can be. …

BAPTIST LYNCH, URSULINE CONVENT,
VALLE CRUCIS, JULY 31st[4]
… After our commencement was over, I wrote invitations … to Ladies living, removed from the Church privilege, and told them that you wished us to offer them the spiritual advantage of a Retreat at Valle Crucis &c, which we would open on the "Feast of Mount Carmel" (July 16) DV They all answerd most gratefully, and appreciated your care of their souls—but really, it was amusing—one had her husband and children,, another her health—&c &c all *prayed to be excused*

I thought of Gospel—

BAPTISTA LYNCH, URSULINE CONVENT AND INSTITUTE,
VALLE CRUCIS, 21 AUGUST[5]
… Mrs. Octavia Pulliam writes she will enter our Noviciate in Sept. DV. and bring as her dower about $10,000, should she ever be professed.

Now if we only succeed in our "claims," we shall begin to think of building and also if we can sell our lots in town advantageously. Everyone says Columbia is becoming a more important place, the year prosperous in general, crops good, so we too will look on the bright side . . .

. . . John . . . and his family are quite fortunate to escape the prevailing indisposition in Columbia. The prevailing waterworks were so dreadfully out of order as to affect the health of the city. Four children died, of the scholars of Nazareth. We rejoice at having been instrumental in preparing them, by instructing them. . . .

BAPTISTA LYNCH, [URSULINE CONVENT], SEPT 4th[6]
. . . Our school begins very well—already 8 pupils and we hear of others. . . .

On Tuesday Sept. 2nd Mme *Charles* and Co. left for Tuscaloosa. . . . I consider Sister Charles anything but well, and fear she is going, like her Rev Brother—however she would not defer a duty on account of her suffering state. She and Mr H. Weed of Richmond want to place in your hands a Deed of 1000 acres of land which they own in Virginia and which [is] now being rendered valuable by R.R. passing thru or near it. . . .

HENRIETTA LYNCH, CHERAW, 13th SEPT[7]
. . . If you had seen the joyfulness springing from Maries heart, to know that she could go again to the convent I am sure you would be sufficiently repaid. I think I see the joy brimming from your own countenance answering hers. . . . I trust that you will have occasion to be proud of Marie all the days of your life. I hope she will render herself worthy of her Christian education. . . .

Josie will begin his school in your mother's little house, which is nicely improved. I trust that Mr. Lynch will experience a happy turn of fortune. We have had a long trial lasting ten years it is time for a change. . . .

BAPTISTA LYNCH, URSULINE CONVENT, VALLE CRUCIS, FEAST EXALTATION HOLY CROSS, [SEPT. 14][8]
. . . When I read the articles of Education I feel as if I had some of Mr. Gilmour's desires (Boston) for a "monster-house" and well filled—or what I would like better, our schools dotted all over the country working during scholastic year, and we all reunite for Vacation, to renovate &c like this year.

Ah! My—When *can* you cease to be a "carpet-bag bishop." . . . I do trust the time is near at hand . . . when I think of *all* you have done! Surely, you have not much more that is pressing. It is wonderful the immense amount you have accomplished! No wonder that Abp. Purcell said, "no other man could have done so well"! (DG) . . .

FRANCIS LYNCH, CHERAW, SEPT. 18[9]

. . . Circumstances have placed me at disadvantage and while you have done so much to relieve them they are not sufficiently mastered, for me to assert and maintain a manful business. . . . When I look around me to see what is to be done, the fact is always the same. To prosecute business to advantage, my available means is too limited. To overcome this, I have been trying to sell lands. But for the fire I think . . . the difficulties with me would have been about surmounted. But now, with the prospect of good gains from the tanning business, which ought to yield a gain of 3000$, want of capital to employ in it shuts me off. It is not that I feel incompetency for the business, but circumstanced as I am, I have not the advantage, common to business men, of business credit.

. . . May there not be some rich Catholic who would lend me five thousand dolls for three pct. With this I wd settle outstanding debts and place about 2000$ in active tanning operations and try and turn it over 4 times a yr for making 25p[ct] each time. It requires more means to get along, and more difficulties to be overcome . . . I fear the continuance in this position may lose me my energy. . . .

JOHN LYNCH, COLUMBIA, SEPT 23[10]

I recd your telegram this morning. Went immediately to the City Clerks office for the information and find he has given to the Sheriff Dent execution for city taxes on the *convent lot* for the years 1865, 66, 67, 68, 69, 70, 71, 72, and 73, . . . Total $1820[75]. Also, on the lot near Mr. McGuinnis, for the same time [period] . . . Total $134[40].

. . . I was under the impression that you settled it. . . . There is an execution against me for this year's tax. I have shown the recpt and they claim that it was for last year. John Bauskett says: it is for this year. . . .

I am sorry to say our city fathers and clerks are seeming to run a race with the state officials and cannot be beaten fair. . . . The prospects in the present corrupt state of the government is [*sic*] decidedly poor. . . .

JOHN LYNCH, COLUMBIA, S.C. SEPT. 26[11]

. . . The patent I can hear nothing of. If I do not get relief I fear I shall be crushed. . . . So long as I could sleep well, I did not mind it so much, but remaining awake all night, trying to think how to turn for some relief, and not having found it by morning is not refreshing. . . .

JOHN LYNCH, COLUMBIA, S.C., OCT 8th[12]

. . . You say to me have courage. . . . It seems to me the times cannot get much darker. . . . Even the University is a failure this year. The trustees some time ago removed LeBorde for a . . . Revd Mr. Fox (rad), then removed Dr. Reynolds to give Dr. LaBorde a place. Since Prof. Rivers has resigned to take the prestcy of a college in Maryland his place has been filled by another *rad* who was in Chapel Hill for a while, afterwards minister to Greece; at the same time, turned out old Dr. Barnwell (the Prest) and Dr. Faber filling one of the chairs and leaving the other vacant. Dr. Le Borde is the only one of the old professors remaining. Three of the new ones are preachers, viz Babbet (Episcop) Cummings and Fox (Methodist) they have the ear of the trustees and rule, thinking themselves very smart. They have tinkered at the old concern until the bottom is about to fall out. The college opened with 6 students, all sons of professors in academic and 2 in med. class. Afterwards Sect. of State *Hayne* entered his name as Med student . . . the other two withdrew. So we have as yet in the med school, a class of one coloured individual for four professors and the demonstrator to work on.

I hardly think the legislature will make an appropriation of nine thousand dollars a year to teach even the sect. of state to practice medicine. Under the present state of things there has not yet been a lecture given, and I do not think there will be this week. The faculty held a meeting on Monday and elected Dr. LeBorde chairman for the year. Dr. Tally regretted the entering of the coloured student. Thinking it would prevent our getting a class. Mr. Fox thought it would be the means of getting a larger class than ever before, but they would be neither white nor black but Brown. He is inclined to be facetious . . . What an awkward position I am in. If I had a practice that would support me, or any thing else I could honorably do I would quit in disgust, but what can I do [?] . . .

P.S. . . . So far, I have kept my mouth shut, even at the faculty meetings. It is no fault of mine, still I feel mean.

HENRIETTA LYNCH, CHERAW, 8 OCT[13]
. . . My dearest Bishop we have been in such straits since the calamity of the fire that you would be surprised to see how we have lived on. We looked forward to the winter to brighten our prospects but as your Brother Francis does not know where to turn to get a cent he has not been able to put up a Gin . . .

I have to beg and entreat of you, my beloved Friend, to let us have some money, please we are in such need that I know if you could see all, you would do what you could. . . . There is a box of machinery at the depot for over a month I think and Mr. Lynch cannot withdraw it for want of means. Our privations are so great that I think our enemies would take pity on us.

Let me entreat of you, dear friend, to fix the property in such a way that our home will not be taken from us. But for you, we would have perished long ago, I am sure. . . .

JOHN LYNCH, COLUMBIA, S.C., OCT. 11th[14]

. . . Monday, it was found that there were only nine students, seven of them professors' sons, the other two medical students. In the afternoon Secretary of State, Hayne, registered his name as a student of medicine, whereupon the two others withdrew. Since then there has been no accession to the classes, consequently no lectures have been delivered. On Monday Dr. LeBorde was elected prest. On Wednesday Drs Tally and Gibbs handed in their resignation . . . on Thursday Dr. LeBorde handed in his expressing great regret, acting only on the advice and solicitation of friends. I was also advanced but respectfully declined, taking the ground, that when I accepted the chair I knew that at some time I would have coloured students, and that I was not answerable for the number of the class. I was employed by the trustees to teach; they were to see to providing the class. I had nothing to do with the number or colour, might only regret the smallness or that they were not brighter. This seems to please the Trustees who are put out at the resignations and say they will fill the vacancies immediately, and that the University *shall* be sustained, even if there are not half a dozen students in it. Will it, is a question. Will the Legislature be advised by the trustees and make the appropriation[?] Do you approve of my quietly remaining waiting to see what will turn up. It is true I will have to face public opinion but I have courage and can fight my own battles. . . .

BAPTISTA LYNCH, URSULINE CONVENT, VALLE CRUCIS, OCTOBER 12th[15]

. . . Our school has filled in to the capacity of the House, viz 16 boarding pupils and we have three day scholars from the *neighborhood*—one . . . is Judge Carpenters' little daughter. . . .

Mrs Pulliam arrived on Wednesday 8th—entered her retreat and today made her formal entrance into noviciate after holy Communion and received the plenary indulgence of Rule. We are mutually pleased and we trust [she] may persevere. . . .

[P.S.] Any chance for us at Washington?

BAPTISTA LYNCH, OCTOBER 13th[16]

. . . On Saturday evening—after reading what you said about your Taxes and knowing you had to pay ours too I wrote to Mrs. Carpenter requesting her to ask her husband, Judge Carpenter to call on Monday morning. . . . I consulted Mother who approved. . . . John . . . said I had done wrong in so acting &c . . . I [responded that I] hoped divine Providence would draw some good out of my mistakes . . .

This morning Judge C. called. I found him pleasant, sensible and satisfactory—says he will, with pleasure, do anything for us that he can . . . Yes, he is the judge of Columbia—he said he . . . will inquire about Taxes, assessment and see if parties will lessen the amount and let me know when he has done something. . . .

BAPTISTA LYNCH, VALLE CRUCIS, FEAST SS. SIMON AND JUDE [OCT. 28][17]

If you only knew what a delightful tonic—stimulant—sedative and ever so much else, your letters are to me you would write oftener. Yet, I should not say that either, for I would not have you fatigue your sight or self in any way, to write to me.

. . . We are still anxious for a nice German young lady of good education for a postulante for general work. We are obliged to pay out $4⁰⁰ four dollars every week for "Help" but perhaps it is more satisfactory since it is to one of Daniel's daughters and to Nate's wife we pay it. But any way, we want one good postulante to help Sr. Monica make fires etc. when they cannot come.[18] . . .

Old Mr Jacob Cohen used to say, that "a woman arrived quickly by her just instincts, at the point, which a man reached after many circuitous reasonings." Presuming on that, I am going to tell you what has often come into my mind about you. It is this—If you could select three or more among your Priests and sell them your property (legally) they, thus becoming legally the trustees of all church property and your property, will be responsible for all debt of same . . . and you . . . stay all the time at home . . . without molestation from day one, respecting money.

Oh! How happy we would all be to see you . . . go about preaching everywhere in the towns and villages you could do *so much good*. After all your fatigue north you have only collected about $600. I know *that is better* than nothing, but . . . you are not growing younger to be traveling and exposing yourself in this *way*. . . .

. . . The move of "Jay Gould" on the Wall-Street chess-board has shown the South, the necessity of creating her own cotton factories and people are warm on the subject, so, out of evil good will arise. . . .

RB CARPENTER TO BAPTISTA LYNCH, AT HOME
[COLUMBIA], OCT 28th[19]

. . . I have had several interviews with L.C. Carpenter esqr. Chairman of the
Com. Of Ways and Means of the Board of Aldermen . . . and he has assured
me that the taxes on your property shall be remitted, and I have no doubt it
will be done. I have thought it the more prudent course to ask this as a favor
to a charitable and religious institution rather than to demand it as a right in
accordance with the old maxim in reference to extricating one's hand from the
lion's mouth. . . . I have made inquiries and find the state taxes all satisfied. . . .

FRANCIS AND HENRIETTA LYNCH, CHERAW, 9th NOV.[20]

. . . A few days ago I wrote you hurriedly and now write to say that Messrs
Buist have sent to the Sheriff the Judgment in favor of G.W. Williams and
Co. with instructions to push it. My feelings would prompt me, not to trouble
you in the matter but I know you would prefer that I acquaint you of the cir-
cumstance as also, that your goodness will prompt you to help me through the
trouble, if you can.

Being all the while at the mercy of my creditors, the appalling feeling
unmans me. . . .

I had begun to have brighter hopes, for I had bargained off lands to the amt
of near 6000$ with some prospect of disposing of more, granting long terms
to the purchasers—say 1/5 or ¼ cash, the remainder in small installments,
properly secured. Yet I much fear, if pressed and sold out that my programme
will fail . . .

. . . The lands that I bot of Dr. Sanders 1180 acres for which I paid $20,000
could be deeded to you and made the security for a loan of 5000$ as estimated.
. . . I will do what I can but perhaps all my efforts may be futile. Man proposes
but God disposes. . . .

My dear Bishop and Father,

Your brother Francis has been in great distress of mind this whole day,
because he has no means to prevent the Sheriff advertising the sale of his property in this week. I beg you, do come to his assistance . . . and relieve the weight
of his mind by Telegraphic dispatch. . . .

FRANCIS LYNCH, CHERAW, 10 NOV[21]

. . . On conferring with the sheriff, I learn that before he will levy, he will
apprize Messrs B and Busit, that they can get nothing by such a course and
that they must prepay to him, the costs before he will act. So unless you
have committed yourself to the paymt I will endeavour to compromise in

the settlmt of it. . . . I hardly think this claim will be pressed under existing
circumstances. . . .

FRANCIS AND HENRIETTA LYNCH, CHERAW. S.C., 13 NOV[22]

. . . Messrs Busit and Busit advised me that they will wait thirty days on the
claims . . . Still I do not see how to meet it . . . Perhaps something is in store
for me. Much of my open lands are adapted for meadows and Col Cash tells
me that from 50 acres he will get $3000 for the hay gathered from it. So if sales
cannot be affected a good revenue may be reached in this way. . . .
My very dear Bishop and Father,

    . . . Mother Superior is dunning me for $5 weekly for Marie's board if I can
send it her, but unfortunately I have so few scholars I cannot respond to her
request. I am perfectly tortured by the straits surrounding us, just at the time
that our children have to be educated. . . . I will leave to your own generous
impulse and judgment, my very dear Bishop and Father, whether to comply
with this request or not, remaining as ever

    Your very grateful child, H. M. Lynch.

BAPTISTA LYNCH, URSULINE CONVENT, NOV. 14[23]

. . . Mr. Stephens of Georgia says he will do all he can for us, if our claim
is heard in Congress. Mr. Boyce says the same . . . but Judge Aldrich thinks
nothing can be done with present administration in power since Grant vetoed
a similar claim which passed both houses in Congress last session. Of course a
convent is the last Institution that he would favor. Still he might be overruled
if Gens Sherman and Ewing could be gained. . . .

JOHN LYNCH, COLUMBIA, S.C., NOV. 18th[24]

. . . I have been advised to have a small school house erected on all three of the
lots, and open a school in each even if it be for Negroes. This will if properly
managed exempt them from both state and city taxes. . . .

    I was introduced to the new professor who fills Dr. LaBorde's chair, (a co-
loured man). Prof Greener of the Howard School Washington, D.C. . . . I am
getting on finely with my lectures . . . [but] as yet I have no money . . .

JOHN LYNCH, COLUMBIA, S.C., DEC. 1st[25]

. . . I am selfish enough to wish you could find *two* good physicians, who would
be fully able to fill the chairs of "Anatomy and Surgery" and "Practice and
Obstetrics" who for health would be willing to move to Col and accept the
chairs in an university which are not filled, nor do I expect them to be this year,

without someone applies who has a reputation. You might find a *companion* for me. I have none in the present faculty.

FRANCIS LYNCH, CHERAW, SC, 17 DEC[26]
Messrs Busit and Busit have advised me of our having paid to them the claim they held on me, in for G.W. Williams and Co. I thank you very much, Dr Brother for this great kindness and although it now seems beyond my reach, I hope to be able to show in some measure my high appreciation of the very many acts of goodness I have recd of your noble generosity. . . .

BAPTISTA LYNCH, URSULINE CONVENT, 20 DECEMBER[27]
I do not think you could have read my several letters or you would have been here today at the earliest.

I must now beg you to come without delay—before Christmas. I am sorry we must give you this trouble. . . .

17

"I AM AT THE MERCY
OF CREDITORS"

January–June 1874

The Spanns had returned from Galveston to Washington Country where Charles tried his hand, once more, at planting, although
with regrets that he had no alternative for labor than the exenslaved. Like the Lynches in South Carolina, the Spanns much
preferred to employ Irish immigrants on their land, but the heavy
Black majority in the county kept immigration to a trickle.

Francis Lynch's selection for grand jury duty was, to him, a
strong indicator of the political winds in South Carolina shifting
in his direction. Despite being relentlessly plagued by thousands
of dollars of entangled debt which put his property in imminent
danger of being seized, Francis maintained his renewed optimism
that "brighter prospects are in store for me . . ." In his desperate
search for a path toward financial recovery, Francis devised various schemes, mostly involving land sales, by which he could secure enough capital. No matter how creative Francis' plans were,
in the end, his bishop brother's largesse was the main safeguard
against this branch of the Lynch family realizing the worst consequences of indebtedness, including the lack of the most basic
necessities of food and raiment. Once again it fell to Henrietta to
alert her brother-in-law about their dire state.

The "tax vampires," as Baptista Lynch dubbed them, spared
no one's property, even that of bishops and women religious.
The Ursulines' unoccupied town lots became a natural target of

taxation. "I have . . . almost come to the conclusion," Baptista admitted to Patrick, "that we should be broken up root and branch by them." That fear subsided considerably when a widowed postulant brought with her a substantial dowry, which provided the opportunity, at last, to build a free-standing chapel for the Ursulines and their students. Meanwhile, the convention in Columbus called to discuss strategies for achieving tax reform buoyed hopes that better times were indeed coming.

John Lynch's situation appeared to brighten when a potential agent turned up with a proposal to sell his mine to European interests. Within days, his prospects darkened again when the legislature failed to appropriate funds for a vacant position in the medical school to which John had been appointed, in addition to his regular chair. That failure raised doubts about the university's survival, and with it, that of the medical school. As John summed up the developments to Patrick, "it seems the more I struggle the more I get in the maze. There is something always in the way, just at the wrong time." The political unrest was jeopardizing business transactions, including the sale of repositories of precious metals. Within a couple of weeks, nonetheless, John, probably at the assurance of the trustees, was feeling so confident about the school's survival, that he acquired complete ownership of the mine, to maximize the income he could anticipate from any sale.

Meanwhile, his eldest son, Robert, grew increasingly desperate to escape Edgefield, a place devoid of economic opportunity but awash in violence, much of it the work of the paramilitaries resisting Reconstruction. Learning that his Uncle Patrick would soon be in Philadelphia, Robert implored his long-standing patron to find a position for him there, where he and his wife would not only have a chance to rise above their present poverty but know the sacramental blessings that their priestless church in Edgefield could not provide.

BAPTISTA LYNCH, URSULINE CONVENT,
VALLE CRUCIS 9 JANUARY[1]
. . . What is your program about going north and when will you find it convenient to give the white veil to our postulante? . . . You will be pleased to hear that she wishes to have the blessed privilege of building our Convent Chapel, and have it begun at once. She . . . may not be able to get the entire sum in hand as needed but will ultimately. . . .

FRANCIS LYNCH, CHERAW, 11 JANUARY[2]

... My efforts to better my condition financially by sales have not really availed
anything as yet ... for lack of money. But for the panic I think I wd have made
fair sales. ... Not having succeeded in the premises, I am at the mercy of creditors ... I cannot tell what is before me.

The tide of immigration will mend matters surely, but may be too late for
me, though I hope not.[3] ...

FRANCIS LYNCH, CHERAW, 15 JANUARY[4]

... I received your most welcome letter with the check enclosed in it. Another
time enabling me to bridge over hanging troubles, ... I wish I was more de-
serving of such favors.

My endeavours to sell lands, seem to me to almost be a success, but the
scarcity of money, or something else has so far defeated their fulfilment—I am
still trying. ...

MARY LYNCH SPANN, WASHINGTON CO, TX, 17 JANUARY[5]

... You are aware, my dear Brother, that since our return to the country, Mr.
Spann has been steadily aiming to get his farm in a prosperous condition once
more; by patience and perseverance he has effected something, the great difficulty is the uncertainty of labor, the Negroes being more numerous than whites
in this County, prevents immigrants from settling here; however Mr. Spann is
well pleased to have made some progress; fortunately he is blessed with very
good health and a cheerful disposition and has more energy of character than
when a young man being always interested in the politics of today both of the
old and new world; as we are faithful readers of the "Freeman's Journal," are
familiar with the awful and unnatural condition of Rome, you who are so familiar with everything there, must feel horrified, at the outrages, constantly
taking place. ...

Conlaw is doing well in a hardware store in Galveston ...

FRANCIS LYNCH, CHERAW, 21 JANUARY[6]

... In my present condition my life is wasting away. This should not be so. But
a feeling of insecurity so hinders me that it has an unnerving effect.

... It would be most gratifying, if you could [loan $3500 to] put me beyond
danger.—And then all that could be realized from sales of property and of
profits from business ...

If this cannot be done, sooner or later I may expect to be sold out. ... I
shall await with great interest your answer, for I have the hope that brighter
prospects are in store for me. ...

BAPTISTA LYNCH, URSULINES, VALLE CRUCIS, 31 JANUARY[7]

. . . Please instruct me about chapel plans which I will send you. . . . I think Mrs. Pulliam can command the money $4000—at any time . . .

I think it would be well, to advertise in the Columbia papers when we do begin—that it is a gift—for it would look badly after owing for lots and petitioning for remittance of Taxes! To start off like we had money in reserve—which we have not of course. . . .

Do you start for Nassau next week as Rev. Dr. M thinks?[8] . . . No doubt you will do great good—as you do every where you go—Madame Etienne and myself and I suppose all the rest, if they could express themselves as freely to me as she does—have come to the conclusion that we have never seen any man—even among Bishops—possess all the good and fine qualities with which Divine Providence has blessed you. . . .

JOHN LYNCH, COLUMBIA, 22 FEBRUARY[9]

I was called on a few days ago by Mr. E.B. Roberts . . . he is out here looking after an interest in a copper mine . . . hearing through Conlaw of my copper mine, . . . [he] proposes trying to sell it for me . . . I have written to Mr. Courtenay seeking some information, about him, he seems to be a business gentleman, says he has crossed the ocean fifty four times &c. &c. . . .

I have not yet been able to get the Trustees together, but expect to do so this week.—and expect to succeed . . . When I do, I will begin to think the tide has turned at last, . . . Hope is an excellent medicine, but it will not fill the pockets, or pay debts. . . .

ROBERT LYNCH, EDGEFIELD C.H., 10 MARCH[10]

. . . I have long since, come to the conclusion that farming and making money are incompatible, so that I am thrown on my pen to do it, and at present, in the south, that is very hard, if not impossible. Kate wants to go where she can have the benefit of the church, and as far as that goes, so do I. It is now over eight months since we have had Mass, and we are too poor to go to Augusta. With one word, you can get me a good place, and it would be a charity, my dear Uncle. . . . We would like to live in Philadelphia, . . . I am buried here, and what little I do know, is of no service to me. The way things are now in Edgefield it is perfectly awful; no less than seventeen murder cases on docket, four of them condemned to be hanged already this court. For God's sake, my dear Uncle, help me to leave this God forsaken country . . . I am willing to take any place that you may see fit to get me, and that you think me competent to fill. . . .

JOHN LYNCH, COLUMBIA, 10 MARCH[11]

... When I last saw you, I was in fine spirits. I thought I saw my way out of the wilderness, but it seems the more I struggle the more I get in the maze. There is something always in the way, just at the wrong time. I had every member of the board of trustees pledged to give me the salary for the Chair of Anatomy, in addition to my own, when the Legislature made a set [sic] against the appropriation for the vacant chairs, and scared them so, they were afraid to do anything, so I am as bad off as ever. My only consolation being, "what I never had I never lost."

The appropriation is now all right for this year, but I sometimes think the university will be obliged to fail, ... I am trying to prepare for it; by getting Mr. Roberts to sell the mine for me. ...

BAPTISTA LYNCH, COLUMBIA, MARCH [12?][12]

... Can not you and [Bishop Wood] together send us two good young lay sisters particularly, and a German teacher postulant? They are very much needed. The lay sisters would save us considerable expenses every week paid out to help for the washing and the German Teacher is now considered a "sine qua no" to a corps of teachers. ...

JOHN LYNCH, COLUMBIA, S.C. 26 MARCH[13]

I write to let you know that I today concluded the purchase of the balance of the Mary Mine, 3./8ths for one thousand dollars, payable 1st Nov, 71, 72 and 73, in equal installments, giving a line on my quarter salary falling due at that time, as security. ... I know I can do nothing with it just now, but times cannot last as they are, and I will try and find some one who has a fancy for dabbling in copper mines—and hope you will not forget to mention it whenever and wherever you have a good opportunity, I *now claim* the \whole mine, with charter of company &c &c. ...

The university is getting on first rate, appropriation made as last year—after passing this year I think there will be very little danger. ...

BAPTISTA LYNCH, URSULINE CONVENT, VALLE CRUCIS, 26 MARCH[14]

... It seems to me things are daily looking brighter and I trust these representatives from Tax-payers Convention, whose patience and perseverance I admire will effect a good work—which will make real estate saleable &c. ...

FRANCIS LYNCH, CHERAW, 9 APRIL[15]

. . . In the lives of the Saints, I have read of spiritual dryness. It seems to me, I am troubled in a worldly sense in somewhat the same way. The 60 acres of land I sold . . . (because of judgmts on me) had to be sold for Shffs titles. . . . This sum the Shff applies to the oldest judgmts. . . .

I think you will pardon my feelings of dejection, sometimes. Seven years is said to bring about a change, already there are some inquiries for land, a capitalist was looking at my lower plantation for a stock farm and seemed pleased with it, very likely will buy in the fall. It is admirable for that purpose. If my 1700 acres bring me at 15$ 25,500 . . . , I would like to do something in a prosperous career that would inspirit me with confidence. . . .

FRANCIS LYNCH, CHERAW, 30 APRIL[16]

. . . With . . . 2500$ . . . I could tan 3000 sides pr ann with 7000 Splits from same . . . Margin 2500. Selling all merchantable stock at a city mkt with more working capital this might be doubled. Yet now I find myself financially crippled simply because of the judgmts on me and credit gone because of them. . . . Could you not borrow six thousand dolls. for three years . . . And with proper guarantees of insurance, this tanning business is one that may well be sought after for the safe investment of funds.

Effecting an arrangement in this way, thrift and life will drive away despondency. . . .

I have to attend U.S. Court as a grand juror on 4 May. . . .

BAPTISTA LYNCH, COLUMBIA, 12 MAY[17]

. . . I have been greatly exercised on the subject of taxes and had almost come to the conclusion that we should be broken up root and branch by them—Revd Dr M is even bluer than I am. John is more courageous, but he told me we should have to pay $800 or $1000, no doubt. . . .

I wish you could send on to me $500—and we will settle afterwards—we have sent out Bills for collection, but they are uncertain—John says he will stay the sale, but I do not know if he can. . . .

BAPTISTA LYNCH, COLUMBIA, 15 MAY[18]

I . . . now, write to say we have collected money enough to pay the taxes on all but the *convent lots* . . . the state tax of which is $334.62 and beyond our ability to meet. . . .

I wish you find a purchaser . . . However, you never failed yet so I am expecting money from you in this to prevent sale. . . .

HENRIETTA LYNCH, CHERAW, 21 JUNE [19]

... I mean humbly to ask of you to give me means to get tablecloths and sheeting and longcloth for the very decency of life, until things take a better turn, if they ever do. We are very poor. In war times we were counted respectable to what we are now. We keep but one servant for two long years, just to cook, and we do the rest. ...

Please burn when read

My Beloved bishop . . . I will pray you let me have the sum of $100 for our necessities—may God reward the same.

18

"THE WIND SEEMS TO BE VEERING NOW"

July–December 1874

In the wake of the state and congressional elections in the fall of 1874, Baptista Lynch wrote her brother, "The wind seems to be veering now, and I hope things are on the mend." She was anticipating that, with Democrats regaining power both locally and nationally, economic improvement would follow, creating much more favorable conditions for solving their fiscal woes. 1874 proved not only that the political winds were veering; they were providing tailwinds of hurricane force for the Democrats. The election produced an unprecedented congressional realignment, with the Democrats who had been in the political wilderness for the past fifteen years going from a 110-seat deficit in the House of Representatives to a 60-seat majority. Daniel Chamberlain, John Lynch's choice for governor, was one of the few Republican survivors of the tidal wave that swept Democrats into office across the country. Much of the Democratic political success in the South was due to the growing terror that paramilitary bands like the Ku Klux Klan carried out against Blacks and their Republican allies. Baptista Lynch may have dismissed the exponentially rising violence as the normal political struggle for the spoils of office, but this was political violence of a magnitude that was more and more becoming a race war. The immediate message of the election was a clear repudiation of Congressional Reconstruction. The death watch began for the three states in the former Confederacy in which Republican governments survived: Louisiana, Mississippi, and South Carolina.

John Lynch's calculation was that Daniel Chamberlain, even though a Republican "and a carpetbagger," would be better positioned to improve the economy, and thus make it more feasible to sell a mine. John's chances of survival at the medical school, he also had to believe, would be far better with a Republican in the governor's mansion. But ultimately, John Lynch's fortunes rested, not with the governor, but the trustees appointed by the governor. When, at year's end, they failed to meet to make appointments for the coming academic term, John found that he "cannot study, consequently, cannot write; thereby may loose [*sic*] what I think is my opportunity in the medical world (scientifically)."

If John Lynch thought that his financial crisis could not worsen, a lawsuit brought against him and his family threatened imminent ruin. In the first year of the war, John Lynch had been made guardian of Sue Caldwell and given $3,000 to provide for her tuition and other expenses at the Ursuline Academy in Columbia. The suit charged him with fraud in using the funds to cover his own expenses, including the tuition of his own children at the academy (Apparently John Lynch had invested most of the money in Confederate bonds). Desperate for the thousands of dollars needed to satisfy the claimants, both John and Baptista turned to Patrick, the sole Lynch who had the standing to secure a loan to cover the money owed the Caldwells.

Caught in his own web of impoverishment, Francis Lynch understandably was "cast down for means to employ his energies." Debt seemingly had put beyond reach his plans for reprising the success he knew in manufacturing during the war. Channeling the Canaanite woman in the New Testament, Henrietta Lynch persisted in her appeals to her brother-in-law bishop, even in the face of his failure to respond to her earlier pleas. When one has not the wherewithal to put food on the table for her children or medicine for their sickness or other "necessaries," one can give no thought to pride in humbling oneself beyond measure.

The Ursulines themselves were experiencing the effects of the economic downturn, as evidenced by their reducing the stipend they were able to provide to their retreat director (from $60 to $50). Being named defendants in the Caldwell suit threatened to worsen their finances even more. All the more urgent grew the need for their friends in Washington to persuade Congress to appropriate $100,000 as compensation for the loss of their academy and convent. These latest lobbyists proved to be no more productive than earlier ones.

A more immediate challenge at Valle Crucis involved two Ursulines whose disruptive behavior represented the newest threat to the hallmark tranquility of the convent school which Baptista so cherished. One was a recently vowed nun, DeSales Clarke, whose erratic, at times violent behavior, endangered herself as well as others. A much more undermining force was Mary Ellen Clagett, a malcontent ever pressing to assert her independence within the community. Clarke, whom Baptista judged to be incapable of making decisions for herself, fortunately had a family in Maryland whom Baptista summoned to Valle Crucis. Both religious superior and family members concluded that she needed medical treatment.[1]

Theresa Clagett's behavior was so disruptive that Baptista ordered the Maryland native to seek treatment at St. Agnes Hospital in Baltimore, which had a section dedicated to treating persons with mental illnesses. Baptista had appealed to Patrick, who was now their canonical superior, to make clear to Clagett that she would be unable to return to their community. While in Baltimore in August, Bishop Lynch visited Clagett who, together with the Sister administrator of the hospital, pleaded that Clagett had been suffering from a medical condition that was treatable and she should be allowed to return to Valle Crucis. When Patrick reported this to Baptista, she refused to accept that as an explanation for Clagett's chronic misbehavior over the past dozen years. When Clagett subsequently requested permission to rejoin the community, it set in motion a series of events which led to Patrick and Baptista Lynch having an unprecedented falling out in their very special relationship. As superior of the Ursuline community, Baptista had always adroitly managed to maintain a certain level of independent leadership within the patriarchal structure that gave her bishop brother virtually absolute authority over them. Not this time. Patrick, perhaps still harboring some regret that his sister had dragged him into the orchestration of Augusta England's departure from the Columbia community, told Baptista that, in his judgment, she deserved a second chance in the community. Baptista, in response, professed her members fully ready to obey their bishop, so long as he would grant them at least two years' relief from her disruptive presence. And one other condition, Baptista noted. For the Community's common good, should Clagett return, conscience would compel them to declare a moratorium on receiving any postulants, so long as she remained among them. To the shock of Baptista and the rest of the community, Clagett did return, just before Christmas. When Bishop Lynch showed up for his Christmas visit, he found Baptista's mind closed to any arrangement which would allow Clagett to remain in a community which effectively had disowned her. That was, for Patrick, one disguised challenge too many. He departed without notice, leaving his sister distraught over the rupture of their relationship.

JOHN LYNCH, COLUMBIA, 10 JULY[2]

... You ask about *that tax.* I had the note discounted and paid it, but could not get the penalties removed, had to talk strong to keep them from adding *fifty* percent extra. I wrote you that a note made to pay the city taxes, falls due on the 14th and until the Trustees act for me, I will have to continue renewing, for fear you may not receive the letter I sent. I enclose a few blanks. I will use them prudently. I have recd my third quarters Salary and have made the final payment on the mine, there is now no difficulty except finding a purchaser which I am even more anxious to do now than when I saw you. ... If you remain any time in N.Y. please see Courtenay and find out if Roberts has gone to Europe. I wrote to both of them, some weeks ago, but have heard nothing from them. I fear they are tired of me. ...

JOHN LYNCH, COLUMBIA, 16 JULY[3]

The annoyance I alluded to in my last letter to you, has commenced today in the form of "U.S. Subpoena . . . "To John Lynch, C. Lynch, F. Lynch, Jno. H. Kinard, of South Carolina, and Ladies Ursuline Community of Columbia a Chartered Corporation in a bill of complaint of Susan A Caldwell by her mother. . . Agnes M. Caldwell citizens of Maryland" "The defendants are to enter their appearance in this suit in the clerk's office on or before the first Monday in August . . . if it is possible, I would much prefer . . . raising the amt. by a sale on mortgage of the mine. . . . I know you have your hands full, . . . but as the cord draws tighter, . . . no one else can I turn to with any hope. . . .

BAPTISTA LYNCH, COLUMBIA, 23 JULY[4]
... Dr. David Clarke and Miss Sallie Clarke came down day before yesterday, and he as physician says a change of air and scene are essential to preservation of mental health of his sister, and that he will with your permission, take her on north himself, at the time appointed. ... Will you please send me her "obedience" or "passport" or "furlough" for one year. ... (Of course, the Ursulines are not obliged to keep her). ...

BAPTISTA LYNCH, URSULINE CONVENT,
VALLE CRUCIS, AUGUST 1st 1874[5]
... I would so much prefer to speak, than to write our troubles—as now I must do—It seems that Satan is resolved to do his work and again (Clagett) has acted in the same way as last winter. We think she is dangerous to herself and to others—What shall we do? She may precipitate matters so that we cannot wait, but I hope not. ...

BAPTISTA LYNCH, COLUMBIA, 2 AUGUST[6]
... I think that (Clagett) is getting like one incapable of *any* self-control and that perhaps the only way to save *any* reason will be, to disengage her from every restraint possible. Therefore I would suggest to settle on her *for life* $2000 to revert either to you or to the convent who ever donates it. We have not it *now* but will charge ourselves with it, if you think it best. The convent will lose an able-bodied hard worker, but better that, than as it is. She has ... chosen her future home among her Maryland relatives, ... Outside of all religious views, she disturbs us very much just now on the eve of our Retreat ... For a year or two past there has been a weak spot on the top of her head, so tender that she could not bear the weight of her hand on it. I think physical causes contribute to the difficulties—and the habits of life are culminating. ...

BAPTISTA LYNCH, COLUMBIA, 8 AUGUST[7]
... Since writing ... our painful intelligence about (Clagett) ... [we] are anxious to hear from you on the subject. ... But taking into consideration what you say about the baptism of Aldrich and that the tempers of a woman are not precisely the thing to occupy a Bishop's time, I do not think you will. However, no one here has power to act in the case. ...
　　... Poor little De Sales is still quite feeble after her attack of diphtheria but is about again. ... The house was peaceful for awhile. ...

HENRIETTA LYNCH, CHERAW, 10 AUGUST[8]
... Our town is in great affliction. So many children with Diphtheria sick and
dead and dying. ... I trust we will be spared.

My dear beloved Father, tho it may seem impertinent to be so bold I am
put to this step involuntarily, to beg of you again a sum to carry us on thru
this season of scarcity, when Mr. Lynch does not see 10 cts, and cannot get
credit for 10 cts. I was forced to let him use the last for the house all to $25. ...
Your brother Francis is harassed to death by his debts every day. No one pays
him. ... If you will kindly give me for our present wants, please send cash in
a letter. ...

JOHN LYNCH, COLUMBIA, 15 AUGUST[9]
... I am sometimes reminded of the old man we read of name Job and am
tempted.

BAPTISTA LYNCH, COLUMBIA, 26 AUGUST[10]
... I wrote to ... Miss Clagett. Poor child! What a lesson. She could hardly
credit that I have, in an informal way ascertained the sentiments of the Community—Lay Sisters as well as Choirs—and there is but one voice respecting
her—viz—that she may never return, where she was never at peace. ... How
little did we foresee the ways of Divine Providence. But all things happen for
the best. ...

Yesterday Dr Clarke and Miss Sallie Clarke arrived and took Sister de-
Sales on North—they have acted so handsomely in every way, ... The poor
little thing looks wretchedly and I would not be surprised if she did not live to
return. She is in the best of disposition and made her Retreat well. ...

Mr and Mrs John Bauskett called today. ... His principal business was
to get me to sign a paper, prepared by M.P. O'Connor Esqr. of Charleston,
showing that *our Convent did not connive* with John in defrauding his creditors.
What an accusation! ... Mrs Caldwell and family, must belong to the Victor
Emmanuel sort of Catholics, to summon a *convent* and *you*, her *bishop*, on such
terms as these into open Court. ...

JOHN LYNCH, COLUMBIA, 29 AUGUST[11]
... With Six thousand dollars I could not only pay off the Guardian claim but
every other debt I owe outside of the family. ... If I could by any way, with the
mine, raise the money, I would at once get an order from the probate court, to
invest it securely for the time of Sue Caldwell's minority, and then ask to have
another guardian appointed. ...

BAPTISTA LYNCH, COLUMBIA, 4 SEPTEMBER[12]

. . . I have received letters from Sister Mary Ann and Miss M.E. Clagett who spoke to you, as they write I presume. But we cannot change our judgement. Has it been her health for the last 12 years?

. . . We would . . . humbly request two years reprieve, that we may enjoy awhile that religious peace, which her absence affords and which gives to our house another atmosphere—and also assure you, that should she return we would feel bound in conscience to refuse all candidates so long as she lived in our house, such has been the incalculable injury she always has done, and no doubt always will do, to the religious spirit.

. . . I write this plainly, my dearest brother, that knowing both sides you can better judge and also you may not compromise yourself in any way. I cannot tell you how *sorry* I am, that you have this trouble.

I suppose you think from the papers, that we are all commotion down here. But not at all. It is some part of the politician to make out this fuss . . . It is all nonsense and for their own monied interest, nothing more. . . .

BAPTISTA LYNCH, URSULINES, SEPT. 8[13]

. . . As to Miss M E Clagett's reports of herself—you can place no reliance on it—Would you think it well for a man to introduce a mad dog among his others—or a wild bull among his cows? We would as soon see her among us again—not one of our Community would be willing. They have borne and forborne until it ceased to be a virtue . . . and I blame myself for ever consenting to her Profession which she never kept—nor had any vocation for—so far as I am capable of judging we have sent her $10 to buy the few articles of clothing we had not, to give her and will send more and pay her board (DV) but never want to see her again. . .

BAPTISTA LYNCH, COLUMBIA, 6 OCTOBER[14]

. . . I will say nothing new about Miss Claggett . . . She knows the words of Rule and conditions of membership. Viz "that it is for the greater glory of God, the salvation of my soul, and the good of the Community" "These three conditions . . . *never* were fulfilled by her—and judging from the past, . . . her most earnest desire is to be liberated from all bondage, as she was always expressing, and go out into the World, and live independent—She was never happy in the Convent, never in her right element and it is so delightfully peaceful since she, and poor little D S—have gone! . . .

JOHN LYNCH, COLUMBIA, 7 OCTOBER[15]

... You ... remark that the "Mine difficulty is based on the political state of S.C." That being the case, I will expect to be releaved [sic] in Nov. after the election of D.H.C. I think he will be elected and have tried to persuade myself that he is the *best* man in the state for the position at this *particular time*.[16]...

BAPTISTA LYNCH, COLUMBIA, 8 OCTOBER[17]

... I do hope the affair of Miss Clagett[18] does not distress you. If you knew as much as we do, and what a good actress she is—how emotional—you would not allow it to do so....

BAPTISTA LYNCH, COLUMBIA, 10 OCTOBER[19]

... Mr B would not allow the sheriff to come out, but brought it himself. He sent me word that he had "accepted service" on it and that Mr B DeSaussure said, if we would pay ¼ ($850°°), for which we are sued $3400) in 15 days—he would not push the matter for one or two years? I wish you could borrow $4000, for us, and let us pay entirely for the lots and give a mortgage on them to whoever would lend us the $4000.

... (Shall we sue persons who owe us over a year for board and education of their children? We never have.) ... It is difficult to know which is best to do—whether to let the lots be sold at sheriffs sale (which seems to me bad, unless we could run them up on buyers—not likely now) Or, try and pay within 15 days—say 23rd inst. $850 and stay further suit for a year or two—or what I prefer—viz. Borrow $4,000—pay entirely Bond and mortgages and get rid of all debt here over lots—and sell at our own price as soon as possible.

Which of these three ways is best—and which most feasible? ...

We could wait awhile, put up a cheap fence and a couple of cheap cabins to rent @ $5, or $10 per month and make lots pay their own expenses—then sell when the government allows the sun to shine.... The wind seems to be veering now, and I hope things are on the mend.

BAPTISTA LYNCH, COLUMBIA, 14 OCTOBER[20]

... Hon. R.B. Carpenter wrote me yesterday, that he had placed our interest, in the hands of "Senator Robertson" of Columbia,[21] and had a personal interview with him, and he said he would do what he could for us—and he will prepare and present our claim or case in Washington.

I now write to let you know this, and to ask you, would you not please get some of your friends to speak to the members of Congress there, where you are, and interest them in the case, so that when it comes up in Congress, it will have such *influential backing*, that it will be sure of success? Would not "Butler" whose wife and daughter are Catholic, take an interest in it? and are there not other Catholic members who could take a *Catholic* interest in the matter—not mixing politics, for *we will not compromise ourselves in any way.* I told Judge Carpenter so, when he so kindly offered to take the matter in hand. . . .

BAPTISTA LYNCH, COLUMBIA, 20 OCTOBER[22]
Your welcome letter of date 17th is at hand with enclosed bank cheque of $850—for lots.
Thank you, thank you a thousand times for coming to our aid in the emergency. . . . how I do hate to sink your money in those old lots. But I learn there is a prospect of selling them after the elections and if so, I do hope we may be able to refund by the time you come home. . . .

If Judge Carpenter does not recover more rapidly from the effects of his fall, most likely court will not be held, and we not sued—"It is an ill wind, that blows nobody good." . . .

JOHN LYNCH, COLUMBIA, 2 NOVEMBER[23]
. . . I have no one to turn to, except mother and yourself. . . . The crushing pressure of the times would be nothing to me, individually, but as the head of a family, most of whom are dependent; and my anxiety to see them, independent, without having to submit to the many crosses, the world is always throwing in the way makes *me anxious.* Anxiety begets despondency, despondency begets a disease of the nervous system, which once established, *may* never be eradicated. This, I fear, is producing its effects on me . . . I hope that Chamberlain (although a R and Carpetbagger) will be elected gov. I believe him to be honest, and with his promises carried out . . . we will have a different state of affairs in S.C. I hope then to see confidence restored (measurably) and capital flowing into the state to develop its manufacturing and mineral resources, then will the "Mary Mine" be known, and those who have been struggling to keep the shaft in place, be relieved . . .

. . . The trustees have done nothing for me as yet. . . . I cannot study, consequently, cannot write; thereby may loose [*sic*] what I think is my opportunity in the medical world (scientifically) . . .

. . . Robt has found employment in Kinards store as . . . cashier, small salary as yet . . .

BAPTISTA LYNCH, COLUMBIA, 4 NOVEMBER[24]
. . . It distresses me my dearest brother to hear that you have been so much worried and I greatly fear that poor child—Miss Clagett has been somewhat the cause of it. . . . Poor child. I do hope she may find happiness somewhere.

She certainly never did here and has for the last ten years, at least, been begging for the liberty she now possesses and the association of her family in Maryland. . . .

BAPTISTA LYNCH, COLUMBIA, 18 NOVEMBER[25]
. . . "DeSaussure Miller and party would not come to terms so Bauskett and they will only have to fight it out in Law. Rev. D^r M said I had better put the $850 out at interest for five years @ 7 percent . . .

Now, that the elections are over, and every one seems to see the 'silver lining to the cloud," we will expect cotton to advance and for money to become more generally circulated. Please advise me what to do with your money . . .

In my last I enclosed the copy of my letter to Miss M.E. C. St Agnes Hospital.[26] . . . It always makes me feel so uncomfortable to act without knowing that you approve fully of what I do—even when I feel that I have done right, as in this instance. I know were you here, you would see as we do. . . .

HENRIETTA LYNCH, CHERAW, 22 NOVEMBER[27]
. . . This 29th inst. will be the birthday of your brother Francis. . . . There is a gift I wish you to extend to him—An overcoat with cape as is now worn, sent by Express. Mr. L lent the Dr his shawl years ago to go North and it was lost by him, he has nothing fit since.

The next gift I desire you to extend to my family wants is the sum of $100— not being unmindful of past sums and favors, but trust Oh! Ever so much, of your leniency and native goodness, mon bon Père. . . .

BAPTISTA LYNCH, COLUMBIA, 18 DECEMBER[28]
. . . Yesterday another letter came from [Miss Clagett], the same threat repeated and snapping her fingers in our face since she had you to back her, and our voice was nothing.

This morning, she arrived . . . and forced herself upon us—against our expressed will. Again I consult the wish of the Community—and they are unwilling to have her association.

I have not seen her—treated her as an unwelcome guest, but given her every bodily comfort—until you act, we are powerless. . . .

FRANCIS LYNCH, CHERAW, 22 DECEMBER[29]
. . . It is an old adage "tis better be born lucky than rich." And so I felt and had reason to feel so, when a few days ago, Henrietta took me into a room and showed that in opening a package received by Express from N. York so hand-

some and elegant [an] overcoat from Drolan and Co. N.Y. that my feelings of gratitude to the donor were indescribable. . . . Needing just such an article, . . . be sure it was selfishly appropriated, and most highly appreciated. . . .

JOHN LYNCH, COLUMBIA, 30 DECEMBER[30]

. . . Outside of the mine, if I get the expected help from the Trustees, I see my way clear of debt, but with a sale as you proposed, I can get along independently. . . .

BAPTISTA LYNCH, COLUMBIA, 28 DECEMBER[31]

My Darling precious Brother,

I am miserable, at the thought of giving *you* pain. It distresses me, that in doing, what I conceive my duty, you are displeased. I never could endure to displease any superior, how much less *you*, my ever kind and loving brother. Not only my eyes, but my very heart weeps at the remembrance of your troubled appearance. My every breath seems an aspiration for you. Oh! How I wish, we could judge differently—

I do hope, your letter for New Orleans may bring a favorable reply. If not, we will for love of *you*, reconsider your last proposition, much as we know it will cost us—

Revd Dr M returned, saying he had seen you off on the N.Y. train. . . .

How can I wish you a happy New Year? And yet I will for where God is, there is happiness and I know He always dwells in your heart and soul. . . . [32]

I embrace you my dear precious brother, and Kneel in spirit—asking your blessing and prayers. . . .

19

"OUR BLESSED LITTLE ANGEL
BREATHED HER LAST
ON MONDAY MORNING"

January–June 1875

For Baptista Lynch the first five months of 1875 must have been wretched ones. She found herself estranged from her "dearest brother," the one she ever wanted to be in contact with, if not physically, then at least by mail. Yet it seems that from the beginning of the year until June, no letters were written, nor visits made. In the latter month, Patrick had taken the initiative toward reconciliation, probably by a surprise visit. During which he learned of the tax due on the town lots, which he subsequently paid, providing the opportunity for Baptista to feel free to resume her cherished, if all too one-sided correspondence.

To keep his finances afloat John Lynch desperately tried to salvage two major investments (the mine and the Beaufort lots) which both seemed to be lost causes. His major potential source of income—his faculty position at South Carolina University— was in danger of being eliminated with the proposed closure of the medical school in reaction to Blacks dominating its rolls. John's plan was to secure a top-notch physician to teach part of the curriculum, with John teaching the rest. In one stroke it would raise the academic standards, essentially to ensure that few, if any, students graduated. This was reform, born of desperation that might be seen as protecting the academic integrity of the institution but was also clearly intended to provide financial relief for its promoter.

Francis Lynch, despite his various efforts to increase his revenue, including the allocation of more of his land to sharecropping, still found it necessary to depend upon his bishop brother to meet his outstanding debts, which were compounded by the irascible behavior of a business partner as well as by the taxes the Reconstruction government imposed upon all property owners. If only for his brother's sake, Francis projected an optimism that the return of prosperity to his family was very much on the horizon. He professed to be more concerned with Patrick's precarious health, a concern shared broadly within the extended Lynch family.

Francis's economic misfortunes may have reduced the family to a poverty level they never expected to know, but Henrietta was determined to maintain their middle-class status, at least by keeping up a certain genteel appearance publicly. So, she, like her husband, turned to her brother-in-law for money, not to stave off the bill or tax collectors, but to dress for church in the way the Lynches had long been accustomed. Indeed, their situation had become so precarious that Henrietta decided to celebrate their twentieth wedding anniversary rather than wait another five years for the traditional milestone, little knowing what their condition would be by then. So, for June 26, they planned a modest marking of their two decades of family building, along with the ninth birthday of their youngest, Theresa, who was, at least to her aunt, the child with the most promise. By the time that day arrived, celebration had given way to a deathwatch in the Francis Lynch family.

LOUISA BLAIN, CHERAW, 29 JANUARY[1]
. . . I think only one of H[ennie]'s children will take after their great Uncle. Kate Theresa, is very bright and intelligent, fond of reading, reads well and understands what she does read. Fond of books and has a very inquiring mind. Unfortunately she will not take after him in good looks. . . .

FRANCIS LYNCH, CHERAW, 28 FEBRUARY[2]
It has come to my mind that you have been quite unwell, in New York, and I can assure you—all of us were very much grieved. And join in the hope that you have fully recovered, and request that you will come home and rest yourself. . . . Rest and quiet are great restoratives and we hope you will have recourse to them. . . .

FRANCIS LYNCH, CHERAW, 5 MARCH[3]

The pleasure shared by all of us, in learning from your letter, of your improved health and return to the city can better be imagined than expressed. For the contents (the ck) in yours, please accept my sincere thanks. It was unkind in Mr W. to have written you on this matter. However the settlemt is made and he is paid in full.

I am sorry I cannot yet apprize you of having made any perfect sales of land though I had much of it bargained off. This year I have rented for cotton near 200 acres, to be manured by the renters, who are to pay ¼ of gross crops—my bearing ¼ of the cost of fertilizer as shall be purchased and applied—The income from this crcp, ought to bring near six dolls. p^r acre while the area rented for grain crops ought to bring more being of larger extent. . . .

Meanwhile I would like to borrow on the basis of rents 400$ for a short time to cover my taxes, payable the 14th of this month—More than this sum is promised me by four parties, owing me; but I fear their coming in time. And taxes are inexorable. . . .

FRANCIS LYNCH, CHERAW, 21 MARCH[4]

Thinking it probable you have returned to the city . . . I feel impelled to trouble you in the matter of my taxes, to meet them I lack about three hundred dolls. The treasurer has waited on me a week, and I much fear the penalty of 20 p^{ct} will be incurred, if they are not paid in a day or two. If you can assist me pray do so. . . .

FRANCIS LYNCH, CHERAW, 22 MARCH[5]

This afternoon I recd your telegram, . . . and called on the county treasurer. . . . He will await the transmission of the money, which please send to me 300$ p^r Express . . .

. . . Most anxious on my part to turn the tide. . . .

FRANCIS LYNCH, CHERAW, 24 MARCH[6]

Last evening it was my good fortune to receive yours of 20th together with its enclosure ck for four hundred dolls. As I had not drawn on you, I made use of the ck and will finish paymt of taxes this morning. . . .

HENRIETTA LYNCH, CHERAW, 19 APRIL[7]

I write to you this letter that by your helping hand I may get relief I now need. I need an outfit to wear at Church by which I may look genteel, at least and know you would wish to see me have it . . . Music scholars, because of the stillness of business, fail me. You know how embarrassed my dear husband is, between his debts and the strife to keep up with those he keeps around farming. . . . Our children keep at home see no pleasure. Since the war I have to give up to them sometimes a pair of shoes, and many little things. This is why I am often as now, unable to be genteel in my dress to attend Church. . . . May God's hand be extended to bless you, whose hand has been ever ready to help our family, is a prayer I now make and hope to make forever more on behalf of my best friend.

If you can let me have $30 I take the great liberty asking this sum.

HENRIETTA LYNCH, CHERAW, 23 MAY[8]

. . . The 26th of June next, is the 20th Anniversary of our Marriage and . . . instead of waiting for the 25th Anniversary, when I will be older and less able to enjoy it, I will ask a favor with the clinging of a child towards a parent. I beg you . . . to make me a present of a sum of money, whereby I can relieve some of my immediate wants. . . . This day the 26th was made doubly a festive day by the birth of Francis of whom I hope God will make another priest. . . .[9]

FRANCIS LYNCH, CHERAW, 23 MAY[10]

. . . I feel much more confidence in the mastering my business and that the tide is on and upward. That a prosperous career is opening on me I am truly indebted to your exceeding great kindness. . . .

BAPTISTA LYNCH, COLUMBIA, 1 JUNE[11]

How good and kind of you to send me that money to pay for *those lots*. I am so afraid you embarrassed yourself to do so. . . . The $1500 I have given you credit for on our books. . . . How relieved and thankful I am to get it! (D.G.) . . .

FRANCIS LYNCH, CHERAW, 26 JUNE[12]

. . . When I wrote to you that our daughter baby had diphtheria, I little thought of its becoming such a serious case. The Dear child is yet in an exceedingly critical way, and we all dread danger. Daughter and Marie are up this week, because of her low state. May we ask you to be mindful of her. . . .

JOHN LYNCH, COLUMBIA, 28 JUNE[13]

I have today finished my duties at the University until next Oct. Unless I can get the Trustees to elect a competent professor to fill the vacancy in the Medical School, I will be transferred into the Academic course to lecture on Comparative Anatomy, Physiology, and Hygiene. The larger number of the class will be Negroes.

As the law does not require but two professors in the Medical School, I propose to say to the trustees, that if they will procure the services of a first class physician who will undertake to teach Anatomy, Surgery, and Obstetrics, I will teach Mat. Med. Physiology and Pract. Med. thereby filling all the necessary chairs. A Demonstrator of Anatomy can be easily procured. If we commence by placing the standard of examination high it will matter very little who attends the lectures so we have a class, they cannot graduate until they stand the examination, which in every case shall be written in the presence of the professors without any assistance from notes, mem-books or other students, and 75/100 being the lowest mark for graduation.

In your travels have you met any one qualified, whose health would be benefited by a residence in the South during the winter months, who you think could be induced to accept the position[?]

. . . I am beginning to become seriously alarmed. I see no prospect of selling the mine, hear nothing from Roberts, have written again to Courtenay but have heard nothing from him, and to crown all I learned the other day that the Beaufort property had been advertised and sold for taxes. . . . I will have to redeem it, if possible, for I consider it valuable as wharf lots, if Beaufort ever grows, which is probable. The judgement I told you of one a note of $425—with interest has been pressing me. I have made an offer to give my last quarters salary, due Oct. 31 in payment and the party accepted the proposition, the quarter due July 31 is all promised to the Bank and a few small accts for my goods for the girls I will have to turn around for the money to support the table, and pay Mrs Caldwell's interest when it comes due, also the balance due in the Bank.

So you see I have cause to feel alarmed. . . .

LOUISA BLAIN, CHERAW, 28 JUNE [14]
I can only say that our blessed little angel breathed her last on Monday morning at ½ past one. I do not know how I will stand it. I try hard to be reconciled but it is so hard. She spoke up to the last moment . . . We are all fatigued, but I fear for Ma and Hennie they have gone through so much. Hennie has had palpitation of the heart which has given her great fright. I think after getting some rest she will feel better. She begs me to say to you that if there is any one she would like to see it is you and begs of you if you come to Charleston next month to come up and see her as she wishes to speak to you on matters of importance. Mr Lynch is better and stronger than he was last evening. . . . What would we not give to have you with us at this time. Pray earnestly for the others not to get sick. . . .

20

"OUR POOR HEARTS
ARE BROKEN"

July–December 1875

In Theresa Lynch's sudden death from the diphtheria epidemic that struck Cheraw in the early summer, Henrietta found consolation in the knowledge that her youngest would be spared the loss of innocence that comes with adulthood and a cruel world from which parents could no longer shield them. Henrietta took the occasion to remind Patrick of what he knew too well: that he was the mainsheet anchor for her family, its ultimate security. A reminder that twice accompanied her plea for new support: providing the tuition for their daughter Ellen to continue the family tradition of having their girls educated under the guidance of their Ursuline aunt. As Henrietta explained to her brother-in-law late in the year, despite teaching music for the past four years, the family could still not live without charity. And to make matters worse, Francis's workmen had abandoned him, presumably because of his failure to pay them. Locals, she told Patrick, could not figure how such an upright man as Francis could fail to prosper. Sadly, character too often is a liability in the pursuit of prosperity.

John Lynch's frustration about the ostracism he had endured as a physician in Columbia boiled over when his own parish priest, his patient, sought medical treatment from a local non-Catholic doctor. It suggested that John's failure to support himself and his family by his medical practice might stem as much from a boycotting of university faculty as from the poverty of his patients. As he admitted to his bishop brother at one point, "I have little practice," whether it be per fee or (in effect) pro bono. As for his greatest potential asset, his mine, John increasingly worried that he had made a grave mistake in entrusting virtually all its documentation to a foreigner who seemingly had disappeared. Meanwhile too many of his boarders were acquaintances who had invited themselves and paid nothing. The financial stress had serious psychological consequences which John was all too aware of from his inability to concentrate on his scientific investigations. Writing itself became difficult. Worse, his inability to assist his sons in establishing themselves affected their health as well, as the malaise became intergenerational.

His best chance of securing a dependable income continued to be the university; only now his best hope lay with an appointment, to a chair of science, in the college rather than in the medical school. At least his supporters within the university had indicated that the trustees were so inclined. Of course, all depended on the legislature's appropriating the funds, as well as acting favorably on Lynch's claim that he was owed house rent for the six years he had been on the university's faculty.

Relations between Baptista and Patrick did not immediately return to normal. The summer apparently passed without a single letter from the Ursuline to her brother bishop. In the past, it was not uncommon for Baptista to write Patrick several times in a single week. When she did write in late September, she indicated that her information about his doings came from others within her network. As she pointedly noted about his intentional silence, "I am very thankful ever to hear of you, since you will not let us hear from you." Despite the awkwardness pervading her letter, the Ursuline could not refrain from nagging her brother, in her inimitably oblique manner, about penning a pastoral letter to promote the Jubilee or Holy Year which Pope Pius IX had declared.

HENRIETTA LYNCH, CHERAW, 11 JULY[1]

Our poor hearts are broken! Sad affliction has come upon us! Our little baby is not here now, to follow us step by step and fling her little arms around us to comfort us—My drink is mingled with my weeping. I am all alone, alone. We all made an idol of her and knew it not. The first time her fears were displayed she said "Ma am I going to get better." "Yes, my Darling you are going to get better." "Ma Ma make me say prayers." And I did so. This she did whenever by our cries her fears were moved. On the first night of her agony—which lasted a week—after resisting as it were the power of death, a faintness came and the loving angel threw one arm around her father's neck, drew him to her mouth and kissed him, threw the other arm around me; did the same and then let fall one arm to becon [*sic*] her dear Ma Blain to come to get *the Kiss*.

As her father enters the door at night he misses the Angel of Light! . . . Almighty God has cared for her sensitive heart; she could not pass thro this rough world. Those little fingers so delicately formed, that none but an angel could press without pain will now touch the Harps that stand in the presence of the God of Hosts. The sweet prayer taught her by her Ma Blain was lisped with her dying breath and our little prayer—My God I love every body. Her last words to her Doctor. I am *mighty sick*. Three minutes more and her last breath mingled with the breath of Angels, and her pure soul passed. The little birds of the air who were coming at that first hour of the Sabbath morn to "sing out their lay"[2] Let the tearing of our hearts be expressed in her own dear little song: "Oh! How I loved her *none* can tell." Our sweetest nightingale

. . . We have all been very sick. Your dear brother sank under the blow, saying he could not be reconciled. He loved the child too dearly. God, no doubt, has come to his assistance. I want to give all to God in future. I want to meet my child, but, I want badly to see you that you may calm my soul. . . .

LOUISA BLAIN, CHERAW, 23 JULY[3]

. . . My intention to become a religious is still the same—and all those doubts and objects that I spoke to you about when I last saw you, have been removed. My earnest desire is to join before this year is out about 8th Dec at the furthest.

. . . The other day Hennie . . . was telling me how much Ma felt being separated from me and how she did not think she had the strength to stand it. . . . I wish you to reflect and answer me . . . as you have always been *my Beacon* in life. I beg . . . of you to . . . say if, I am obliged to give up all thought of a religious life during my mother's life time; . . . I cannot see it in that light for I may stay on and never be able to give her much help. . . . The only thought is to save my soul and to retire for the rest of my life. . . . A very great change has come over me since the last two months and I believe some times I have no heart as I do not feel for others as much as I did at other times. All this makes me very unhappy and unsettled in mind; I think my people should give me more encouragement when I wish to do what is right. . . .

JOHN LYNCH, COLUMBIA, 28 AUGUST[4]

. . . This has been a hard year for me. Very little practice and poor pay. Robt and John are getting such small salaries they are unable to assist me. Robert has been able to pay me only five dollars a week for himself and family. . . . Mrs

Jno Spann and Son with us since May. Hattie Keitt spent two months, and Mary Henderson three months on a visit. Self-invited all this takes money. You can imagine if I am not busy practicing, that I must be trying to furnish a table and procure necessaries for a large family. Half of whom are invalids. I do try to study but I can neither read nor write with any satisfaction. . . . Do you see any prospect for me soon. . . .

HENRIETTA LYNCH, CHERAW, 13 SEPTEMBER[5]
. . . We have been affected by severe coughs and cold.

Your dear Brother, Francis is struggling on, but has so severe a trial he can with difficulty find workers, his old ones, Munson and Cadieu, having left him. I don't see how he stands it—all his affliction and these daily crosses. . . .

As time passes so rapidly it is now the season to think of sending our daughter Elinor to the Convent, that she may have the same advantages as her sister, above all as they both have to subsist by teaching. We are trying hard to get her there by October, and hope we may succeed.

Again your child, H.

BAPTISTA LYNCH, COLUMBIA, 11 OCTOBER[6]
We were very happy to hear of you, through a letter from Sister de Sales Clarke, at the Ursuline Pittsburg—who wrote and mentioned that you had the kindness to call after receiving my last letter, and give her her enclosed note—

I am very thankful ever to hear *of* you, since you will not let us *hear* from *you*

Our school is more prosperous this year than last, and our House crowded for this season—having 14 scholars (D.G.) . . .

JOHN LYNCH, COLUMBIA, 9 NOVEMBER[7]
. . . Of course I cannot say anything certain about the University, but believe if the appropriation is made for it, I will be included as a prof in the Scientific department. I have also a claim before the Trustees (not yet taken up) for compensation for house rent, for the past six years. If they can get it up, before the sitting of the Legislature, the chance is that I will receive it, If I do I will feel comparatively easy—and can read and study with some satisfaction, an impossibility as matters now are. . . .

HENRIETTA LYNCH, CHERAW, 1 DECEMBER[8]
We received your dear letter including the check—actions, of charity, such as these are rewarded by God, alone. . . . He, who rewards even a cup of cold wa-

ter, given in His name, will look down upon this very deed of yours and record it with the hundreds of others you have extended.

We are all anxious to teach but find it hard here, to get scholars, without scholars we are very badly off. The academy carries off the few who learn. . . . I know it will please you to hear me say that I have taught music for 3 or 4 years it was a great help, but as we have such expenses it is on this account we have to call on you so, . . . Every body says Mr. Lynch ought to prosper, he is such a good man. My beloved bishop, accept again our love and kindest wishes. It is all we have. . . .

BAPTISTA LYNCH, COLUMBIA, 31 DECEMBER[9]
New Years Eve 1875

We have been expecting the pleasure of a visit during this Xmas. Octave and especially on the Feast of Holy Innocents, but this year you have disappointed alike children and nuns. . . . When you do come I hope the rainy season will have given place to sunshine. Your presence will bring that to our hearts anyway. . . .

21

"NO ONE THINKS HER
CONVERTED"

January–June 1876

For John Lynch the walls of indebtedness continued to close around him. Lacking a horse in an area where house calls are an expected part of any doctor's practice proved a major deterrent to the maintenance of his practice, much more its expansion. That liability further solidified the poor reputation that misfortune and his perceived collaboration with the Radical government had established. Despite his enlightened approach to medical care, his practice continued to regress, the victim of an overcrowded profession in an area still struggling to recover from the economic devastation the war brought. That he was a Catholic scalawag only further diminished his ability to attract patients.

He reported to his brother that "the spirit of retrenchment is running wild through the legislature," the consequence of the anti-tax, anti-Reconstruction movement, and the foreshadowing of the barebones government which full Redemption would bring. An austerity program, for John Lynch, had all-too-real consequences, inasmuch as his university salary was his major source of income. Despite his protracted efforts, potential buyers failed to materialize for his next best asset, his undeveloped mine. Nor could his children provide any relief. The third Lynch generation fared no better than their elders in finding their way in the New South.

As he awaited the legislature's action regarding his future in the university, John Lynch continued to teach his all-Black class.

When those few students did surprisingly well on an exam that he himself found challenging, instead of complimenting the students for attaining scores in the C to A-plus range, Lynch took the unexpected high scores as a confirmation of the special treatment the Blacks need in the form of lectures, textbooks being beyond their grasp. With his scientific bent, one would expect that he would want to test their ability to comprehend written material as well as the oral intake from his lectures, but prejudice provides no incentive for conducting such a comparison. In closing his mind to the possibility that Blacks have an intellectual horizon that can expand under the right circumstances, Lynch shortchanged his Black students' academic prospects. Nonetheless, the experience appeared to be but further confirmation of a discovery that John Lynch had made quite late in life: that he could best practice medicine through teaching the doctors of the next generation.

When, in late March, the legislature finally passed the act that assured his position, John Lynch felt on the cusp of the economic salvation he has been seeking for far longer than he cared to remember. All the more crushing was the disappointment of learning, six weeks later, that he would have to wait the better part of a calendar year to receive his salary. From the governor John Lynch got the disturbing news that it was very unlikely that the legislature would approve the faculty position in the university that John was so banking upon for economic relief. It would seem that John Lynch was a payback victim of Reconstruction politics for casting his lot with the "Radical University."

Francis who, like John, continued to use his connections to the Republican governor to advance or protect his interests had no more success with Chamberlain than he did with any other prospects for aid outside of his family. His immediate family's condition continued to be dire, lacking the most basic provisions. Their situation was made even more critical when the matriarch, Eleanor, arrived from Valle Crucis for the summer. Henrietta once more had to go on rhetorical bended knees to her most dependable rescuer, to beg yet again for relief from the wolf at the door.

The Lynches also came to take responsibility for their deceased sister Julia's two children, Sarah Phoebe and Conlaw Pinkney. In 1862 Eustace Pinckney had remarried. Gravely concerned that his children by Julia were receiving no Catholic formation in a household with a Protestant stepmother, Patrick Lynch, in the spring of 1876, arranged for Phoebe and Conlaw to move to Valle Crucis, Phoebe to become a student and Conlaw to join his cousin, Jimmie, in working on the farm under William Meriwether's supervision.

More than a year after Baptista defied her brother's decision to allow Mary Ellen Clagett to rejoin the community, the Ursuline superior relented, citing a vow that she took that if God restored Madame Etienne to health, Baptista would once more allow Clagett to wear the habit at Valle Crucis. Harboring no illusions about Clagett's reformation, Baptista was pleasantly surprised at the positive impact the reclamation of their prodigal member had upon the community which had unanimously chosen to expel her.

The centenary of the nation's independence proved to be a major celebratory occasion even in South Carolina. Charleston, at the epicenter of a second major rebellion, had its own special celebration on the Fourth. Perhaps the eagerness to celebrate national independence reflected their own growing anticipation that South Carolina, along with the other former Confederate states, would soon know their own, if limited, autonomy, free of foreign military occupation.

BAPTISTA LYNCH, COLUMBIA, 24 JANUARY[1]

... The enclosed letter explains itself—I cannot account for such a change in myself. You must have offered the Holy Mass, for that intention. It must be the fruit of prayer—for when Mm Etienne was so low, I promised the almighty that if He would restore her to health I would—so far as in me lay—give the Habit to Miss C[2]—No one thinks her converted yet all have concurred and some are gratified at seeing mercy shown to her. It has had a good effect in every way I believe and we are doubly happy, in being able to contribute to your wishes and happiness ...

JOHN LYNCH, COLUMBIA, 8 FEBRUARY[3]

... I suppose you see by the papers that the spirit of retrenchment is running wild through the whole legislature. Already they reduced the salaries twenty per cent, and they may probably abolish some of the chairs before they are done. If they do, mine will go first. This is a fine prospect for me, with my first quarter salary on to Feb 1st, already anticipated, on my note to E.I Scott and Son ... My Insurance $50 [due on the] 28th State and City taxes to meet, and Cantwells judgement, about $375⁰⁰ only stayed until May 1st. . . . and Mrs Caldwell's interest to be met next Nov. Is not this a frightful condition to be in, especially when I have only the balance of my salary to depend on, together with what little may be made from the boarders (which is very little), and my small practice. I did hope to get the practice of the Penitentiary, after the legislature leaves. But the salary is now only $500 a year, with a prospect of being reduced to $300. I do not think I can afford to pay a daily visit the year round at that price. I also hope to get from the trustees something in place of house rent, due as professor, but with the spirit of retrenchment and the antagonism existing between the governor and other members of the board of trustees I fear my chance is small. Looking at all these points I sometimes become confused and would like advice. I know I have reduced my indebtedness during the past year about nine hundred dollars and expected to reduce it at least five or six more this year, but you see my present prospect. If my position in the college falls, I will not be able to live in Columbia. . . . If I could find someone who would lend me enough money to pay out my indebtedness in full, and enable me to purchase a good horse, as to put myself in the way of practice again, I might . . . support the family and pay out. I know that I understand my profession as well as anyone in the country and if I could get myself before the people properly, I could command a practice, if the patients would pay. . . . I had great hopes from the family at one time, but am getting discouraged and fear they are also. . . .

BAPTISTA LYNCH, COLUMBIA, 17 FEBRUARY[4]

Did you remember that this is the famous anniversary of the burning of our convent by the Federal Army under Genl Wm T. Sherman? As usual we give half day's holiday to our pupils and keep it, a sort of thanksgiving day, for our preservation in that awful time from all dangers and insults to Ursulines and pupils.

God is very good to us—how truly grateful we ought to be for the many blessings we enjoy! . . .

JOHN LYNCH, COLUMBIA, 1 MARCH[5]

By reference to the papers, you will see that I have to commence lent, not only by fasting, but with trouble, occasioned by the striking out of my professorship from the list in the general appropriation bill, this occurred from my not having attended the legislative meetings, and bolstered up my claims. I knew nothing of it until I read the bill this morning. I was shocked for a little while, seeing all my castles (in air) for the year, demolished. But after Mass, went to the State House and saw the Chairmen of the Committees who both excused, or tried to excuse themselves by saying they had been deceived as to what I was doing—were informed that I was doing no duty. I referred them to Trustees report, in which I am reported as delivering five lectures during the week, and examining applicants for licence [sic] as pharmaceutists [sic]. I happened to receive two applications this morning appointing a day to come before me for examination. Those I exhibited, showing the expense and inconvenience to them if obliged to go to Charleston for examination. This had considerable effect and I hope if the bill is approved by the Governor, to have a bill amending the bill passed, so as to restore me to my position, or rather pay. . . . Judge Willard thinks I will succeed, but if I do not, I will not be able to pay taxes, or debts; which I hoped to clean out this year, with the exception of what I owe to you, and Mrs Caldwell. . . . The Gov. has not done anything about brother Francis's business yet. I think he will wait for the legislature to adjourne. I have not had a chance to speak to him since you saw him. Except for a few moments this morning, on my own case; he seemed worried, very much. . . .

JOHN LYNCH, COLUMBIA, 4 MARCH[6]

. . . The trustees . . . tell me to go on. I shall receive my pay, as long as they keep me in office. . . . I have continued my lectures, and attended the faculty meeting today as if nothing had happened. There was no allusion to it in the meeting, which looks significant. . . .

FRANCIS LYNCH, CHERAW, 6 MARCH[7]

Your truly valued favor of 3rd inst is recd together with your ck for $350 enabling me to pay my taxes. I cannot sufficiently thank you for this great kindness, in addition to the many favors for which I am so greatly your debtor.

This year nearly every acre of my open lands is occupied and with the blessing of God the returns from them, will be better than ever . . .

BAPTISTA LYNCH, COLUMBIA, 12 MARCH[8]

. . . I saw John lately. He is very busy with those state-house people and writes me that you sent up C to look after his interest. . . . He is so disappointed that he failed to get that office for Francis but mother and I say it is for the best. He would be handled in the newspapers like others and censured perhaps by the envious. . . .

JOHN LYNCH, COLUMBIA, 19 MARCH[9]

. . . I made the effort to amend the appropriation bill, passed the house without dissenting voice, but in the Senate, Beverly Nash opposed it, and called for the Ayes and Noes. . . . It was killed. I made another effort . . . the House insisted on the amendment, and called for a committee of conference, this was appointed on Friday last and will meet tomorrow or Tuesday. The Prest of Senate (Glover [?]) told me he would appoint a favourable committee and Nash should not be on it. . . . I have feard they might not get it through before they adjourn which will be on Thursday. . . , have held my intermediate examinations on Friday, am gratified and surprised at the result. I gave as questions, what would have been considered a very good paper for Medical Students. Their answers range from 74 to 94 (100 being considered maximum) and this from my lectures alone, unassisted by text books, proving to me that knowledge can be communicated to a crude mind better by teaching through lectures than from books. . . .

. . . I begin to think teaching is my vocation. . . .

JOHN LYNCH, COLUMBIA, 22 MARCH[10]
. . . The Act has passed both houses and only awaits the signature of the Gov. to become a law. Tomorrow I expect to draw the first quarter's salary, at the rate of two thousand a year. This will last till next Nov. . . .

JOHN LYNCH, COLUMBIA, 11 MAY[11]
. . . Practice is so very poor here, and so many physicians striving for that. I have been thinking of getting up a course of lectures on the principle [sic] processes in the body, and taking a trip up the country this summer, to see if it would not pay. I understand we are to receive no more salary—until next Febry. I must look out for other means. . . . .

JOHN LYNCH, COLUMBIA, 13 JUNE[12]
. . . Dr M is in rather a peculiar condition . . . I fear you will have to give him relaxation from duties, and let him have change of scene for a while. He is running too long in one grove, beginning to wear. It is change, not medicine that he needs, although he has functional derangements which may ultimately prove serious, brooding over them only makes them worse—change might dispel them. . . .

HENRIETTA LYNCH, CHERAW, 28 JUNE[13]
. . . Your dear mother has arrived safely and is well. I feel I must ask you if you can possibly give us any help you will kindly do so, for we are really in need of provisions . . . We could establish a Convent of perpetual Abstinence verily! I know you are much pressed for money but I leave it to yourself. I will tell you the thing just as it has been. Mr. Lynch passed thro' his humily [sic] asking the store keepers to let him have without success. [sic] He has had his trial of it. I know if you can I do not ask in vain. I leave it all to God.

22

"VERY MUCH ENTHUSIASM PREVAILS FOR THE SUCCESS OF THE DEMOCRACY"

July–December 1876

In 1849, Patrick Lynch had successfully utilized Charleston's newspapers to lobby for artesian wells as the chief source of the city's water supply. A quarter-century later a local drought provided an occasion for expanding the well system that municipal officials had adopted at Lynch's urging. In the summer of 1876, the city council formed a committee, headed by Lynch, to assess the feasibility of expanding the city's artesian well system. Subsequent testing by Lynch convinced him that the new well would meet the city's expectations.

Civic service may have put Charleston in Patrick Lynch's debt, but it could not eliminate the pressing debts, not only those of the diocese which he headed, but his personal financial obligations, many, if not most of which accrued from his on-going assistance to a very extended family. The kinfolk now pleading for Patrick's monetary support included the third generation of Lynches. But his siblings and their spouses remained the chief sources of familial solicitations of his assistance. That assistance was largely made possible from loans the bishop was forced to take out. How much, if any, of his benefactions to family and friends derived from his fundraising tours, we do not know.

Baptista Lynch discovered, in William Meriwether's protracted absence from Valle Crucis just how crucial his presence was to maintaining the needed discipline for her nephews working the farm. Even if he proved unable to meet his responsibilities as chaplain, still his very presence ensured the good behavior of her nephews. As it was, the family workforce at Valle Crucis kept changing with relatives leaving and coming for various reasons.

A dozen years into the Valle Crucis era, Baptista at last realized that they could no longer sustain themselves by relying on the income derived from tuition and board as well as the farm. The size of the manor house prevented any expansion of enrollment. With Meriwether's absence, the farm was no longer producing what they previously could expect from it. Given those stark realities, Baptista had to look to her original plan of satellite communities to begin schools that would provide the revenue to sustain them. All the while she was suffering from what John Lynch eventually diagnosed as hookworm, which would explain the fatigue and out-of-sorts feelings of which she increasingly complained. Baptista's off-hand remark that she had "gotten to dislike the pen so much" suggests that John's suspicion that something was seriously wrong with Baptista was well-founded. For this prodigious letter writer suddenly to find writing a burden should have sent out alarms to all those who knew her well.

To offset the chronic surfeit of rain which had ill-disposed fields to produce a successful crop, Francis Lynch wanted to drain his fields and build up the soil level to improve crop production but was unable to obtain the loans needed for the supplies to carry out his experiment. Once again, he turned to Patrick. At the same time, Francis, still intent on reestablishing his credentials in the tanning industry, was exploring new processes which he hoped would enable his doing so.

John Lynch discovered that in the midst of a political counterrevolution there was little interest in lectures on physiology, much less in paying for them. When the position of attending physician suddenly became available at the state penitentiary, John leapt at the opportunity, even though the pay was meager and working conditions miserable. When there was but one port to which one could find shelter from the storm, one did not hesitate.

By September Columbia was fully caught up in Wade Hampton's Red Revolution, as the Redeemers sensed they were on the cusp of final victory over the remnants of Reconstruction. At Valle Crucis, barely three miles from the capital, Baptista Lynch had enough awareness of the violence that the counterrevolution was cultivating (she deems it simply "political excitement"), that she felt compelled to assure her bishop brother in Charleston that "I feel no fears whatever." Did she harbor any thoughts that the local redeemers would consider her a collaborator for socializing with the Yankee occupiers and taking their aid? Over in Cheraw, Francis Lynch reported to Patrick that "Very much enthusiasm prevails for the success of the Democracy." Although Francis seemed to ignore the lethal activity of the Red Shirts and other agents of violent voter suppression which was a critical part of Wade Hampton's "campaign," the references to "harvests" and the extinction of "yellow fever" appear to be Francis' oblique indication of his aspirations for the resurgent Democratic Party in South Carolina. Those political hopes may well have sprung from his own wretched economic condition, one so bad that his wife found herself begging Patrick to adopt their younger daughter "for a few years" in order to assure that she will be able to enjoy the upbringing that they had been able, with the bishop's help, to provide for their older one in better times.

In Columbia, John Lynch had much more at stake in the Reconstruction government's survival, which was becoming less and less likely as the terror campaign spread in South Carolina. He seemed to portend this outcome at some level, when he told his brother that he had little hope that the Redeemers would cut him any slack for joining the faculty of the Radical University out of financial necessity. Whether Hampton won or not, whether the university survived on not, John Lynch would be forever considered a scalawag who betrayed his own by failing to boycott the university.

As the 1876 campaign concluded, Baptista, despite her earlier dismissal of campaigning as so much distracting noise, revealed just how much the Lynches, including those within the walls of Valle Crucis, had been swept up into this final phase of Redemption. A new generation had a new cause to which to pledge their selves: the restoration of white supremacy. Baptista had reinstated the tradition of "storming heaven" with prayer, now in the formula of the Litany of the Saints, for the triumph of the crusade that she saw Hampton personifying: that of reestablishing the proper order so that "truth and honesty and humanity" might once again center political society. With Hampton's apparent triumph at the ballot box, the Ursulines were ready to contribute to the celebration of their redemption. In 1861 it had been the sewing of flags for South Carolina units to carry into the war; now it was laurels to decorate the streets in honor of their conquering heroes. Baptista manifested the general joy that Redemption generated among Columbia's white community, along with the expectation that Redemption would at last open the way to the renewal of the prosperity that had eluded them since Sherman swept through the region. Redemption would revive public confidence in society's direction that would increase enrollment at their school as well as raise real estate prices for the property they had long sought to sell.

When the outcome of the election in three southern states, including South Carolina, was disputed, apprehension mounted about the possible undoing of the redemption they had thought was an accomplished fact. That apprehension was only heightened for Baptista by the burning of the nearby Hampton home, a fire that Baptista was quick to blame on their former bonded work force. With racial war looming in the popular imagination, it was no surprise that parents were waiting to see how events played out before allowing their daughters to enroll at Valle Crucis. And so, as the centennial year drew to a close, all eyes were on Washington to see how or if the mounting crisis was solved.

BAPTISTA LYNCH, COLUMBIA, 2 JULY[1]
... Lilly ... writes me that Conlaw and Phoebe are ready to come at any time. ... I hear since Jimmie's sun stroke or sickness he intends leaving when Revd. Dr Meriwether returns. That may be only talk. Any way let Conlaw and Phoebe come by last of August or Sept. 1st It will be a mutual benefit. ...

PATRICK N. LYNCH TO JAMES ROOSEVELT BAYLEY,
CHARLESTON, 3 JULY[2]
... After returning from St. Augustine I shall have to go North to get some money if possible for I have got through this year so far only by borrowing— and now I must *pay* or go to jail or be disgraced and bankrupted. ...

BAPTISTA LYNCH, COLUMBIA, 5 JULY[3]
... How is Revd Dr Meriwether. We all are anxious to have him return, ... we who know the "ins and outs" of things think it would be much better to have

the Rev. Dr at home, even if he did not say Mass the whole year, but required our constant nursing—just for the sake of his presence here and the safe and respectable protection he gives the place. . . . the sooner the better, for Ewd and Jimmy. . . . [who] go from bad to worse. . . . They are remarkably fine boys but I fear, without the Doctor's presence and good influence on them, there is danger ahead. . . . They are young and Rev. FF only irritates them. . . . [4]

BAPTISTA LYNCH, COLUMBIA, 7 JULY[5]
. . . I am so much obliged to you, my dearest brother, for keeping before me our "Annual Retreat" . . . that pleasant welcome I used to give retreats, when I could look on them as a sufficient reward for a whole year of labor I feel no longer and nothing but a sense of duty makes me now undertake one—I suppose it is the painful association occurring at that time, which gives me the feeling—certainly it is not that I do not love prayer and meditation for I do, more than anything else.[6]

I am very glad, that you will bring Eustace's children up with you to Charleston and hope they will come to Valle Crucis Sept 1st. . . . Augusta says that Conlaw is a splendid farmer and Phoebe also very bright and intelligent. I hope the dear children will be happy and improve and remain together for awhile after leaving their father's house. . . .

HENRIETTA LYNCH, CHERAW, 14 JULY[7]
It is under the title of Father Brother friend Benefactor, I call on you to ask what is a real and a lasting obligation. To enable a young person by means of a good education to feel a confidence to pass thro this terrible cold world. Verily! "Out in the cold World out on the street." These thoughts are called for by our inability to send Elinor back to the Convent. All means of paying for her failing us, I want you to adopt her for a few years, and to take all the expense of her coming and going. . . . Elinor needs now two good years more. . . . I trust . . . my appeal shall not be in vain. . . .

BAPTISTA LYNCH, COLUMBIA, 29 JULY[8]
. . . Seeing that "Valle Crucis" cannot support itself even when the house is crowded as it was last session, because every year the "dead-heads" have us missing from $1000 to $14000 unpaid and only promised never to be collected. I have been thinking of asking you to let me go to Greenville and see what prospect we would have there for a Day-School and (3 Nuns) Perhaps we could rent a house, and establish a school there which would support itself and make known the Faith. Our chapel would be a nucleus for Catholics and be ready for

the Priest until the Church is built. Perhaps those persons desiring to induce immigration by assenting to build a church, would also assist to establish a Catholic school. What do you think of it?

. . . If you do not write to the contrary, I propose starting immediately after the "Retreat" to see about it Unless the Holy Ghost intervenes. . . .

C. A. LYNCH, GREENVILLE, 4 AUGUST[9]
Dear Uncle,

You may be surprised to find this letter from me and wer [sic] it not that I am real [sic] in need I would not write. I have a good chance to make money and am Genl Agt for a large house in Tennessee but have nothing to commence on. I have money owening [sic] me but it will be 60 and 70 days before I get it. I also have a good trade. I have been struggling and trying in every way to succeed but have always been thrown back in some way. If I do not get assistance I will be obliged to give up the place as agent and let someone else be appointed. . . . I have not forgotten your kindness in letting me have $50.00 once before . . . I have kept the pledge[10] taken in the city and intend to keep it. . . . If you can let me have $100.00 dollars I will succeed and return same to you with interest as soon as possible. . . . I am your affect nephew, C A Lynch

FRANCIS LYNCH, CHERAW, 4 AUGUST[11]
Yesterdays mail brot me your valued letter with the ck you were so kind in sending me. It is very timely. . . .

The result on my drained farm promises to be satisfactory while the crops generally are good on my lands.
During the past two months, I have in tanning had recourse to leaves of Sumac and sweet gum . . . So far I am more than pleased. Next week I will hope to send a small parcel of leather, so tanned to Baltimore where I hope it will take good rank. . . .

BAPTISTA LYNCH, COLUMBIA, 10 AUGUST[12]
. . . It seems to me to be a necessity- either to make a Branch house in Greenville as I proposed or to enlarge this house so as [to] receive more pupils. Otherwise it is a sinking business as far as temporals go.

For the spiritual I am truly thankful to say—a better community as a whole I do not think you would find anywhere (D.G.) . . .

FRANCIS LYNCH, CHERAW, 16 AUGUST[13]
Your esteemed favor was duly recd with the enclosure of ck for fifty dolls.

which to me was a great boon at this time, and for so greatly obliging me, you have my sincere thanks. . . .

The little trial that I made of underdraining lands of which I spoke to you, is satisfactory. In very dry and hot weather, the effect on the cotton was admirable, the plant all the while vigorous. Of late the fall of rain was too much for the surface to fully absorb. Deeper plowing and subsoiling will attain this end. This is the key to farming on my lands. . . .

PATRICK N. LYNCH, [REPORT OF ARTESIAN WELL COMMITTEE, CHARLESTON, 29 AUGUST.[14]

Some weeks ago, on your motion, the City Council was pleased to appoint a Scientific Committee to examine and record the stratifications of the new Artesian Well, then about to be commenced by Mr. Spangler. . . . We have collected as carefully as possible under the circumstances specimens of all the strata through which the well has passed in reaching its present depth of 670 feet. Those specimens are now being analyzed. When this is done . . . the specimens on hand will be turned over by us to the City Engineer or any officer or committee whom it shall please the city Council to designate.

. . . Everything encourages us to look forward towards a successful completion of the work undertaken. . . .

JOHN LYNCH, COLUMBIA, 6 SEPTEMBER[15]

I have returned from Greenville disheartened. . . . I went up at an unfortunate time. Everybody seemed wild about politics. Democratic clubs meetings, nominations, &c together with Catholic festivities, Baptists, Methodist and Presbyterian revivals, withall there seemed to be no money. . . .

Today I was offered the position of physician to the penitentiary, the incumbent having sent in his letter of resignation. I feel compelled to accept it, as I have virtually nothing else to do, if the college closes. I would be obliged to find some other field, to make a living for the family in. Atlanta has been recommended to me, as having a large Catholic population, and only one Catholic physician (Dr. C. Pinckney) as yet. If it had not been for Ellen and mother, I would have gone long ago. This position of physician to penitentiary will be neither pleasant nor profitable. Still it is doing something and I cannot afford to be idle while I have debts to meet and the family to support. I did hope to establish a new business by lecturing on physiology but have lost heart. If I had succeeded I could have paid out of debt in a short while, and been independent of the College. As it is, I have to take my humiliating position, and wait for my pay, which is given so grudgingly that half the good is taken out of it. . . . It is inconvenient to be without a horse. Still he is expensive. I shall try to get on without one for some time yet. . . .

BAPTISTA LYNCH, COLUMBIA, 6 SEPTEMBER[16]
I hear you will remain in Charleston while the fever lasts or, at least until you ascertain that it is not yellow fever. That is just like *you*, who are, as I have always thought, "the most Christ-like man" I ever knew.

Where there is sickness, suffering of any kind, there you are to be found (D.G.) You will tell me it is a priest's mission and duty how much more the Bishop's—the father of all. I rejoice that it is your pleasure, as well as duty. . . .

I cannot get over your tired look when last here, my dearest brother, and the way your clothes hung on you—so gloomy in appearance and no doubt were after so many nights of unrest. . . . You really ought . . . not over-work yourself . . .

BAPTISTA LYNCH, COLUMBIA, 18 SEPTEMBER[17]
I have an idea that you may run up here if you know all the rumours about the proposed torch light procession which sensationalists love to repeat. I feel no fears whatever

. . . We will look anxiously for you.

BAPTISTA LYNCH, COLUMBIA, 21 SEPTEMBER[18]
. . . We are thankful now to be out of the city, where political shouting and yelling keep ones nerves shocked all the time. . . .

JOHN LYNCH, COLUMBIA, 22 SEPTEMBER[19]
. . . I am very much engaged just now prescribing at the Penitentiary, not less than 30 to 40 cases to prescribe for each day—the great number trifling, a few serious. It takes from 2 to 3 hours to get around. I commenced paying two visits a day, but have now reduced to one, without I am sent for, in which case they send a wagon. . . .

I am sorry to say sister Ellen is not as well as I would like to see her, although she is attending to her duties and looks well, if she is not relieved soon, she will begin to fail in body. From studying her own case, which is more troublesome than dangerous (ascarides).[20] . . . I am prescribing for her but it is not satisfactory to me to be writing, when I ought to see the case. Still, I can do no better just yet. . . .

. . . John is still out of employment. Robert has been elected to take charge of the Oddfellows Academy. He gets the Academy rent free, and gets his salary from the pupils. . . . I tell him if he succeeds, and Thompson is elected school commissioner, he may take his place, as principal teacher in the city. . . .

FRANCIS LYNCH, CHERAW, 26 SEPTEMBER[21]

. . . As may be seen in the papers, the political campaign is opened here. Gnls. Hampton and Kershaw and other able speakers are here now. Very much enthusiasm prevails for the success of the Democracy. . . .[22]

JOHN LYNCH, COLUMBIA, 6 OCTOBER[23]

. . . The exercises of the University commenced this week. I have but four in my class, three intelligent mulattos, and one stupid black fellow, who went to sleep twice during my lecture today. The whites of the class have withdrawn from the university. The fiscal year terminates 31st of this month. There is no appropriation provided for my chair yet, in the bill for next year. New Trustees will be elected by the next legislature, and I expect most of the profs. will be removed. Whether their places will be filled this year is questionable or whether any appropriation will be made. The present trustees are no account and have done nothing during their term of office. I have written several communications to them on business, none have been attended to or noticed, the excuse has always been, no quorum.

The question with me now is whether I ought to resign, to take effect Nov 1st or hold on and wait the action of the new trustees. What action will be taken about the University if H[ampton] is elected, you no doubt know better than I do. If it was not for the salary I would not wait a day, but can I afford to resign? Will it be better for me to continue my lectures until Nov. 1st and then quietly stop on the plea that there is no appropriation for my chair . . . and wait the action of the trustees, until I resign or am removed. I still will be a professor and entitled to pay, and if the University is revived, I may be retained.

It is evident that the University as now conducted is a disgrace to the state. Consequently those connected with it are in a disgraceful position . . . If you think I ought to resign, please write me . . .

P.S. I have just read the proclamation in this Evening's Union Herald. It is hard to restrain the feeling one must have when he feels the tyrant's lash.[24]

BAPTISTA LYNCH, COLUMBIA, 2 NOVEMBER[25]

. . . Every one else gives place now to Genl. Wade Hampton, one of So. Ca.'s noblest sons! Grand preparations are being made to give him an ovation in

Columbia tomorrow and the *hearts* of our best people and the gentry of the state are in it. We are saying the "Litany of the Saints" daily, begging God's blessing on the Cause of honesty, truth, and humanity which he and his Conference represent. . . . You see their kind friendship for our Convent for the past 18 years, is appreciated, nor do I forget, how the Genl came in person last year, and offered to sit up with Rev. Dr. Meriwether. . . .

. . . After the elections are over, I suppose people will send their children to school. They are afraid to do so yet, but I have no apprehension.

. . . The Hampton procession—decorations &c are all the young people can talk of and even our little grandniece, Kate's child, knows how to "Hurrah Hampton!" . . .

BAPTISTA LYNCH, COLUMBIA, 8 NOVEMBER[26]
. . . About the elections—we have not been at all nervous—some complimentary notes passed between the Misses Hampton Mrs Col Haskell and ourselves and we sent evergreens to help decorate the city on Saturday—but we are very quiet and are real "Know-Nothings" by choice these days. I trust the apprehensions of others may prove groundless. . . .[27]

JOHN LYNCH, COLUMBIA, 16 NOVEMBER[28]
. . . On Tuesday I was called on for pew rent, could not pay it . . . If I did not pay, they would have to close the pew. I answerd to do so, if they chose, and bowed them out of the office. . . . I know I am stubborn, but I am also a law abiding man and as I consider *you* as *Law* in this case I bring it to your earliest consideration that I may have the benefit of your advice before doing anything I might be sorry for hereafter . . . In any other community I believe I could succeed in my profession; here, I cannot do anything. There are but three families of the congregation who employ me (i.e. that are able to pay anything) and their practice would not shoe [*sic*] me a year. I do all the charity practice that presents itself, and attend to the religious gratuitously and willingly. I give the clergy no trouble, nor do I interfere with the affairs of others. I am neither a hypocrite, nor sycophant. This may sound pharisaical. Still I believe it to be the truth. My family do what they can, to contribute towards the harmony and good of the church, but I cannot help seeing a marked difference shown, between them and the rest of the congregation. . . .

BAPTISTA LYNCH, COLUMBIA, 17 NOVEMBER[29]
. . . I hope these election commotions may soon be over and our school fill in.

[Letter no. 2 Nov. 1876]

Every body seems perfectly elated by the result of the elections! and are saying
many extravagant things of all they wish to do in showing their devotion to
Genl Hampton and all expect bright and prosperous days as heretofore—Real
estate has gone up already.

BAPTISTA LYNCH, COLUMBIA, 1 DECEMBER[30]

. . . I will not pretend to repeat the daily bulletins of political events in the
City. . . . They have not said much however of the burning out of our neighbors
the Misses Hampton. Their servants set fire to the house early in the evening
about 8 o'clock and must have kerosened it for in 15 minutes it was reduced
to ashes—the ladies having only time to save their lives and some silver and a
little clothing. It is supposed they were bribed to do it . . . I am so glad you are
out of the state—and hope you will not return until things are more decided.

Everyone is in perfect admiration of Genl Hampton's masterly inactivity
and endurance. He is truly a noble man!

Sallie Burt's uncle Mr. Abner Atkinson was yesterday at Rev. Dr. M's—
spent Thanksgiving Day with him. He is in Columbia as one of the "election
rioters" and under false accusation. He says that he was miles away from the
place and quietly at home that not only he, but a neighbor who has been dead
about 3 years and another about 2 years and an old man 82 years of age are
indicted for the same! Which goes to show, that this new element down here,
catch the names of property holders who were rich before the war and determine to get money out of them, by hook or by crook. Mother says it puts her
in mind of Ireland, when the Orangeman used to swear to anything against
the Catholic—

Mr. Atkinson says they have a big blubber-lipped negro there swearing
against them, but he really does not see how they can make anything out of it.
Still he has been here expecting his trial all the week. On [his] expense—and
sadly needed at his home where his crop is not yet attended to, nor is there any
one able to take his place there.

What a government! This is only one instance of the many things being
enacted of cruelty and injustice. . . . I hope soon we shall see a different sort of
government. . . .

23

"GOD IS GOOD!"

January–June 1877

As a new year began, the Lynches, like most white South Carolinians, nervously awaited the outcome of the still undecided presidential and gubernatorial elections. Both the incumbent governor, Daniel Chamberlain, and his Democratic challenger, Wade Hampton, claimed victory. Hampton had received about a thousand votes more than Chamberlain, but the Republican-controlled board of canvassers nullified the returns of three counties, including Edgefield, where fraud and violence had ensured that Samuel Tilden, the Democratic nominee for president, and Hampton would prevail. In January, two governments gathered in Columbia, one committed to Chamberlain and one to Hampton. In Washington, a special electoral committee of fifteen had been formed from the Congress and the Supreme Court to determine which party had won the three former Confederate States of Florida, Louisiana, and South Carolina. Whichever way the committee ruled, the Democrats saw themselves in the catbird seat. If Tilden was declared the winner of South Carolina, then Hampton could claim the governorship, confident that Tilden would not deploy the few Federal troops still in the state to keep the Republicans in power. If Hayes, there was reason to believe that Home Rule would still be their immediate future, given Hayes' indications that it was time to end Reconstruction.[1]

Baptista Lynch, as noted previously, had strong interests in wanting Wade Hampton in the governor's house. The Hampton family's estate outside of Columbia was close by Valle Crucis.

Over the near dozen years since their forced relocation there, the Ursulines had been frequent recipients of the Hamptons' generosity. Not least, Hampton's coming to power meant an end to the oppressive taxes which Baptista admitted to having "been so harassed by them, that the very word makes me sick and nervous …" Baptista saw nothing wrong in using social connections to secure political favors, particularly when they concerned taxation. Indeed, she was even ready to follow advice to fudge a property's valuation, so long as it brought tax relief. Hampton's decision to return the state capital from Charleston to Columbia, Baptista recognized, would greatly increase the value of the real estate that the Ursulines had over the past decade been trying in vain to sell. And finally, with native friends back in power, the Ursulines would never be in a better position to press their war claims with Congress.

By the time Wade Hampton took the oath as governor, he had become for Baptista Lynch the avatar of the Christian politician. For the late June commencement of the Ursuline Academy, Baptista had her community prepare two special musical odes in honor of their special heroes of Lost Causes, one for Wade Hampton and one for the prisoner of the Vatican, Pope Pius IX.

The Democrats might have succeeded in reclaiming power in South Carolina, but, with Rutherford Hayes in the White House, Republicans still controlled Federal patronage. A rising generation of Lynches, like the former one, assumed that their bishop uncle had powerful enough connections in Washington for him to be an effective lobbyist in obtaining some federal position for them in their home state. For all that the Lynches found offensive about the federal government, the financial security it offered was something not to be spurned to preserve one's ideological purity.

Even as the era of military occupation came to a close, the tentacles of Northern capital took an ever-tighter grip on the Southern economy, which the Lynches experienced in various ways, whether in securing a loan or finding a possible purchaser of property. Nonetheless, the overthrow of Republican government opened economic as well as political opportunities, at least to Francis and John Lynch's thinking. Here at last was their chance to get out from under the debts that plagued them. Francis, the former shoe supplier to the Army of Northern Virginia, believed, in the present economic conditions, the tanning industry was poised to take off from its current stagnation. He intended to be part of the boom. The sad reality, however, was that, even in a South in which home rule had been restored, Francis remained a financial outcast, unable to raise the credit that was absolutely essential to conducting business. Patrick Lynch still found himself the only person standing between his brother's family and ruinous poverty.

John Lynch calculated that he could make good on nearly all of his indebtedness, with the exception of that owed to Patrick, if the sure-to-come booming economy enabled the state to make good on the salaries he was due from the university and penitentiary. The bullish times which Redemption would inaugurate would also somehow transform his suspect mine and underwater properties into attractive acquisitions for flush investors. Meanwhile, his position as medical doctor of the penitentiary exposed him to the Dickensian conditions prevailing there, including the abusive practice of hiring out convicts.

FRANCIS LYNCH, CHERAW, JAN 3[2]

. . . In regard to business, the fruits from the past year were better in corn and hay than cotton, while this last alone brings money. . . . The few acres underdrained last year, showed the advantage of such preparation. As soon as the weather and land permit, it is my purpose to underdrain more. . . .

I am about done ginning for the season, and desire to push the tanning, which business seems to have touched bottom, and now is encouraging. I feel that I now possess the basis for a successful business, if the wheels can be made to turn for a while. . . .

BAPTISTA LYNCH, URSULINES, JAN 6[3]

. . . Now, that Genl Wade Hampton is so wisely working things, I trust the prospects generally may improve. . . . What if we could effect the sale of lots on Main Street . . . Perhaps you could now find a purchaser for that valuable property. Judge C—[4] says he . . . estimates the whole [of it at] $24,000. We ask $25000 [$734,906] . . . Have been paying taxes at assessed value. But as the Hampton family are such good friends, of the Convent, perhaps we shall not be taxed again.

John called on the Governor H, who was very affable and made kind inquiries for the Mother Superior. I am glad the Convent merits the friendship of such noble people (AMDG).

If we could only sell that town property and concentrate all we have at Valle Crucis, where we have some land to help support us, it seems to me, it is the best thing we can do, especially as our day school is in the city. We see by it, and by our letters from sister convents, that we could not find support in the city. . . . Several other convents in cities write me on the eve of dissolution for want of support. So there must be some other means besides the school now when times are stringent.

. . . My hobby now is to get every thing in readiness and . . . to build . . . another story on this house during this coming summer if possible, which will unite the entire house under one roof and make dry, comfortable sleeping rooms for pupils and community. Perhaps Mme Ursula's money could do that. . . .

JOHN LYNCH, COLUMBIA, JAN 7[5]

. . . I still believe Hampton will be Gov. and Chamberlain will have to give up. . . .

BAPTISTA LYNCH, URSULINES, JAN 11[6]

. . . The belief here is that after March [new governor Hampton] will bring his capital here when real estate will go up one hundred percent. So every body is cheerful in hope. . . . We agitate the subject and pray every night about it and for God's blessing on our temporal affairs.

It seems to me *now* is the time to put in our claim in Congress . . .

BAPTISTA LYNCH, URSULINES, FEB 12[7]

. . . The political lookout seems to arrest the attention of every one and indeed prayer is needed for the whole country. . . .

JOHN LYNCH, COLUMBIA, FEB 16[8]

. . . My mine must wait for a year or two. So if it comes in, in time for Sue Caldwell, I am satisfied.

. . . Are very much occupied at the hospital of Penitentiary. Had 9 cases of pneumonia sent in on me from a farm down the river. Where 150 convicts are hired. The greater number were in a dying condition. 4 have died, the balance will get well I think, but I have spent the best part of my time for the past 10 days with them.

. . . Eliza has engaged to board 8 members of the Legislature when they meet, at $40 per month. She will have to pack them, like sardines. . . .

C.S. LYNCH, CHERAW, FEB 22[9]

. . . You know that I am in my twentieth year, and have not as yet commenced business. This year, it is my wish to farm. But I have not the means, . . . Though father is very anxious to help me, he is not able. I would require about two hundred dollars. With that amt I would be able to get a horse, wagon and necessary implements, . . . If you will be kind enough to do what you can for me, I will pledge the whole crop to the repayment of your gracious obligation. . . .

BAPTISTA LYNCH, URSULINES, FEB 22[10]

. . . How worthy of all praise is Gov. Hampton! What beautiful self-government and Christian fortitude. He ought to be a Catholic, and may I pray . . .

BAPTISMA LYNCH, URSULINES, FEB 27[11]

. . . . Brother John . . . in his note of yesterday . . . expressed his hopes rising and the political logjam clearing and Gov. Hampton *certainly* to be inaugurated. God grant it.

What a government!!! . . .

BAPTISTA LYNCH, COLUMBIA, ND.[12]

. . . Genl. Hampton is declared the accepted Governor. I hope since Charleston initiated such a good step every other county will follow and the taxes will go into the right channel—as well as moderate. I have been so harassed by them, that the very word makes me sick and nervous, for which I am impatient with myself. . . .

FRANCIS LYNCH, CHERAW, APR 27[13]

. . . Now that political troubles are over, and prosperity of business are reviving, I . . . wrote to Mr. C.J. Lowndes, Charleston, as to the feasibility of borrowing 1500$ from the Bank of Charleston, on easy terms, stating that I wanted one full renewal, and after then, paymts of 300$ to insure further renewals naming 90 d as the term of notes.

Mr. Lowndes kindly answered that on my sending him a bankable note for the sum, he would submit it, for me, to the Bank. This I consider as equivalent to saying the note would be discounted. And I believe that with it, in time to secure a good supply of tan bark, as well as hides, I can fully protect this note, and do a good profitable business in the meanwhile.

. . . If not distasteful to you I would ask that you be my security on the note, to be offered at bark. . . .

BAPTISTA LYNCH, URSULINES, May 1[14]

... We are teaching the children "Hampton's March" on piano, harp, and guitar and also the "Ode to Pope Pius IX"—both of which are very pleasing, and are to be played also at our Commencement. Sister Michel arranges them for the harp, Sr. Ignatia for the piano, and Sr. Bernard for the guitar. ...

FRANCIS LYNCH, CHERAW, MAY 11[15]

Last week was recd your kind letter and with it, the endorsement asked for. I thank you greatly for your ready compliance with my request.

Mr. Lowndes on my behalf submitted the note ... for a simple discount, without renewals, would not be to me so acceptable. So the note was returned to me. True had this arrangement been effected it would have been very liberal to the borrower considering the manner now of banking.

... With good facilities the past six months were very inviting of activity in the hide and leather business. And now prices are attaining fancy figures. To me these are as phantoms until I can make avail of them. This end would have been attained had the discount been made. ...

JOSEPHINE G. LYNCH, GREENVILLE, MAY 13[16]

... There is a vacancy on the Greenville and Columbia R.R. as mail agent. It pays well, and being in the United States employ, one is always sure of their salary. Dear Bishop could you not assist [Conlaw] to procure this place you are so well acquainted with the influential [sic] men who are at the head in Washington, or the member of Congress from this state, I feel confident he could fill the place and give satisfaction to all parties. ...

HENRIETTA LYNCH, CHERAW, MAY 16[17]

... My very dear father and friend, I regret from my heart that in addressing you I have to make an unpleasant request, but in a fit of despair, I may almost say, I turn to you to ask the means of carrying on the house in these months of impoverishment and dire necessity. Mr. Lynch can get no credit from stores, not even the value of $1 and we need truly as I ask you. By my past knowledge of your warm heartedness, and of your unbounded kindnesses to our family I need fear no rebuff and may close with the assurance that with both hand and heart I shall be helped by ...

FRANCIS LYNCH, CHERAW, JUNE 5[18]

... The contingencies of a business must be promptly met to assure success in it. It is not enough to say they will be met in time. They must be timely met.

Now I have several hundred sides of leather in tan, within 60 days I can place 200$ worth of leather in debt and a larger amt within 60 days more. And yet in the prosecution of this business in its legitimate way and of my farming interests, I have so exhausted all my available means, that on Saturday last I failed to raise 20$ town tax. On yesterday was notified that 28$ covering penalty would suffice if paid by Friday morning next. If not then paid, that 12$ additional would attach, making 40$ to be pd.

. . . I must look to you [to] back my credit by endorsement . . . If you can conveniently have a note for two hundred dolls for sixty—discounted, please do . . .

JOHN LYNCH, COLUMBIA, JUN 9[19]

. . . My Penitentiary salary continuing, I hope to be able to live, until the University will reorganize, when I hope to be reelected to some chair, say physiology and chemistry. If I once get seated, I hope it will be for life. . . .

BAPTISTA LYNCH, URSULINES, JUN 20[20]

. . . We received a letter from sister Mary, who will be here to meet you, at our Commencement. (D.V.) . . . Very likely you and mother and herself may all come out to Valle Crucis together on 27th or the morning of 28th. . . . Mary and Mother . . . will go over to Cheraw then for the summer. . . .

ELEANOR LYNCH MEMORIAL CARD, JUN 26[21]

> PRAY IN CHARITY
> FOR THE SOUL OF
> **MRS. ELEANOR N. LYNCH**
> WHO DIED JUNE 26TH, 1877

BAPTISTA LYNCH, URSULINES, TO SIBLINGS, JUN 27[22]

I am with you in spirit all the time and near our precious mother. Let us bless the Almighty that we are the children of such a mother! What a true Catholic Christian she has always been! The truly valiant woman and how faithful. Almighty God would not be outdone in generosity. His goodness to her fills my soul with deep gratitude! He preserved her from the imbecility of age—and from its ordinary helplessness. She possessed her every faculty to the last. Always cheerful, strong and sweet. She was the support, counselor, and model of all who approached her, whether the mature in years or the playful schoolgirl. All found in her a *true mother!*

Oh! How much have *we* to be grateful for—that she was not bed-ridden and helpless, like so many at her age! and that she had the happiness to die surrounded by her own loved and loving family. That her sickness was of short duration, that God mysteriously and mercifully consoled her by *your* presence, my dear sister and then—such a death! Truly precious in the sight of the Lord! it is "asleep in the Lord."

Let us picture her happiness and our dear father on their union in heaven and with their children already gone before her!

God is good! God is merciful and they can chant "The mercies of the Lord, I will sing forever!"

The greatest sacrifice I have ever made since leaving home to become a nun, I made yesterday, when I could not go to mother. You, my dearest brothers, can share that with me, since it pleased God that you also, could not be with her at the last.

But she who always had such superiority of understanding, knew that our hearts and prayers were with her and that "God doth all things well." . . . (R.I.P.)

24

"EVERYBODY SEEMS PLEASED WITH THE RETURN OF HOME RULE"

July–December 1877

In mid-July workers in Martinsburg, West Virginia went on strike against the Baltimore and Ohio Railroad after the company cut wages for the second time in a year. Like wildfire the work stoppage spread, halting rail traffic and the industries dependent upon it across much of the country. In Pittsburgh, state militia opened fire on strikers who had seized control of rail switches. Twenty died, which touched off more violence and killing in Baltimore, Chicago, and St. Louis. Although the strikes did not penetrate as far south as South Carolina, news of the unprecedented scale of strikes and their ensuing violence did breech the cloistered walls of the Ursuline Academy at Valle Crucis. Baptista Lynch's sympathies were with the workers, even though she could not embrace unions or strikes as instruments for attaining justice. Her fundamental conservative streak revealed itself in her confidence that charity, such as that exercised by a benevolent organization like the Vincent de Paul Society, was the best approach to protecting labor from the oppression that was the consequence of greed.

We do not know Patrick Lynch's reaction to the labor earthquake that shook America to its core that summer. A year earlier, the bishop had given a lecture to the St. Vincent de Paul Society in New York on the topic of "Society and the Poor." It represented his best effort at addressing what was coming to be known as "the Social Problem," i.e. labor's quest for social justice and the role that government should play in that quest. The bishop made clear that labor deserved a fair share of the wealth they helped to produce. But instead of calling for the social reform that would meet the workers' cries, Bishop Lynch pointed to the necessity of religion, not only as the great preserver of social order, but as a propaedeutic for good citizenship. Part of that training was inculcating an acceptance of the lot they had been given in society. Patrick Lynch understood poverty as a permanent human condition, a consequence of original sin. The world which Adam and Eve made is one marked by a fundamental inequality. The best one can do is to alleviate the suffering and want that poverty entails. And religion is eminently the key to developing the compassionate spirit that issues in works of charity, works that prove to have a chain reaction in imbuing that same urge to give in those who have received. Since government intrinsically lacks that spirit, its attempts to address poverty and its offshoots inevitably results in coldness, abuse, and the dystopia of the workhouse. Like his Ursuline sister, Patrick Lynch could only look to private charity, either exercised by pious individuals or religious communities, as the only reliable means of achieving a semblance of social justice.

Bishop Lynch singled out the various Southern Relief Societies that formed in the war's immediate aftermath as an example of the immense good that private charity could do. What he did not mention was that the greatest beneficiary of the Southern people was the Freedmen's Bureau which extended aid to Black and white alike. That, alas, was a government organization. In part, this ignoring of public relief and recovery programs arose from the two-sphere model through which Lynch, like so many of his fellow prelates viewed the Church-State relationship. The Church had nothing to say about the state's obligation to provide for the general welfare, the ways in which it could protect and promote fundamental rights. That, like slavery, was outside the Church's scope. Rerum Novarum was still more than a decade in the future.

Urinary infections plagued Patrick Lynch throughout his adult life. In August of 1877, while in Massachusetts on his latest fundraising expedition, a particularly severe outbreak hospitalized him. In three extensive operations over the course of several days, surgeons attempted to crush stones in his bladder. For Baptista Lynch, who concerned herself about few things more than Patrick's health, these operations were the worst fulfillment of her chronic fears. She constantly had prescribed safeguards or remedies for his ailments. Once she even had a druggist ship Bishop Lynch a case of water from Glenn Springs, a spa noted for its healing waters. If her bishop brother would not go to the springs, she would bring them to him, if only in bottled form.

Baptista rejoiced that her "grand old state" of South Carolina was once more under the control of those "interested in her welfare." That welfare, of course, was largely limited to those who had thrived under the ancient regime before the war. The mudsills and their provocateurs had been cast down. The networks of privilege which held South Carolina society together had been restored. The Lynches saw an early return from that network when Robert Lynch was appointed to a potentially profitable position in the federal custom house at Charleston. Baptista, all too aware that the Ursuline failure to obtain justice from the federal government was largely responsible for Patrick's seemingly perpetual fund-raising tours, finally secured a full-time representative in Washington.

By the late 1870s, Baptista faced a dilemma in navigating a path between remaining true to the educational apostolate to which she had dedicated her religious life, and meeting the demands which the standardization of American higher education was raising. Securing a charter seemed to her the best way to gain legal protection for the independence of their academy. She proposed to her brother that they move expeditiously, to take advantage of the current sympathetic legislature before it adopted some of the intrusive investigations that were becoming standard practice throughout the western world. The charter Baptista also saw as their possible fiscal salvation, inasmuch as it might well open the door to state financial relief. That external aid had become a greater need as enrollment at the academy became exclusively Catholic, in part the consequence of the evangelical boycott of convent schools in the postbellum era, especially in the South.

BAPTISTA LYNCH, URSULINES, JUL 12[1]

... A letter came to me from Mrs Brownfield ... saying how anxious she felt and she did hope you would not be transferred to another diocese. ... I would not be surprised if there were some truth in the rumours. At all events, I am happy to see you are considered worthy of so much esteem and honor in the Church, as I know you to be—and, although I am the one who would have just cause to fear such a transfer, I would see it with such a pride in, and for you, my dearest brother, as to silence all else. ... I want you to feel perfectly free to act, with my will according fully with yours, whatever that may be in the case. ...[2]

BAPTISTA LYNCH, URSULINES, JUL 19[3]

... I find that sister Mary is out here for her own health. Brother John is prescribing for her, and she feels better. ...

BAPTISTA LYNCH, URSULINES, JUL 24[4]

... Brother John ... came out this morning to take Jennie Whitwell to the depot. Her father wrote us to send her on under care of conductors to Cleveland, Ohio. All arrangements possible were made to secure her safe travel, but in these days of RR strikes it looks risky to say the least of it. ... What terrible news from Pittsburg today—I could see the burning of Columbia over again! Awful! ...

One cannot help sympathizing with the laborers when they are defrauded by rich employers. Cannot those RR. Kings be reasoned with? I would think St. Vincent de Paul's society would be the best protection for the defrauded laborer. Are the "Train Men's Union" and "Engineer's Brotherhood" secret societies? and are many Catholics among these strikers? Poor unfortunate fellows! ...

PATRICK N. LYNCH, LECTURE ON SOCIETY
AND THE POOR, N.D.[5]

An issue of the highest importance, and pregnant with vast consequences, seems looming up before this country, and the minds of not a few are turned to it with anxiety.

A civilized society is divided into classes, and ranks. ... Sooner or later one class or another obtains a certain degree of power or of prominence. Passions and prejudices are aroused, and the struggle before almost unnoticed becomes an angry clashing leading at times to the most disastrous results.

... However Socialists and Politicians may speak sweetly or enthusiastically of the equality of all men, we feel it is all theory. In practice men are unequal in too many respects. In body, some are strong. . . . Others are weak. . . . In mind, some are . . . gifted with powers of deep thought and abstruse reasoning, others have sound practical judgment. . . . While others again are . . . shallow, or variable as the wind. In character too they may differ, . . . conscientious, respecting rights and loving justice, or, on the contrary, . . . destitute of principle.

Before God, there are saints, and . . . sinners. . . . Before men, there . . . [are] those to whom wealth seems to come almost unsought, [and] those who toil and struggle to gain their daily bread,—These differences . . . do what the world may, . . . cannot be totally eliminated. The Highest authority has declared, that the poor we shall always have with us. . . . So long as men differ in their faculties and powers, . . . so long may we look for inequalities, sufferings, and evils.

. . . Divine Revelation tells us, that man . . . by his own act, he fell, and that these evils are consequences . . . [of] his fallen condition. . . . Yet much of their extent, and of their intensity . . . depends in no small degree, on society itself. Wise and prudent legislation on the part of government, and among individuals and classes, a mutual recognition of their respective rights, and a general spirit of active kindness on the part of those who have the means, towards those that suffer, will not fail to restrict and to alleviate them. On the other hand, tyranny and class legislation, and a course of oppression and injustice in the walks of daily life, a prevalence of selfishness and of greed in a community, . . . How often . . . has such a course entailed its own punishment, in outrages, tumults and sanguinary convulsions of society. Happy is the people, which . . . by legislation and by those social agencies which escape the legislator, . . . seeks earnestly to lessen the number of the unfortunate in its bosom, and to mitigate the woes they suffer.

Until recently we might in America look on this as a foreign question . . . A homestead was within the easy reach of every one. Our people were as yet uncorrupted by the luxuries of modern times. Labour and industry were held in respect. In every bosom there was a sense of personal independence, and a dislike, an abhorrence, of subjection to, or dependence on another. Each one labored quietly, in his own way, seeking his own prosperity, and the vast multitude of our citizens could easily attain a modest independence. Our whole population seemed . . . middle class. . . .

But every one feels that a change has come over the country. . . . The paths of honest slow plodding labour and trade with gains small but sure, no longer satisfy the impatient cravings of a rapid accumulation of wealth . . . [through] speculation. Physical labor . . . we leave . . . to the newly arrived immigrants. . . .

Capital and labour are being dissociated. The former is being accumulated in fewer hands, and the classes of labourers is [*sic*] increasing, who own little else than their hands, . . . The rich are becoming richer, and the poor poorer.

. . . We see Unions, associations, societies, combinations, springing up among them on every side. Strikes interfere with the course of trade and the quiet of the country, and proclaim the increasing dissatisfaction. . . . Shall the struggle of classes, so productive of disasters [in Europe], be inaugurated here? . . .

How many hours of toil may be required each day, of the labourer, without injury to his health and welfare? What wages shall be held a just and sufficient remuneration of that labour, these . . . are questions intimately and at once affecting the relations of society and the poor. Yet . . . I do not feel competent to treat that phase of the theme.

I purpose rather to treat the subject under another view, . . . How may the poverty, the misery, the sufferings, which after all, do and will exist, be most effectually alleviated, by us. Are there any agencies, beyond that of political and legislative action, which can and should aid in their grand work? . . . Religion, . . . coming from Heaven, claims preeminently the first place.

. . . What duty more sacred to her than to nurse the sick, console the dying and bury the dead. . . . She is ever blessing the world, with her miracles of charity. . . .

Religion is necessary for all. To him who has wealth, it is specially necessary in view of the judgments of a world to come. To the son of toil it is also necessary . . . he comes to understand what in truth is man's life on earth—a journey, painful and laborious it may be, but leading to the only true home of happiness. He accepts the ruggedness of his path . . . for it has been touched by the hands of the Savior himself, who deigned to toil in poverty when on earth. . . .

To him the world, with its variations of rank, conditions and duties, and its differences and inequalities, is, as it were, a vast Basilica built by the hand of God, . . . Each stone . . . has its appointed place and duty from the hand of the architect. . . .

. . . Fill his mind with the hard selfish precepts of modern political economists, and what may you look for. . . . In his bitter hopeless poverty [the worker] stalks the streets, glaring is the vast edifices of the wealthy, . . . dreams of fairy land . . . which he cannot share. . . . Let the days of Terror in the French Revolution, tell to what horrors, Philosophical speculation, casting Religion out of the heart of a people and arousing their fell [*sic*] passions, can swiftly bring a country.

There is no preservative for Society like Religion. . . .

JOHN LYNCH, COLUMBIA, AUGUST[6]

. . . I have not yet received a cent of the $50,000 appropriation for deficiencies of last years salaries . . . I am sorry to say the Penitentiary is not paying regularly.

. . . Honest government will bring better times after a while.

BAPTISTA LYNCH, URSULINES, AUG 5[7]

. . . Sister Mary. . . spends the greater part of her time on the bed—and seems quite debilitated by the heat. She says that . . . last summer she was good for nothing and this summer as soon as she gave way, Mr. Spann and her children hurried her away to her native air, hoping it would restore her. But so far, it has not. . . .

Little Annie Carpenter—our former pupil came over a day or two ago to ask your address for her father. Poor man! I suppose he will try and get you to help him by your influence, as he helped us when in difficulty about our taxes—by his influence, which at that time, was great. I pity him and my gratitude prevents my joining the cry against him. But of course, he and all his party can never live here after the exposé now being made.[8]

What a wonderful change in the tide of events! and when Ex-Governor Moses has turned state's evidence before the investigating Committee what disgraceful disclosures will be made! Strange, strange, state of affairs and how it redounds to the glory of South Carolina! . . .

JOHN LYNCH, COLUMBIA, AUG 19[9]

It is hardly necessary to say how much I was grieved, to hear of your late suffering, and pained to know that you have to undergo an operation. I am only thankful as it has become necessary that you are under the hands of so skillful a surgeon. . . .

. . . Sister Mary has improved wonderfully, her complexion is as clear as ever, and she sleeps and eats well. . . .

BAPTISTA LYNCH, URSULINES, AUG 19[10]

I am just in receipt of yours of 16th inst and how it fills me with anxiety. . . . I can think of nothing now, but of your own dear self. . . . Do let us hear by telegrams daily, how you are getting on—Oh! how anxiously will we pray for your speedy recovery, and then how relieved, you will feel! . . .

BAPTISTA LYNCH, URSULINES, AUG 21[11]

Brother John has just sent me the telegram, giving us the grateful intelligence

that you have stood the operation well and are comfortable. *Deo Gratias* is
heard on all sides. . . .

BAPTISTA LYNCH, URSULINES, AUG 28[12]
Your telegram of today to brother John fills us with anxiety—tomorrow
Wednesday, you say will decide the necessity of another operation . . . Your
many years of over-work my dearest brother, are now telling against you and
you will have to stop for awhile to rest—We are all of opinion that as soon as
you are well enough to do so, you must come to Valle Crucis and stay quietly
for three or four months . . . After which you will be able to resume your labors, but not in such a break down way as when you were ten years younger. . . .

BAPTISTA LYNCH, URSULINES, SEP 4[13]
. . . Could you have seen us all when we read your telegram of 1st inst. saying
"Discharged. Well but weak. Will write soon" What joy . . . ! How many Te
Deums, Laudates and other prayers arose from our grateful and glad hearts!
. . .

BAPTISTA LYNCH, URSULINES, SEP 10[14]
. . . You may remember, that young "Hon. Robt Aldrich" tried to pass a Bill
of Exemption from taxation for us, in the last session of the Legislature, but
failed. He now writes to me, that some of the Committee on Education . . .
entertain extraordinary views in regard to our Community &c. But says, . . .
[he has] dissipated their false notions, [and the chair said] . . . that if he would
bring in another bill, at next session, in the shape of "a Charter for any school,
and in the Charter, embrace the exemption desired, he thought Mr. A. could
get it through. . . .

Brother John and I think it well to get this Charter—it is what convents are
doing all over the world . . . to meet the public and other schools. . . .

BAPTISTA LYNCH, URSULINES, SEP 21[15]
. . . Senator M.C. Butler has been to V.C. and I gave him our papers and he
expresses himself very kindly on the subject. But says it will be a slow process
and while he will do all in his power for us, it will [be] advisable for us to get
a lawyer in Washington City to attend to our interest in the matter. (the lobbying, &c) . . .

We ask of Congress one hundred thousand dollars and offer ¼ one fourth
of whatever amount we get from Congress to pay for lobbying our claim
through on fee—The ¾ we keep ourselves. I think I see you smile and say. "You

may *when* you get it" Never mind. We have strong backers and our Blessed Lady and St. Joseph the strongest of them all. I don't believe I would work half as hard as I am doing in this matter—if you were in easy circumstances. But I am so anxious that our Convent should not be an incubus to you and to see you able to rest at home with us. . . .

BAPTISTA LYNCH, URSULINES, SEP 26[16]
. . . Every one seems to be "patting each other on the shoulders" and promising better times—but at present all business seems at a stand still and money very scarce—Still the newspapers speak of amusements, fashion, etc.

. . . Sister Mary . . . is feeling stronger but is not looking any better or stronger. . . .

I want you to administer on the estate and let a sale for division take place before Sister Mary returns to Texas; you can do so by proxy. We each stand in need now of the proceeds. . . .

It seems to me, to be highly desirable that we should get this "charter" now, when we can do so with so much less trouble, than we could get it in a few years—not only on account of it freeing us from all taxation but also for future usefulness. You have not been able to see all the moves respecting education, &c and my letter would indeed be a folio, if I were to tell you of the circulars coming to us from Europe and Ursulines all over the world—suffice it to say, they and other convents, are subjecting themselves to a public examination by an "educational Board" in order to obtain *this charter* or right to give a diploma, that they may cope with the infidel schools of the day, who would seduce youth from convent education.—the only Convent in this country so far as I know, who has done this is, that of "Mt. de Chantal—Wheeling, W.Va. But in Rome, Italy, In Belgium, France and Germany Ursulines have been obliged to do so—and I take it to be most fortunate for us, if we can now get this honor without publicity or any inconvenience such as they had to undergo—in order to keep up their Institution. . . .

BAPTISTA LYNCH, URSULINES, OCT 4[17]
. . . I suppose you know that the University is closed for a year. Some one set fire to its buildings a few nights ago . . .

My dearest Brother—you may remember that I asked you to loan us some money before you went north, which for the first time, you could not conveniently do—It was to settle up our grocers Bills at the close of scholastic year . . . these bills have not been paid, and have increased necessarily, so that now, I would be glad to get $500, if I could see fairly, a prospect to return it by Jan. 1st.

I got Mrs Pulliam to try and get that much, but she could not—then I sent out bills in every direction—but so far, we have not received anything . . .

BAPTISTA LYNCH, URSULINES, OCT 22 [18]
. . . [Regarding the charter] Mr. Aldrich wants to have all the papers in hand ready and written up before coming to Legislature the last week in November. . . . I am all the more anxious, as the taxes become due Nov. 1st and this will exempt us from them. And I am sorry to say our school was never so poor at this season. . . . I also hear, the Parsons have been threatening with excommunication, their flock, who send their children to convent schools. Any way, we have not a Protestant in our school and fewer Catholics than usual at this season of the year. . . .

BAPTISTA LYNCH, URSULINES, NOV 2[19]
. . . I enter today on my 55th year! A good round age—and far more than I ever expected to attain. Our school is so very small . . . Mme Etienne's . . . health is decidedly better since our novena to our Blessed Lady of Lourdes and taking the water from the fountain. . . . It was dredged up from the fountain a short time ago, by Frank Gray of Augusta Georgia and brought to her.[20]
    . . . The session of Legislature . . . will assemble 26th November as usual. Every body is so happy to enjoy such a good, *honest home rule*—that harmony reigns—and it is like a rest, after a storm—All that is needed now, is for the ball of internal improvement to be set in motion[,] and things will go on swimmingly—Factories made—mines worked—real estate change hands &c &c Fiat. . . .

BAPTISTA LYNCH, URSULINES, NOV 6[21]
. . . You do not know, my dearest Brother, how much your letter made us feel when you express yourself as feeling sad, to come home with empty pockets. What matter is it about your empty pockets in comparison to your coming home well! How truly grateful we are, to have you as you are! D.G.
    Never mind about the pockets . . . have you not reduced the debt of the dioceses most wonderfully! Have you not by your own personal exertion, rebuilt the Cathedral Chapel, bought a residence for its clergy, given orphanage for Boys &c &c &c—not to speak of the aid you have given to the widows and orphans left destitute! . . . It is a privilege and an honor for which we should be and are grateful to serve the poor and destitute, as you have been . . . doing all your life. . . .

BAPTISTA LYNCH, URSULINES, DEC 12[22]

... Sister Mary left V.C. on Sunday 9th. ...

Brother John writes me that Mr Robt. Aldrich told him and I suppose you also—that he was moving favorably our Charter. ...

... Mme Etienne has received [a letter] from Miss Daisy Aldrich, in which she says—Papa is very much interested with the noble theme (our claim) and I think he would like nothing better than to plead in your behalf." That sentence prompts me to ask him to be our lawyer and plead our cause ...

... Prospects for our school are beginning to look more promising ...

BAPTISTA LYNCH, URSULINES, DEC 15[23]

... We hear something of more pupils coming after Xmas and the passage of the "Usury Law"[24] will no doubt be of great benefit to the country at large. ...

I am sorry you are going to N.C. ... Let the young people do the active work now, and you do the head work for them. That is what I do now.

... Is it not a comfort to see the work [the state legislature] are doing and realize, our grand old state is again in the hands of those interested in its welfare. ...

Did you hear that Robert has a place in the Custom House, Charleston, and he and Kate will live down there. ...

BAPTISTA LYNCH, URSULINES, DEC 23[25]

... We have no Xmas tree this year—not a child in the house. Each of the few we have will spend Christmas with her family. ... It is the first Xmas I have ever spent so. ...

25

"THERE IS NO MISTAKE THAT FARMING IS EVER A FAILURE"

January–June 1878

From the correspondence Baptista Lynch and her community had from relatives and former students, one senses the scale of the northern migration which landed Southerners in New York, Boston, Bridgeport, and other cities they judged to hold better futures than the ones they faced at home, particularly in port cities like Charleston, which were not sharing in the economic growth occurring in the emerging postwar South. The old district of the city still remained a massive ruin, a stark reminder of the persistent poverty that prevented rebuilding so many of the structures, like St. Finian's and St. John's Cathedral.

The hard times which war and Reconstruction had precipitated had narrowed peoples' vision for their children. The tradition of parents preparing their children to do better than they themselves had done fell victim to the parents' own immediate needs. Education was first to suffer from this change in priorities. Female students and their parents came to value home economics far more than they did the fine arts. Teaching music was unfortunately the only means that Henrietta Lynch had of providing some revenue for her family. Despite her rock-bottom charge of eight dollars for a year's music lessons, she found herself a music teacher without pupils.

Patrick Lynch remained not only the financial rescuer for the various branches of the family, but its chief agent of placement for the Lynch men of the third generation. Conlaw S. Lynch, Francis and Henrietta's older son, had been working the farm at Valle Crucis on a hand-to-mouth basis. Back home in Cheraw, none the better financially for all his labor at the farm south of Columbia, Conlaw naturally looked to his uncle to use his influence to secure him a position in a "counting house." Francis was clearly disappointed that his eldest son had chosen not to follow in his path by taking up the tanner's trade. But, from his father's own bleak postwar experience, who could blame Conlaw for looking elsewhere for business opportunities?

Robert Lynch, the first of his generation to enjoy his bishop uncle's support, himself found that clerking, even for the secretary of state in Columbia, could not remove him and his growing family from the "pathways of poverty." And so, he turned once more to his uncle to support his moving to Charleston, where an opportunity had arisen for him to return to the tanning business in which he had first apprenticed in France. Despite his uncle Francis' woes in trying to resurrect his own tanning operations in the postwar period, Robert confessed that having his own tan yard had long been his career dream.

John Lynch, having staked his fortunes to the "Radical University," mainly out of financial need, now found himself in danger of being pushed aside, as the university was re-organized, or "de-radicalized." He realized he was in no position to compete with the Le Contes and other distinguished professors whom the new administration was courting. To his relief, John retained his position on the faculty and at the Penitentiary, but this income wasn't nearly enough to liquidate his debts. Needing $3,500, John's only hope was to attract a loan from someone who would have faith in his selling his unworked mine and underwater lots in Beaufort. The Republicans had a better prospect of bringing back Reconstruction.

Back taxes continued to haunt Baptista, forcing her to the extreme, and probably illegal device of having John devalue their town property to reduce their taxes. An unexpected infusion of tuition allowed Baptista to meet their immediate tax delinquency without resorting to any fiscal legerdemain. The Ursuline, however, was determined, not just to minimize her taxes but to avoid them altogether. One means to achieve that was by securing a charter for the Ursuline academy. John Lynch agreed to be the point man in lobbying the state legislature. The other potential relief lay in the sale of the former academy site, which the nuns had kept as a possible place for their new building. Baptista welcomed the revival of the real estate market, even if driven by Northern money for luxury vacation homes. She cared little about the geographic origin or purpose of prospective buyers, so long as they had the means to lift the albatross of the town lots from them, together with the tax burden they carried.

The death of Pope Pius IX was a blow to American Catholics, particularly those in the South who had so identified with him in their mutual suffering at the hands of hostile governments. Indeed, the affection and personal loyalty that Pio Nono had evoked from American Catholics over his long reign was unprecedented. This familial relationship led to the "Holy Father" becoming their standard invocation for the spiritual head of Roman Catholicism, a title that surely would have baffled John Carroll, and probably John England as well.

Redemption had not only reinvigorated white society in South Carolina, but the white Catholic community in particular, as the building or renovation of its churches indicates. At a time when Patrick Lynch found his fundraising in the North to be producing diminishing returns, Catholics eagerly relied on fairs and other special events to raise money locally. Confidence in their future buoyed their commitment to the rebuilding of the institutional church.

PATRICK N. LYNCH TO JAMES GIBBONS, CHARLESTON, 22 JAN[1]
... Pity for a poor crushed episcopal Micawber who awaits something to turn up in the shape just now of six hundred dollars to meet engagements maturing in two weeks, and who is too crazy to write as he would like to do. In fact, I question if a man, under sentence of death, feels more gloomy and sad than I do—and have done ever since Christmas. ...

R[OBERT] A. LYNCH, COLUMBIA, JAN. 23[2]
... When you were last in Columbia you were kind enough to promise Kate that you would use your influence in obtaining me employment under Mr. Baldwin. ... With a position which would pay me anything like a decent salary I could in two or three years save enough to start a small tan-yard, a thing I have been trying to do for ten years. ...

JOHN LYNCH, COLUMBIA, JAN 26[3]

... The University bill has just passed the House today. If it passes the Senate, which I think it will, I must stir myself. I think it is the intention to try and induce the Le Contes to return. If so, I will have but a poor chance. ...

BAPTISTA LYNCH, URSULINES, JAN 31[4]

... It is only that "Tax Bill" that we must settle as soon as we can—we should have paid it in '77 for '76. I intend to ask John to assess the property at a lower value so as to reduce the tax for the future—in the way that Judge C. instructed me before. I will presume on your permission apropos. ...

BAPTISTA LYNCH, URSULINES, FEB 1[5]

I write you only a few hasty lines saying that Mr. Ewd R. Hays . . . and Barnwell brought two daughters today and paid us on *acct* $150 which we will put at once in brother John's hands to pay those taxes for 1876—due in 1877 but overlooked by mistake and sent in recently. This relieves me and you too considerably just now—D.G.—so, you [need] not go collecting now. ...

BAPTISTA LYNCH, URSULINES, FEB 13[6]

... I want to give you the pleasant news of the success of Rev. Father's [Fullerton] Fair in Columbia- Every body is gratified and it realized $1000. ...

I am a great advocate for "Fairs"—Hot-Suppers Concerts—and Pound-party, to help defray the expenses of good works for the church. It is so much nicer to let the congregation share the burden than have the priest have the onus and it will be so much better to have the "Fair" every year in Charleston, and you stay at home, than have you traveling to collect. ...

The election for Judges came off, and I am happy that Judge Aldrich is elected . . . Judge Mackey, too, was reelected. ...

CONLAW [S.] LYNCH, CHERAW, FEB 15[7]

My father instructs me to write you begging you to be the means of my getting a situation in Charleston or some other city. If I was left my choice I would prefer Baltimore or some other northern city. I am not particular as to the kind of business but would like to get into a "Counting House" where I could work my way up. Do not stand back on account of salary. Anything is preferable to being idle. . . . I am depending entirely on you. If you fail to get me a situation I will be idle until Fall without a suit of clothes to my name. ...

JOHN LYNCH, COLUMBIA, FEB 16[8]

The convent Charter bill passed its third reading in the Senate today . . . You
will have to exert your influence with the Compt. Genl. and Attorney Genl.
to keep their eyes *from* the Constitution while reading the law, I fear. . . . No
money from Penitentiary or anywhere else yet.

HENRIETTA LYNCH, CHERAW, FEB 28[9]

. . . We see tight times to obtain a cent, all that was made at cotton went for
taxes, there is no mistake that farming is ever a failure. It is only to obtain
that which pertains to health and the necessaries of life that I dare intrude on
your benevolence . . . I have taught for years . . . but scholars refuse to come
at any price. They would learn cooking, faster than music in this refined age.
I feel that I was born to teach and am in every body's way unless I see myself
teaching. . . .

BAPTISTA LYNCH, URSULINES, MAR 1[10]

. . . I am very grateful about our Bill passing the Legislature—exempting us
from taxes. . . . Brother John who worked hard for us says we are much indebted to Hon. Robt. Aldrich and Mr. *Wyler* of Lancaster—whom you may
remember, as . . . your lawyer [for the] McKenna will case. He and his wife . . .
seem to be ready to become Catholics.

BAPTISTA LYNCH, URSULINES, EVE LAETARE
SUNDAY [MARCH 30][11]

. . . I was delighted to hear yesterday . . . that you . . . were looking remarkably
well—D.G. You will feel even better when you come and see Sister Theresa[12]
in her black veil and satisfactory. . . .

BAPTISTA LYNCH, VALLE CRUCIS,
GOOD FRIDAY [APRIL 19][13]

. . . You heard no doubt Robert has succeeded in obtaining the office with a
salary of $800 per annum. Very glad. . . .

HENRIETTA LYNCH, CHERAW, JUN 7[14]

. . . I know this season of drought, we have passed thro it many a year only
thro your kind unselfish hand opening the purse strings. . . . People of this
renowned town turn up the chance of taking music lessons at $6 pr year. . . .
They get rich by keeping their children from learning. . . .

26

"WHEN YOU SHALL LIVE AT HOME, YOUR DIOCESS WILL BECOME A PERFECT HOTBED OF CATHOLICITY"

July–December 1878

Student enrollment at the Ursuline Institute, barely above single digits, provided neither the revenue nor the rationale for expanding their cramped facilities on the old Keitt estate. So badly reduced was their annual enrollment that Baptista found herself hoping that the yellow fever scare in the Low Country might prompt more parents to send their children to the Ursuline Academy in the safer upcountry. What fear of Yankee invasion had produced for them in 1862, Baptista hoped the threat of the yellow plague would accomplish nearly two decades later. Moreover, their efforts to secure compensation from the federal government continued to fail. Still, in their struggle to recapture the status that their academy had known during the war, Baptista attempted to maximize the attention that the school could generate at its most public event of the academic year: its commencement exercises. What had begun as an exhibition of student accomplishments for the pleasure and edification of parents and friends became a major public event, which drew former students, as well as regional residents, including public officials whose presence conferred a certain gravitas to both occasion and institution.

Baptista, remembering all too well their forced removal from

Charleston in the 1840s, was determined not to repeat that sad history in Tuscaloosa. When, in 1866, she had led a band of Ursulines there to begin an academy, she expected that her friend, Bishop John Quinlan, would, unlike Patrick Lynch's predecessor in Charleston, make the Ursulines the legal owners of the house that would serve as convent and academy, as their constitution required. More than a dozen years later, despite his overall support, Quinn had not done so. To make matters worse, he was sending a priest to Tuscaloosa as their chaplain who had demonstrated his hostility to the nuns' apostolate. The community in Columbia decided to condition the supply of two additional nuns to the satellite house on the Ursulines' becoming the legal owners of the convent academy, with the Bishop holding a mortgage on the house. "Business is business," Baptista reminded her brother.

Time and again she reminded him that the sooner he began to make his presence felt throughout the region, by becoming the pastoral bishop he was meant to be, the sooner would they realize their life-long dreams of converting South Carolina, or at least its upper class, to Catholicism. She was reviving, in a more positive manner, John Moore's plea to the Archbishop of Baltimore in 1865. In effect, they were both echoing St. Paul: unless the people hear the gospel preached, how shall they believe? In her brother Baptista saw the unique preacher who had the power to change hearts and minds to embrace the Faith. As for their own need to have a priest to reanimate their vocations during their annual Retreat, Baptista, in an assertion of spiritual autonomy one could hardly imagine her voicing a decade or more earlier, assured her brother that they were perfectly capable of being their own directors, as they had done before.

John Lynch's financial struggles had not caused him to abandon his life-long engagement with the intellectual world. Indeed, his desperate need to retain his faculty position at the university led him to attempt to utilize his medical experience over the years to propose a meta-theory identifying the marrow of life in the universe. His relative success in mitigating the symptoms of consumption by the measured administration of ether inspired him to identify the substance as the prime matter of the universe. John acknowledged that the common reaction would be that he had lost his mind. But this Lynch had a very rational goal behind his eccentric speculation. Winning acceptance for such a theory within the scientific community, as unlikely as that might be, would, he calculated, secure the reputation that would qualify him for the prestigious position of Professor of Physiology. Which chair would afford him the financial security at last, to concentrate his remaining productive years on further scientific development.

Henrietta was in such a desperate state that she made no elaborate appeal to her brother-in—law's generosity, but simply begged for any help he could immediately send to feed her family. She laid bare their utter poverty—not even a dime could they claim to own. She admitted to being on the brink of losing her very bearings over her inability to provide for them. Husband, son, her very self: all find themselves totally dependent on their bishop kin to enable them to meet the most fundamental needs that middle class families simply take for granted. To such a level had life sunk for the Cheraw Lynches that Henrietta's sister, Louisa Blain, who probably of all those within the extended Lynch family had been the one living most hand-to-mouth, became a major supporter of her brother-in-law's family, sending five dollars one week, two dollars the next, according to her own fluctuating ability to help from such meager income as she realized with her tutoring.

Despite the family's driving ambition to recoup its fortune and status in the new world, the third generation lagged far behind the second's achievements. This had to grate especially on Eliza Lynch, John's wife, who, more than any other of the Lynches, was so sensitive to class as a crucial marker of Southern society. The cruel irony was that poverty had come to consume the family at large in South Carolina. Lillie's breakdown seems a metaphor for the extended family's condition.

Six months after her extended visit to South Carolina, Mary Lynch Spann reported that her return to her native state had given her "a new lease on life." Less than a month later, a telegram brought shocking news about the Lynches' oldest daughter.

BAPTISTA LYNCH, URSULINES, JUL 2[1]

It is about 10 o'clock P.M. all are at rest—the house quiet and our commencement over this afternoon. To me it was very indifferent, but every body seems pleased and gratified—so "alls well that ends well" Col R.M. Sims Secretary of State and Mrs. Sims were here.... Several other old pupils, some now mothers of families were here, and all seem warmly attached to the Convent....

BAPTISTA LYNCH, URSULINES, JUL 8[2]

... I received a long letter from Mme Charles of Tuscaloosa—their school does better than usual, but Bishop Q says that unless they can pay the whole interest each year = $650°° !!! the house must be sold. Heretofore, Sister Charles has by great exertions paid yearly $350°° interest—which is a heavy rent for that house, in that locality. But if any one can manage it, she can.

"Bishop Q also says that . . . if he does not find two [additional nuns] there from Valle Crucis there is no hope for that convent to continue. He will return Sisters Charles and Joseph to V.C. and find a home for Sr. Theresa in some other convent." How wise, our Constitutions are, in prescribing that the House &c shall be secured, before any sisters are sent. . . . *I ask your permission to act with our Sisters* . . . what we . . . shall find to be for the best. . . .

Our letters from Barnwell are enthusiastic . . . I am so glad you went there and did so much good! When you shall be able to live at home, and go around in that way, your Diocess will become a perfect hotbed of Catholicity.

. . . Do not trouble yourself about our Retreat. In Bank Street we each took her book and went off to herself and made an excellent Retreat. We can do so again.

JOHN LYNCH, COLUMBIA, JUL 21[3]

... My principal reason for writing is to ask you where I can find the best articles written on the subject of "that boundless ocean of matter, called ether, which penetrates between all atoms, and fills the immensity of space with its eternal vibrations and undulations." . . .

I have formed an opinion on the formation, uses, and relation of the substance to the life of man. This opinion . . . is the result of at least thirty years study of our subject. I feel that it is correct. . . . If not contrary to the teaching of the church, my own opinion, is as good as any one else. If I can support it by good and sufficient reasons. . . .

HENRIETTA LYNCH, CHERAW, JUL 26[4]

... It is the disagreeable task again that I undertake. It makes me sad. We are truly needy, having not even 10 cents to handle thro the long summer. If the privation of genteel dress is a passport to Heaven then I can enter there, but, this is not what I would annoy you but of the wants of the table. . . .

LOUISA BLAINE, CHARLESTON, AUG 3[5]

... This week I had a letter from Cheraw for you . . . I know they are dreadfully in want for the necessaries of life at this season nothing doing and no credit. I sent them what I got in this week from my scholar but it was only two dollars. I entreat of you . . . to help them . . . as soon as you receive this. . . .

BAPTISTA LYNCH, URSULINES, AUG 4[6]
. . . Another letter from Mrs. Ryan Brown tells us of the conversion of her cousin Mrs. Mary Tobin—She had been *almost* a Catholic for years but your sermon at the Dedication of Barnwell Church decided her. . . . I do hope you may soon have the "ways and means" in your hands to stay at home and going quietly from place to place in your own Diocess bringing souls to a knowledge of the True Faith. . . .

BAPTISTA LYNCH, URSULINES, AUG 11[7]
We are deep in our Retreat and enjoying it very much. I speak for myself, and as many as I have spoken with say the same. . . .
    . . . I hope the alarm about yellow fever may give us pupils from the low country. . . .

JOHN LYNCH, COLUMBIA, AUG 22[8]
I have just returned from Madam Etienne's funeral. She died yesterday morning very quietly after having received all the sacraments the day before. May she rest in peace.

HENRIETTA LYNCH, CHERAW, AUG 26[9]
You made me the promise you would [do] anything for me, let come what would to others. It seems now that that time has come . . . Conlaw, our son is decidedly unwilling to engage in the Tanny and he can not be constrained. He has seen his father humbled to the earth, has witnessed his struggle from 10 years up to this day's struggles to bow the heart in grief, so that his father wishes not to constrain or to prevail o'er him. It would be slavery over again. . . . Being reared as a teacher it was my ambition to have my sons *learned* men, scholars a pride to their name. Poverty held her sway. Let me now at least . . . ask this mighty favor of you, that you give the means to Conlaw to go to Baltimore that in person he may find a situation. . . . I, as his mother, say . . . that he deserves a helping hand . . . He has served us from a little boy up; . . . I raise my voice in his praise for he helped in time of need. . . . I fall on my knees before you to ask in this case all the help it needs: . . . I will now be done, trusting this affair in God's hands. You understand it well, it needs no more. . . . .

JOHN LYNCH, COLUMBIA, SEP 3[10]

. . . I am preparing an article for the Legislature on the Barbarism of the so called S.C. Penitentiary, which if I read before them, will make them open their eyes. . . . It is on "Animal Heat" as generated and expended in the so called Penitentiary, physical effects on convicts &c, &c. . . .

BAPTISTA LYNCH, URSULINES, SEP[11]

. . . I have written to M Charles, that rather than have the convent so broken up, we would send two Sisters by next session—*on condition*, that she had the deeds in her hands and legally registered for the property they now occupy— she giving the Bishop a mortgage on the property and bond as security. . . . I do not forget, that the omission of this acct, turned our Charleston nuns out of house and home—and deprived them unjustly of all they had expended in local improvements. . . .

    . . . Whatever is to be done, we have to do promptly. . . . But I want the Deeds of purchase to be in hand first. . . .

    St. Francis Assisi said to his monks, that God had mercifully preserved them from the pest of a wife's but the devil had raised up these Sisters to torment them. I suspect Nuns sometimes, feel like uttering the same sentiment—only vice versa . . .

    Another point of Tuscaloosa, I fear that the Bp is going to place as pastor there—that individual whose letters accidentally came into my hands. I object—and will not allow our sisters to accept his ministry—if I can prevent . . .

BAPTISTA LYNCH, URSULINES, VALLE CRUCIS
NEAR COLUMBIA, S.C. SEPT. 16th[12]

You have received ere this Brother John's letter telling you that our beloved Sister Mary has gone to a better world (RIP).

    . . . She was so superior to me in every way, that I loved to look up to her and be guided by her wise yet always modest counsel—In her married life she reminded me of our precious mother—and that is saying *everything.* . . .

BAPTISTA LYNCH, URSULINES, OCT 3[13]

. . . Mary . . . was sick in bed about a month before she died and was suffering just like our precious mother.

    The Doctors said she had malarial poison in her system and heart disease from which she must have been suffering for a long time. (R.I.P.)

    . . . Our next work is our "Claim on Congress . . . We hope to see Senators Butler and Gordon in a few days. They have promised us their influence . . .

and others also. I will get Sister Ignatia Dunn to work this, a good deal for I do not feel like it now. . . .

LOUISA BLAINE, CHARLESTON, OCT 12[14]

I wrote to you this week telling you that Mrs Ryan and her little daughter were sick and for fear that Lilly would break down I insisted on her getting help but with all she did break down and is most fearfully insane. I brought her down on Thursday night thinking it would do her good but she screamed and went on so I was obliged to take her back to her mother today Saturday. They are trying to keep her in, but I fear she will at any moment heart [*sic*] herself. . . . The [Charity] Sisters and I have done all in our power. She has a woman . . . to mind her but for all that she is so violent it takes more than one. I telegraphed Dr. Lynch but he has written to say he cannot come. Come without delay and take her away if you do not it will be done by strangers. . . . Come at once . . .

BAPTISTA LYNCH, URSULINES, OCT 24[15]

I cannot tell you how thankful and relieved I am, that you arrived in Charleston when you did—to take in hand our dear Lilly's case. For like our own precious mother, you see at once how matters stand and what must be done—and do it. . . .

Sr. Theresa wishes you could send Lilly to St. Agnes Hospital where many such go, instead of to Mt. Hope—[16] But *we* do not know, as you do, what is for the best, and the dear child may be violent. . . .

BAPTISTA LNCH, URSULINES, NOV 17[17]

. . . In two weeks Congress will meet—we all want our claim to come up at once, and be rushed right through.

Of course, it is through prayer, we hope for success but we will work all we can . . . This is the last term for Patterson. His successor will be Gov. Hampton and of course, it would be entirely out of place, for him to take the cause in hand. . . .

BAPTISTA LYNCH, URSULINES, DEC 14[18]

. . . Brother John is looking very badly. I really feel anxious about him—there seems to be a giving away of his whole system and today, I saw the erysipelas in one side of his face and near his temple and yet he is faithful to his duty at the Hospital and does not give up. No doubt he over-exerts himself. He certainly edifies me and I only wish he could pay his debts and feel easy . . .

HENRIETTA LYNCH, CHERAW, DEC 26[19]

... Many happy Christmas days to you and health and God's blessing.

My dear Bishop I hope I will not be subject to censure when I tell you that now after one year I would like you to let C. Pinckney be put to whatever situation he intends. Knowing my indebtedness to you, although we had but one room for our boys I gave up my bed to Francis and let C.P. share our Conlaws bed. . . . Our boys having given up their room regularly to visitors I am not surprised that they wished to leave home when of age. . . . I have not slept in my room for one year and I know you to be too great an advocate of the marriage state, to advocate separation of man and wife. But for my high regard for your opinion I might never have cared to marry.[20]

We all sleep—the females in my mother's room. . . . I waited the full year and hope your charity will read the thing clear. . . .

LILLIE LYNCH, MOUNT HOPE RETREAT,
NEAR BALTIMORE, DEC 30[21]

... I am striving earnestly to be a good little Angeline and child of Mary and try to be amiable and obliging to those around and give the good Sisters as little trouble as possible. When strong enough I have been permitted to assist the sacristan. Was that not a privilege? I ... try to employ my time much as we did at Valle Crucis. When suffering I unite it to the Passion of our Lord. . . .

27

"THIS DEPRIVES ME OF THE LAST FRAIL PLANT I HAD TO LEAN ON FOR THE SUPPORT OF MY FAMILY"

January–June 1879

In his annual report to his diocese's chief foreign benefactor, the French Association for the Propagation of the Faith, Bishop Lynch presented a grim picture of their finances. As they began a new year, he had less than "a hundred francs" in hand. All the indicators pointed to their raising in the coming fiscal year perhaps a half of the revenue they managed to accrue during the past one. The sad truth, he confided, was that South Carolina had still not recovered from the impoverishment that the war brought. If anything, for too many, conditions had worsened. "Every year I find greater depth of misery among those who fifteen years ago were wealthy."

On Tuesday, May 13, Lynches of the second and third generation were among the thousands who gathered on the State House grounds in Columbia for the dedication of the Confederate memorial. If the South had regained quasi-autonomy in its political and social affairs, it still needed to wrest control of the narrative of the war which had resulted in its temporary loss of statehood. The Columbia dedication marked one of the earliest manifestations of that revisionism, undertaken by the female memorial associations and the Confederate veterans' organizations in erecting the monuments and writing the memoirs which celebrated what became known as the Lost Cause. It represented the redemption, in stone and historiography, of the South's raison d'etre: white supremacy.

A quarter century earlier, John Lynch had hoped to use Patrick Lynch's rising reputation in Charleston to give John an advantage in establishing a medical practice there. Instead, he had moved from Cheraw to Columbia, with its promise of a larger pool of potential patients and of the presence of two institutions with a permanent need for physicians. Now, twenty-five years later, John Lynch found himself a double victim of the new order of Redemption in the state's capital: locked out of both the medical school of South Carolina University, as well as of the penitentiary. At the latter facility, John Lynch's dismissal was part of an austerity regime that had no place for humanitarian care, especially for felons. Those dying, no longer a threat to society, were simply let loose, to die where they might. The last thing the Redeemers intended to provide was health care.

John Lynch's attempts to secure revenue by putting his papers on the market or securing engagements for lectures proved equally fruitless. Nor could his resident children provide any income. The upshot was a family reduced to a level of hand-to-mouth living that the Cheraw Lynches already knew. Like Francis, John appealed to his bishop brother for relief. Rescue from immediate financial peril came in Patrick's assuming a new mortgage on the mine. Then, unexpectedly came an opportunity seemingly too good to be true: the promise of a practice in Atlanta, subsidized by wealthy Catholics. A regional medical association meeting in Atlanta provided an occasion to explore the offer. The informal gatherings around the sessions gave John Lynch the opportunity to demonstrate his cutting-edge medical knowledge. The short shrift he was given by the Atlanta Catholics he met boded poorly for any hope of a subsidized practice, a reality which John was not willing, as yet, to acknowledge.

Virtually as soon as Henrietta Lynch had insisted that Patrick Lynch remove his nephew Conlaw from their home, the Cheraw Lynches found themselves hosting an even more invasive guest: their alcoholic pastor slipping rapidly into dementia. Henrietta again had the painful duty of telling her bishop brother-in-law that their resident priest was no longer capable of taking care of himself, much less serving as their pastor. The priest, alas, was only the most acute of the family's problems.

BAPTISTA LYNCH, URSULINES, JAN 4[1]

... I trust my precious brother your sickness is more fatigue, after all that hard work and travel than anything else—and after you get a good rest at home, you will feel quite well again.

... Sister Ignatia—whose father lived in Washington D.C. and who knows something of Congressional doings has relieved me of writing and has found in Mrs Lloyd Mackay and Judge M. old acquaintances and enthusiastic workers and she also is an old acquaintance of Senator M.C. Butler.[2] I have left the work to her ...

JOHN LYNCH, COLUMBIA, JAN 8[3]

On Monday last, without warning, and quite unexpectedly to myself and friends, the new Superintendent of Penitentiary, sent me a note, stating that my commission with the institution as surgeon would cease from that date, ... This deprives me of the last frail plant I had to lean on, for the support of my family, and I am sorry to say, my practice is principally charity, and in the family, with the exception of a few families ... whose practice does not amount some years to ten dollars. This is a poor prospect.

... Can you advise me on this, my sixtieth birthday, what to do. I am too old to commence life anew am fit for nothing outside my profession, as a physician or teacher. Is there a chair of Physiology in the Charleston College? ...

But there is another, and equally as embarrassing a matter to me. Sue Caldwell's Guardian Bond. I have earnestly hoped and prayed that I might be able to sell the Mary Mine, before the time of settlement would arrive. But ... I am afraid my hopes are dissipated. At one time you offered to take the mine and relieve me of the debt. At that time I executed a mortgage of the mine to you, in consideration of your security on my Guardian Bond, ... I am willing and anxious to make any arrangement that will secure you, and relieve myself.

. . .

PATRICK N. LYNCH TO ASSOC. FOR THE PROPAGATION OF THE FAITH, CHARLESTON, JAN. 10[4]

May I take the liberty of laying before you the present condition of this Diocess of Charleston and of respectfully entreating you to place it again on the list of the Dioceses to which you accord your liberal charity.

. . . The sad prospect before me for 1879 fills my heart with sad forebodings, and in my almost despair, I appeal again to your charity. . . . For thirteen years my labors have been arduous. . . . Especially had I to provide for the special wants of the enfranchised Blacks. . . . The situation was rendered more difficult by the course of civil government, to which, in punishment for the War of secession, this state of South Carolina, my diocess, was subjected. . . . The rich became poor, and the poor were almost starving. . . . I hoped that in two or three years this miserable condition would pass away, and that some measure of prosperity might return. . . . But the prosperity has not come. Every year I find greater depth of misery among those who fifteen years ago were wealthy.

. . . We have met our running expenses, and have not allowed the debt of the Diocess to increase. But it leaves me at the end of the year without a hundred francs, and with a feeling that in 1879 I cannot look for one half of what we managed to obtain from the people and elsewhere, during the past year. And yet, the interests of the church call for as much, if not more. . . .

But what troubles me most now, is the debt still due on the Church, Presbytery and School in Charleston which some years ago I provided for the Emancipated Catholic Negroes. That church is a source of consolation to me for the fervour of those simple good souls, for such are they made by the influence of our Holy Faith, and by the conversions made there by the zealous priests labouring among them. I have spent on the buildings almost 100,000 francs, of which sum 12,000 francs are still due, and every six months I have to pay a heavy interest on it. Would to God that your charitable allocation would relieve my sad heart of this heavy burden, and enable us to labour more cheerfully in the work of the Lord. . . .

BAPTISTA LYNCH, URSULINES, JAN 20th[5]
I . . . have heard from Washington that our claim although presented must await next Congress. . . .

JOHN LYNCH, COLUMBIA, JAN 24[6]
. . . I see that the new Supt and Doctor at Penty have been making a clean sweep of the sick, two of the inmates of the Hospital died, and today ten of the worst cases—some in a dying condition were pardoned and sent home. . . . This is inhumane. But the idea seems to be, to save every doll possibly (poor fellows!) . . .

JOHN LYNCH, COLUMBIA, JAN 26 [7]
Your letter of the 24th containing check on N.Y. for $210⁰⁰ . . . was recd this

morning. I am very much obliged and relieved, although mortified at being obliged to call on you for assistance. I hope the time will soon arrive when I may be able to reciprocate, although the lookout at present is gloomy.

. . . I have . . . gotten up a few scientific lectures which I think are excellent . . . my idea was to give one or two *free* lectures, . . . I have never yet had an opportunity to *show* what I *know* or can *say*. . . I know this is visionary, but what better can I do[?] . . . I might invent, and take out patents. What could I do with them . . . [?] I have no talent for trading. . . .[8]

JOHN LYNCH, COLUMBIA, FEB 6[9]

. . . I can sit in the office all day, and rarely have a visitor. Those who do call are unprofitable. . . . It really seems to me, I am under a cloud. And cannot clear myself. . . . Offered to sell some papers, but could find no one with money who would purchase. . . .

BAPTISTA LYNCH, URSULINES, FEB 10[10]

How good and kind of you—to pay the taxes! . . . I am so much obliged to you. . . .

HENRIETTA LYNCH, CHERAW, FEB 13[11]

On this subject I should have written long ago, it is of Rev. Father Cullinan. . . . [who] has taken again to his old failing . . .

Bishop we cannot stand it. . . . A tavern room is not more disgusting in the puddles of tobacco spit but, when a man so far forgets himself as to blow his nose in his hands at table repeatedly, I tell you I crawl. . . . We are only mortals! Even if Mr. C. at your command stops drinking, it is not possible he will now give up these horrid practices. His hands and person are so neglected and as you know when he drinks he wants every body to see him. Servants and every body knows it. . . . Mr C's memory is failing him very much. . . . I think him unmanageable. . . . To lose him I would be truly sad. But on the rules of cleanliness and civilization as well as in temperance an entire reform must take place. . . .

. . . Since the above Marie has come from Mrs. F's saying that last night the house was nearly burned down by Rev. Mr. C. in one of these fits. Mr. F . . . was roused by the smell of fire and entering was nearly stifled. It seems he had thrown in the fire a large quilt from off his bed. . . . They say they really think he wants to destroy himself, and it was miraculous that the hay under the house did not set them all on fire. This is the second time the floor was burned . . . We really think that his mind is leaving him. . . .

JOHN LYNCH, COLUMBIA, FEB 27[12]

... It seems that my case is not an exception to the general rule. The world will now try and put me as low down as they can. My having (as they seem to suppose) lost everything by losing my salary. Sometimes I do feel as if I could not see my way clear, but I have *faith*. ... If man deserts me, God will not, in the long run. ...

... Now that the Spirit of Emigration to the south has started, I hope you may hear of some miners or speculators in mines ... I have nothing to fall back on except the mine, Beaufort lots, and the prospect of a professorship when the University opens again. I know I cannot make a support at my profession here, without an entire new population. ...

BAPTISTA LYNCH, URSULINES, MAR 10[13]

... Poor Archbishop Purcell! How I do feel for him![14] I think this is a terrible blow to the Church in this country, because, I have no doubt, that every diocese nearly and all our Church institutions are in much the same condition—fearfully in debt and if pushed could not pay. I sincerely trust this Cinn. action may not sound the tocsin and precipitate matters with others, laboring to sustain the Church and her institutions under difficulties and debts, which must exist necessarily.—Whoever it was that pushed Abp. Purcell need not expect the blessing of the Almighty on themselves or children to the fourth generation. I now admire your wise management and may God bless your work and efforts. ...

JOHN LYNCH, COLUMBIA, MAR 13[15]

I received yours of 4th March containing a check for ($400.00) four hundred dollars, and cannot say whether I was more pleased or mortified. ... But you do not know how much service the $400 did. ...

BAPTISTA LYNCH, URSULINES, LAETARE SUNDAY [MAR 23][16]

... I ... got a letter from the saintly Archbishop Purcell. He says six months ago, he never thought such a calamity could befall him and he seems overwhelmed ... The Archbishop says he does not see his way out of his difficulties. I will write to him and think of suggesting that he would presume to refund by installments in 50—40—30 or say 20 years monies loaned him *without interest* by other dioceses ...

BAPTISTA LYNCH, URSULINES, APR 16[17]

... As ... for Tuscaloosa—I fear that convent must go—I suppose the Bishop of Mobile is unable to forward the money and continue it. Everything is for the best anyway. . . . Then we will see about opening a school up in . . . some place in the Diocese. . . .

JOHN LYNCH, COLUMBIA, APR 1[18]

. . . Another idea has been suggested by a letter from Conlaw, he says "Col. T.M. Acton one of the proprietors of the *Atlantic Constitution* will call on (me) some day next week, and will make me a proposition." "Col. A. is an Irishman and a good Catholic and has great influence with the leading Irish in Atlanta." "Col. A. will propose that I move to Atlanta. . . . Whether he has sickness or not in his family, will pay so much a year. Will guarantee the best Catholics and richest in the Church to do the same . . . " He thinks it would pay at least five thousand dollars a year!" . . . Now if such a proposition is made to me in good faith, in my present condition, I do not see how I could refuse it, although . . . the proposition has not yet been made, and I may not be tempted. . . .

JOHN LYNCH, COLUMBIA, APR 26[19]

. . . Twenty some years ago I attended as "delegate" the A. Med Association. In Charleston. Next month it meets in Atlanta. I would very much like to attend again and am trying to raise the money and at the same time get an appointment as delegate from our county Med society. It might benefit my health, by the change—and would give me an excellent opportunity of seeing the people without saying anything about going over to live. What do you think of the matter?

JOHN LYNCH, COLUMBIA, MAY 1st[20]

. . . I today received my credentials as delegate, will expect to start Saturday night . . .

Mr. Woodward has just called . . . to see if Col. Acton[21] had been to see me, when I told him he had not, he said he would write to him tonight, that I would be in Atlanta attending the Convention. I am not anxious to move, nor will I, without a very great inducement is offered . . .

BAPTISTA LYNCH, URSULINES, MAY 6[22]

. . . A letter from Tuscaloosa today from Bp. Q[.] who will continue the Convent. . . .

BAPTISTA LYNCH, URSULINES, MAY 13[23]

. . . Brother John has returned from his Atlanta trip, very much benefited and looking ten years younger. I can see how you preserve your freshness by travel and change of place. . . .

Julia has gone to witness the unveiling of the monument. Conlaw is down from Greenville.[24]

JOHN LYNCH, COLUMBIA, MAY 13[25]

. . . Arrived in Atlanta 5 A.M. [Monday] . . . Col. Acton . . . called in the afternoon . . . and took me with another physician to ride all around . . . the city. When he left me at the hotel he said he could call after ten or so in the morning to see me. I did not meet him afterwards. He was particularly pleasant, and all his introductions alluded to *our relationship,* and former acquaintance. . . .

Although I did not make any speeches, . . . I flatter myself that I had as much attention paid to me as any other private in the ranks, . . . [in] a conversation at the hotel with a party of MDs from the west, on the very subject [as the president's upcoming address], [I] had expressed my views very clearly enough to elicit discussion the next day after the address . . . several times . . . had pleasant conversations [with the president as well as] the most distinguished and literary members, and as the subject invariably turned on the prest address . . . I was always at home, and . . . I no doubt gained a little more respect . . .

. . . One of the most pleasant weeks I ever spent. . . .

BAPTISTA LYNCH, URSULINES, JUN 1 PENTECOST SUNDAY[26]

. . . Poor dear old Archbishop Purcell. . . . I know you strained a point to give him that $100 which is as much from you as was any one's offering, and more, for it was a beautiful act of self denial—which will draw down a blessing for you. . . .

HENRIETTA LYNCH, CHERAW, JUN 8[27]

. . . In winter heretofore our wants have been supplied by cotton business, but Mr Lynch can get no supplies to carry him on in summer, because of backwardness in the former year. I request of you a sum to enable me to set some one to cook. If they see the money they will come. I pray again and again that you will mercifully respond to the call of your child, and may God in his mercy bless you. My temper is like vinegar my trials seem so hard to bear, I am always calling on the name of the Lord. . . .

28

"JUST NOW EVERYTHING LOOKS GLOOMY"

July–December 1879

Visitors to Valle Crucis expressed their delight that the years of "hard times and bad government" were behind them, but those at Valle Crucis themselves were not really sharing in the new order that the Redeemers claimed to be establishing. One needed look no further than the harvesting of the fall crops by the entire community at Valle Crucis to dispel any such notion. What the enslaved labor on the estate would have been responsible for before the war, now fell to those who previously would have been spared such work. Financial impoverishment was not the sole downside of life at Valle Crucis. There were the mental disorders of individual members of the community, which put a particular strain on Baptista. The mother superior found herself constantly weighing the Community's welfare against the toleration of the abnormal behavior of individual members.

Nothing unsettled John Lynch to the degree that the Caldwell lawsuit did, in accusing him of defrauding the estate of which he had endeavored to be a faithful guardian. As though flailing for an explanation for his financial woes, John blamed the entire community of Columbia for shunning him professionally, for never giving him the chance to build up a practice. In his mind, the condition of his house, the lack of a horse, his real estate failures, his being part of the Radical University, all had poisoned the community against him. And now he had to bear the disgrace of seeing this ostracism inflicted upon his daughters. The shaming that John had for so long felt, the second generation must now share. That stigma, interestingly, had forced all his sons to bet their futures on finding success, not in the professions, but in business, as their Uncle Frank had, if only briefly.

One aspect of the Old South that had survived both war and reconstruction were seasonal fevers. The summer of 1879 was an especially deadly one for typhoid, nowhere more so than in Cheraw. The Lynch household escaped this latest plague, just after Patrick Lynch had removed the demented, alcoholic priest from their midst. Henrietta deeply appreciated her brother-in-law's intervention, but, unfortunately, she had more to ask of him. At a time when the third generation Lynch males were seeking business opportunities, Francis Jr. had long aspired to practice law. Perhaps anticipating that Patrick had thoughts of their first-born son becoming a priest, and thus keeping alive the family tradition of which Patrick himself was such an important link. Henrietta noted that, had Francis Jr. grown up in a different environment, perhaps he would have been the one to succeed his uncle in the priesthood and beyond, but that was not to be. Henrietta's plea was a simple one to her brother-in-law: give her son the opportunity to fulfill his dream.

Whatever the quality of his instruction, Josey Blain was successful enough in attracting students to become the object of the attacks of a local Methodist minister. The cultural war over education, which had been largely limited to urban areas where the rapidly growing parochial school network was centered, now reached upcountry Carolina, where the Catholic menace was nothing church-sponsored, but the most modest of operations by a disabled Catholic layman trying to provide some income for his extended family. Henrietta's brother had unfortunately found himself in the crosshairs of an institutional fight.

JOHN LYNCH, COLUMBIA, JUL 5[1]

. . . It is now six months since I left work at the Penitentiary Hospital, and although I have stuck close to my office I am not succeeding at all. . . . I have made applications for writing, book Keeping, and such like work, but can find no one who has it to give out. You can readily perceive why I am so anxious to make a speedy sale of the mine. . . .

LOUISA BLAINE, CHERAW, JUL 11[2]

… Last Sunday my brother was denounced from the pulpit by the Methodist Minister. He told his people not to send their children to that school and so on. …

FRANCIS LYNCH, CHERAW, OCT 2[3]

Appreciating your anxiety in the matter of the urgent claims to provide for which, I received your ck for twelve hundred dolls. and a blank ck, this latter I have not used. … It is exceedingly fortunate that you have been so good to come to my relief, and I cannot sufficiently express my thankfulness and appreciation. Be sure of all our prayers. …

BAPTISTA LYNCH, URSULINES, OCT 7[4]

… Our school has now 14 Boarding pupils with a prospect of more—which is better than it has been in October for years—D.G.

… I cannot express to you—how much your last welcome letter comforted and strengthened me. … As you say—it is well to lose our self-sufficiency and if I only realized that it led me nearer to God, it would make me very happy.

… Y have done for us far more than we had any right to expect and we owe you a large debt of gratitude as a community. When we read the *"Circulars"* of other convents, we realize more fully our own blessed condition—for which under God, we thank you our ever good and kind "Father Bishop" …

JOHN LYNCH, COLUMBIA, OCT. 12[5]

… Just now, everything looks gloomy. I hope you are progressing in your undertakings, and that the time is not far distant when I may be able to assist, instead of being a burden to you. … But meantime I am not collecting sufficient to supply the table; Insurance, taxes, and winter clothing for the family, have to be looked after …

I am tired seeing my daughters humiliated and disappointed, they have made every effort to assist me, as far as their talents will allow, but the same spirit which prevents *my* rising in my profession in this community, prevents their succeeding in their endeavours. I cheer them up as much as possible. *I know* that if I sold my mine, painted my house, bought a horse, and made an independent appearance generally, there would be a revolution in sentiment. …

LOUISA BLAINE, CHARLESTON, OCT 17[6]

… I heard from Cheraw this week. … Our Rev father[7] has been to Sumter, and I want you to write and beg him not to leave Cheraw again until you go there. He gave great trouble last week and up to Saturday. Was in a very bad state (he said Mass on Sunday but some think it would have been better if he had not). . . .

HENRIETTA LYNCH, CHERAW, OCT 24[8]

. . . Our son Francis[9] is a pride to our hearts. He is truly noble and pure with the humility of a little child he says his prayers daily and will at any time kneel to offer a prayer pointed out by Ma to him. . . . Surrounded as we are by Protestants he has given no sign of turning to the Priesthood which with other surroundings might have been all different, but he has said that his aspirations always have been, to be a lawyer.

Francis would need much more study before he could think of such a thing. . . . Is now 17 years of age. . . . Your mantle of dignity, nobleness and learning I hope will fall on Francis. I see no scion of your family of whom you may be so justly proud. . . .

FRANCIS LYNCH, CHERAW, OCT 26[10]

. . . Sometime in March last, in response to an inquiry from the representatives of the late Mr. Cragin of Boston, in regard to my bond there, I took the liberty of suggesting that on account of the difference in value of currency perhaps they would consider 300$ now and 6 pr ¢ int as equivalent to the 500$ in 1867. Lately I have recd an intimation of assent provided some paymt would now be made on it. To this my reply was the paymt would be impracticable now. Thinking that among your friends, some one, on such good security, would loan 300$ to be returned in four annual instalments, with interest, not over 7prct . . .

BAPTISTA LYNCH, URSULINES, OCT 30[11]

. . . Every body is busy gathering in the crop. We began yesterday to plow and dig potatoes which gives plenty of work to all hands. . . .

. . . Our visitors all seem to be cheerful and satisfied with the state of the country and times, and the cry of "hard times" and "bad government" no longer are to be heard (D.G.).

BAPTISTA LYNCH, URSULINES, DEC 6[12]

. . . Columbia is quite lively now. Court in session and everybody rejoicing at easier times—in general (with a few exceptions)

29

"I FEAR I AM LOST IN THE LABYRINTH"

January–June 1880

Writing her bishop brother on January 1, Baptista Lynch pointed out that ex-President Grant had been in the capital of South Carolina as the year and decade ended. "Appropriate day," she commented, "the last day of the old year." As the avatar of the failed attempt to impose a new order on the South, Grant's presence in South Carolina as an old year gave way to a new one seemed especially fitting. For Baptista, Grant represented a discredited experiment that, mercifully, no longer plagued the South, nor the nation.

Francis Lynch continued to pursue his two professions, that of planter and tanner. For the latter he had a team of presumably Black laborers peeling bark for the tannery he still hoped to revive, if only he could come by the capital needed to procure the supplies that would enable him to operate. There was the rub. He could not pay for the labor to harvest his oat crop. Meanwhile his legal debts would not go away. Amid these difficulties Francis saw a serendipitous conjunction of circumstances—the opportunity to obtain railroad bonds as capital with which to secure supplies whose costs the extension of the railroad to the vicinity of his plant were already greatly reducing.

More than two decades earlier, Francis Lynch had turned to New York for the skilled labor he considered crucial to the success of his tannery. Once more he reached out to the North, not for labor, but the capital that would enable him to recapture the place he once held in the regional tanning industry. In attempting to find accommodating creditors, he had paradoxically more success in Boston than in South Carolina. The bottom line, nonetheless, was an increase in debt. Still his perennial optimism enabled him to insist to his brother Patrick that his tanning business could produce enough revenue through stepping up its output, if only he had the means to purchase the leather needed for production. So again, he turned to his brother for the $1,000 that would enable him to procure the supplies needed to turn his fortunes around. Once again Patrick became his lifeline for preserving Francis's farm and business.

Ironically it was Henrietta Lynch whose correspondence probably got to the gist of things better than did that of any of the Lynches, including those with far more education. In striking contrast to her husband's perennial wishful thinking, she manifested a remarkable ability to probe beneath the surface and bear witness to the larger impact that, say, an alcoholic priest had—and didn't have on their community. The mental decline that alcohol abuse had fostered put not only their parish priest in harm's way but did enormous damage to the Catholic community, particularly the younger generation so badly in need of good example. The price, Henrietta found, was the loss of that generation, morally and spiritually. Into that vacuum the Protestant churches reached out to exploit the Catholic failure. And Henrietta had the courage to remind her brother-in-law that he alone had the authority and means to redeem their scandalous situation. To his credit, Patrick Lynch did so.

"Fear I am lost in the labyrinth and need a guide:" was John Lynch's dire assessment of his situation as 1880 neared its midpoint. He had no paying practice of medicine, there were no boarders to provide a supplemental income, his investments attracted no buyers. Neither family nor society could come to his assistance. The Church's condemnation of fraternal organizations like the Elks closed off that avenue to wealth and reputation. And so, as so many times before, in desperation John turned to his brother for the advice and assistance that he could not find elsewhere.

BAPTISTA LYNCH, URSULINES, JAN 1 1880[1]

... "Rosa Murray" left for home yesterday (31 Dec) Mr Chas Logan who called for her—informed us that "Ex-president Grant would meet her at the Depot! Expected in Columbia! Appropriate day—the last day of the old year! ...

FRANCIS LYNCH, CHERAW, JAN 21[2]

... It affords me pleasure to tell you, that I have so arranged the debt I owe, in Boston, as to have substituted in satisfaction for it; 4000$ at 6 pct interest from 1st inst and payable in four annual payments. This was exceedingly generous on the part of my friends there, who have always evinced to me a large liberality.... What is of great importance to me is such business arrangements as will enable me [to] do a larger tanning business, from the fruits of which to make provision for my obligations. Ample facilities in this way the past year would doubtless have enabled me to pay full this claim by this time. The margin between the cost of producing leather and the wholesale price of it in N.Y. does away with all risks, and actively done should yield 3000$ pr ann.... Confident of succeeding, I am endeavoring to procure 1000$ worth tan. Bark ...

CONLAW [S.] LYNCH, CHERAW, JAN 22[3]

I recd your kind letter with draft enclosed. I wrote the bank instructing them to hold the amt ($465°°) subject to my Drft in partial amounts.... I am very grateful for the confidence you have placed in me....

BAPTISTA LYNCH, URSULINES, FEB 2[4]

... I have gotten several letters from Tuscaloosa recently and just as I expected, the house is to be sold in order to pay Cincinnati debt, so, of course our good Sisters will come home ... Some time ago, I wrote them, that I thought it only just to the good Bishop Quinlan, to return him the property they could not pay for and not trespass longer on his kindness &c. But I suppose they wished to hold on to the last. Now, however, I think they must act definitely ...[5]

FRANCIS LYNCH, CHERAW, MAR 2[6]

... The preparations for planting are good, and prospects promise well so far. Conlaw has profited well from his experience and his attention in that quarter affords me the better opportunity for pushing the Tannery. The prices of leather have added to its lucrativeness and I want to make 2000$ clear from it the present year. If my plans are ably seconded, I will hope to do more.

... The extension of the RRd towards Wadesboro will enable my procuring tan bark in quantity and much lower cost and it seems financially suicidal to forego so good an opportunity for success. Do not say that I am too sanguine. . . .

BAPTISTA LYNCH, URSULINES, LOW SUNDAY [APR 4][7]

. . . I am only sorry my dearest brother that you need to take the Lithia waters and hope they will give you that relief, which they are said to give. Brother John seems to suffer in the same way a good deal lately. Let me be thankful you can get the remedies—it is what thousands are unable to do.

. . . You will be glad to hear that our pupils continue to increase—so that now, our house is crowded. This is owing partly to our lowering our terms to suit their means. We have our hands full of work and are thankful to get it to do. . . .

I wish you could get a wine-keg of the Glen-springs waters to cure you. . . .

HENRIETTA LYNCH, CHERAW, MAY 2[8]

. . . Mr. Lynch is very unfortunate as a business man, but in his walk before God he stands without a blemish, prayerful as a Saint and strict in every religious duty. . . . That Rosary he has recited for 365 days, every year, till now it numbers 25 years, will not fail in the sight of a just God to obtain your rewards and an interest an hundredfold, I trust. . . .

. . . Every one in town has asked when were you coming they seemed anxious to hear you preach. . . . They are grossly ignorant of our Faith and have now lost 15 years wherein so much could have been done. . . . To be very candid with you our children need all the good preaching and example they can see. I sue on their account. . . . I wish a winning priest could come up. . . .

BAPTISTA LYNCH, URSULINES, MAY 3[9]

. . . Why does the thought of writing to me, make you feel sad . . . you, my dearest Brother are too much like our precious mother, not to have her large heart and large mind, and wisdom, and do you remember her sage expression "we must take the world as God sends it"

The newspapers are talking a great deal of "the strong man" You my dearest Brother, have ever been *the strong man* to me—Yes, ever since your boyish arms bore me up, and saved me from drowning even till now—when we've both grown old together. . . . I love to think of you always as well and strong and bright, and cheerful, and equal to any emergency, as I always believe you to be with God's blessing. . . .

Yesterday, we saw in the newspapers something of the Cardinal having a co-adjutor and began to think that might be the trouble—if it is not money difficulties. But whatever it may be, you may count on our earnest prayers. . . .

5th May
. . . I was much pleased with Julia and Jemmie agreeing together to make a novena that their father may be elected on Monday 10th inst. to Professor's chair in University. The election will take place on that day, it seems. . . .

LOUISA BLAINE, CHARLESTON, MAY 21[10]

. . . I am so sick at heart that sometime I do not know what I am saying or doing. I cannot live in this way any longer. I am going to try my best to find a situation in some family were [sic] I can at least support myself. I would go right to the Sisters if I had only the means but I do not wish to go without a cent. I am broken hearted and feel sometimes as if God has forsaken me. . . . Of course if I can get scholars by the first of the month I will remain where I am but I must try and see what I can do. What I want you to do is this to send me $30 by the end of this month if you can not the whole amount send me 20 and the rest as soon after as you can. I know and feel it is a great shame to ask this of you but I promise you to try my best to put a stop to it. . . .

JOHN LYNCH, COLUMBIA, JUN 7[11]

. . . I have been undertaking to collect something on my old debts. If I send John with bills he is snubbed or insulted. If I go myself, I am either put off by the cry of poverty, or promises, which are not fulfilled. We have no boarders for the reason, none are offering, are trying to get some. While in this condition, Mrs. Caldwell from N. Ca writes, "her daughter will be of age this month," must be prepared to settle. [After two more such letters] I sent the following answer ". . . I have been mindful of the fact that Miss S. would become of age this month, . . . I expect to make a final settlement with the Court within the time allowed me by law." . . . I am depending on the sale of the mine for the means. . . . It would be a pity to be obliged to a forced sale for this debt, when the property would be sacrificed . . ."

What am I to do? and how go about it. I am entirely off the track, fear I am lost in the labyrinth and need a guide. If I could do as my professional brothers, join all those clubs and societies, thereby making myself popular, I might see a chance of fighting an even game. . . . I may be mistaken, but I fear I never will be able to make a support in this place, without a change of population or sentiment. . . .

FRANCIS LYNCH, CHERAW, JUN 14[12]

Last spring . . . I pressed forward during the season for peeling tan bark and have procured a fair supply . . . In doing this with farm work I have expended my available means and if permissible would like to borrow 3000$ to be returned after our renewal of note, as was done the past year. Having a large crop of oats . . . none harvested, I am put to, for money to pay for having it done. Of oats I hope to have a surplus for sale in. Cotton Crop doing fairly well. . . .

30

"THE POPE DID NOT DO RIGHT TOWARDS BISHOP LYNCH"

July–December 1880

In the late spring of 1880 newspapers began speculating that Rome would soon appoint Patrick Lynch coadjutor archbishop of New York, which bestowed the right to succeed the current archdiocesan head, Cardinal John McCloskey. Patrick's family had mixed feelings about his transfer to a northern diocese, in particular New York, but the rumors should not have surprised them. Given Patrick Lynch's close friendship with John McCloskey, he seemed a natural choice. Indeed, McCloskey initially favored Lynch as his co-adjutor, but then changed his mind. Probably few had a better read on the bishop's health than did the New York archbishop who evidently concluded that Patrick Lynch was in no condition to assume the leadership of the largest diocese in the country. Unlike John McCloskey, Patrick's own family, especially his Ursuline sister, could not face the reality that the health of their spiritual and financial bellwether had become precarious.

The giant roadblock to John Lynch's economic recovery was the Caldwell suit. It would seem that the crux of John Lynch's failure to pay to the Caldwell daughter the funds he held in trust for her was his having invested them in Confederate bonds which, by 1880, had long been worthless. In effect, he was being sued for his uncalculating patriotism to a failed country. Once again, he turned to Patrick for direction, if not rescue, in dealing with his financial quandary.

Thanks to his brother assuming at least some portion of the debt owed to the Caldwells, John finally settled the suit. Perhaps the relief from that financial weight spurred John to come up with a plan to turn his mine into an asset rather than an albatross. Rather than continuing in his long-frustrated search for a buyer, John conceived the notion of chartering the mine as a means of attracting investors to supply the capital to operate the mine. John Lynch wishfully assumed that he and his associates were going to find investors for a mine for which he had been unable to find any buyer. He was reduced to the generic hope that "times will improve soon," even as his own health badly deteriorated as summer bled into fall.

Henrietta seems to have reached her boiling point from the ineffectiveness of the two men closest to her: her husband and her brother. Francis had simply too many irons in the fire: in the form of responsibilities which he was incapable of fulfilling. Henrietta urged her brother-in-law to advise Francis to concentrate on planting, by having him lease his tannery for others to operate, as well as by removing him as executor for his mother's estate.

JOHN LYNCH, COLUMBIA, JUL 7[1]

. . . The sudden news of the death of poor Conlaw was a great shock to me . . . What I learned at first, was that he had died after an illness of some days from typhoid fever, that he had the priest with him. . . . Mr Woodward tells me—after paying all the funeral expenses, and other small debts he may have about town he will not owe a dollar and may have a little left for Josephine. Mr Woodward will continue the business he has built up for a while . . . for the benefit of his children. . . .

BAPTISTA LYNCH, URSULINES, JUL 8[2]

. . . Brother John . . . is looking thin and old—but is greatly consoled by his visit to Greenville and seeing and hearing for himself and they all realize how deeply grateful we should be, that Conlaw was consoled by the Sacraments and that he was respected and beloved by all who knew him—leaves an honorable name—a spotless reputation among men. . . . (R.I.P.)

. . . You really *must* rest your system. . . . You must not tire yourself even at a thing so interesting and scientific and useful to the city.[3] When 6 days were taken to create the world, was it not to teach the lesson "to make haste slowly? . . .

FRANCIS LYNCH, CHERAW, JUL 9[4]

. . . I wrote you in N.Y. a short time ago, saying I . . . would need to borrow money from Bank, to be repaid from leather . . . I must ask of your endorsement on my note. . . . By this means I can get to do enough tanning, to feel its fruits in meeting obligations. . . .

BAPTISTA LYNCH, URSULINES, JUL 23[5]

I see in the newspapers of New York, Charleston and Columbia! mention of the affairs concerning you . . . I presume a definite answer has been given at Rome. Have you received it? Let me know when you do please. Until then I will treat it as a mere newspaper item. . . .

HENRIETTA LYNCH, CHERAW, JUL 25[6]

. . . As Mr. Lynch says often that I have a better head than he—just let me ask your reflection on this—Do you think it would be better for him to turn all his thought to one business alone and let that be the planting as it seems almost a miracle to have means to carry both on, he managed for instance to have some bark gathered long ago and while the drought lasted there the bark remained, no money to pay hands to bring it up and store it in the cars, but a continual regret as the rain falls that the bark is rendered useless. This has been the case as far as my memory goes. Now this thought is mine that perhaps some man around would like to hire the concern . . . If you think it for Mr. L's good it is for you to advise, of course, not me. . . . So now I have told it all to you how things really are. . . . Then there is my brother . . . Josey it is true is to be pitied as far as his health goes. . . . But you know when debt is due there is something wanting in him too. . . .

BAPTISTA LYNCH, URSULINES, JUL 26[7]

I am so much obliged to you for your welcome letter of 23rd inst. and am very happy to know the "Glenn Springs" waters are benefiting you. . . . Those who have visited the Springs, say it is just the same, as if you dipped it up out of the springs. When your case begins to get low, please let Mr. Barlot know it then, and . . . get you a supply again. . . .

JOHN LYNCH, COLUMBIA, JUL 26[8]

. . . I am glad to see you are *beginning* to take some care of yourself, and from your own, and the account of others, you, no doubt, are beginning to see the necessity of your taking physical and mental rest.

I saw the article in the papers referring to your probable transfer to other fields of labour. I hope not, not only for your own sake but for the sake of others. Still if it is for the good of the church, and the glory of Almighty God, we must quietly submit. . . .

FRANCIS LYNCH, CHERAW, JUL 30[9]
. . . If it be the will of God that you be called to a larger field, we would rejoice in it, if it be in accordance with your desires. . . . Still I hope you would pardon the natural feelings of regret that would fill us on your departing from the Diocese.

JOHN LYNCH, COLUMBIA, AUG 5[10]
. . . You have led me to believe that you see a way for me out of the difficulty [Caldwell], having full confidence in your financial abilities, I have quietly waited for a purchaser of the mine. Your last letter induced me to decline the offer of the London broker, but I have not yet heard from your friend in Charlotte; and am getting sick with waiting . . . Please write to me and let know what *I* shall do, what *you* expect to do, and when you expect to be able to assist me in satisfying Mrs. C that I do not intend cheating her daughter. . . . The . . . family in usual health, myself the worst off. Don't expect ever to be well again. Very little practice and less pay. Hope times may improve soon.

JOHN LYNCH, COLUMBIA, AUG 10[11]
. . . I am beginning to think that my cross in this world is, and will continue to be stress for money. . . . I hope I may soon get a good offer for the mine, so that I may not only get a relief myself but may repay you all you have been kind enough to assist me with. . . .

HENRIETTA LYNCH, CHERAW, OCT 31[12]
. . . We are all truly sorry that you did not get the appointment as coadjutor Archbishop, but as God knows what is for the best, we think some other high position is in store for you at the South, in the midst of your own people. However you are so much of a philosopher that very little affects you. . . .

JOHN LYNCH, COLUMBIA, NOV 14[13]
I recd the enclosed letter this morning. . . . I showed it to Judge W. who . . . advised me to write the following proposition . . . Viz. "If you will give myself and the Bishop a release in full of all demands, duly executed by Miss Sue Caldwell, upon the ascertainment of the amount due, the money will be placed at your disposal . . ."

I would suggest that . . . you place at my disposal, either in the Bank of Charleston or Columbia $2450—to be used for that purpose. I shall use it for no other. . . .

JOHN LYNCH, COLUMBIA, DEC 18[14]

. . . I suppose that your friend Genrl DeSassure has informed you that the *Caldwell* business has been satisfactorily arranged. I can only say my mind has been relieved for which I thank *you*. . . . An idea suggested itself to my mind. And on consulting with friends, I find it feasible, viz. Get a charter! And stock the company. . . . Maj Hart of Yorkville . . . said to me, he could get a charter from the Clerk of court and if . . . I could . . . get five thousand dollars, bona fide, cash subscribers here, he would guarantee to get the balance of a capital of sixty-thousand dollars subscribed at once between Richmond and Baltimore. . . . Fifty-dollars a share or twelve hundred shares. I have spoken to Senator Robinson who speaks favourably. . . . Francis says he does not see why it should not be a grand success. But to do so we must first secure the services of a first rate practical miner in Copper, as superintendent . . . I have taken the liberty of using your name as one of the corporation, but not officially. The name used was Jno Lynch, P.N. Lynch and Jas F. Hart, with their associates." . . . As you are now at home, I will not proceed further until I hear from you, whether you approve or not. . . .

FRANCIS LYNCH, CHERAW, DEC 24[15]

I recd yours by last mail and have already sent the ck of twelve hundred and forty dolls that you kindly sent me, to Mr Sumner Albee Boston. . . .

31

"THE HOUSE WOULD FALL DOWN IF YOU HAD NOT BEEN ITS PROP AND SUPPORT"

1881–1882

Over the last year and a half of Patrick Lynch's life, the volume of family correspondence to him plummets. Of Patrick's eleven siblings, only three remained: John, Francis, and Baptista. As John's health continued to worsen in the spring and summer of 1881, his letters to his brother became limited to those short periods when his health temporarily revived. No correspondence survives of Baptista, who, since the 1840s, had been Patrick's most prolific correspondent. There was, as she once suggested, a special bond between the two, forged in Patrick's saving her from drowning in their youth.1 There were no reports of health problems. She had given several hints to Patrick in recent years that, with declining energy, she was delegating her responsibilities to others, including letter writing. But writing her brother had never been a burden for her. If anything, it was an addiction, as she frequently admitted. Whether it was health or the (unlikely) misplacement of her letters, the extraordinary correspondence of Baptista Lynch to her brother ends abruptly on July 31, 1880.

The third generation of Lynches accounts for much of the family correspondence to the bishop during 1881–1882. Financial struggles continued to dominate the lives of the third as well as the second generation of Lynches. Given their economic insecurity, it is not surprising that most of the correspondence of both the second and third generations amount to solicitations for their bishop brother/uncle to secure handouts or loans. No one was more proficient at relentless quasi-demands for money than Louisa Blain, who had long mastered an approach of softening her outright demands with apologies for being so direct. At times the tone betrays a certain aggressive entitlement, suggestive of magpies relentlessly snapping at their prey, as though fully aware of how effective such posturing has previously been in opening Patrick Lynch's (perceived) substantial purse to meet their needs. On rare occasions, they overplayed their imposition, even for someone as indulgent as Patrick Lynch. No one, in this regard, was more presumptuous than Francis's oldest son, Conlaw, for whom the bishop had done more than for any other Lynch of his generation, apart from Lillie Lynch. In the end, nonetheless, Patrick Lynch provided the money to Conlaw, perhaps out of respect for Conlaw's mother who had pleaded with her brother-in-law to do what he could, not only to aid Conlaw, but to relieve Conlaw's father from the necessity of being both planter and tanner. There could be no greater contrast in tone than that between the epistolary solicitations of Conlaw and Henrietta Lynch, the one with its dunning character; the other assuming the child-like persona best calculated to secure a favorable outcome in such a patriarchal culture.

John Lynch's own health was in sharp decline. Lacking the money to consult another physician, he pretended that his best medical course was to trust in God and in his own diagnostic experience by treating himself. It should surprise no one that, despite the alarming physical symptoms (fast pulse, swollen ankles, weight loss), he focused on the "languor" he was experiencing and concluded that hypochondria was at the root of his perceived ailments. And yet, the fact that he felt compelled to put his affairs in order, preeminently by effecting a sale of the mine, points to his recognition that his illness ran deeper than any psychosomatic treatment could cure. "I know the end will be for the best" became his epitaph. To his dying hour, even as his mental faculties dimmed, he labored to clear his debts, putting a bank note under his pillow to deal with it on a tomorrow that never came.

Even though Francis feared that his brother Patrick was himself seriously ill, the rare opportunity to regain the prosperous condition Francis knew during the war prompted him to ask his

brother to secure a loan of $5,000 from a Boston firm to provide
Francis with the capital to become a co-founder of a chartered
company manufacturing fertilizer. Francis himself had long since
lost the business standing to negotiate such a loan for himself.
So, one last time, he turned to Patrick to be his angel in enabling
Francis to realize economic redemption.

Patrick Lynch's health was indeed disintegrating. Nonetheless, throughout 1881 and into 1882, the bishop kept up his extensive itinerant fundraising, now in its fifteenth year. By the
summer of 1881, the retirement of the war debt was at last within
reach. The time had come, the bishop decided, to begin to rebuild
the cathedral whose ruins had dominated the lower city since fire
had roared through it nearly two decades earlier. Louisa Blain,
for one, understood the importance of restoring the magnificent
neo-Gothic structure Patrick had been chiefly responsible for
erecting in 1854, as a symbolic revival of institutional Catholicism
in South Carolina.

1881

CONLAW S. LYNCH, CHERAW, JAN 17[2]

I write to know if I could raise the sum of Four or Five hundred dollars in
Charleston for the purpose of carrying on my business. I would like to give
my note, payable next December of January if you would endorse it. I would
be willing to give as high as 12%, though a less per cent would be much more
desirable. Several Charleston houses, Walker and Trenholm, for instance, are
letting persons about here have money. And even money at 12% is more desirable than a lien. I wish you would do the best you can . . . It is a matter of
necessity for me to raise money at present and if I can not get it this way I will
be obliged to make sacrifices which will be very injurious. I have the saction
[*sic*] of my father in the course I am taking. . . .

CONLAW S. LYNCH, CHERAW, FEB 8[3]

I wrote you some time since but as I have recd no answer I fear that my letter
miscarried. . . . I now renew the request as it is an absolute necessity. Please
write at once. . . .

JOSEPHINE LYNCH, GREENVILLE, FEB 9[4]

. . . I have been very much worried about business matters. . . . My dear Conlaw
had his business in such a confused state it was discovered afterwards that

he died terribly in debt. I have already been sued by one house and another threatening . . . I feel very much crushed at times to think there should be any reflection on his memory. Dear Bishop, I again appeal to you to give me one hundred dollars. . . . I am trying to get a position as housekeeper or anything that is respectable. . . .

CONLAW S. LYNCH, CHERAW, FEB 22[5]

We doubt when you read the following request you will think I am very presumptuous. I want you to endorse for me to the amt. of two hundred dollars. Though I have spent the whole amt you procured for me, I have no doubt but that you would approve of every transaction that I have made. I have bot three mules and am going to run four plows on shares with choice hands and two for myself with an extra horse to enable me to do every thing in proper time.

As to the amount of cotton that I control this fall, I do not consider sixty bales an overestimate, tho' less than forty will meet all my obligations . . . So please do your best for me my dear uncle. . . . I intend to take charge of Pa's ginning in the fall and make one press do the packing for two gins. . . .

CONLAW S. LYNCH, CHERAW, MAR 11[6]

I have just recd your letter and am ever so grateful for your kindness. . . . I will gladly acquiesce in any arrangement you may see proper to make. . . .

CONLAW S. LYNCH, CHERAW, APR 14[7]

. . . As to how I am getting on, I must say I am doing very well. My oats about 25 acres, are as fine as any I have seen. Of the sixty acres cotton land I have lint on forty five acres rakings at the rate of 10 two horse loads per acre. Each load weights over a ton. . . .

I am draining out the central ditches on the plantation which have not been cleaned out in twelve years and more, and therefore very expensive. . . . If I succeed in finishing the ditches . . . they will greatly benefit a large portion of the plantation which has not been producing any thing in proportion to its fertility. . . .

Labor is very much demoralized. I find it necessary to keep in constant employment several hands to keep them from scattering as I know from experience that if they get away, it will be impossible to obtain labor when it is needed. . . .

JOHN LYNCH, COLUMBIA, JUNE 6[8]

. . . Am very glad to hear you are in good health and will visit us so soon. I will send word to Sister Ellen as soon as possible. I know she will be delighted. . . .

I have suggested to [Dr. Meriwether] to go to New York: to some hospital.
. . . Jimmie . . . has taken charge of the farm since 20 of last month when
Dr. M. wrote for him. . . . There is no one I esteem more as a priest, or respect
more as a gentleman than Dr. M. but if I am not much mistaken, you will soon
lose his usefulness, if you cannot divert his mind from himself. . . .

LOUISA BLAINE, CHERAW, JUN 7[9]
Your kind letter and the enclosed came to hand last evening and I thank you
from the bottom of my heart. . . . If I would get hold of 200 I would go north
in Aug and take Marie. . . .

Now I want you to do what I am about to ask without fail and let me have
it by Fridays mail. It is to let me have $10 if you never grant me another favor
anyhow grant this one. Be kind and dearest friend do this for me or my heart
will break. . . . As I am on this disagreeable subject I must beg you to let me
have ten more by the end of next week, or the week after if you can. . . . Do not
let it be later than Monday next . . . or it will be too late. . . .

LOUISA BLAINE, CHERAW, JUN 14[10]
Last evening I received a letter from Marie in which she mentioned you had
put into her hand a sealed envelope and she would open it the next day and give
it to the party for whom it is intended. I feel truly grateful to you for this and
all you have ever done for me and thank you with all the sincerity of my heart.
There is nothing in this world that I would not do for you or yours to prove
my gratitude. . . .

HENRIETTA LYNCH, CHERAW, JUN 21[11]
. . . You have a claim on each, individually, because you are our prop and staff.
My sweet little baby used to say if "Ma Blain was not here the house would fall
down from its top." And now I repeat her words and say the house would fall
down from its top, if you had not been its prop and support. . . . You it was who
in the midst of trouble and perplexities without number brought back a ray of
sunlight to our hearts and hearths. . . .

CONLAW S. LYNCH, CHERAW, JUL 4[12]
I wrote you a hurried letter sometime since asking you to send me $50 if you
possibly could. I am in very straitened circumstances and have not a cent. I
wish you would do what you can for me and as soon as you can. . . . I have
thrashed out 800 bushels which is very good considering the crop was short all
thro' the country . . .

CONLAW S. LYNCH, CHERAW, AUG 1[13]

When I last heard from you, you sent me $25⁰⁰ in your great kindness saying you would send the other $25⁰⁰ soon as you could. I owe a debt of $25⁰⁰ another one $15⁰⁰ borrowed money which I have promised to settle on the 4th August. . . . If you can by any means let me have $40⁰⁰ in that time you will do a great favor and guaranteed payment. . . .

P.S. Do please answer at once.

LOUISA BLAINE, CHERAW, AUG 7[14]

. . . I know you think me the boldest beggar you ever came across and so I am. I am in great trouble and I entreat of you to help me. I promise if you will do what I am about to ask, I will return every cent you gave me this year if that house on Broad St. is ever mine, I will ensure you 1000 any how.[15] I know your good and noble heart too well to think you will not hear this appeal of the poor outcast and beggar. . . . I want you to let me have $20 every month or $10 every two weeks just as it suits you until December. That will make four months and I promise after that to leave you alone. . . . I am so sad I do not know what to do, as I ask you in charity to answer this and relieve my anxiety of mind. . . .

CONLAW S. LYNCH, CHERAW, AUG 9[16]

I wrote to you at Charleston some ten days ago not knowing that you were off. I stand very much in need of some money at present. There is a balance of $25⁰⁰ on the $200. Could you make it $50⁰⁰. I had to borrow $20⁰⁰ . . . which I promised to pay the first part of August. Please send me the fifty dollars immediately, if possible. Cotton is doing well. . . .

LOUISA BLAINE, CHARLESTON, AUG 16[17]

I arrived here on last Thursday—found your very kind letter awaiting me, how can I find words to express to you my gratitude and thanks. God alone can reward a heart as forgiving and charitable as yours. . . . Do not trouble yourself to send me anything more until Sept first week, if you can do so, conveniently then, I will be truly grateful . If you can send me $20 in that month and $20 in Oct that will do. I think I can get on after that if my prayers are heard. . . .

JOHN LYNCH, COLUMBIA, AUG 22[18]

. . . I have not been well a day since I saw you. In fact kept going gradually downhill, until I had lost in weight twenty four pound, and was nearly past getting about, appetite entirely gone, constant nervous fever, feet and ankles swollen, pulse never less than 100. . . . I have been much worse off than I let any of the family know. I really believe if I had all my temporal affairs arranged satisfactorily, I would not be here now, but knowing their condition, and believing that no one else could arrange them, stimulated me, to exert myself towards throwing off the very great languor which had taken possession of me.

If I had a similar case in another I would pronounce it Hypochondriasis. Therefore, have not consulted any one. Knowing I must have employment both mental and physical, before I can get well, . . . I hope to be able to sell the mine during the Atlanta Exhibition as the mine will be represented, through the State Commissioner (Col. Butler) . . .

LOUISA BLAINE, CHARLESTON, AUG 26[19]

As I saw by yesterday's paper the cheering news of rebuilding the Cathedral I felt as if I would like to write you a few lines of congratulation, for whatever gives you happiness does the same to me. God grant that you may see it erected without too much labour or anxiety of mind. I heard Mrs. De Carudene say that now her daily prayer would be that you will be the one to consecrate it, more than one heart will join in that prayer. . . .

JOHN LYNCH, COLUMBIA, SEP 3[20]

. . . I am anxious to make a sale [of the mine] as soon as I can, on your account, and to enable me to arrange my temporal affairs in time, for I feel that a radical change must be effected, if I ever expect to get well again. I am asked by friends to consult physicians on my case. I know my condition, and know what is necessary, then why make an object of myself and consult those in whom I have but little confidence, and if they should advise or suggest what I believe to be necessary, but cannot carry out, it would amount to a farce. Therefore I have concluded to trust to a healthy constitution and faith, together with such medicines as the immediate symptoms call for, placing myself in the hands of Almighty God, I know the end will be for the best. . . .

FRANCIS LYNCH, CHERAW, SEP 30[21]

. . . My neighbor Capt. Pollock has for some few years been preparing a Fertilizer which has deservedly won much favor, the demand for it has so grown, that the measure of his capital in it about 600$ is insufficient for the supply. . . . He has assented to the formation of a chartered company of 500 shares of 100$ ea. He and I to hold the larger measure of the stock—which on the selling of 1000 tons, as he has been selling it, (and for which a good deal is already bespoken) will yield an annual dividend of full 15p^{ct} on the stock, most likely exceeding 20p^{ct}.

. . . The stock will have a high market value after having declared a dividend. In order to profit well, by this enterprise which Capt P. has already established, in the enlargement of it, I would like to borrow 5000$ for two yrs placing that amt of stock in the Pee Dee Fertilizing Company (the to be chartered name) as collateral security.

I see no risk in this business, . . . Any one having money to loan would hardly find a safer way. . . . If desirable the repaymt of it could be made soon after the first dividend in Dec 1882. . . . The annual revenue to me from this source will be hardly less than 4000$, if I should succeed in the first steps. . . . It is not often in one's life that such opportunities offer. I must act soon to avail of this. . . .

ELIZA LYNCH TO FRANCIS LYNCH, COLUMBIA, OCT 10[22]
Dear Uncle Francis,

I was so disappointed that the Bishop did not come up to Columbia to see dear Father. Will you write to the Bishop *for me* dear Uncle, and say Father seems to be growing weaker every day. Yesterday he was weaker than I have ever seen him and slept nearly all day. Today he is on the sofa in the sitting room sleeping all the time. He suffers so much, his head becomes giddy and he has palpitation of the heart, whenever he walks even across the room. I only pray he may not have a fall at any time, though we do not allow him to [go] out alone. Could you not come over to see him, on some of the excursion trains, for I think it would do him a great deal of good, to see you. . . .

ELIZA LYNCH TO BAPTISTA LYNCH, COLUMBIA, OCT 10[23]
My Dearest Aunty,

. . . Will you please write to the Bishop, for *me* and say he must not be surprised to hear at any time that dear Father has been taken from us. . . . Yesterday he was weaker than I have ever seen him before and slept nearly all day—today he is on the sofa in the sitting room sleeping all the time. I had hoped that the cold weather would help him, but he does not improve. Pray dear Aunty, that he may not be taken from us yet. . . .

R.A. LYNCH, COLUMBIA, NOV 9[24]
. . . I will gather up the titles to the mine property so that there will be no trouble in that direction. . . .

I do not think there will be any trouble about disposing of the mine at a good figure—the one difficulty will be on the terms of sale. . . .

1882

FRANCIS LYNCH, CHERAW, FEB 3[25]

Since early last month, I have been saddened on hearing of your indisposition
yet hoping in each successive letter to learn that you were yourself again. I
much fear the exertion of preaching has rather retarded the improvement I
was happy to hear had set in with you. I now promise myself the great pleasure
of visiting you soon. And will most gladly have you accompany me home, if you
will permit so. The country air might serve you very beneficially. Such would
be our prayer. . . .

R.A. LYNCH, COLUMBIA, FEB 9[26]

I arrived home safely Tuesday morning at 5:30, and found all well. I sincerely
hope that you are continuing to improve as rapidly as you seemed to be doing
on Monday.

I send you a copy of a letter [from Oscar Lieber] which I found in Father's
papers relinquishing all claims to the York property. This letter, although not a
regular quit claim deed, will, coupled with the undisturbed possession, confer
a perfect title. . . . Hoping that you will find no further trouble about the titles
and that the property may be shortly disposed of so as to relieve the family. . . .

Epilogue

Death Comes for the Bishop

Spending the fall of 1881 as he had been doing for fifteen years—fundraising in the North, Patrick Lynch was unable to get to Columbia to be with his brother John, who died on October 20. Nor was Patrick able to honor Henry Northrup's invitation to preach at his consecration as Bishop of North Carolina in early January of 1882. Patrick's own failing health had forced him to return home from New York at the beginning of the year. Home air and treatment brought no respite from his decline. In late February, his brother Francis arrived in Charleston in response to warnings about Patrick's sinking condition. On Saturday, February 25, the bishop fell into a coma. A last-ditch operation failed to revive him. Less than a month shy of his sixty-fifth birthday, Patrick Lynch died on Sunday morning, February 26, of what the coroner determined was "chronic suppurated cystitis."[1]

"We Are All Catholic"

In 1858, Rome's announcement that the new Catholic Bishop of Charleston was a local priest who over the past decade had become a major contributor to Charleston's civic and intellectual life inspired the Chamber of Commerce at its annual banquet to toast that in Patrick Neison Lynch's appointment, "we are all Catholic." The city's reaction to the bishop's death was a resounding restatement of that solidarity. As the *New York Times* reported: "the mourning was as sincere as it was general."[2] The bells of the city tolled throughout the day of his funeral, on Wednesday, March 1. The Court of Common Pleas closed in honor of the departed prelate. His funeral drew thousands who thronged Broad Street outside the pro-Cathedral. The city's political, religious, and social elite led the procession which carried the bishop's remains to the vault beneath the ruins of St. John and St. Finbar. The obituaries fittingly highlighted the scope and persistence of his intellectual interests. "Bp. Lynch," the *News and Courier* wrote:

was one of the most remarkable men of the day. Breadth of view
was one of his marked characteristics. Endowed with a mind
highly analytical in its nature, he was, nevertheless, comprehensive
and far-reaching in his conception and treatment of every subject.
. . . His report on the new well, as chairman of the scientific committee appointed by the City Council, was completed and submitted last week. . . . At the time of his death he was . . . engaged upon
a work [for the *Catholic World*] intended to demonstrate, in the
light of the latest archeological and ethnological discoveries, the
absolute agreement of science and the Mosaic revelation.[3]

Back to Columbia

Patrick's death left Baptista Lynch, as the convent's annals reported, "completely prostrated for some time." All too conscious of the fact that Patrick
Lynch had made it possible for them to return to South Carolina, the Ursulines, in their annals for 1882, naturally wondered whether his successor might "prefer to bring other Religious into the Diocese to labor in our
stead?" and ask the Ursulines to leave, as Patrick Lynch's predecessor had
done thirty-seven years earlier. Fortunately, Patrick Lynch's successor, Henry
Northrop, was a close friend of the Ursulines.

On August 31, 1886, an earthquake struck Valle Crucis, whose aftershocks
persisted for two weeks, leaving a badly damaged main house but miraculously
injuring no one. Indeed, the annals claimed that the earthquake had, to some
extent, revitalized Mother Superior Baptista, who had become a semi-invalid
by that time. She abandoned her wheelchair for a cane. But the natural disaster accelerated the decline in enrollment at the academy, no longer inflated by
Lynches supported by the Bishop of Charleston. By the close of the academic
year in June of 1887, there were but five students. Bishop Northrop decided
that the Ursulines had been "buried in the woods" long enough. It was time to
return to Columbia where they could have day students as well as boarders.
Ironically, the Preston mansion, the place in which some of the community
had taken refuge after being burned out of their academy and convent in 1865,
was again available. As the annalist noted, "the house is unsuited for school
purposes—being only a dwelling house for a large family." There being no
other option, the Ursulines purchased the mansion for $27,500 ($911,251 today), through the sale of Valle Crucis and loans provided by Bishop Northrop
and a female friend of the nuns.

In mid-July 1887, sixteen nuns and two students made the three-mile trip
from Valle Crucis to Columbia in two omnibuses and a carriage bearing their

ailing mother superior, along with her beloved niece, Caro Michel Spann. The trek reprised the one made by nuns and students twenty-two years earlier, when Sherman's troops were swarming the land. This time there were no menacing Yankee soldiers, only some Black men who came out of their cabins along the road to extricate one of the busses whose rear axle had sunk up to its hub in the mud. Immediately upon arriving at the mansion, the community began a novena for their superior's recovery. Baptista refused to join in it, saying, "I am afraid to die and I am afraid to live. I wish only the will of God." On July 28, 1887, Ellen Baptista Lynch died. That November she would have turned 64.[4]

The Ursulines continued, for five more decades, to press the war claims that Baptista had begun shortly after war's end. Her successors had no more success than their foundress. Finally, in 1938, the Columbia Ursulines merged with the Ursulines of Louisville and gave up their quest for economic justice for a war crime long forgotten by the nation, if not by Southern whites.

The Measure of Success

Despite their expectations, Redemption did not restore the halcyon days the Lynches had enjoyed before the fortunes of war betrayed them. Despite the best efforts of two generations of Lynches, they did not become part of the New South which promised paths to financial success and renown. Instead, disappointment and failure continued to plague the family, symbolized by Patrick Lynch's being passed over as the next archbishop of New York, a see his kinfolk especially had long assumed he would one day occupy as a fitting recognition of his extraordinary gifts and service to the American Church.

Ironically, Francis Lynch, who seemed, at least psychologically, the most fragile of the siblings who survived the war, outlived them all, dying at the age of eighty in 1901.[5] Well before the new century, Francis had finally regained his reputation as a respected businessman in Cheraw, if not the prosperity he had briefly known when the Confederacy was at high tide. With Francis's passing, the last page closed on the second generation's quest to fulfil the two commitments which Eleanor and Conlaw Peter Lynch had made in staking their future in America: that their first-born would dedicate his life to the Lord's service, and that they would do all that they could to regain the wealth and prestige that their respective families had known in pre-Cromwellian Ireland.

As it happened, of Eleanor and Conlaw Lynch's immediate progeny, not only did their oldest child become a bishop; his sisters, Ellen and Catherine, became superiors of their respective orders. And the second youngest daughter, Anna, wanted very much to become a religious, but honored the Irish tradition of a daughter remaining at home to assist her aged parents. Among the third generation, two of the daughters of Mary Lynch Spann, Ellen and Caroline, became Ursulines. Tuberculosis claimed Ellen (Sr. Gertrude) in 1865, barely a year after her profession. Her younger sister, Caroline (Sr. Michael) became the second Lynch offspring to serve as mother superior of the Columbian community. Anastasia Gertrude Lynch (1857–1938), the second youngest daughter of John and Eliza Lynch, entered the novitiate of the Sisters of Charity of Our Lady of Mercy at the unusually advanced age of forty-three.[6] Following in the footsteps of her maternal aunt, Anastasia (Sr. Agatha) spent the next four decades teaching at Charity academies in the state. One could make the case that the only Catholic family which made a greater contribution to the institutional church in the nineteenth century were the biracial Healys who counted among them a bishop, a vicar general, a university president, as well as a superior of a women's congregation. Unlike the Healys, the Lynch contribution was not confined to a single generation but flowed through two.

On his return from the Second Plenary Council in Baltimore in 1866, Patrick Lynch had stopped at Fortress Monroe to visit Jefferson Davis, still being held prisoner as the former head of a confederacy of breakaway states. One of the bishop's designs in visiting the former Confederate president was to restir any attraction Davis might have had as a student at St Joseph's College in Bardstown. Converting the Southern elite class had long been a goal of Patrick as well as his Ursuline sister. Baptista confessed that such a transformation had long been the "utopia" she had been dedicated to bringing about in South Carolina. But the relatively meager harvests of the postwar period proved disappointing, as a new Protestant crusade against Catholic education tended to accelerate the move toward making Catholic schools a central part of the Catholic ghetto which, for various reasons, the hierarchy was instituting in the late nineteenth century, ranging from schools to cemeteries.

Baptista would have been far more disappointed had she been able to foresee the faith drainage which would occur among Lynch descendants over the next six generations.[7] She had been particularly concerned about the religious fate of the four children of her two siblings who had died very early in their married life. She persuaded her brother Patrick, to effectively rescue Mary Elizabeth (Lillie) and James Thomas Lynch, from an alcoholic, abusive stepfather. At the same time she convinced Patrick that Conlaw Lynch Pinckney and Sarah Phoebe Bellinger Pinckney would not receive a Catholic upbringing in a household with a Protestant stepmother. Baptista eventually arranged for the four nephews and nieces to move to Valle Crucis where the girls took up studies at the academy and the boys worked as farmhands while receiving private tutoring from the chaplain, William Meriwether. Baptista even secured tentative approval from Lillie Lynch's mother, Augusta, for her daughter to enter the Ursuline novitiate in Quebec. Lillie's subsequent breakdown and hospitalization put an end to that hope of yet another Lynch becoming a religious.

Geographic mobility increasingly dispersed the generations of Lynches across the country and beyond. By the 1990s, one Lynch descendent was living in the Fiji Islands. In general, a majority of John and Eliza's children and grandchildren maintained their middle-class status while accruing a mixed record of sustaining their ancient faith through several generations. Robert Lynch (1843–1928) moved to Boston with Kate and their five children where he practiced law; in his retirement he became very active in archdiocesan charity organizations. John Lynch (1848–?) moved to central North Carolina where he married and worked as a clerk in a department store. Eliza Lynch (1847–1929), the eldest daughter, became the companion and caretaker of her mother until the latter's death in 1910. Mary Gertrude Lynch (1851–?) married Robert Pringle Mayrant, a Confederate veteran. Her sister Eleanor (1852–1943) married Donald McQueen, a construction supervisor. Two of the five McQueen children made careers in the US Navy. For over a half-century James Bernard Lynch (1860–1945) worked as a clerk for the Southern Railway in Columbia. Julia Lynch (1862–1944) married George Powell Miller, a bank cashier in Columbia, where they raised a family of five sons and four daughters.

Conlaw Lynch (1857–1930), the oldest child of Francis and Henrietta Lynch, without his uncle's financial support, eventually abandoned farming. By 1900 he was a train conductor; a decade later he had become a real estate agent. His younger brother Francis (1867–1930), did not realize his boyhood dream of becoming a lawyer, but did manage to get out of Cheraw, moving to New York City, where he secured a position at Wanamaker's, one he held for the rest of his life.

In 1880, Henrietta Lynch had characteristically written about her two surviving daughters:[8]

> Eleanor is a general favorite receiving attention from young gentlemen and older ones . . . her singing . . . and the nonsensical prattle she carries on pleases them . . . Her sister, Marie, three years her elder, won the respect of the adult females in the town for her allaround skills ranging from piano to home economics.

As predicted, Eleanor Lynch had no trouble securing marriage proposals, including one from M. Carnot Bellinger, of a prominent South Carolina family. Eleanor subsequently had two children, Patrick Lynch Bellinger (1885–1962) and a daughter, Eleanor Bellinger (1887–1902), The sole Lynch named for the third bishop of Charleston, Patrick Bellinger became the most accomplished of all the descendants. When Eleanor died at the age of thirty-eight, in 1897, her siblings, Marie and Conlaw, neither of whom had married, raised her children. Somehow, without apparent connections, Pat Bellinger received an appointment to the US Naval Academy. In the pre-World War I years, Bellinger was instrumental in developing the Naval Air Force. He served in both world wars, including as Rear Admiral commanding air operations of the Atlantic Fleet during World War II. He was buried with Catholic rites at Arlington National Cemetery in 1962.

The Lynches never managed to come remotely close to recovering in America the riches that had been wrested from them in Ireland. Collectively they wrought something of greater value and longer lasting, something revealed in the municipal mourning that marked Charleston's observance of Patrick Lynch's death. From being near penniless exiles in a strange land, the Lynches, over the course of four generations, had made singular contributions to church and state which would long outlive them. Conlaw and Eleanor Lynch would have been more than proud of what their offspring had wrought.

Notes

Introduction

1. Francis Lynch to Patrick Lynch, Cheraw, July 4, 1849, 6 M3, CDA.
2. David C.R. Heisser and Stephen J. White, Sr., *Patrick N. Lynch 1817–1882: Third Catholic Bishop of Charleston* (Columbia: University of South Carolina Press, 2015), 32.
3. Moore to Martin Spalding, Charleston, February 23, 1865, 35 J11, AASMUS.
4. Moore to Spalding, Charleston, August 26, 1865, unclassified, CDA; Moore to Spalding, Charleston, Sept. 16, 1865, 35 J13, AASMUS.
5. Patrick Lynch to Charles G. Schwartz, Rome, September 1865, unclassified, CDA.
6. Patrick Lynch to SPF, January 9, 1879, 67 G4, CDA.
7. July 3, 1876, Bayley Papers, 40 K10, AASMUS.
8. It is instructive to compare Patrick Lynch's $100 contribution to the rescue plan with the $1000 which John Purcell sent to the Columbian Ursulines in 1866 (Baptista Lynch to Patrick Lynch, Valle Crucis, July 16, 1866, 15 SS, CDA.
9. Heisser, 194.
10. *From Slave to Wage Laborer in South Carolina, 1860–1870* (New York: Cambridge University Press, 1994), 18–29, 103–110.
11. Saville, 139.
12. Baptista Lynch to Patrick Lynch, Valle Crucis, July 29, 1876, 19 M11, CDA.
13. See 20 T7, CDA for Baptista's report about Sallie Burt.
14. Ursulines, December 15, 1877, 20 G6, CDA.
15. Email correspondence with Brian Fahey on September 30, 2024.
16. See Baptista Lynch to Patrick Lynch, Ursulines, February 12, 1877, 19 S10, CDA; same to same, February 17, 1877, 19 T2, CDA; same to same, Ursulines, February 22, 1877, 19 T4, CDA; same to same, Ursulines, July 19, 1877, 20 A7, CDA.

1. "Everything Starts Anew Now": January–May 1866

1. 34 U8, AASMUS.
2. Edward Sorin, CSC (1814–1893), provincial superior of the Congregation of the Holy Cross and president of Notre Dame University in South Bend, IN.

3. The Marists, or Society of Mary, a French congregation which had sent its first priests to the Confederacy in 1863, at the invitation of Archbishop John Odin of New Orleans.

4. 15 M3, CDA.

5. 15 M4, CDA.

6. Lucas Jones, the agent Patrick Lynch had employed to solicit donations for the Columbian Ursulines in the Northern states.

7. 15 M7, CDA.

8. Adelbert Ames (1835–1933), Medal of Honor recipient for his heroic leadership at the First Battle of Bull Run. In 1868 he was appointed governor of Mississippi and later represented the state in the US senate.

9. 15 M10. CDA.

10. 15 N1, CDA.

11. Her deceased Ursuline daughter, Ellen Gertrude Spann.

12. 15 N2, CDA.

13. 15 N3, CDA.

14. John McCloskey, Archbishop of New York.

15. 15 N5, CDA.

16. Augustin Verot (1794–1876), the French-born bishop of Savannah.

17. 15 N6, CDA.

18. 15 N7, CDA.

19. 15 N8, CDA.

20. John Smith Preston (1809–1881), whose Columbia mansion the Ursulines briefly occupied after being burned out of their convent school.

21. 15 N10, CDA.

22. Douglas Blanding DeSaussure (1832–1882), a lawyer and politician who was a delegate from South Carolina to the Philadelphia convention which Andrew Johnson had called in order to form a new political party.

23. 34 W3, CDA (draft).

24. 15 P1, CDA.

25. 15 P2, CDA.

26. 15 P4, CDA.

27. 15 P7, CDA.

28. 15 P8, CDA.

29. 15 P9, CDA.

30. Joseph LeConte, (1833–1901), professor of chemistry and geology at South Carolina University.

31. William Gilmour Sims, who wrote *Sack and Destruction of the City of Columbia, S.C.* (Columbia, S.C.: Power Press of Daily Phoenix, 1865).

32. 15 P10, CDA. This marks the formal beginning of the community's attempt to

seek compensation for their losses. Inasmuch as the US Senate had already refused to seat John Lawrence Manning because it did not recognize the South Carolina Senate that had sent him to Washington, Manning was in no position to help. It should be noted that the school's enrollment, including boarders and day students, never approached 200 before or during the war. This request represents not a need to replace but an aspiration to expand. Baptista had no doubt about the justice of their claim. It was, as she told her brother Patrick in April, "a thing as plain as that the sun shines!" (Baptista Lynch to Patrick Lynch, Valle Crucis, April 6. 1866. 15 P9, CDA). The horrors of that night were still all too fresh: their abandonment by their Federal guard, almost immediately replaced by other soldiers hellbent on ransacking and putting the convent to the torch. To Baptista and her sister nuns, it made no difference that the initial arson had likely been the work of fleeing Confederates; what the Ursulines saw was a mob of drunken soldiers, engaging in the worst sort of hard war that had become so identified with Sherman's army. Marion Brunson Lucas, in his *Sherman and the Burning of Columbia,* concluded that the conflagration was less the climax of Sherman's hard-war policy and more than an accident of war (Columbia: University of South Carolina Press, 2000), 46. That may be a reasonable allocation of responsibility for Columbia's burning, but it would have given no comfort or satisfaction to those who had had to endure the cruelty and the outrages of that terrible night. The winds might have spared the Ursulines' site that evening; Sherman's soldiers made sure that that favorable outcome never occurred. For the nuns, February 17 became a quasi-holy day to be remembered as the night in which God had permitted them to join Christ in this dying to self that the loss of nearly all their earthly possessions made possible.

33. 15 R1,CDA.

34. 15 R2, CDA.

35. Apostleship of Prayer.

36. Benedict Sestini, SJ (1816–1890), an Italian refugee who, in 1866, founded the *Messenger of the Sacred Heart,* which became the chief channel for the spread of the devotion of the Sacred Heart among Catholics in the United States. The Apostleship of Prayer was the pious voluntary association dedicated to the practice of the devotion.

37. *The New York Tribune.*

38. 15 R4, CDA.

39. 15 R9, CDA.

40. The fiftieth wedding anniversary of Conlaw Peter and Eleanor Lynch.

41. 15 R3, CDA.

42. 15 R6, CDA.

43. 15 R8, CDA.

44. 15 S3, CDA.

45. General Braxton Bragg (1817–1876) commanded the Army of Tennessee from April of 1862 to November of 1863.

2. "Practice Free, Times Hard, Money Very Scarce and Getting Scarcer": June–December 1366

1. 15 S1, CDA.

2. 15 S4, CDA.

3. 15 S5. CDA.

4. 15 S6, CDA.

5. 15 S8, CDA.

6. 15 S9, CDA.

7. 15 S10. CDA.

8. 15 T2, CDA.

9. Charles Croghan, who during the latter part of the war had served as a chaplain at the hospital the Mercy sisters had conducted in White Sulphur Springs, Virginia.

10. 15 T3, CDA.

11. With much of the Congress and nation turning against his pro-South Reconstruction policy, Andrew Johnson attempted to create a new political party, a coalition of Conservative Republicans and Democrats, which he labeled the National Union Party. Johnson's adherents from both North and South held a convention in Philadelphia in August 1866 to advertise their bi-sectional support for the president's program.

12. 15 T6, CDA.

13. 15 T7, CDA.

14. 15 T8, CDA.

15. 15 T9. CDA.

16. 15 T10, CDA.

17. During the war John Lynch had purchased shares in the Mary Copper Mine in York County, SC, as an investment. In the late 1850s the company which had discovered the ore deposits had sunk a shaft down nearly 60 feet and dug a 160-foot tunnel. The mine, with a railroad line less than three miles distant from the mine and its reported discovery of phosphate enhanced the mine's prospects. Then came the war. Mineral scavengers descended on the abandoned mine to cart off any valuable ore they could chance upon. In time the buildings were razed or removed. When John became a partner, he little realized the plight of the mine. The worse his financial situation deteriorated, the more he came to delude himself about the mine's promise, so much so that he went into further debt by purchasing all the mine's shares to become sole owner (John Lynch to Governor Francis H. Pierpoint, Columbia, September 22, 1876 [draft] CDA).

18. 15 W1, CDA.

19. There was wide-spread speculation that the bishops at their upcoming council would approve the establishment of a Catholic university which would be dedicated primarily to clerical education. Baptista took the occasion to remind her bishop brother that female education should be a matter for their consideration as well.

20. 15 W2, CDA.

21. Peter Guilday, ed. *The National Pastorals of the American Hierarchy, 1791–1919* (Westminster [MD]: Newman Press, 1954), 220–21.

22. 15 W3, CDA.

23. 15 W5, CDA.

24. 15 W6. CDA.

25. 15 W 7, CDA.

26. "My hope is that I will never despair, so long as I live."

27. 15 Y3, CDA.

28. 15 Y4, CDA.

3. "In All Probability This Will Never Be a State Again but Be Part of a Kingdom": January–June 1867

1. Saville, 142.

2. 16 A1, CDA.

3. Baptista seems to imply that their Black workers have usurped the assigning of work and the determination of how precisely it is to be done.

4. 16 A5, CDA.

5. 16 A6, CDA.

6. 16 A7, CDA.

7. John Francis Maguire (1815–1872), an Irish Member of Parliament, had come to the United States to write a book about the Irish in America. During his tour of the country, Maguire visited Charleston, where Patrick Lynch hosted him.

8. James Lynch had died in September 1860, leaving his pregnant wife, Augusta Pinckney Lynch, and a two-year-old daughter. Lillie. James' widow remarried, but not wisely, as it turned out. Her new husband proved to be an alcoholic prone to violence. Augusta had two more children with him. He claimed to be unable/unwilling to raise children not his own. Why the Pinckneys, who were much better situated than the Lynches, did not step in is unknown. It fell to Patrick Lynch and his siblings to provide for Lillie and James (See Louisa Blain to Patrick Lynch, Charleston, October 9, 1870, 17 D4, CDA).

9. 16 A8, CDA.

10. 16 A9, CDA.

11. 16 B1, CDA.

12. William Aiken (1806–1887), former governor of South Carolina and the owner of the largest rice plantation in the South.

13. George Peabody (1795–1869), Massachusetts-born, London banker who in 1866 established the Peabody Education Fund of $3.5 million to "encourage the intellectual, moral, and industrial education of the destitute children of the Southern States."

14. 16 B2, CDA.

15. Augusta Lynch, widow of James.

16. 16 B3, CDA.

17. Should be "Visitandine."

18. Secretary of War Edmund Stanton (1814–1869).

19. Likely Sarah Wise Meade (1851–1913) or Henrietta Meade (1853–1944), daughters of General George Meade.

20. Michael Domenec (1816–1878).

21. 16 B4, CDA.

22. 39 M6, CDA.

23. 16 B6, CDA.

24. Francis Patrick McFarland (1819–1874), Bishop of Hartford, CT.

25. 16 B7, CDA.

26. 16 B10, CDA.

27. 16 C1, CDA.

28. 16 C4, CDA.

29. Ambler Weed (1817–1871), the brother of Sr. Charles and a priest in the diocese of Richmond. Like his sister, the Rev. Weed, formerly an ordained minister in the Episcopal Church, was a convert.

30. 40 C5, CDA. Sullivan had organized the association. She was the wife of Algernon Sydney Sullivan, a New York judge whom the Lincoln administration had imprisoned during the war for his pro-Confederate activities.

31. 40 E6, CDA.

32. 16 C7, CDA.

33. 16 C8, CDA.

34. 26 C10, CDA.

35. 16 D1, CDA.

36. James L. Orr (1822–1873), governor of South Carolina from 1865 to 1868. Even though Orr had raised a regiment for the Confederacy and had served in the Confederate Senate, his original opposition to secession apparently cast doubt on the depth of his Confederate nationalism, a doubt which Baptista apparently shared (Dan T. Carter, *When the War Was Over: The Failure of Self-Reconstruction in the South, 1865–1867* [Baton Rouge and London: Louisiana State University Press, 1985], 94).

4. "You Have No Idea of the Scarcity of Money Here":
July–December 1867

1. General Daniel Sickles (1819–1914).
2. 16 D2, CDA.
3. Camilla Ahern, Irish-born lay sister.
4. 16 D4, CDA.
5. John Bauskett (1800–1867), a lawyer, from whom the Ursulines had acquired the American Hotel in Columbia in the summer of 1859. Father of Kate (1847–1891).
6. Transfer Case I, EE, CDA.
7. 16 D9, CDA.
8. 16 D10, CDA.
9. 16 E1, CDA.
10. Notice of taxes due on their property.
11. 16 E2, CDA.
12. Martha Huchet (1821–?), mother of three daughters at Valle Crucis.
13. The Feast of the Presentation, which commemorates the bringing of the infant Jesus to the Temple by his parents.
14. Emily Virginia Mason (1815–1909) of Virginia became a benefactress of women's education in the South in the postwar era. It would seem that the Ursuline Academy was among the institutions Mason had already aided.
15. The convention which met in Columbia to form a new state government and to write a constitution for it, as dictated by the Reconstruction Act of 1867.
16. 16 E3, CDA.
17. Louis Claude Marie Chambodut (1821–1880), as a seminarian in Lyons, France, had responded to an 1845 plea from Galveston, Texas for missionaries.
18. 16 E6, CDA.
19. 16 E7, CDA.
20. 16 E8, CDA.
21. 16 E9, CDA.
22. 16 G1, CDA.
23. Edward Canby (1817–1873), military governor of South Carolina.

5. "These Attacks I Think Indicate Consumption":
January–June 1868

1. 16 H1, CDA.
2. 16 H3, CDA.
3. 16 H4, CDA.
4. 16 H6, CDA.
5. 16 H10, CDA.

6. The sharp-spiked chain, or *catena*, was a standard ascetical instrument which was applied tightly to an upper leg as a penitential exercise. It was particularly utilized during Lent.

7. 16 K1, CDA.

8. Douglass B. De Saussure (1842–?), attorney. His wife, Martha (1849–?).

9. These appear to be notes Lynch prepared for an 1868 lecture to be given in New York or some northern city.

10. South Carolina, of course, had the largest Black majority of any state (57% in the antebellum era). Nowhere was there greater fear about Black government than in South Carolina. As for 2/3rds of the freed persons working, that statistic most likely reflects the retirement of freedwomen from the fields in the new social order. Land was the top priority for so many freedmen. Land had indeed been promised, and, in many cases, granted in 1865, especially in the low country around Charleston, only to have President Andrew Johnson order the land returned to the owners who had abandoned it.

11. 16 K2, CDA.

12. 16 K3, CDA.

13. 16 K5, CDA.

14. Abram Ryan (1838–1886), the priest poet whose 1865 verse, "Conquered Banner" touched off the revisionist history of the war which became known as "The Lost Cause."

15. 16 K6, CDA.

16. 16 M2, CDA.

17. 16 M3, CDA.

18. William Beverly Nash (1822–1888), while enslaved, had worked as a porter in a Columbia hotel. In the postwar years Nash, as one of the earliest political organizers in the Black community, quickly became one of the state's most influential leaders (Eric Foner, *Freedom's Lawmakers: A Directory of Black Officeholders During Reconstruction* [New York and Oxford: Oxford University Press, 1993], 159).

19. 16 M5, CDA.

20. 16 M7, CDA.

21. *The Charleston News and Observer.*

22. *Banner of the South*, the diocesan paper for Savannah, which Ryan had begun in March of that year.

23. 16 M9, CDA.

24. 16 M10, CDA.

25. Sr. Augustine.

26. 16 N1, CDA.

27. 16 N4, CDA.

28. 16 N5, CDA.

29. 16 P1, CDA.

30. 16 P2, CDA.

31. 16 P3, CDA.

6. "The Rub with Us Now Is Wether We Can Get the Necessaries of Life": July–December 1863

1. 16 P5, CDA.

2. James Dooley (1841–1922), whose sister, Florence, had been a student at the Ursuline Academy during the war.

3. 16 R9, CDA.

4. 16 P8, CDA.

5. Henrietta's invalid brother who lived with them, along with their mother.

6. 16 P9, CDA.

7. Caroline Spann (1852-?).

8. 16 P10, CDA.

9. A reference to the consecration in Baltimore of James Gibbons as the first vicar apostolic of North Carolina on August 18, 1868.

10. 16 R1, CDA.

11. A reference to Augustine England.

12. Claude Mary Dubuis (1817–1895), Bishop of Galveston, 1862–1892.

13. 16 R3, CDA.

14. 16 R5, CDA.

15. Patrick Leahy (1806–1875), Archbishop of Cashel.

16. 16 R6, CDA.

17. Abram Ryan.

18. 16 R7, CDA.

19. Andrew Cornette, SJ (1819–1872), a member of the faculty at Spring Hill College.

20. 16 R8, CDA.

21. 16 R10, CDA.

22. 16 S2, CDA.

23. 16 S3, CDA.

24. 16 S4, CDA.

25. 16 S6, CDA.

7. "I Feel as if I Were in the Embrace of a Boa Constrictor": January–June 1869

1. Annals, 1869, AUCL.

2. 16 W8, CDA.

3. 16 T9, CDA.

4. 16 W1, CDA.

5. 16 W3, CDA.

6. The Eighth Provincial Council of Baltimore.

7. Cornelia Reilly Lynch, Hugh's widow.

8. 16 W4, CDA.

9. Bicycle.

10. 16 W6, CDA.

11. 16 W7, CDA.

12. An inkling that she has read Darwin, or at least about his work.

13. 16 W9, CDA.

14. Francis Lewis Cardoza (1836–1903), a mixed-race Charlestonian, who, in 1868 was elected Secretary of State for South Carolina. As such, Cardoza had oversight of the South Carolina Land Commission.

8. "Sr Borgia Believes the World Is Near Its End": July–December 1869

1. 16 Y3, CDA.

2. 16 Y5, CDA.

3. Louisa Macnamara (1832-?). sister-in-law of John Lynch, and member of the Mercy Sisters of Charleston.

4. Robert Kingston Scott (1826–1900), first Republican governor of South Carolina.

5. Anna Lynch, the youngest surviving Lynch of the second generation.

6. Adilene Brisbane (1808–1872), a choir sister.

7. 16 Y7, CDA.

8. Lillie Lynch Ryan.

9. 16 Y8, CDA.

10. 16 Y9, CDA.

11. 16 Y4, CDA. Should be 16 Y5, CDA.

12. 16 Y6, CDA.

13. For Rome, to participate in the ecumenical council which Pope Pius IX had called.

9. "Rev Dr Meriwether Hopes It Is Not True You Have Not Gone for the Immediate Definition": January–June 1870

1. 17 A1, CDA

2. Presumably at the U. of South Carolina.

3. 17 A2, CDA.

4. 17 A4, CDA.

5. 17 A5, CDA.
6. 17 A6, CDA.
7. 17 A8, CDA.
8. 17 A7, CDA.
9. 17 A9, CDA.
10. 17 A10, CDA.
11. 17 A11, CDA.
12. 17 B1, CDA.
13. 17 B4, CDA.
14. 17 B5, CDA
15. Canon law forbade Catholics from participating in the liturgical worship of other Christian denominations.

10. "No Man Seems to Know Whether He Is Standing on His Heels or His Head": July–December 1870

1. 17 B7, CDA.
2. Conlaw Lynch (1845–1880), John Lynch's second oldest child
3. Abram Ryan.
4. 17 B8, CDA.
5. 17 B9, CDA.
6. Edward D. Boone (1833–1916), of one of the founding Catholic families of Maryland, was then vice-president of Loyola College.
7. A reference to the threat of war between Prussia and France.
8. 17 B10, CDA.
9. 17 B11, CDA.
10. William W. Holden (1818–1892), had dispatched troops to the piedmont counties of his state to counter Klan violence and intimidation. When the force arrested some one hundred suspected Klansmen, Holden declared martial law to enable the prisoners to be tried in military court. State Democrats petitioned federal courts for the release of the suspects on the ironic grounds that Holden had violated the Habeas Corpus Act of 1867, enacted to protect Southern Blacks and their white allies. The court ruled in favor of the plaintiffs and ordered the captives set free. Holden's campaign against the Klan led to a Democratic sweep in the state's elections that fall. A month later, the now Democratic-controlled legislature impeached the governor and removed him from office.
11. The Franco-Prussian War which had begun on July 19. The subsequent defeat of the French and the overthrow of Napoleon III as emperor led to the withdrawal of French forces in Rome and its subsequent fall to the armies of unification in mid-September 1870.
12. 17 C1, CDA.

13. 17 C2, CDA.

14. 17 C3, CDA.

15. 17 C4, CDA.

16. 17 C6, CDA.

17. 17 C8, CDA.

18. 17 C9, CDA.

19. 17 C11, CDA.

20. 17 D2, CDA.

21. Lucius Bellinger Northrop (1811–1894), former commissary general of the Confederacy.

22. The patriarchal tradition endured within this Irish American family, with the eldest son succeeding as the formal head of the household upon the death of the father. With the Irish such relationships were complicated by the informal power of the mother. Eleanor Lynch certainly continued to command a great deal of power within the family, no matter whom she designated as successor to her husband.

23. 17 D3, CDA.

24. 17 D4, CDA.

25. "Friend" has been written over "child." "D" stands for "Daughter," by which name Louisa was known among the Blaine family and her Lynch in-laws.

26. 17 D5, CDA.

27. When Italian troops had seized Rome in September. Pope Pius IX had taken refuge in the Vatican, the beginning of an "imprisonment" which would extend over the next six decades.

28. 17 D6, CDA.

29. 17 D7, CDA.

30. 17 D11, CDA.

31. 17 E1, CDA.

32. 17 E2, CDA.

33. 17 E3, CDA.

34. Anna apparently died on Dec. 26 or Dec. 27. She was thirty-five.

35. 17 E5, CDA.

36. Anna was buried in St. Peter's graveyard, Columbia, despite Conlaw's insistence that Anna wanted to be interred in the family gravesite at St. David's Cemetery in Cheraw, next to her twin brother, Bernard.

11. "How Long, O Lord, How Long?" January–June 1871

1. 17 G3, CDA.

2. 17 G6, CDA.

3. Alfred Proctor Aldrich (1814–1897) and Martha Ann Aldrich (1819–1891), parents of Sarah Aldrich (1846–1928).

4. 17 G7, CDA.

5. 17 G9, CDA.

6. Caro Spann.

7. 17 G10, CDA.

8. Ellerbe Brogan Crawford Cash (1823–1888). His wife, Eunice Ellerbe (1828–1880), was his cousin.

9. 17 H3, CDA.

10. 17 H1, CDA.

11. 17 H7, CDA.

12. 17 H 8, CDA.

13. 17 H 9, CDA.

14. 17 H10, CDA.

15. 50 H7, CDA.

16. 17 K1, CDA.

17. 17 K5, CDA.

12. "It Looks Like Antebellum Times": July–December 1871

1. 17 K7, CDA.

2. Caldwell.

3. Emma Dennison (1844-?).

4. Unclassified letter, CDA.

5. James A. Ward (1813–1895).

6. 17 K10, CDA.

7. 20 S2, CDA.

8. 17 M3, CDA.

9. Baptista's oldest brother is evidently the sole family member for whom she is ready to break cloister, an action she first contemplated taking during the war when Patrick refused to move his residence beyond the range of the Union guns bombarding Charleston.

10. 17 M7, CDA.

11. 17 M8, CDA.

12. 17 M9, CDA.

13. 17 N1, CDA.

14. The Great Chicago Fire.

15. The immense losses that the diocese of Chicago will undoubtedly suffer from the disastrous fire, Baptista realizes, will create a competitor to Patrick's own diocese in seeking relief funds from the American Catholic community.

16. 17 N2, CDA.

17. 17 N6, CDA.

18. Discounting was the banking practice of reducing the interest due on a financial transaction.

19. 17 N7, CDA.

20. 17 N9, CDA.

21. 17 N10, CDA.

13. "To Me It Appears More Difficult to Regain Than to Have First Gained": January–June 1872

1. 17 R1, CDA.

2. 17 R2, CDA.

3. 17 R3, CDA.

4. At the state fair.

5. 17 R4, CDA.

6. 17 R5, CDA.

7. 17 R6, CDA.

8. 17 R7, CDA.

9. 17 R8, CDA.

10. 17 R9, CDA.

11. 17 R10, CDA.

12. 17 S1, CDA.

13. 17 S3, CDA.

14. 17 S4, CDA.

15. 17 S5, CDA.

16. 17 S6, CDA.

17. 17 S7, CDA.

18. The Ursuline council was composed of nuns elected by the Community to serve as advisors to the mother superior.

19. 17 S10, CDA.

20. 17 T1, CDA.

21. 17 T2, CDA.

22. 17 T3, CDA.

23. Oscar Montgomery Lieber (1830–1862), had headed South Carolina's Mineralogical, Geological and Agricultural Survey.

24. Francis Lieber (ca. 1798–1872), renowned jurist and political scientist who had taught at the University of South Carolina for two decades before the increasingly repressive intellectual climate drove him to Columbia College in New York City.

25. 17 T5, CDA.

26. 17 T11, CDA.

27. 17 W2, CDA.

28. 17 W3, CDA.

29. 17 W5, CDA.

30. John Dougherty, of Loyola College, their spiritual director.

31. Josephites.

14. "The Idea of a Religious Invoking a Malediction on the Head of Anyone!" July–December 1872

1. Otto H. Franke, *One Hundred Years of the General German Orphan Home in Baltimore, 1863–1963* (Baltimore: General German Orphan Home, 1963), 50; Charles Warren Currier, *Carmel in America: A Centennial History of the Discalced Carmelites in the United States* (Baltimore: John Murphy & Co., 1890), 293.

2. 17 W6, CDA.

3. The college commencement at the University of South Carolina which normally would take priority over the Ursuline Institute as a communal attraction.

4. 17 W7, CDA.

5. 17 W8, CDA.

6. 17 W9, CDA.

7. 53 D7, CDA. This letter is not in Baptista Lynch's hand.

8. The section of the community's annals extensively detailing the destruction of the convent contains this exchange between General Sherman and Mother Baptista: "As [Sherman] approached with extended hand, he said, in a bright and cheerful tone and manner 'Ah! Sister these are times in which to practice Christian fortitude and patience.' 'You have made them thus to us, General,' she replied, extending her hand in an equally cordial and cheerful manner" (Annals, AUCL, 49).

9. 17 W11, CDA.

10. 17 Y1, CDA.

11. 17 Y2, CDA.

12. 17 Y4, CDA.

13. 17 Y6, CDA.

14. 17 Y7, CDA.

15. 17 Y8, CDA.

16. 17 Y9, CDA.

17. 17 Y10, CDA.

18. 18 A2, CDA.

19. 18 A4, CDA.

20. On Saturday evening, November 11, fire broke out on Summer Street in downtown Boston. For the next twelve hours the fire swept across some sixty-five acres of the city, leaving in its path nearly 800 ruined buildings and as many as twenty Bostonians dead.

21. 18 A5, CDA.

22. 18 A7, CDA.

23. 18 A10, CDA.

24. As a cloistered order, the Carmelites' monastery was off limits to outsiders, with the exception of the Speakroom.

25. 18 A 9, CDA.

26. 18 B1, CDA.

27. 18 B2, CDA.

28. 18 B3, CDA.

29. 18 B5, CDA.

15. "The Taxes Seem to Carry Everything Before Them!" January–June 1873

1. Catherine had joined the Carmelites at the advanced age of thirty (Annals, Baltimore Carmel, 1873. Courtesy of Sister Connie Fitzgerald, ODC).

2. 18 C1, CDA.

3. 18 C3, CDA.

4. To raise money by having a noted priest give a lecture at their place.

5. 18 C4, CDA.

6. 18 C6, CDA.

7. 18 C7, CDA.

8. 18 C9, CDA.

9. 18 D4, CDA.

10. 18 D8, CDA.

11. 18 D9, CDA.

12. 18 D10, CDA.

13. 18 D11, CDA.

14. 18 E1, CDA.

15. 18 E7, CDA.

16. 18 E8, CDA.

17. 18 E11, CDA.

18. 18 G1, CDA.

19. 18 G3, CDA.

20. 18 G4, CDA.

16. "Our Privations Are So Great That I Think Our Enemies Would Take Pity on Us:" July–December 1873

1. 18 G6, CDA.
2. 18 G10, CDA.
3. A seventy-acre plot between the railroad and the river.
4. 18 H1, CDA.
5. 18 H3, CDA.
6. 18 H5, CDA.
7. 18 H7, CDA.
8. 18 H8, CDA.
9. 18 H10, CDA.
10. 18 K1, CDA.
11. 18 K2, CDA.
12. 18 K3, CDA.
13. 18 K4, CDA.
14. 18 K5, CDA.
15. 18 K6, CDA.
16. 18 K7, CDA.
17. 18 K9, CDA.
18. Bautista shows a sensitivity to the impact the addition of a lay sister will have upon the Blacks whose loyal service the community has been so dependent upon.
19. 55 Y5, CDA.
20. 18 K11, CDA.
21. 18 M1, CDA.
22. 18 M2, CDA.
23. 18 M3, CDA.
24. 18 M4, CDA.
25. 18 M5, CDA.
26. 18 M11, CDA.
27. 18 M9, CDA.

17. "I Am at the Mercy of Creditors": January–June 1874

1. 18 N3, CDA.
2. 18 N4, CDA.
3. The persistent expectation that immigrants, ideally Irish ones, would soon be arriving in such numbers as to provide the labor in staple agriculture which enslaved Blacks traditionally had done.
4. 18 N5, CDA.
5. 18 N7, CDA.

6. 18 N8, CDA.

7. 18 N9, CDA.

8. The Bahamas were part of the Charleston Diocese.

9. 18 P2, CDA.

10. 18 P3, CDA.

11. 18 P4, CDA.

12. 18 P7, CDA.

13. 18 P5, CDA.

14. 18 P6, CDA.

15. 18 P9, CDA.

16. 18 R1, CDA.

17. 18 R3, CDA.

18. 18 R4, CDA.

19. 18 R6, CDA.

13. "The Wind Seems to Be Veering Now": July–December 1874

1. Joseph Mannard, in his research into the Georgetown Visitandine community in the 1820s, discovered a similar pattern of mental breakdowns, when the convent was facing "tremendous problems concerning finances due to declining enrollments in the academy, leadership turnovers, and malcontent nuns about how to live an 'authentic' Visitation religious life." (Email, December 21, 2021; also see Mannard, "'Our Prospects Are Mighty Dark . . . Still I confide in God': The Ordeal of the Sisters of the Visitation in Antebellum Wheeling," *American Catholic Studies* [Spring 2020], 28n31).

2. 18 R11, CDA.

3. 18 S1, CDA.

4. 18 S3, CDA.

5. Patrick Lynch Miscellaneous Papers, CDA.

6. 18 S5, CDA.

7. 18 S7, CDA.

8. 18 S8, CDA.

9. 18 S9, CDA.

10. 18 S11, CDA.

11. 18 T1, CDA.

12. 18 T4, CDA.

13. 18 T3, CDA.

14. 18 T6, CDA.

15. 18 T7, CDA.

16. Daniel H. Chamberlain (1835–1907).

17. 18 T8, CDA.
18. A line has been drawn through "Clagett," as though to hide the information.
19. 18 T10, CDA.
20. 18 T11, CDA.
21. Thomas J. Robertson (1823–1897), a Republican, served in the US Senate from 1868 to 1877.
22. 18 W2, CDA.
23. 18 W3, CDA.
24. 18 W5, CDA.
25. 18 W6, CDA.
26. St. Agnes Hospital, operated by the Daughters of Charity in the southwest suburbs of Baltimore.
27. 18 W8, CDA.
28. 18 W11, CDA.
29. 18 Y1, CDA.
30. 18 Y2, CDA.
31. 18 Y3, CDA.
32. Baptista, in her conversation with her brother, had been quick to emphasize that the decision to dismiss Clagett was not hers alone. It was the consensus of the community that Clagett had, for over a decade, failed to demonstrate that her actions were "for the greater glory of God, the salvation of my soul, and the good of the Community," as their Rule required. But if Baptista Lynch thought that this appeal to the Ursuline Constitution would cause her brother to defer to the community's judgment, she was mistaken. Four years earlier, Baptista, appreciative of the key role that her brother Patrick had played in relieving the community of Augustine England's bedeviling presence, had secured a rescript from Rome which gave Patrick Lynch, as Bishop of Charleston, ultimate authority over the Ursuline Community in South Carolina. Now she was paying the price for wanting her brother, rather than the Order's Constitution, to have the last word in all matters regarding his sister's community.

19. "Our Blessed Little Angel Breathed Her Last on Monday Morning": January–June 1873

1. 19 A2, CDA.
2. 19 A5, CDA.
3. 19 A7, CDA.
4. 19 A10, CDA.
5. 19 A11, CDA.
6. 19 B1, CDA.

7. 19 B4, CDA.

8. 19 B7, CDA.

9. The Lynches had five children: Marie, nineteen; Conlaw, seventeen; Ellen, fifteen; Francis, thirteen; and Theresa Henrietta, eight.

10. 19 B8, CDA.

11. 19 B9, CDA.

12. 19 C2, CDA.

13. 19 C3, CDA.

14. 19 C4, CDA.

20. "Our Poor Hearts Are Broken": July–December 1875

1. 19 C8, CDA.

2. Song (Celtic).

3. 19 C10, CDA.

4. 19 D2, CDA.

5. 19 D3, CDA.

6. 19 D8, CDA.

7. 19 E1, CDA.

8. 19 E2, CDA.

9. 19 E5, CDA.

21. "No One Thinks Her Converted": January–June 1876

1. 19 G6, CDA.

2. The Maryland-born Mary Ellen Clagett (1831-?) had entered the community in 1859 as a lay sister and been given the name Theresa. That Baptista was still referring to her as "Miss Clagett" points up Baptista's persistent conviction that putting a religious habit on someone does not make her a nun.

3. 19 G8, CDA.

4. 19 H1, CDA.

5. 19 H3, CDA.

6. 19 H4, CDA.

7. 19 H6, CDA.

8. 19 H7, CDA.

9. 19 H9, CDA.

10. 19 H11, CDA.

11. 19 K5, CDA.

12. 19 K10, CDA.

13. 19 M1, CDA.

22. "Very Much Enthusiasm Prevails for the Success of the Democracy": July–December 1876

1. 19 M3, CDA.
2. 40 K10, CDA.
3. 19 M5, CDA.
4. Folchi.
5. 19 M6, CDA.
6. This would seem to apply to the crisis surrounding Mary Ellen Clagett in August of 1874.
7. 19 M8, CDA.
8. 19 M11, CDA.
9. 19 N1, CDA.
10. The pledge to abstain permanently from alcoholic beverages. Theobald Mathew (1790–1856), the Irish Capuchin, had made the taking of the pledge the centerpiece of his crusade to reform "the alcoholic republic" during his American tour from 1849 to 1851. In the late 1850s, Conlaw's father, John Lynch, had himself battled a drinking problem that threatened to ruin his career as well as his marriage. After experiencing several lapses in his observance of the pledge, John Lynch became a successful teetotaler for the remainder of his life.
11. 19 N3, CDA.
12. 19 N4, CDA.
13. 19 N5, CDA.
14. 61 A5, CDA. Draft.
15. 19 N6, CDA.
16. 19 N7, CDA.
17. 19 N11, CDA.
18. 19 N12, CDA.
19. 19 P1, CDA.
20. Intestinal worms.
21. 19 P2, CDA.
22. The popular term for the Democratic Party.
23. 19 P6, CDA.
24. At Governor Chamberlain's pleading, President Grant had issued a proclamation ordering "all persons engaged in unlawful and insurrectionary proceedings" in South Carolina to disperse within three days.
25. 19 P8, CDA.
26. 19 P9, CDA.
27. White supremacist groups like the Klan had no monopoly on the violence

which marred the presidential campaign of 1876 in South Carolina. In the fall, on two occasions Black Republicans, incensed at the presence of Black supporters at Hampton rallies, had killed six whites. Still, as Eric Foner noted: "the campaign of intimidation launched by Hampton's supporters far overshadowed such incidents" (*Reconstruction: America's Unfinished Revolution, 1863–1877* [New York: Harper & Row, 1988], 574).

28. 19 P11, CDA.
29. 19 R1, CDA.
30. 19 R2, CDA.

23. "God Is Good!" January–June 1877

1. Eric Foner, *Reconstruction*, 574–81; Thomas Holt, *Black over White: Negro Political Leadership in South Carolina during Reconstruction* (Urbana and Chicago: University of Illinois Press, 1977), 173–74; Williamson, *After Slavery*, 411–12.
2. 19 S2, CDA.
3. 19 S4, CDA.
4. Carpenter.
5. 19 S5, CDA.
6. 19 S6, CDA.
7. 19 S10, CDA.
8. 19 T1, CDA.
9. 19 T3, CDA.
10. 19 T4, CDA.
11. 19 T6, CDA.
12. Unclassified, CDA.
13. 19 W6, CDA.
14. 19 W8, CDA.
15. 19 W9, CDA.
16. 19 W10, CDA.
17. 19 W11, CDA.
18. 19 Y3, CDA.
19. 19 Y5, CDA.
20. 19 Y6, CDA.
21. 19 Y7, CDA.
22. 19 Y9, CDA.

24. "Everybody Seems Pleased with the Return of Home Rule": July–December 1877

1. 20 A4, CDA.
2. On July 11, an article appeared in the *New York Sun* which denied that Bishop Lynch was going to be named coadjutor to Cardinal McCloskey, with the right of succeeding him as Archbishop of New York. As the Charleston prelate explained, he had "reached an age when he should seek a coadjutor than a coadjutorship."
3. 20 A7, CDA.
4. 20 A9, CDA.
5. Transfer Case I, P, CDA. Sponsored by the St. Vincent de Paul Society of New York City.
6. 20 C7, CDA.
7. 20 B3, CDA.
8. Lewis Cass Carpenter (1836–1908) was a Connecticut-born lawyer who, after the war, had relocated to South Carolina where he edited the *Daily Union* of Columbia. The paper had a contract with the state government to promulgate the laws and other official business. In 1877 Carpenter was accused of inflating by more than threefold the figures on checks he received for the paper's work for the state. A biracial jury convicted him.
9. 20 B7, CDA.
10. 20 B8, CDA.
11. 20 B10, CDA.
12. 20 C5, CDA.
13. 20 C9, CDA.
14. 20 D2, CDA.
15. 20 D6, CDA
16. 20 D10, CDA.
17. 20 E2, CDA.
18. 20 E6, CDA.
19. 20 E7, CDA.
20. Pilgrimages to Lourdes became popular among Catholics, particularly those in the South, in the period after the Civil War. Apocalyptic events, like the collapse of the Confederacy and the fall of Rome, seemed to induce Catholics to look to Lourdes as a confirmation of God's continuing presence, through the apparition of Mary, no matter how absent the divinity seemed to be in worldly affairs.
21. 20 E8, CDA.
22. 20 G5, CDA.
23. 20 G6, CDA.

24. A law which limited the rate of interest which could be charged for a loan.
25. 20 G9, CDA.

25. "There Is No Mistake That Farming Is Ever a Failure": January–June 1873

1. 73 M10, AASMUS.
2. 64 Y2, CDA.
3. 20 H6, CDA.
4. 20 H7, CDA.
5. 20 H9, CDA.
6. 20 H10, CDA.
7. 20 K1, CDA.
8. 20 K2, CDA.
9. 20 K3, CDA.
10. 20 K4, CDA.
11. 20 M6, CDA
12. Mary Ellen Clagett.
13. 20 M10, CDA.
14. 20 N7, CDA.

26. "When You Shall Live at Home, Your Diocess Will Become a Perfect Hotbed of Catholicity": July–December 1873

1. 20 P1, CDA.
2. 20 P8, CDA.
3. 20 P4, CDA.
4. 20 P9, CDA.
5. 20 P10, CDA.
6. 20 R1, CDA.
7. 20 R2, CDA.
8. 20 R6, CDA.
9. 20 R7, CDA.
10. 20 R9, CDA.
11. 20 R10, CDA.
12. Patrick Lynch Miscellaneous Papers, CDA.
13. 20 S6, CDA.
14. 20 S9, CDA.
15. 20 T4, CDA.
16. St. Agnes Hospital had a wing devoted to the care of patients suffering from psychological ailments, but, unlike Mt. Hope, did not bear the stigma attached to a mental institution.

17. 20 T10, CDA.
18. 20 W7, CDA.
19. 20 W8, CDA. Clearly Henrietta has deeply resented Patrick's condition that Pinckney devote his time to study for a year before he would use his influence to secure a place for him elsewhere. She lays out in stark detail what that agreement has meant for their domestic living arrangements, including removing her from her marriage bed. Her formulaic closure stamps her repressed feelings.
20. A few months after marrying Francis Lynch in 1855, Henrietta suddenly returned to the home of her widowed mother in Charleston. Patrick Lynch was, at least in part, responsible for persuading Henrietta to return to her husband and resume their life together.
21. 20 W9, CDA.

27. "This Deprives Me of the Last Frail Plant I Had to Lean On for the Support of My Family": January–June 1879

1. 21 A3, CDA.
2. As a candidate for the US senate in 1876, Butler was a major implementer of the "Edgefield Plan" of 1876, which utilized fraud, intimidation, and violence to overthrow the Republican government in South Carolina.
3. 21 A4, CDA.
4. 67 G4, CDA.
5. 21 A6, CDA.
6. 21 A8, CDA.
7. 21 B1, CDA.
8. Persuading others to invest in them.
9. 21 B4, CDA.
10. 21 B5, CDA.
11. 21 B6, CDA.
12. 21 B9, CDA.
13. 21 B10, CDA.
14. Some four decades earlier in the wake of the economic chaos brought on by the Panic of 1837, Edward Purcell, the archbishop's brother, had established an informal bank. Purcell's "bank" in the cathedral rectory gradually grew into a major interest-earning depository for Cincinnati's Catholics. In three decades over $13,000,000 had been entrusted to Edward Purcell's safekeeping. By the 1870s, its reputation was rock-solid. Undeservedly so, as Edward Purcell was a careless investor of the money Cincinnati Catholics had put into his safekeeping. It finally caught up to him in October 1878, when a local bank failed, and the rumor surfaced that Edward Purcell had a great portion of his investments there. It fell to his seventy-eight-year-old brother to admit to the packed cathedral that the

rumors were true. The money was not there (M. Edmund Hussey, "John Baptist Purcell: First Archbishop of Cincinnati," in Gerald P. Fogarty, SJ, ed. *Patterns of Episcopal Leadership* [New York: Macmillan Publishing Co., 1989], 103–05).

15. 21 C1, CDA.
16. 21 C2, CDA.
17. 21 C5, CDA.
18. 21 C6, CDA.
19. 21 C8, CDA.
20. 21 C10, CDA.
21. Thomas McCarroll Acton (1821–1895), newspaper owner.
22. 21 D1, CDA.
23. 21 D2, CDA.
24. On Tuesday, May 13, the Ladies Memorial Association unveiled the Confederate monument, which depicted a Confederate infantryman on guard duty.
25. 21 D3, CDA.
26. 21 D7, CDA.
27. 21 D8, CDA.

28. "Just Now Everything Looks Gloomy": July–December 1879

1. 21 E9, CDA.
2. 21 G2, CDA.
3. 21 H8, CDA.
4. 21 H9, CDA.
5. 21 H10, CDA.
6. 21 K1, CDA.
7. Cullinane
8. 21 K3, CDA.
9. The seventeen-year-old was the youngest of the three children still at home. The 1880 census listed him as clerking in a store.
10. 21 K4, CDA.
11. 21 K5, CDA.
12. 21 M1, CDA.

29. "I Fear I Am Lost in the Labyrinth": January–June 1880

1. 21 N1, CDA.
2. 21 N4, CDA.
3. 21 N5, CDA.
4. 21 N9, CDA.
5. The collective decision of the American hierarchy to come to the relief of the Archdiocese of Cincinnati when the bank which the Purcell brothers had

established failed in 1878 apparently became the occasion for Bishop Quinlan to terminate what he considered to be a struggling operation by selling the building which housed the convent and academy.

6. 21 P3, CDA.

7. 21 R5, CDA.

8. 21 S3, CDA.

9. 21 T10, CDA

10. 21 S4, CDA.

11. 21 S7, CDA

12. 21 S10, CDA

30. "The Pope Did Not Do Right Towards Bishop Lynch": July–December 1880

1. 21 T3, CDA.

2. 21 T4, CDA.

3. The city of Charleston had asked Bishop Lynch to head a commission to study the need to expand the city's water supply.

4. 21 T6, CDA.

5. 21 T9, CDA.

6. 21 W2, CDA.

7. 21 W3, CDA.

8. 21 W4, CDA.

9. 21 W6, CDA.

10. 21 W7, CDA.

11. 21 W10, CDA.

12. 21 Y7, DCA.

13. 21 Y9, CDA.

14. 21 Y11, CDA.

15. 21 Y13, CDA.

31. "The House Would Fall Down if You Had Not Been its Prop and Support": 1881–1882

1. See Baptista Lynch to Patrick Lynch, May 3, 1880.

2. 22 A1, CDA.

3. 22 B1, CDA.

4. 22 B2, CDA.

5. 22 B4, CDA.

6. 22 C1, CDA.

7. 22 D2, CDA.

8. 22 G2, CDA.

9. 22 G3, CDA.

10. 22 G4, CDA.

11. 22 G5, CDA.

12. 22 H1, CDA.

13. 22 K1, CDA.

14. 22 K3, CDA.

15. In the 1880 census, Louise Blain was listed as living in the home of her aunt, Anna M. Fugas, a schoolteacher, at Eighty-One North Broad Street (US Census, Charleston, S.C., 92).

16. 22 K4, CDA.

17. 22 K5, CDA.

18. 22 K6, CDA.

19. 22 K7, CDA.

20. 22 M1, CDA.

21. 22 M3, CDA.

22. 22 N2, CDA.

23. 22 N3, CDA.

24. 22 P1, CDA.

25. 22 T1, CDA.

26. 22 T2, CDA.

Epilogue

1. Inflamed, infected urinary bladder (Heisser, 181).

2. March 2, 1882.

3. Heisser, 181–84.

4. Annals, 168–78.

5. His wife, Henrietta, had predeceased him by fourteen years.

6. The sisters' entry book listed Anastasia's age as thirty-eight, five years younger than her actual age. We do not know the reason for the discrepancy. We do know that it was rare for convents to admit candidates who were over forty (Sr. Anne Francis Campbell, OLM, to Nina Blythe Googe, Charleston, May 3, 2005, copy, CDA).

7. This survey of Lynch descendants is based on two genealogical studies of the second to eighth generations of the progeny of Conlaw Peter Lynch and Eleanor McMahon Neison ("Lynch Family: Line of Conlaw Peter Lynch and Eleanor McMahon Neison, of Clones, County Monahan, Ireland and Cheraw, South Carolina," compiled by Henry de Saussure Copland, October 1993, CDA; additional notes on the Lynch Family genealogy provided by Nina Googe, 2005, CDA).

8. See Henrietta Lynch, Cheraw, to Patrick Lynch, Cheraw, Jul 25, 1880, to Patrick Lynch, 21 W2, CDA.

Index

Acton, Thomas McCarroll, 285–86, 344n21

African Americans, 326n10

Agatha, Sr SMC. *See* Macnamara, Louisa

Ahern, Elizabeth, 85, 97

Aiken, William, 56, 324n12

Aldrich, Alfred Proctor, 19, 24, 43, 60, 137, 181–82, 191, 263, 268, 331n3

Aldrich, Martha Ann, 159, 263

Aldrich, Robert, 260, 269

Aldrich, Sarah, 24, 43, 137, 159, 137, 159, 182

American Hotel, 82, 174

Ames, Adelbert, 320n8

Angela, Sr. Mary OSU. *See* Brownfield, Natalie

Anthony, Sr. OSU. *See* Kearnan, Cecilia

Antonia of the Purification OCD. *See* Lynch, Catherine

Apostleship of Prayer, 32

Atkinson, Abner, 243

Augustine, Sr. Mary OSU. *See* England, Nora

Baltimore Plenary Council, 37–38, 46–47

Banner of the South, 84, 325n18

Baptista, Sr. Mary OSU. *See* Lynch, Ellen

Barr, Sarah (Sallie), 127

Barry, Cecilia, 74, 78

Barry, Teresa, 164

Bauskett, John, 55, 68, 71–72, 74, 325n5

Bauskett, John, Jr., 188, 208, 212

Bauskett, Sophia Crane, 74, 78

Bayley, James Roosevelt, 8, 162, 165, 173

Beauregard, Gustave Pierre Toutant, 3

Bellaclas, J.B., 49

Bellinger, Eleanor, 318

Bellinger, M. Carnot, 317

Bellinger, Patrick Lynch, 317–18

Benedictines (Latrobe), 21

Bermingham, Timothy, 61, 90, 96, 150

Bernard, Sr. Mary OSU. *See* Burt, Sallie

Bertheville, Laure de, 84

Black Codes, 6

Blaine, Joseph; injured, 121–22, 128; opens school, 187; under attack, 288–89

Blaine, Louisa, 16, 35, 117, 346n15; assisting the Lynches, 83, 218, 273–75; spiritual turmoil, 223, 308; as supplicant for financial assistance, 8, 304, 307–8

Blaine, Louisa J., 223

Boone, Edward D., 126, 128, 329n6

Borgia, Sr. OSU. *See* Brisbane, Adilene

Boston, 56, 118, 272, 334n20

Boyce, William Waters, 182, 193

Bragg, Braxton, 322n45

Brisbane, Adilene, 84, 93, 107, 112, 328n6; companion with Sr. Augustine, 91,

Brisbane, Adilene (*cont.*)
94, 105; dowry, 158; Georgia lands, 81, 98, 103–4, 106–7; health, 97–98, 112–13, 145–46, 148, 150, 153, 155
Brownfield, Frances, 81, 93, 256
Brownfield, Mary, 93
Brownfield, Natalie, 78, 81–82, 93, 129, 133
Burt, Sallie, 243, 250
Burton, Henry Stanton, 62
Butler, M. C., 281, 343n2

Caldwell, Agnes M., 69, 145, 181, 219, 230, 295, 300
Caldwell, Susan A., 295
Camilla, Sr. OSU. *See* Ahern, Elizabeth
Canby, Edward, 74n23
Cardoza, Francis Lewis, 107, 259, 328n14
Carpenter, Anne, 259
Carpenter, Lewis Cass, 191–92, 211, 247, 268, 341n8
Cash, Ellerbe Brogan Crawford, 138, 140, 331n8
Cash, Eunice Ellerbe, 331n8
Catholic Association, The, 171, 178
Catholic World, The, 116–17, 314
Centennial celebration, 229
Chairs, Octavia, 85
Chamberlain, Daniel, 203–4, 211, 228, 231–32, 245, 336n16, 339n24
Chamber of Commerce, 313
Chambodut, Louis Claude Marie, 71n17
Charity, Sisters of, 277
Charles, Sr. Mary OSU. *See* Weed, Mary Otis
Charleston, 2, 246, 265
Chase, Salmon P., 34
Chicago, 148
cholera, 32–33, 41–42
Cincinnati, Archdiocese of, 56

Clagett, Mary Ellen, 68, 73, 95, 104, 205–13, 229, 269, 277, 337n32, 338n2, 339n6
Clarke, David, 207–8
Clarke, Minerva, 67, 207–8, 224
Clarke, Sarah (Sallie), 207–8
Columbia, postwar condition, 23; postwar revival, 112, 149, 290; restoration as state capital, 246; targeted as seat of rebellion, 167; water failure, 187
Corcoran, James A., 115
Cornette, Andrew, SJ, 96, 327n19
Corrigan, JN, 167
Court of Common Pleas, 313
Crogan, Charles, 43, 322n9
Cullinane, John, 283, 289–90
Cummings, Sr. de Chantel VHM, 57
Cuthbert, Mary, 35

Daniel (freedman from Valle Crucis), 22, 32, 53, 72–73, 191
Davis, Jefferson, 27, 316
Denison, Emma, 78, 81, 83, 85–86, 91, 93, 145, 250, 281, 331n3
DeSales, Sr. Mary OSU. *See* Minerva Clarke
DeSaussure, Douglass Blanding, 26, 79, 82, 178, 302, 320n22, 326n8
DeSaussure, Martha, 326n8
DeSaussure, William F., 28, 53, 210, 212
Domenec, Michael, 57, 324n20
Dooley, James, 91, 327n2
Dougherty, John SJ, 162, 165, 173, 333n30
Dubuis, Claude, 93, 327n12
Dugan, Pierre, 166

Edgefield, 196, 203, 212, 245
8th Baltimore Provincial Council, 105, 328n6
Election of 1876, 234–36, 240–43

Emmet, Robert, 78

England, John, 11, 76, 90, 112, 169, 267

England, Nora; as community disrupter, 11–12, 41, 76, 83–85, 87; in Ireland, 105, 181; sanctions imposed upon, 86; transfers to Ursuline community in Ireland, 90–91, 93–96; in Tuscaloosa, 42, 70, 78

Enright, Mary, 85

Etienne, Sr. Mary OSU. *See* Vassas, Carrie

Ewing, Charles, 167

Fahey, Brian, 14

Fairs, 68, 76, 132, 148, 267–68

Fer, James, 61

Ferre, Rosalind, 95

Fillon, Leo, 4

Fitzgerald, Edward, 14

For Church and Confederacy, 3, 16

Fort Sumter, 3, 27,

Franco-Prussian War, 127, 139, 329n11

Freedman's Bureau, 6, 22, 76, 90, 254

Fullerton, Francis, 169–70, 268

Garasché, Laura C., 27–28, 78

Gertrude, Sr. Mary OSU. *See* Spann, Ellen

Gertrude, Sr. Mary MSC. *See* Lynch, Anastasia

Grant, Ulysses S., 90–91, 241, 291, 293

Greenville, 238–39

Hampton, Wade, 14, 53, 234–36, 241–43, 245, 247, 277

Hamptons, 168, 182, 186, 236, 243

Harris, Kate, 78

Hayes, Rutherford B., 245

Hayne, Henry E., 189

Healy family, 316

Heiss, David, 16

Holden, William W., 127, 329n20

Huchet family, 24, 70

Ignatia, Sr. Mary OSU. *See* Denison, Emma

Johnson, Andrew, 4, 6, 9, 320n22, 322n11, 326n10

Jones, Lucas, 3, 33–34, 42–43, 50, 96, 320n6

Josephine, Sr., 274

Kearnan, Cecilia, 74, 104

Keitt, Ellison Summerfield, 6, 71–72

Keitt, Hattie, 90

Kelly, Patrick, 162, 164

Ku Klux Klan, 148, 150, 203

LaBorde, Maximilian, 189–90

Ladies Memorial Association (Columbia), 344n24

Lafitte, Edward, 50

Lamb, Sr. Martha OSU, 84

Leahy, Patrick, 94

LeConte, Joseph, 29, 31, 320n30

Leopoldine Foundation, 5

Lieber, Francis, 160, 332n24

Lieber, Oscar Montgomery, 160, 311, 332n23

Lincoln, Abraham, 4, 6, 9

Lost Cause, 246, 344n24

Lourdes, 327n15, 341n20

Low Country Digital Library, 15

Lyceum, 22, 51

Lynch, Anastasia, 316, 346n6

Lynch, Anna (daughter of John Lynch), 85

Lynch, Anna, 55, 112, 328n6; as caretaker

2–3, 9; on Cheraw homestead, 131, 132–34; death of, 134, 330n34, 330n6; health of, 28–29, 32–33, 35, 38–40, 124, 128–30; on servants, 121–22, 322

Lynch, Bernard, 2

Lynch, Catherine; on Anna's death, 135–37; death of, 176; entrance into Carmelites, 2, 334n1; health of, 137; on her brother becoming her archbishop, 153, 165, 169; new convent, 161; sale of old convent, 160–62, 165–66, 172–74; as superior of community, 119, 173–74

Lynch, Conlaw A., 125, 148, 329n2; death of, 298; postmortem discovery, 305; seeking his uncle's help, 76, 85, 237, 250

Lynch, Conlaw Peter, 9, 28, 315; death of, 121; golden wedding anniversary, 33–34; health of, 11, 120, 129; leaves Ireland, 1; loss of labor, 9; sued 77; as town builder, 1

Lynch, Conlaw S., 278; as Anna's intercessor, 134; as bishop uncle's beneficiary, 293, 304–8; as borrower, 179; as farmer, 249, 293, 306; later careers, 317; seeks position elsewhere, 268, 275; as speculator, 89, 91; takes total abstinence pledge, 339n10

Lynch, Cornelia Reilly, 105, 328n7

Lynch, Eleanor, 317

Lynch, Eleanor Blaine, 112, 224, 237, 317

Lynch, Eleanor Nieson, 9, 243, 315; in Columbia, 133; death of, 251–52; death of husband, 121; golden wedding anniversary, 33–34, 321n40; health of, 30, 124, 129; leaves Ireland, 1; as patriarch, 330n22; returns

to Cheraw, 228, 232; on servants, 71; at Valle Crucis, 96, 130–32, 137

Lynch, Eliza, 317

Lynch, Eliza Macnamara, 132, 273

Lynch, Ellen, 97; and Blacks, 37, 323n3, 335n18; Columbia Day School, 24–25, 31, 163–64, 168, 175–76; early years, 2; dealing with disruptive sisters, 11–12, 207–15, 229, 269, 287; death of, 315; diocesan debt, 112; election of 1867, 71; election of 1868, 90–91, 97–98; election of 1876, 240, 242–43, 339–40n27; on economy, 72, 191 261; on evangelical war on Catholic education, 272; her estimation of Patrick, 294; as evangelizer, 12–13, 26, 55, 72–73, 316; fairs, 82, 84, 95, 132, 148, 268; fallout with Patrick, 213, 215, 222, 224–25; financial challenges, 56, 60–61, 70, 81, 106, 125, 127–28, 135, 158–59, 175, 234; former work force, 22, 32, 53; Franco-Prussian war, 135, 138; frustration at bishop's perennial absence, 110, 123, 125, 130, 187, 191, 271, 275; as fundraiser, 19, 37, 50, 58, 82, 334n4; and Hamptons, 242–43, 245–46; health of, 76–78, 106, 137, 234, 240, 303, 314; impact of Patrick's death, 314; as Patrick's beneficiary, 7–8, 111, 113, 200, 211, 289, 303; on Patrick's episcopal prospects, 150, 256, 294–95; plans for community and region, 37, 39, 52–53, 78–79, 116, 121, 126, 187, 234, 237; political views, 133, 246; portrait of, 16; on railroad strikes, 253, 256; on real estate boom, 267; rebuilding plans, 22, 52, 54–55,

57–59, 105–7, 123, 186–87, 198, 267; on Reconstruction, 5–6, 19, 52, 135–36; on Redemption, 14, 234–35, 246, 249, 255, 259, 262–63, 282; as retreat giver, 38–39, 186; satellite communities, 68, 237; seeks charter for academy, 152, 154, 255, 260–61, 266, 269; seeks rescript from Rome, 1, 18; on self-directed retreats, 272, 274–75; as spiritual counselor, 123; on taxes, 191, 196, 200, 246, 249, 261, 266, 283; as teacher, 127; and third generation, 265; Valle Crucis, 11, 126, 146; vision for diocese, 7; war claims, 3, 19, 29–31, 164, 167–68, 176, 182, 185–86, 193, 204, 210–11, 255, 260–62, 276–77, 281–82, 315, 321n32; on women's education, 46, 323n18

Lynch, Francis; adopts sharecropping, 22, 216; in Baltimore, 119; financial exigences, 7, 77, 89, 91–92, 124, 128, 132, 145, 149–52, 154–56, 158, 160, 166–67, 175, 177, 180, 184–85, 188–90, 192–93, 195, 197, 200, 201, 204, 208, 212, 216, 218, 228, 232, 235 237, 249–50, 269, 273–74, 286, 290; as fraternal beneficiary, 7, 28, 32, 76–77, 131 156–58, 177, 194–95, 212–13, 215, 217, 231, 238, 250, 289, 292, 299, 301, 304–5; health, 83, 178; immigration as labor solver, 197, 335n3; as investor, 309–10; loses workers, 18, 317; as planter, 18, 34, 44, 71, 77, 149, 160, 216–17, 231, 234, 238–39, 259–60, 291, 296; and Redemption, 14, 235, 241; selling lands, 180; shoe supplier during Civil War, 3–4; as tanner, 53, 73, 75, 117, 124, 131, 149, 165, 173, 177–78, 180, 200,

221, 224, 234, 247, 250–51, 291–94, 296; taxes, 154–56, 178, 217, 231, 250; war claims, 10, 22, 83

Lynch, Francis, Jr., 278, 290, 344n9

Lynch, Henrietta Blain, 1, 30, 46, 338n9; advocate for sons, 275, 288, 290; financial exigences, 7, 89, 91–92, 128, 180, 201, 208, 212, 216, 218, 232, 235, 237, 250, 269 273–74, 286; health of, 4, 18, 42, 83, 112–13, 219, 180; on her brother, 299; on her husband, 221, 225, 294, 298–99; as housing relatives et al. 228, 232, 278, 280–81, 283; impact of diphtheria epidemic, 208, 218, 221–22; as music teacher, 180, 218, 221, 265, 269, 288, 292, 343n19, 343n20; spiritual needs of Cheraw, 294; testament to Patrick, 180–81, 187, 221, 224–25, 307, 343n20

Lynch, Hugh, 3, 75, 77

Lynch, James, 2, 55, 323n8

Lynch, James Bernard, 146, 295, 307, 317

Lynch, James Thomas, 131, 229, 236–37, 316, 323n8

Lynch, John, 146, 223, 240, 295, 317

Lynch, John Hugh, 53, 79, 132, 146, 277; Atlanta prospect, 239, 280, 285–86; birth at sea, 1; Caldwell lawsuit, 204, 206, 208, 281, 287, 295, 297–98, 300–301; as certifier for pharmacists, 152; as consultant, 127; death of, 313; feeling ostracized, 211, 221–22, 227, 242, 284, 287–89, 295; financial struggles, 9–10, 69–70, 89, 132, 146–47, 150, 164, 166, 174, 178, 181, 183, 186, 188–89, 215, 219, 223–24, 259, 280, 289, 292, 295, 300; health of, 105, 222, 294, 303–4, 308–10; lecturing prospects, 239; medical

Lynch, John Hugh (*cont.*)
practice of, 38, 45, 161, 166, 221–23, 232, 283; medical school professor, 110–11, 113, 117, 152, 159, 161, 178, 189, 199, 218, 222, 224, 227–28, 230–31, 241, 259, 266, 295; as mine owner, 32, 46, 56, 139, 150, 152, 164, 166, 196, 198–99, 210, 219, 227, 281, 284, 298, 300–301, 309–11; moves to Columbia, 2; as parish leader, 136, 138; patents of, 92, 94, 146, 174, 188, 283; as Patrick's beneficiary, 8, 86, 147, 153, 157, 159, 172, 182, 261, 280, 282–84; penitentiary medical director, 230, 234, 239–40, 251, 266, 269, 281; real estate investments, 186, 219, 284; relations with government officials, 76, 164, 169, 204, 230–31; as scalawag, 112, 190, 234; scholarship of, 146–47, 272–74, 276, 280, 283; taxes, 99, 106–7, 200, 205–6, 229; trip to New York City, 95–96; victim of Redemption, 14, 234, 242, 280; and Ursuline charter, 267
Lynch, Josephine, 125, 148, 250, 305–6
Lynch, Julia, 2, 295, 317
Lynch, Kate Bauskett, 68, 148, 267, 317
Lynch, Marie, 138, 218, 283, 307, 317
Lynch, Mary Elizabeth (Lillie); as beneficiary, 8, 138, 304, 316; in Charleston, 117, 128; in Cheraw, 111–12; mental crisis of; 273, 277–78, 317; at Valle Crucis, 132
Lynch, Mary Gertrude, 317
Lynch, Patrick; as administrator of Lynch estate, 26; at Baltimore Plenary Council, 38–39; at post Appomattox condition, 98; background, 1; as lecturer, 51, 56, 253–54; on pope's temporal power, 136; on

Pope Pius IX, 139; postwar challenges, 4–5, 20, 112, 267; real estate investments, 107; as rebuilder, 7, 305, 309; taxes, 71; on society and labor, 253–54, 256–58; at Vatican Council, 13–14, 121; and yellow fever, 146, 148, 240
Lynch, Robert; in Boston, 317; employment, 76, 211–13, 222, 240–41, 255, 263, 266, 269; marriage, 68–69; seeks aid from uncle, 84, 179, 196, 198, 266–67; as tanner, 77, 266–67
Lynch family, 14–16; correspondence of, 14–16; election of 1876, 245; embrace of Lost Cause, 279–80, 286; their fortunes of faith, 316–17; their lasting contribution, 315–16, 318; in the New South, 227; and Redemption, 246, 315; third generation, 227, 230, 233–34, 246, 273, 303–4

Mackey, Lloyd, 268, 281
Macnamara, Louisa, 111, 328n3
Madden, Richard C., 16
Maguire, John Francis, 55, 323n7
Mannard, Joseph, 336n1
Manning, John Lawrence, 30, 321n32
Marists, 320n3
Mary Ann, Sr. SM, 209
Mary Copper Mine Co., 322n16
Mason, Eliza S., 71
Mason, Emily Virginia, 71, 325n14
Mathew, Theobald, 339n10
Mayrant, Robert Pringle, 317
McCloskey, John, 17, 297, 320n14
McDonough, William, 45, 125
McFarland, Francis Patrick, 58, 324n24
McGill, John, 55, 130
McMahon, Peter, 104
McNally, Thomas, 104

McQueen, Donald, 317

Meade, George, 98, 324n19

Meade, Henrietta, 57, 324n19

Meade, Sarah Wise, 57, 324n19

Memphis, 6

Mercy Sisters, 136, 322n9, 328n3

Meriwether, William, 40, 42, 78, 104; on
    Bishop Lynch, 44, 59; as chaplain,
    85, 125, 166, 170; as community
    benefactor, 136, 139, 141; on day
    school, 170; as farm manager, 35,
    45, 52, 55, 68, 72, 81, 104–5, 109, 111,
    152, 157–59, 233–34, 236–37; health
    of, 62, 232, 307; on papal infallibil-
    ity, 120; plans for the academy, 116,
    118–19

Methodist Female College, 126, 178

Michel, Sr. OSU. *See* Spann, Caroline

Miller, George Powell, 317

Moore, John, 4

Moses, Franklin J., 259

Mount de Chantel, 261

Nash, William Beverly, 53, 83, 231,
    326n14

Nassau, 198

National Union Party, 43, 322n11

New Orleans, 6

New York Ladies Southern Relief Asso-
    ciation, 51–52, 58, 60–61

New York Tribune, 17

Northrop, Henry, 314

Northrop, Lucius Bellinger, 130–31

O'Connor, Michael P., 116

Orr, James L., 44, 62, 324n36

Panic of 1873, 183, 185

Papal infallibility, 116–17, 120

Papal States, 132, 139

Parker, Mrs. William McKensie, 60

Patrick of the Cross OCD. *See* Kelly,
    Patrick

Peabody, George, 56, 314n1

Peace Convention, 43

Pee Dee Fertilizer Co., 310

Pelham, Charles, 120–21

Pellicier, A. D., 44

Perry, Benjamin Franklin, 6

Persico, Ignatius, 83, 85–87, 91, 94

Pierpont, Francis H., 322n16

Pinckney, Conlaw Lynch, 228–29,
    236–37, 278, 316

Pinckney, Eustice Bellinger, 237

Pinckney, Sarah Phoebe Bellinger,
    228–29, 236–37

Pinckney Family, 2, 323n8

Pius IX, 27; death of, 267; declares Ju-
    bilee Year, 222; link with Southern
    Catholics, 267; loss of Papal States,
    132, 140, 246, 330n27; and Sacred
    Heart Devotion, 152–53

Porcher, Mrs. Phillip J., 60

Preston, John Smith, 26, 43, 320n20

Preston Mansion, 314

Prestons, 168

Pulliam, Octavia, 186, 190, 196, 198

Purcell, Edward, 343n14

Purcell, John Baptist, 284, 286, 343–
    44n14, 344–45n5

Quigley, Thomas, 110

Quinlan, Thomas, 110, 125, 154, 169, 272,
    274, 276, 285, 293

Railroad strikes of 1877, 253

Reconstruction; presidential, 6; congres-
    sional, 6, 53, 203–4, 245, 71n15

Redemption, 227, 229, 247, 267, 282

Rerum Novarum, 254

Roberts, E.B., 198–99, 206, 219

Robertson, Thomas J., 210, 337n21

Roman, Belle, 62, 67, 125

Ryan, Abram, 82–84, 86, 95, 125, 376n14

Ryan, Mary Augusta Pinkney Lynch, 55, 111–12, 131, 237, 277, 317, 323n8, 324n15, 329n3

Sacred Heart Devotion, 152–53, 161

Saint Agnes Hospital (Baltimore), 337n26, 342n16

Saint Finian's and Saint John's Cathedral, 265

Saint Vincent de Paul Society, 253–54, 256

Saville, Julie, 9

Scott, E.J., 57, 62, 168–69

Scott, Robert Kingston, 111, 153, 328n4

Sestini, Benedict, SJ, 32, 321n36

Shadler, F.J., 104, 126

Sherman, Ellen Ewing, 164, 167, 186

Sherman, William Tecumseh, 10, 30, 34, 167, 182, 186, 189, 193, 236, 333n8

Sickles, Daniel, 6, 34, 43,62, 67, 325n1

Sims, William Gilmour, 320n31

Society for the Propagation of the Faith, 5, 13,145, 148, 279

Sorin, Edward (CSC), 21

South Carolina, University of; appropriations from legislature, 196, 199, 225, 230; boycott of, 183–84, 190, 221, 230–32, 241; closing of, 215, 261, 266; college, 189; integration of, 110, 183, 218; "Radical University,"183–84, 228, 287; reorganization of, 178–79, 189; trustees, 189–90, 196, 198–99, 204, 218–19, 224, 230–31, 241

South Carolina Legislature; chartering the Ursuline Academy, 262–63,

269; about the penitentiary, 276; retrenchment, 227–29; on the university, 10, 178, 222, 231, 241, 268

Southern exodus, 265

Southern Relief Societies, 254

Spalding, Martin, 4, 165

Spann, Caroline, 49, 90, 112, 250; in Charleston, 117; enters novitiate, 127–28; as Ursuline, 138, 316; at Ville Crucis, 92–93

Spann, Charles, 117, 259; during the Civil War, 3; as head of St. Mary's College, 119; as lawyer, 53, 71; moves to Texas, 2; as planter, 19, 23, 38, 48–49, 197; preference for immigrant labor, 195, 197; in retirement, 132

Spann, Conlaw, 49

Spann, Ellen, 23, 316, 320n11

Spann, Mary Lynch, death of 273, 276; health of, 256, 259, 261; moves to Texas, 2; on parish community, 48; on son's vocation, 49; visits Columbia/Cheraw, 90, 92–94, 97, 251, 263; in Washington County, 119, 132–33, 193

Stack, John, 166

Stanislaus, Sr. Mary OSU. See Fennell, Fannie

Stanton, Edmund, 57, 172, 324n18

Stanton, Patrick OSA, 173

Stephens, Alexander, 182, 18, 193

Sullivan, Algernon Sydney, 324n30

Sullivan, Mary Mildred, 60–61, 324n30

Tax Convention, 140, 196, 199

Theresa, Sr. Mary OSU. See Clagett, Mary E.

Thomasine, Sr. Mary OSU. See Barry, Cecilia

Tilden, Samuel, 245
Tobin, Mary, 275
Torre, Rosina della, 16

Ursula, Sr. Mary OSU. *See* Dignam,
  Ursula
Ursulines, 261
Ursulines, Tuscaloosa, 116, 124; and
  Bishop Quinlan, 110, 125, 154,
  169, 272, 274, 276, 285; closing of,
  284–85, 293; enrollment, 46, 89;
  origins, 38, 41–42, 44–45, 47–48;
  strategies for saving the community, 67, 116–18, 130, 152–53
Ursulines of Brown County (OH), 106
Ursulines of Opalousa, 95, 118
Ursulines of Quebec, 22, 96
Ursulines of Valle Crucis, 10–11, 110, 314;
  academy enrollment, 107, 11, 24, 28,
  31–32, 34–35, 37, 43, 70, 75, 82, 129,
  138, 146, 148, 158, 172, 190, 22, 261,
  271, 294, 314; celebrating the nation's centennial, 250; choir sisters,
  39–40, 116, 186, 199; Columbia lots,
  26–28, 33, 70, 85, 106, 137, 177–78,
  180, 188, 200, 247; commencement,
  166, 271, 273, 333n3; commemorat-
  ing the 1865 burning, 103, 105, 204,
  230, 333n8; community council, 159,
  332n18; contributions received; 23,
  26, 28, 33, 35; curriculum, 127, 163,
  170, 172; day school, 10–11, 40, 169;
  earthquake at Valle Cruce, 314;
  fairs, 70–71; and farm, 18, 35, 49,
  69; finances, 75–76, 116, 123, 261–62;
  and the Freedman's Bureau, 24–26,
  35, 86, 98; hard times, 204, 287, 290;
  lawsuits against, 90, 208, 210, 212;
  lay sisters, 40, 71, 103, 199; merger

with Louisville Ursulines, 315;
  rebuilding plans, 49, 56, 124; return
  to Columbia, 314–15; satellite
  communities, 64; taxes, 104, 138,
  262, 268
U.S. Catholic Miscellany, 31

Vassas, Carrie, 157, 198; as teacher, 127;
  death of, 275; health of, 229, 262,
  263
Vatican Council, 115–16, 119–21, 139–40
Verot, Augustine, 24, 320n16

Ward, James A., 145, 331n5
Weed, Ambler, 60, 324n29
Weed, Mary Otis, 92; family of, 155;
  health, 187; superior at Tuscaloosa,
  97–98, 125, 153–54, 274
Wheeling Visitation, 261
White, Alonzo, 155
White, Edward, 106
Williams, George W., 156
Wood, James Frederick, 106, 178, 199

Xavier, Sr. MSC, 111
Xavier, Sr. Mary OSU. *See* Pulliam,
  Octavia

Yellow fever, 146, 148, 240, 271

www.ingramcontent.com/pod-product-compliance
Lightning Source LLC
Chambersburg PA
CBHW030744310726
48969CB00005B/1318